Summer Jobs

WORLDWIDE 2011

With an introduction by Susan Griffith

VACATION WORK
The Gap Year Experts

42nd Edition

This edition first published in Great Britain 2010 by
Crimson Publishing, a division of Crimson Business Ltd
Westminster House
Kew Road
Richmond
Surrey
TW9 2ND

A catalogue record for this book is available from the British Library.

ISBN 978 1 85458 565 3

Printed and bound in the United States of America by Sheridan Books, Inc, Michigan

CONTENTS

PART 3: WORLDWIDE

Organisations with vacancies worldwide 253

Africa and the Middle East 286

The Americas 303

Asia 329

Australasia 346

Useful publications 356

WHY A SUMMER JOB WORLDWIDE?

The summer holidays are looming and weeks of gloriously un-timetabled free time are stretching ahead of you. You can do whatever you want – you could go travelling, experience new places, meet interesting people, try out exciting new things – the world is yours for the taking. Or it would be if it weren't for one problem: you're broke.

But why let a little thing like that ruin your summer? You could of course stay at home and slog it out at a local factory, or break your back stacking shelves at the local supermarket. But why would you choose to do that when the alternative is working on a French campsite, teaching English to kids in Italy or mixing drinks behind a bar in Ibiza?

A wealth of CV-improving, mind-expanding and, most importantly, interesting jobs are available throughout the UK, Europe and even further afield. Thousands of students and young people shake off the boredom and routine of living at home by packing their bags and heading off for a summer job worldwide. Why not join them?

The advantages of a summer job away from home

Experiencing new places and cultures

If it's a case of itchy feet you are hoping to cure, how better to see a new part of the world on a budget than to take a summer job? Working away from home is one of the ways that you can afford an extended period of travel. Many of the jobs you will find within these pages offer full bed and board as well as a wage. So all you have to fund is the travel. You will even find that many of the jobs on offer are set in some stunning locations, from remote retreats to 5 star resorts.

By venturing away from your home town or city you will gain greater independence and experience a destination from the inside rather than as an onlooker. If you don't fancy venturing too far from home, jobs abound all over the UK, from working on an activity camp on the shores of Lake Windermere in the heart of the Lake District, to working as a deckhand and tour guide on England's waterways.

But these days, with the number of cheap flights available, your job hunt should not be confined to Britain. With a bit of research you can find budget return flights to many places in Europe. The added advantage of going abroad is that you can also use the trip to improve your knowledge of foreign languages and cultures. Working abroad offers an experience that is quite distinct from straightforward travel. If you are on holiday, you pass through rapidly; you see the sights and eat the food, but you very rarely leave feeling as though you have satisfied your curiosity about a place and its culture. By contrast, a summer job allows you to work at close quarters with local inhabitants, sometimes even lodge with local families, discuss local issues and build lasting friendships. And as for languages, whether you want to start from

A cycling tour being led through Kentucky

scratch or simply brush up your skills, there is no better way to do so than a few months of complete immersion.

Earning some cash

These days getting a decent education can cost a fortune. What with the astronomical financial burden of university tuition fees, added to the not-inconsiderable social and accommodation costs, work-free summer holidays have become the sole preserve of the fortunate few. And the chances are, if you have bought this book, you are not one of them. Don't worry though. Working in the summer gives you the chance to earn money to support a social life, perhaps a holiday and boost your bank balance too.

Enhancing your CV

The summer is a great opportunity to get ahead of the game, and make yourself stand out as a candidate in an increasingly competitive job market. Employers notoriously favour candidates who have demonstrated initiative and spent their vacation time productively. Choosing a summer job that's relevant to a future career choice will stand you in good stead when it comes to entering the real world.

Improving your job prospects doesn't necessarily mean finding an internship with a New York investment bank. High-flying summer work is hard to come by, and anyway might not be that much fun. Increasingly employers are realising that transferable skills are what matter. And whatever you end up doing, it's the way that you sell it on your CV that matters. For instance, if you manage to find work on a holiday barge on the French waterways, you will have demonstrated language and communication skills, leadership abilities, client service and a hardy stomach. Even if you work behind a bar – you may well have demonstrated these same skills plus a degree of numeracy and a faculty for working long hours under pressure. Any summer job can be used to your advantage if you phrase it right on your CV.

The key is to go into it with the right attitude. Extract every last bit of experience that you can from a job that others would just turn up for. You need to go above and beyond – think about what else you can add to your role and show your employers you are capable of handling more. If you're working in a pub or a shop and are good at graphic design take some time and design a new poster or flyer for them. According to careers advisers, employers favour CVs that demonstrate how students have effected some change, regardless of the level or nature of work they have done.

Finding a job that is right for you

Given the opportunities available to enhance your CV, it is crazy to restrict yourself to the mediocre jobs in the local paper or Job Centre. If you want to gain experience in an unusual or competitive field, it is likely that you will have to travel to find the right job and may have to consider work experience placements that don't pay. As has been much reported during the credit crunch and ensuing recession, it is becoming more common for media and other professions to offer internships that carry little or no wage, and a number of them are included in this directory. The new buzzword in this context is 'intern', a concept that is being bolstered and encouraged by the British government. Work Experience is one of the fastest growing sectors in the youth travel industry. The international association of work experience providers called WYSE Work Abroad (www.wyseabroad.org) has more than 150 member organisations. Many are affiliated to language schools which integrate a language course with workplace assignments. Many mediating organisations charge a substantial fee for their services, which may or may not include living expenses.

So, what's the downside?

Well there isn't one really, as long as you are realistic about what to expect. Quite often there is something of a gap between the expectations of the uninitiated summer worker who imagines his job to be some kind of paid holiday in the sun, and his employer who regards him as someone who is there to work. Of course it is inevitable that even the most interesting job will be complicated by the realities of day-to-day living and the expression 'working holiday' can be something of an oxymoron. Wherever you do it, a job is still a job, so it pays to try and think through the potential flaws a position might hold – thorns, heatstroke, isolation, stress – all these practicalities are often overlooked during the grand conceptualisation. Nevertheless, as long as you do your research and ask the right questions of your future employer, there should be no nasty surprises.

Certain obstacles in the mind of the irresolute must be overcome: What jobs can I get? Do I need specific skills? What if I only speak English? This introductory section sets out to allay anxieties and to encourage readers to peruse details of the thousands of summer jobs available. Those who have shed their unrealistic expectations are normally exhilarated by the novelty and challenge of finding and doing a summer job worldwide.

You've already made a good start...

Finding a summer job abroad may strike you as a daunting task, especially in these times of economic recession and high unemployment. However, this book leads you through the process in a

A member of staff at a summer camp

systematic way and provides sufficient listings to help you find a job suited to your needs. Some jobs listed pay very well and come with room and board; others are voluntary and therefore unpaid. Some last for the whole season (June to September or longer); others are just for a couple of weeks. Inside these pages you will find everything you need to know to make the most of your vacation time. Working abroad for a short period will enable the dream to become a reality, the dream of being immersed in a different culture, meeting new friends and earning money at the same time.

The bulk of the individual opportunities in this book are in the UK and western Europe, though the rest of the world is also covered. Entries covering opportunities in a wide distribution of countries or continents are included in the *Worldwide* chapter; while those with a distribution in three or more European countries are in the *Organisations with vacancies across Europe* chapter; others are listed in the relevant country chapter. At the start of each country chapter there are some general notes on employment prospects and regulations on work permits, visas etc. The information in the individual entries has been supplied by the organisations/employers themselves, and is included at their request.

We wish you the best of luck in landing a summer job that you have chosen from the selection within, please note however, that the publishers cannot undertake to contact individual employers or to offer any assistance in arranging specific jobs.

WHAT JOBS CAN YOU DO?

The listings in the 2011 edition of *Summer Jobs Worldwide* are as disparate geographically and occupationally as ever. They range from the practical (building, restoration work, organic farming) to the cerebral (interning at a law firm), and from the artistic (fashion design) to the compassionate (working with the disabled) as well as an impressive array of work camps, hotels, campsites, harvests, couriers etc. Here is a rundown of the types of job available to you worldwide.

Tourism

Working in hotels

If you like the sound of working in some of the most beautiful corners of the world, from high in the Alps, to national parks in the USA, then hotel work might just be for you. The tourist industry is a mainstay of summer jobseekers. The seasonal nature of hotel and restaurant work discourages a stable working population, so that hotel owners often rely on foreign and student workers during the busy summer season.

The earlier you decide to apply for seasonal hotel work, the better your chances. Hotels often recruit months before the summer season, so you should contact as many hotels as possible by March, preferably in their own language. Knowledge of more than one language is an immense asset for work in Europe. Knowing some German (for example) is not only useful in Germany but also in Mediterranean countries where so many German tourists take their holidays. If you have an interest in working in a particular country and want to cast your net wider than the hotels listed in this directory, get a list of hotels from their tourist office in London or from a guide or the internet and contact the largest ones.

If you secure a hotel job without speaking the language of the country and lack relevant experience, you will probably be placed at the bottom of the pecking order, such as in the laundry or washing dishes. Reception and bar jobs are usually the most sought after and highly paid. However, the lowly jobs have their saving graces. The usual hours of chamber staff (7am–2pm), allow plenty of free time and of course you don't have to deal with guests.

Working in hotels, especially in the kitchens, can involve hot working conditions, long hours and low wages; but on good days hotel work is lively, varied and exciting. Before taking a job offer you should always ask for precise details about your duties. Many job titles do not provide a clear definition of the

Working in a hotel kitchen can be hard work but lively and exciting

work and may vary in meaning between different establishments (and countries!). Small hotels tend to employ general assistants for a range of duties as diverse as cleaning rooms to working on reception.

There are loads of benefits to working in hotels. The vast majority provide their staff with accommodation and meals (a deduction may be made from wages for living expenses but in most cases this will not be unreasonable). You can also expect excellent camaraderie and team spirit, the opportunity to learn a foreign language, and beautiful surroundings. You will also be amazed at the ease with which wages can be saved when you are sleeping and eating on site.

Campsites

Camping holiday operators employ a huge number of students and young people for the summer season. The Holidaybreak group, for example, which includes Eurocamp and Keycamp, recruits up to 2,000 campsite couriers and children's couriers.

The courier's job is to clean the tents and caravans between visitors, greet clients and deal with difficulties (commonly illness or car breakdowns), and introduce clients to the attractions of the area. The courier may even arrange and host social functions and amuse the children.

For this kind of work you will be rewarded with on average £100–£135 a week in addition to free tent accommodation. Many companies offer half-season contracts April to mid-July and mid-July to the end of September. Setting up and dismantling the campsites in March/April and September (known as *montage* and *démontage*) is often done by a separate team. The work is hard but the language requirements are nil. The majority of vacancies are in France, though the major companies employ people from Austria to Denmark.

Successful couriers make the job look easy, but it does demand a lot of hard work and patience. Occasionally it is very hard to keep up the happy, smiling, never-ruffled courier look, but most seem to end up enjoying the job since it provides accommodation, a guaranteed weekly wage and the chance to work with like-minded people.

The big companies interview hundreds of candidates and have filled most posts by Easter and sometimes by the end of January. But there is a high drop-out rate and vacancies are filled from a reserve list, so it is worth ringing around the companies later on for cancellations. Despite keen competition, anyone who has studied a European language and has an outgoing personality stands a good chance if he or she applies early and widely enough.

A swimming lesson at a holiday camp

An archery lesson at a sports holiday centre

Holiday resorts

Holiday resorts around the world, but especially along the coasts of the Mediterranean Sea, employ thousands of staff to mount programmes of activities during the day and entertainment at night for holidaymakers. People over 18 who enjoy sports and activities, have an ability to work with kids and adults, and are motivated by working in a fun environment are needed to work the summer season.

Sports & activity holidays

Sports holiday centres often specialise in sea, river or mountain activities and as such they are found in remote and beautiful places around the world. They almost always need to recruit live-in workers. While there are opportunities for some unskilled staff, most vacancies are for instructors in everything from windsurfing to nature studies. To apply for these positions you will need appropriate qualifications and a reasonable amount of experience.

Many specialist tour companies employ leaders for their clients (children and/or adults) who want a walking, cycling, watersports holiday, etc. Any competent sailor, canoeist, diver, climber, horse rider, etc should have no difficulty marketing their skills abroad. A list of special interest and activity tour operators (to whom people with specialist skills can apply) is available from AITO, the Association of Independent Tour Operators (www.aito.co.uk). In the US, consult the *Specialty Travel Index* (www.specialtytravel.com).

Agriculture
Fruit picking

Farmers from England to Tasmania are unable to bring in their harvests without assistance from outside their local community and often reward their itinerant labour force well.

7

Historically agricultural harvests have employed the greatest number of casual workers who have often travelled hundreds of miles to gather in the fruits of the land, from the tiny blueberry to the mighty watermelon. If you are looking for a satisfying job that is limited in duration, allows you to work outside, has free or cheap accommodation and will expand your cultural horizons by flinging you into a hard working environment with people from all over the world, then fruit harvesting may well be for you.

Part of the appeal of fruit picking is the ability to raise a fair amount of money in a short amount of time. Most fruit-picking work is paid at piece rates, so while you may start off barely scraping minimum wage, your pay will rapidly increase as you get more experienced. There is also little opportunity to spend your earnings on an isolated farm and most people are able to save several hundred pounds in say, a 10-day harvest.

Equally appealing is the opportunity to experience something completely different. There are few more authentic ways of experiencing an alien culture than working off the land in the most rural areas. The grape harvest, or *vendange*, in France for example, lures many for the pure romance of participating in an ancient ritual. While mechanisation may have completely replaced casual labour in some areas such as Cognac, the finest Grand Cru chateaux are unlikely to ever completely do away with hand picking.

There is also a tremendous community spirit among fruit pickers, from the North African migrants and huge numbers of eastern Europeans to international working holidaymakers. When thrust into such a hard-working environment, living together at close quarters with a large group of people, it is almost impossible not to make friends. Some of the larger farms offer communal events for workers on their days off, such as barbecues and informal sporting matches. There is often a work hard, play hard atmosphere in fruit-picking camps. During the *vendange* season for example, the free wine provided after (or even during!) a hard day's work often makes for sparkling company. Bear in mind though that an early start, and tiring work are not ideal companions for a hangover.

If your experience of farm work is limited to family excursions to the local pick-your-own orchard, then the reality of fruit picking may be something of a rude awakening. Some physical

Apple picking in France

fitness is a definite prerequisite and having a little experience is likely to make the work far more enjoyable. Without either, you are likely to find the first few days gruelling. Do not become disheartened. More experienced pickers will be happy to advise on technique and, after a week or so, your confidence and your earnings will have increased.

Fruit picking work is harder to find than it was before countries like Latina and Slovenia joined the European Union. But the jobs are still there for the taking and you will find several large farms listed in this book as well as interesting farm work schemes. There is no reason to restrict yourself to agricultural work listed here though. These are the kinds of jobs that are best found on the ground and via word of mouth.

Organic farming

The organic farming movement is a very useful source of agricultural contacts. Organic growers everywhere take on volunteers to help them minimise or abolish the use of chemicals and heavy machinery. Various coordinating bodies go under the name of WWOOF – World Wide Opportunities on Organic Farms. National WWOOF coordinators compile a worklist of their member farmers willing to provide free room and board, and this list is sent to members. Organic producers are looking for volunteers who are genuinely interested in furthering the aims of the organic movement. WWOOF is an exchange: in return for your help on organic farms, gardens and homesteads, you receive meals, a place to sleep and a practical insight into organic growing. The norm is for volunteers to work about six hours a day. Some hosts expect applicants to have gained some experience on an organic farm in their own country first, though this is not usual. If the topic of 'WWOOFing' arises at immigration present yourself as a volunteer student of organic farming organising an educational farm visit or a cultural exchange but without mentioning the word 'work'.

Each national group has its own aims, system, fees and rules. The number of countries with WWOOF farms is exploding, so that just this year, new groups have set up in Portugal, Philippines, Ireland and Cameroon. WWOOF has a global website *www.wwoofinternational.org* with links to both the national offices in the countries that have a WWOOF coordinator and to those which do not, known as WWOOF independents. WWOOF organisations exist in many countries worldwide – developed and developing. Choose your destination country, find out if it has a WWOOF organisation and then join (usually €15–€20 for a year) in order to gain access to contact details of participating farms. Currently there is no international membership scheme. If you are starting in Britain and want to try out the system in your own country, fill out the online membership application form (www.wwoof.org.uk). Membership costs £20 per year or £30 for joint membership.

English language teaching

One billion people speak, or are trying to speak, English around the world and those of us who speak it as a first language tend to take for granted how universally dominant it has become. There are areas of the world where the boom in English-language learning seems to know no bounds, from Ecuador to Slovakia, China to Tunisia. The kind of people who want to learn English are just as numerous as the places in which they live, so there are jobs in this arena all over the world. A good source of information about the whole topic is *Teaching English Abroad* (Susan Griffith, 2010), available from www.crimsonpublishing.co.uk.

Teaching in schools and at summer camps

Many English language institutes run summer courses that require a huge influx of teachers and activity leaders. To fix up a job in advance, make use of the internet sites such as Guardian jobs and www.tefl.com. In a few cases, a carefully crafted CV and enthusiastic personality are as important as EFL training and experience. There is also increasing scope for untrained but eager volunteers willing to pay an agency to place them in a language teaching situation abroad.

In some private language institutes, being a native speaker and adopting a professional manner are sometimes sufficient qualifications to get a job. But these days it is more likely that you will require an ELT qualification (see box below) and possibly also a degree. However, there are plenty of jobs in language schools that do not have this requirement. The majority of residential language schools often take on staff to work as social supervisors and organisers of the extra-crricular programme, including excursions. The bigger ones may also require sports and activity instructors. These positions frequently require no qualifications other than interest and an ability to work with young people.

Short-term teachers are nearly always employed to stimulate conversation rather than to teach grammar. Yet a basic knowledge of English grammar is a great asset when more advanced pupils ask awkward questions. The wages paid to English teachers are usually reasonable, and in developing countries are quite often well in excess of the average local wage. In return you may be asked to teach some fairly unsociable hours since most private English classes take place after working hours, and so schedules split between early morning and evening are commonplace.

Working at English summer camps

Across the UK and Europe, a large number of short-term residential summer camps combine sports and outdoor activities with English tuition. Not only do they create short-term opportunities for teaching English, but they also provide a range of opportunities for camp counsellors, monitors, group leaders, activity instructors and sports coaches. English summer camps usually last from one to four weeks.

English Language Teaching Qualifications

Most language schools require their teachers to have a TEFL or TESOL qualification, though some will take on undergraduates. There are lots of TEFL/TESOL courses and qualifications on offer, varying widely in length, location and cost. Check the advertisements for those that seem most respected before committing to a course. It is important to choose a course which offers teaching practice as this will give you the skills and confidence you need to teach effectively.

One of the most widely recognised certificates is the Cambridge CELTA (Certificate in English Language Teaching to Adults). CELTA courses can be taken at 280 approved centres in the UK and overseas. They can be taken full-time over one month, or part-time over a longer period. For more information and to find a centre, contact Cambridge Assessment (01223 553355; www.cambridgeesol.org/teaching).

The other major certificate, carrying equal recognition, is the Cert TESOL, awarded by Trinity College London. The syllabus stipulates a minimum of 130 hours of scheduled course input over a four to five week period (or part-time over a longer period – anything up to nine months). Contact 020 7820 6100; www.trinitycollege.co.uk. Certificate courses cost between £900 and £1,100 or more, including exam moderation fees.

Working with children

Summer camps

Summer camps, once the preserve of the USA, now take place all over the world, becoming increasingly important as more and more parents go out to work and childcare costs rocket. Activities offered range from horseriding and archery to learning how to perform circus tricks. And in order to maintain a broad appeal, new courses offered in the last few years include recording a CD, film-making and website design. These camps require a huge number of summer workers. Jobs available include sports instructors, monitors and group counsellors. Most camps last from two to four weeks.

Au pairs, nannies and mothers' helps

These days, young British women are much less likely to consider au pairing as a summer job than was formerly the case. Being an au pair is seen as an unadventurous option compared with helping to conserve an Amazon rainforest or teaching English to Nepalese children, which is the type of alternative offered by the many, rather expensive, gap year companies. Nevertheless, au pairing remains an excellent way to acquire fluency in a foreign language. Young women (and sometimes young men) can arrange to live with a family, helping to look after the children in exchange for pocket money.

The terms au pair, mother's help and nanny are often applied rather loosely, since all are primarily live-in jobs concerned with looking after children. Nannies may have some formal training and take full charge of the children. Mother's helps work full-time and undertake general housework and/or cooking as well as childcare. Au pairs are supposed to work fewer hours and are expected to learn a foreign language (except in the USA) while living with a family. The Council of Europe guidelines stipulate that au pairs should be aged 18–27 (though these limits are flexible), should be expected to work no more than five hours a day, plus a couple of

Au pairing can be a great opportunity to learn a foreign language

evenings of babysitting, with at least one full day off per week; they must be given a private room, health insurance, opportunities to learn the language and weekly pocket money. The standard amount paid to au pairs in Europe is currently €260 a month (£75 per week in the UK), plus full board and lodging.

Many au pair agencies now operate only as online matching services. The old-fashioned one-woman agency which used to arrange family placements with the help of a partner agency in France, Germany, Italy, etc. has all but disappeared. This is primarily due to UK legislation passed in 2004 which makes it illegal for any agency to charge au pairs a fee for finding them work, either in the UK or abroad. As a result agencies which at one time sent many British girls abroad are now concentrating exclusively on placing foreign girls with paying client families in the UK.

The same rules do not apply to European agencies, some of which are included in this book. European agencies can charge a substantial fee (for example €200+). Many leading au pair agencies and youth exchange organisations in Europe belong to IAPA, the International Au Pair Association, an international body trying to regulate the industry. The IAPA website www.iapa.org has clear links to its member agencies around the world. A list of agencies can also be found at www.europa-pages.com/au_pair. After satisfying an agency that you are a suitable candidate for a live-in childcare position, you will have to wait until an acceptable match can be made with a family abroad. Make enquiries as early as possible, since there is a shortage of summer-only positions.

The advantage of a summer placement is that the au pair will accompany the family to their holiday destination at the seaside or in the mountains; the disadvantage is that the children will be out of school and therefore potentially a full-time responsibility.

Volunteer work

Despite the title of this book, 'Summer Jobs', quite a few of the listings are for unpaid opportunities. Researching sharks in the Maldives or helping street kids in Honduras this summer could be gripping, but it will never make you rich. In fact it might make you poor because charities and NGOs that accept foreign volunteers usually charge a fee to cover their costs and sometimes also as a contribution to the project. These opportunities can provide marvelous experiences (and good CV fodder) but they will require a financial investment.

Both profit and non-profit organisations offer a range of volunteering opportunities around the world. For example, enterprising summer workers have participated in interesting projects from helping a local native settlement to build a community centre in Arctic Canada, to working with hill tribes in a remote part of northern India.

When starting your research for a longer stint abroad as a volunteer, it is important to maintain realistic expectations. Ideally, your research should begin well in advance of your intended departure so that applications can be lodged and sponsorship money raised if appropriate. When choosing a volunteer sending agency, consider the tone as well as the content. For example, profit-making commercial companies that charge high fees for participating in their programmes are more likely to produce glossy brochures that read almost like a tour operator's, whereas underfunded charities or small grassroots organisations will dispense with the razzmatazz and not be the first ones to pop up on google.

For anyone with a green conscience, numerous conservation organisations throughout the world welcome volunteers for short or long periods. Projects range from making films of primates in Uganda to studying how climate change is affecting a lake in Bhutan. Unfortunately, the more glamorous projects such as helping to conserve a coral reef or accompanying scientific research expeditions into wild and exotic places charge volunteers a great deal of money for the privilege of helping.

A volunteer administers first aid at a summer camp

For further information on volunteering, *World Volunteers*, (Fabio Ausender, 2008) available from www.crimsonpublishing.co.uk, contains advice and listings of all types of humanitarian voluntary work worldwide. The companion volume about conservation opportunities is *Green Volunteers* by the same author. The non-profit World Wide Volunteering (www.wwv.org.uk) has an online database of 1,700 organisations offering a potential total of 1.5 million placements, which is freely accessible to anyone.

Work camps

Although the term 'workcamp' is often replaced by 'volunteer project', the international work camp movement is still widely recognised by that name as every summer it mobilises thousands of volunteers to join a programme of conflict resolution and community development. As well as providing volunteers with the means to live cheaply for two to four weeks in a foreign country, work camps enable unskilled volunteers to become involved in what can be useful work for the community (eg building footpaths, renovating schools and providing aid).

Work camps are perfect for people who want to get some experience volunteering, as participants are not expected to have any skills or qualifications. They are also a great way to meet people from many different backgrounds and to increase awareness of other lifestyles and social problems.

There are work camps each summer in more than 90 countries worldwide, although the strongest movements are still in places like France, Germany and Italy. If you are based in the UK you will find a huge number of work camps that are available to you worldwide through the Concordia website: *www.concordia-iye.org.uk;* as well as IVS *www.ivsgb.org.uk* UNA Exchange *www.unaexchange.org* and Voluntary Action for Peace *www.vap-uk.org*.

Rock climbing at a summer activity camp

Volunteering at summer music festivals

Music festivals are increasing in size and scope every year and behind the scenes huge numbers of volunteers are involved in stewarding, first aid and clearing up the festival site. Each year thousands of enterprising individuals gain entry to sold-out festivals, without paying a penny, by volunteering to fill these positions. Oxfam, for example, recruits several thousand volunteer stewards for a range of festivals in the UK, including Glastonbury (www.oxfam.org.uk/get_involved/stewardingindex.html).

As a volunteer, you are required to work quite hard, but in return receive ample time each day to enjoy the festival atmosphere and see your favourite bands. In the majority of cases, volunteers are also provided with a separate camping area, warm showers and meal passes. You will find the details of individual festivals and how to apply as a volunteer in the individual country chapters of this book.

LANDING THE PERFECT SUMMER JOB

You have two choices: fixing up a definite job before leaving home, or taking a gamble on finding something on arrival. There is a lot to recommend prior planning, especially for people who have seldom travelled on their own and who feel some trepidation about being away from home.

If you have no predisposition to choose one country over another based on previous holidays, language studies at school or information from friends or relatives who live abroad, you are free to consider any job listed in this book. It will soon become apparent that there are far fewer listings in developing countries, simply because paid work in the developing world is rarely available to foreigners. Yet many students arrange to live for next to nothing doing something positive (see the section on *Volunteering*).

Some organisations and employers listed in this directory accept a tiny handful of individuals who satisfy stringent requirements; others accept almost anyone who can pay the required fee, for example agencies that recruit paying volunteers for conservation work in exotic places or to teach English. Some work schemes and official exchanges require a lot of advance planning since it is not unusual for an application deadline to fall three to six months before departure.

The kind of job you find will determine the sector of society in which you will mix and therefore the content of the experience. The traveller who spends a few weeks picking olives for a Cretan farmer will get a very different insight into Greece from the traveller who looks after the children of an Athenian shipping magnate. And both will probably have more culturally worthwhile experiences than the traveller who settles for working at a beach café frequented only by his or her partying compatriots. The more unusual and interesting the job, the more competition it will attract.

More unusual and interesting jobs, like a hot air balloon crew, fill up quickly

10 tips for success

Summer work isn't difficult to find, but about half a million other students will be job-hunting, so it pays to plan ahead.

1. Do your research

With over 50,000 vacancies, this book is a great starting point. But there is nothing to stop you using this directory as a jumping-off point, and doing your own research. Once you have seen how many seasonal jobs there are around, and the kind of places to find them, you are sure to find more. Some people prefer just to turn up in a place and look for work. No matter how thorough this book is, there is no substitute for good old-fashioned word of mouth.

The internet can also be useful. The only problem with it is that the plethora of resources in cyberspace can be bewildering and not infrequently disappointing – the number and range of jobs posted often fall short of the claims. Small-scale employers do not like to use the web as they are bound to be inundated with SPAM and applications from Merseyside to Mongolia. The internet as a job-finding tool works best for those with specific experience and skills, for example people looking for TEFL jobs abroad. See the section overleaf on last-minute job-hunting for some recommended recruitment sites.

2. Timing

Apply early. Companies like to make their staff arrangements in good time. Some of the biggest employers may maintain reserve lists to cover late staff cancellations, so it might pay off to apply after the deadline, but don't be disappointed if you receive no reply.

Remember: most employers much prefer one person for the whole of the season rather than several people for shorter periods. If you are able to work for longer than the minimum period quoted, let the employer know at an early stage. This is often a deciding factor.

3. Cast your net wide

Apply for all of the jobs that appeal to you (plus a few that don't). The more you apply for, the greater your chances of getting a great summer job. But do make sure that you are fully qualified for the job. Check any requirements and special qualifications needed, particularly if good knowledge of another language is called for. If there is any shortfall, emphasise other skills and qualifications that may be useful.

4. Get your approach right

Compose a short formal letter, explaining which position interests you, when you are available and why you think you are suitable.

Try to address the potential employer in his or her language. It is not only polite to do so, but there is a possibility that he or she is unable to speak English.

5. Apply with a great CV

Enclose with your letter a well thought out *curriculum vitae* (CV or résumé). Always target your CV to the job in question, leaving out any irrelevant material and emphasising related achievements. Your CV should be on a single A4 sheet (two sides if you must, but no more) covering the following points and any other details you consider relevant:

- Personal details (name, address, nationality, age, date of birth, marital status)
- Previous work experience, especially of similar type of work
- Special qualifications, especially when they have some relevance to the job in question, eg canoe instructor's certificate, typing speeds or fluency in another language
- Education (brief details of type of education, examinations passed)

Make sure you enclose a small recent passport-sized photo of yourself as this is often required. If you need some tips on improving your CV take a look at www.prospects.ac.uk/cv_content.htm.

6. Apply with care

Check and then double check the spelling and grammar in your application. If you are sending it via email, be sure to remember the attachment. Also if a CV is attached, make sure that it is written in a programme that is readable and receivable by the receiver (in Microsoft Word format or a pdf) and that it contains no viruses.

7. Chase it up

If there is no reply from the employer within a reasonable period of time (say two weeks), it may be advisable to follow up the application with a telephone call or another email. The employer may be impressed by your initiative and perseverance if it is matched by enthusiasm and politeness. If you are making a first approach to a potential employer by phone, smile while you are talking to them – it comes across in your voice.

In a few cases it is expected that applicants should make themselves available for an interview or visit the employer in person. Where this is the case, the applicant is likely to find more success if he or she can back up claims of suitability with a written CV and references.

8. Negotiate

When a job is offered to you, check details of wages, hours and other conditions of work with the employer. Do not be afraid to negotiate; you are always entitled to ask whether or not different terms are possible.

9. Check details carefully

The details given in this book have been supplied by the employer and will normally be correct, but it is wise to obtain written confirmation of them before taking up the position. You should insist that you receive a contract of employment before you set off for your job if the journey involves any great expense, or if the employer seems at all vague about the details of the work you will do.

10. Confirm

When you are offered a job, confirm acceptance or otherwise as quickly as possible. If plans change and you do not want to take up a job you have already accepted, it is only fair to let the employer know immediately. If you are offered more than one job, decide quickly which one you prefer and inform both employers of your decision as promptly as possible.

LEFT IT TO THE LAST MINUTE? DON'T PANIC!

If you're reading this section, you are probably not the kind of well-organised jobseeker who plans ahead! Clearly it is far better to organise your summer job well in advance. The two main industries that survive on seasonal labour are tourism and agriculture, and managers from Canterbury to Cape Town need to have enough seasonal staff lined up before their busy season begins. So, the earlier that you can make contact with potential employers, as close as possible to the date indicating the start of the recruitment season provided in the entries that follow, the easier it will be to secure a summer job. Lecture over.

In the real world, it can be very difficult to focus on finding a temporary job until the summer is almost upon you. The good news is that not all is lost, especially for someone who already has a little relevant experience or a smattering of a foreign language. It is always worth contacting large seasonal employers at the last minute, since there is a high turnover in this field and a huge amount of demand. Eleventh-hour jobseekers from Britain will have to concentrate on the UK and Europe, since obtaining student work visas for Australia, New Zealand, the USA and Canada takes many months.

Patient searches of employment websites can also prove productive. A host of commercial websites promises to provide free online recruitment services for working travellers, and some of the job listings will show immediate start dates. These include the admirable *jobsabroad-bulletin.co.uk*, *www.seasonworkers.com*, *www.natives.co.uk* (originally for ski resort work but now also for summer jobs), *www.anyworkanywhere.com*, *www.coolworks.com* and *www.jobmonkey.com* (though the latter two are mainly for North America). Some of them have

Staff giving wind-surfing lessons

useful forums with detailed postings about the interview process etc. Another useful source of this kind of insider information is *thestudentroom.co.uk*. From time to time good summer jobs crop up on *www.justjobs4students.co.uk* which sends email alerts free of charge. Listings will be thinner than they would be before Easter but possibilities still exist.

As in any job-hunt, networking is often the key to success. It is always worth telling family, friends and friends of friends about your plans in case they divulge the details of potentially useful contacts. And if you have no ready-made contacts in your chosen destination, you can seek them out in advance or after arrival through local clubs and organisations whose interests you share, eg cyclists, Hash House Harriers (social runners), jazz buffs, and so on. Irish pubs abroad often attract the expat community who will offer free advice. To meet locals and get free accommodation, investigate membership in an international hospitality exchange organisation like *www.globalfreeloaders.com, www.place2stay.net* or *www.couchsurfing.org*, all of which are completely free to join. One solution would be to choose an almost-guaranteed option that a mediating agency can fix up for you. Most of these incur a hefty fee, but volunteering on an Israeli Kibbutz for two to six months is a venerable exception. Without much trouble or delay foreign volunteers can make an arrangement through the official Kibbutz Program Center in Tel Aviv (*www.kibbutz.org.it/volunteers*) for a modest registration fee of US$90 at least one month in advance of arrival.

Finding a job on the spot

If your patience gives out before you receive the promise of a job, there is one final recourse, which is simply to gamble on finding a job on the spot. Casual work by its very nature is changeable and unpredictable and can often best be searched out where it is happening. So whether you are going abroad, or just further afield than your home town, it may be that your best bet is to pack your bags and go for it.

Even if a prospective employer turns you down at first, ask again since it is human nature to want to reward keenness and he or she may decide that an extra staff member could be useful after all. Polite pestering pays off. Some go so far as to offer to work for an initial period without pay, hoping to make themselves first choice for any vacancy that occurs, though this may be a gamble too far. Boldness and initiative will usually be rewarded with some kind of remunerated job, though seldom will it be glamorous.

Your chances are better if you are willing to consider jobs that are unappealing and with awkward hours. For example, one job with a high turnover is as a 'charity fundraiser'. Commercial companies hire an army of young people to accost passers-by and try to persuade them to sign direct debit forms to support charities. This activity has been dubbed 'charity mugging' and hence the employees are sometimes referred to as 'chuggers'.

Less-structured possibilities abound. Enterprising travellers have managed to earn money by doing a bizarre range of odd-jobs, from selling home made peanut butter to homesick Americans, or busking on the bagpipes, or doing Tarot readings on a Mediterranean ferry, or becoming film extras in Mumbai.

Top tips for finding a job on the spot

- Collect character/job references on headed paper, a short CV and any potentially relevant qualifications (driving, sailing, cooking, TEFL, computing, first aid). Scan and email copies to yourself so that you can access them anywhere.
- Pack a smart, uncreasable outfit for interviews.

- Take a bilingual dictionary and teach-yourself language course on your MP3 player since you will be far more motivated to use these when you are actually living in the country.
- Broadcast your intentions to third cousins, visiting professors or in relevant chatrooms and be prepared to follow up every lead you are given. Contacts are often the key to success.
- On arrival, seek advice from expats and fellow travellers. If looking for casual work on farms or trying to fix up a passage on a transatlantic yacht, for example, a visit to a village pub frequented by farmers, yachties or the local expatriate community is usually worth dozens of speculative applications and emails from home.
- If going door to door, for example along a waterfront stretch of restaurants, ask at every single place, rather than just the ones that seem appealing. You may have to endure dozens of rejections, but the next door along might well be open to you.
- If there is something you are particularly keen to do but there are no vacancies, volunteer your labour so that you can showcase your ability and enthusiasm and then you will be on hand if an opportunity arises.
- Don't hang around waiting for something to turn up. Go out and sell yourself (not literally).

BEFORE YOU GO: ESSENTIAL PREPARATION

Travel

If you are a student, you can take advantage of a range of special discounts both at home and abroad which enable you to go almost anywhere in the world on the cheap. To qualify for these discounts on train, plane and bus fares, on selected accommodation, admission to museums and so on, you need an International Student Identity Card (ISIC) which is recognised all over the world. The card is obtainable for £9 from www.isiccard.com. The ISIC card is valid for 15 months from 1 September. If you are not a student, but still under 26, you can take advantage of the International Youth Travel Card (IYTC) available from www.isiccard.com for £9.

Both cards are available from STA Travel (0871 2300 640; www.statravel.co.uk), Student Flights (www.studentflights.co.uk) and some other student travel outlets. Applications should include proof of student status (if required), a passport photo, full name, date of birth, nationality, address and a cheque or postal order.

Flying

Specialist youth and student travel agencies are an excellent source of information for just about every kind of discount. Staff are often themselves seasoned travellers and can offer a wealth of information on budget travel in foreign countries. Also check out the no frills airlines and cheap flights websites to compare prices before making a final decision. For complex routings, try Travel Nation (0845 344 4225; www.travel-nation.co.uk). A good starting place for independent flight research are websites that search and compare cheapest fares such as www.cheapflights.co.uk and www.skyscanner.net.

Lifeguard on duty at a swimming pool

The leading youth and budget travel specialist in the UK is STA Travel which can organise flexible deals, domestic flights, overland transport, accommodation and tours. STA is a major international travel agency with 40 branches in the UK and hundreds more worldwide. As well as worldwide airfares, they sell discounted rail and coach tickets, budget accommodation and insurance and many other packaged products, and have branches at many universities.

In the US, discounted tickets are available online from Air Treks in San Francisco (+1 877 247 8735; AirTreks.com) which specialises in multi-stop and round-the-world fares. By far the cheapest airfares from the US to Europe (and Hawaii) are available to people who are flexible about departure dates and destinations, and are prepared to travel on a standby basis. The passenger chooses a block of possible dates (up to a four-day 'window') and preferred destinations. A company like Airtech (+1 212 219 7000; airtech.com) then tries to match these requirements with empty airline seats being released at knock-down prices. Lately availability of transatlantic flights has decreased using this method and flights from Europe are now only out of Amsterdam. The website www.studentuniverse.com is also worth a look for cheap flights.

From the UK to Europe it is usually cheaper to fly on one of the no-frills airlines than it is to go by rail or coach. Airlines like Ryanair and easyJet shuttle between regional airports and scores of European and Mediterranean destinations from Tampere in Finland to Marrakesh in north Africa. The list of airlines below is only a selection. There are new companies and new destinations being added all the time so it pays to keep an eye on the press and use the internet. Note that quoted prices now have to include taxes (that add up to £35 on a return fare to Europe) and that you usually have to book well in advance to get the cheapest fares. These airlines do not take bookings via travel agents so it is necessary to contact them directly.

- *bmibaby* – 0870 264 2229; www.bmibaby.com
- *easyJet* – 0871 500 100; www.easyjet.com
- *Ryanair* – 0871 246 0000; www.ryanair.com
- *Thomsonfly* – 0870 1900 737; www.thomsonfly.com
- *Flybe* – www.flybe.com
- *Jet2* – www.jet2.com

Discount airlines have proliferated on the continent too, so check out www.airberlin.com, www.germanwings.com (German), www.transavia.com (Dutch), www.wizzair.com (Polish), www.smartwings.com (Czech) and so on. Central sources of information include www.flycheapo.com and www.whichbudget.com. Scheduled airlines like British Airways and Aer Lingus have had to drop fares to compete and are always worth comparing. After saying all this, you may wish to consider the environmental impact of flying and move on to the next section.

Rail and coach travel

If you want to reduce your carbon footprint, rail and coach travel are far better options and there are some cheap deals to be found if you know where to look.

InterRail is a great way to visit lots of countries cheaply. In the past, tickets were divided into zones, but this system was simplified a few years ago. Now one Global pass covers the whole of Europe for one calendar month costing approximately £367 for those under 26 and £550 for those 26 and over. A shorter duration of 22 days is also available for £284–£431. If you plan to make a few long journeys in a certain number of days, investigate Flexipasses; they permit five days of travel within 10 days, or 10 days of travel within 22 days. Even cheaper are the one-country passes which can be a useful aid to the job-seeker, permitting (for example) three days of rail travel within a month within France, Germany or a raft of other countries. The InterRail pass also entitles you to discounts on Eurostar and certain ferries in Europe.

A number of specialised agencies sell InterRail products and add slightly different mark-ups. Passes can be bought online at www.interrailnet.com or in person at branches of STA Travel and similar outlets. Websites to check include www.trainseurope.co.uk, www.raileurope.co.uk, www.railpassshop.com or the marvellous site for train travellers everywhere www.seat61.com. Rail Europe can be contacted by telephone on 08448 484064.

Group trek in the rainforest

Eurolines is the group name for 32 independent coach operators serving 500 destinations in all European countries from Ireland to Romania. Promotional prices start at £45 return for London–Amsterdam if booked at least a week in advance. Bookings can be made online at www.eurolines.co.uk or by phoning 08717 818181. So-called 'funfares' mean that some off-season fares from the UK are even lower, eg £17 to Brussels, Paris or Dublin.

One of the most interesting revolutions in independent and youth travel has been the explosion of backpackers' bus services which are hop-on hop-off coach services following prescribed routes. These can be found in New Zealand (Stray Travel, Kiwi Experience and the Magic Travellers Network), Australia (Oz Experience), Canada (Moose Travel) South Africa (Baz Bus) and Turkey/Greece (Fez Travel) as well as in Britain and Ireland. For example Busabout serves 30 destinations in 10 countries. You can buy a pass for a western, northern or southern 'loop' (they are not so good on eastern Europe) or a Flexitrip pass. All are valid for the entire operating season of May to October. One loop currently costs £335. A Flexitrip Pass costs £299 and includes six stops (additional stops can be purchased on board). In North America trips run by Green Tortoise (+1 800 867 8647; www.greentortoise.com) use vehicles converted to sleep 35 people and make interesting tours, detours and stopovers around the Americas and Mexico.

Visas and Red Tape

Visiting a foreign country as a tourist is quite distinct from going there in order to work. Tourist visas are not required in Europe nor to visit North America, Australia or New Zealand. Other countries may require a visa to enter. Up-to-date visa information is available from national consulates in London/Washington or on the internet. For example the visa agency CIBT in London (0844 736021; http://uk.cibt.com) allows you to search visa requirements and costs for individual countries. If you are short of time or live a long way from the embassies in London, private visa agencies like CIBT will undertake the footwork for you and charge an extra £40–£45 per visa.

European Union citizens have the right to work anywhere within the EU and in fact the bureaucratic procedures for nationals of the old EU states have become easier. Recent directives are slowly being implemented and the necessity for EU nationals to acquire a residence permit after three months has mainly been abolished. Usually some sort of registration process is necessary but the paperwork in most countries has been simplified.

The accession of two new countries to the European Union in 2007 (Bulgaria and Romania) in addition to the 10 new countries that joined in May 2004 means that the EU now consists of the original 15 member states (Austria, Belgium, Denmark, Finland, France, Germany, Greece, Ireland, Italy, Luxembourg, the Netherlands, Portugal, Spain, Sweden and the UK) plus Hungary, Poland, the Czech Republic, Slovakia, Slovenia, Estonia, Latvia, Lithuania, Malta, Cyprus, Romania and Bulgaria. However some transitional barriers to the full mobility of labour in the new EU countries will be in place for up to seven years. For up-to-date information on regulations regarding taking up work in all EU member states consult the EURES website at www.europa.eu or the individual countries' embassies in your own country.

Work permits and residence visas are not readily available to Europeans looking to work elsewhere in the world or to North American and Antipodean jobseekers in Europe (see sections on *Red tape* in the country chapters). In most cases, a foreign jobseeker must first find an employer willing to apply to the immigration authorities on his or her behalf well in advance of the job's starting date and before the applicant enters the country. The alternative is to participate in an approved exchange programme where the red tape is taken care of by a sponsoring organisation. The same applies to non-European students looking for seasonal jobs in Europe. Established organisations with work abroad programmes are invaluable for shouldering the red tape problems and for providing a soft landing for first-time travellers.

For example BUNAC (020 7251 3472; www.bunac.org.uk) is a student club that helps students and other young people to work abroad. Likewise BUNAC USA (www.bunac.org) assists a large number of Americans to work in various countries around the world. BUNAC in the UK has a choice of programmes to the USA, Canada, Australia and New Zealand plus volunteer programmes in Peru, South Africa, China, Ghana, India and Cambodia. In all cases BUNAC assists with obtaining the appropriate visa. In some programmes, jobs will be arranged for you, for instance as counsellors or domestic staff at American children's summer camps; in others, it is up to you to find a job once you arrive at your destination.

IST Plus Ltd, in London oversees work abroad programmes for Britons (020 8939 9057; www.istplus.com). Work and teaching abroad programmes for students, graduates and young professionals include Work & Travel USA, Internship USA, Summer Camps USA, Work & Travel Australia, Work & Travel New Zealand, Teach in China and Teach in Thailand.

Many other youth exchange organisations and commercial agencies offer packages which help students to arrange work or volunteer positions abroad. For example Camp America and Camp Counselors USA (CCUSA) are major recruitment organisations which arrange for thousands of young people to work in the USA mostly on summer camps. Other agencies specialise in placing young people (both women and men) in families as au pairs, as voluntary English teachers or in a range of other capacities – see the entries for individual countries.

The Schengen Visa

The Schengen visa allows citizens of member states to cross borders freely without the need for a passport (although some form of government approved identification is needed for air travel). The 15 original Schengen countries are: Austria, Belgium, Denmark, Finland, France, Germany, Iceland, Italy, Greece, Luxembourg, the Netherlands, Norway, Portugal, Spain and Sweden. Estonia, Hungary, Latvia, Lithuania, Malta, Poland, the Czech Republic, Slovakia and Slovenia joined the Schengen Agreement on 21 December 2007, possibly soon to be joined by Romania and Bulgaria.

Non-Europeans need to obtain just one visa (which is free of charge) to enter all these countries. Non-Europeans should be careful not to overstay the 90-day limit of their Schengen visa to avoid a hefty fine. Note that the Schengen visa covers only visitor stays and does not affect your ability to work in a certain country.

What to pack

Even if you are travelling directly to your place of work, don't load yourself down with excess baggage. Most people who go abroad for a summer job want to do at least some independent travelling when their job ends and will find themselves seriously hampered if they are carrying around a 30-kilo rucksack. When you're buying a backpack/rucksack in a shop try to place a

A white water rafting expedition in Colorado

significant weight in it so you can feel how comfortable it might be to carry on your back, other wise you'll be misled by lifting something usually filled with foam.

While aiming to travel as lightly as possible you should consider the advantage of taking certain extra pieces of equipment. For example:

- A Swiss army knife (make sure it is not packed in your airline hand luggage) is often invaluable, if only for its corkscrew!
- A comfortable pair of shoes is essential since most summer jobs will involve long hours on your feet whether in a hotel dining room or in a farmer's field.
- A bin-liner to put inside your rucksack to keep your stuff dry.
- A basic sewing kit for mending backpacks or clothes.
- A couple of metres of light strong cord (such as dental floss) to make a washing line etc.

Ideally, talk to someone who has done the job before who might recommend an obscure piece of equipment you'd never think of, for example a pair of fingerless gloves for cold-weather fruit-picking. You might also allow yourself the odd lightweight luxury, such as an MP3 player or a digital camera. You will need to invest in a universal charger (eg Callpod) to fit sockets around the world. You can always post some belongings on ahead, with the employer's permission. Try to leave anything of either great monetary or sentimental value at home as their temporary absence is nothing compared to their permanent loss.

Good maps and guides are usually considered essential tools for a trip. If you are in London or Bristol, the famous map shop Stanfords (www.stanfords.co.uk) can supply most needs. The Map Shop (www.themapshop.co.uk) does an extensive mail order business in specialised maps and guide books.

Accommodation

The vast majority of jobs listed in this book come with accommodation; usually shared with other workers. Even if there is no accommodation on site, many of the employers listed regularly take on young people from all over the world and are used to helping their staff to find local lodgings.

You should always find out what the deal is way ahead of time. Ask the following questions of your potential employer:

- How much will be deducted from your wages to cover accommodation?
- What facilities (especially for self-catering) are provided?
- How close to your place of work are the lodgings?
- Will there be extra costs for food, utilities, etc?
- Are staff allowed to move out if they find more congenial or cheaper accommodation?

Sometimes the accommodation provided is very basic indeed and you should be prepared for something rather more insalubrious than you are used to at home or at university. Certain jobs may provide more luxurious accommodation, for example hotel/resort work or any live-in job. Live-in jobs of course come with their own drawbacks, such as a lack of privacy and free time.

If accommodation is not provided with the job, try to arrange something in advance, and certainly for the first couple of nights. If necessary make the journey to your destination several days early to fix up a suitable room. In cities, if the backpackers' hostels are full, check craigslist, gumtree, kijiji or equivalent, or try universities, which might rent out student accommodation that has been vacated for the summer or whose notice boards may include details of housing. In holiday resorts, accommodation may be at a premium and you will have to use your ingenuity to find something you can afford.

The original Youth Hostels Federation is now called Hostelling International (www. hihostels.com) and consists of 4,000 hostels in 60 countries. Membership costs only £9.95 for those under 26. Seasonal demand abroad can be high, so it is always preferable to book in advance if you know your itinerary. You can pre-book beds via www.hihostels.com.

Thousands of independent hostels also cater to the needs of backpackers. Bookings at hostels worldwide can be made at www.hostelseurope.com. Some hostel groups issue loyalty cards which bring down the nightly cost, for example VIP Backpackers Resorts, which is especially strong in Australia (www.vipbackpackers.com).

Money

Your average budget will vary hugely depending on where you are travelling. Obviously India and Bolivia are going to be much cheaper than Switzerland or anywhere in Scandinavia. Count on spending at least £25 a day and in Western Europe usually quite a bit more.

The most straightforward way to access money abroad is by using a bank debit card in hole-in-the-wall ATMs. Bear in mind that every withdrawal will incur a fee – as much as £5 – so you should get larger amounts out at one time than you would at home. Some accounts give better deals than others, for example in the UK a Flexaccount at the Nationwide Building Society permits free withdrawals in Europe. Remember that hole-in-the-wall cash dispensers abroad will not show your bank balance, so be sure to set up online banking before you go so you can track your balance wherever you have internet access. Always have a Plan B in case your cash card is damaged or stolen (see next section).

Please note wages in this book are not always quoted in British sterling. Bear in mind that exchange rates can fluctuate. The easiest way to look up the exchange rate of any world currency is to check on the internet for example at www.oanda.com.

Keeping your money safe

Whatever the size of your travelling fund, you should give some thought to how and in what form to carry your money. Always spread the risk by carrying your worldly wealth in various forms.

Travellers' cheques are safer than cash, though they cost an extra 1% and banks able to cash them are not always near to hand, even in Europe. The Post Office sells a Travel Money Card which is a prepaid, reloadable card that can be used like a debit card at ATMs and most shops but is not linked to your bank account. You can purchase it online and load it with sterling, euros or US dollars. Be aware that the exchange rate and transaction fees may not be any more favourable than the rival methods, though it is a useful back-up.

Theft takes many forms, from the highly trained gangs of children who artfully pick pocket in European railway stations to more violent attacks in South African or South American cities. You can reduce the risks by carrying your wealth in several places including a comfortable money belt worn inside your clothing, steering clear of seedy or crowded areas, and remaining particularly alert in railway stations and public transport. If you are robbed, you must obtain a police report (sometimes for a fee) to stand any chance of recouping part of your loss from your insurer (assuming the loss of cash is covered in your policy) or from your travellers' cheque company. Always keep a separate record of the cheque numbers you are carrying, so you can instantly identify the serial numbers of the ones lost or stolen.

In emergencies

If you do end up in dire financial straits and do not have a credit card, you should contact some-one at home who is in a position to send money. You may contact your bank back home and ask them to send money to a named bank. It is much easier if you have set up a telephone or internet bank account before leaving home since they will then have the correct security checks in place to authorise a transfer without having to receive something from you in writing with your signature.

Western Union (www.westernunion.co.uk) offers an international money transfer service whereby cash deposited at one branch can be withdrawn by you from any other branch or agency Western Union agents – there are tens of thousands of them in nearly 200 countries – come in all shapes and sizes (eg travel agencies, stationers, chemists). The person sending money to you simply turns up at a Western Union counter, hands over the desired sum plus the fee, which is £8 for up to £25 transferred, £21 for £100–£200, £37 for £500 and so on. It can also be done over the phone with a credit card, or online.

Thomas Cook and the UK Post Office offer a similar service called Moneygram (www.moneygram.com). Cash deposited at one of their foreign exchange counters is available at the named destination right away or can be collected up to 45 days later. The standard fee for send-ing £500 (for example) is £36.

Health and insurance

The National Health Service ceases to cover British nationals once they leave the United Kingdom. If you are travelling in Europe, you should get hold of a European Health Insurance Card (EHIC) which is free. The EHIC entitles you to free emergency medical treatment anywhere within the European Economic Area (the EU plus Liechtenstein, Norway and Iceland). You can apply for an EHIC in person (go into your nearest post office), over the phone (0845 6062030), or online (www.ehic.org.uk).

If you are planning to include developing countries on your itinerary, you will want to take the necessary health precautions, though this won't be cheap. Malaria poses an increasing danger and expert advice should be sought about which medications to take for the specific parts of the world you intend to visit.

Tap water is unsafe to drink in the more remote parts of the world so it will be necessary to give some thought as to the method of water purification you will use (filtering, boiling or chem-ical additives). Remember that water used to wash vegetables, brush teeth or make ice cubes is also potentially risky. Tap water throughout western Europe is safe to drink.

MASTA (Medical Advisory Service for Travellers Abroad) runs Travel Health Centres throughout the UK (to locate your nearest health centre visit www.masta.org). It also maintains an up-to-date database on travellers' diseases and their prevention. You can also get a Travel Health Brief for £3.99 online, with health information on your destinations (up to 10 countries).

Increasingly, people are seeking advice via the internet; check for example www.fitfortravel.scot.nhs.uk; www.tmb.ie and www.travelhealth.co.uk. The BBC's health travel site www.bbc.co.uk/health/treatments/travel is a solid source of information about travel health ranging from tummy trouble to water quality and snake bites.

Foreign health services rarely offer as comprehensive a free service for emergency treatment as the NHS does; while some offer free treatment, others will only subsidise the cost and any part of the treatment not covered by the free health service is met by private health insurance top up schemes. In some countries the ambulance ride has to be paid for, but not the treatment. The cost of bringing a person back to the UK in the case of illness or death is never covered under the reciprocal arrangements so it is considered essential to purchase private insurance in addition to carrying an EHIC.

Travel insurance

Ordinary travel insurance policies cover only those risks that a holidaymaker can expect to face and will not cover work-related injuries such as treating backs damaged while grape picking, or burns caused by an overboiling goulash in a restaurant kitchen.

The following companies should be able to arrange insurance cover for most people going to work abroad, as long as they are advised of the exact nature of the physical/manual job to be undertaken:

Club Direct: 0800 083 2466; www.ClubDirect.com
Work abroad is covered as long as it does not involve heavy machinery.
Columbus Direct: 0870 033 9988; www.columbusdirect.com
Provides a Globetrotter policy for those working abroad for short or long periods (up to 12 months).
Worldwide Travel Insurance Services Ltd: 01892 833 338; www.worldwideinsure.com
Comprehensive policies for most work abroad from two to 18 months. Manual labour cover can be purchased from overseas for an additional premium.
Endsleigh Insurance: 0800 028 3571; www.endsleigh.co.uk
Offices in most university towns. Age limit 35. Special gap year policy covers working abroad.

PART 1: THE UK

BOURNE LEISURE LIMITED

Haven

Would you like to be part of a business that was voted 2nd in the Sunday Times Top 20 Best Big Companies to work for 2009? Or one that 'The Apprentice' magazine lists as one of the 22 Top Employers to work for?

If the answer is YES, then we are proud to say that we are that company.

Haven operates 36 award-winning family holiday parks throughout England, Scotland and Wales - close to some of Britain's most beautiful Coastal lines, Beaches and brightest resorts and forms part of the Bourne Leisure Group, Britain's largest provider of UK holidays. In 2008 2.5 million holiday makers took a break at our parks.

Our aim is to be the standard against which all other holiday providers are measured. We believe in recruiting the attitude and training the skills as it is the positive attitude of our team that bring our guests back to our business on a regular basis.

If you're confident, friendly and believe work should be fun, we'd love to hear from you.

What's in it for you?; comprehensive induction training, a nationally recognised customer service programme, use of the site facilities and on site entertainment, incentives, team member accommodation at some sites, bonus scheme & performance awards plus up to 25% off holidays within the Group... and that's just for starters.

Our Haven Parks are open to our holiday makers from March – October creating hundreds of seasonal vacancies as well as many permanent opportunities for those wanting to pursue a career within this exciting industry.

OWNERS EXCLUSIVE
COMMITTED TO SERVING YOU

We have everything our customers need to make their family feel right at home. Enjoying the freedom of owning thier own Holiday Home complete with great facilities, located in a fantastic Holiday Park and available any time they choose.

As part of the Owners Exclusive team you be on hand to help make our customers dream become a reality.

There are a number of critical roles available on a permanent basis which play a massive part when assiting our customers in making the right choice when choosing their holiday home: Caravan Sales, Reception, After Sales, Administration, Sales Management, Office Management.

At Butlins our mission is to provide at our holiday resorts excellent services and products which enable the maximum number of families to enjoy a holiday in a safe, secure and appealing environment.

The three Butlins Resorts in Minehead, Bognor Regis and Skegness offer a variety of entertainment and activities for the whole family.

Our guests enjoy entertainment in the "Skyline Pavilion" which is the hub of our resorts, housing shops, bars and restaurants, as well as offering a wealth of contemporary entertainment, street theatre and special events.

Please go to www.bournejobs.co.uk to view our extensive portfolio of opportunities.

EXCLUSIVELY FOR ADULTS

Just for adults, Just the Job, Just for You

We think Warner's is a great place to work, just ask all 2,400 of us!

Working for Warner's is just like being part of a family, you will be an integral and valued member of our team whatever role you join us in; restaurant, housekeeping, bars, retail, entertainments or leisure. Warner prides itself on great customer service in fantastic locations, for example tomorrow you could find yourself serving medieval banquets in the great hall at Littlecote House or working in the spa at Thoresby.

Applicants with a 'can do' attitude will go far with us. If you're confident, friendly and believe work should be fun, we'd love to here from you.

Head Office: Bourne Leisure Ltd. 1 Park Lane, Hemel Hempstead. HP2 4YL
Tel: 01442 230300 – www.bournejobs.co.uk

FINDING A JOB IN THE UK

The summer has always been a period when employers in Britain look for large numbers of additional staff. Even when the recession of the early 1990s was at its worst people still, for example, ate fruit and vegetables and went on holiday, so agriculture and tourism continued to provide a reliable source of short-term work. This is also proving to be true in today's troubled economy. In this chapter we have collected details of job vacancies supplied to us by employers in England, Scotland, Wales and Northern Ireland. The jobs have been arranged under the following headings, complete with some UK specific information about each type of job:

- Business and industry
- Children
- Holiday centres and amusements
- Hotels and catering
- Language schools
- Medical
- Outdoor and sport
- Voluntary work
- Vacation traineeships and internships, the latter providing on-the-job work experience for students in business and industry.

Further sources of information and employment

Jobcentre Plus: The Department of Work and Pensions runs the Jobcentre Plus network where a full range of temporary vacancies can be found by searching on touch-screen terminals known as Jobpoints. Jobcentre Plus advertises all of its vacancies at www.directgov.uk/employment.

Jobseeker Direct: A phone service designed to help you find a full or part-time job. Telephone advisers have access to jobs nationwide and can help match your particular skills and requirements to vacant positions. Contact 0845 6060 234.

Employment agencies: While the number of agencies dealing with temporary work in London can be positively daunting, outside the capital the range is much narrower. It is worth registering with as many agencies as possible in order to enhance your chances of finding work. The jobs offered are frequently office based, though increasingly agencies specialise in different industry sectors. Under the Employment Agencies Act it is illegal for an agency to charge a fee for finding someone a job: agencies make their money by charging the employers.

National institutes: One way of finding out more about Vacation Training opportunities within a specific field is to contact the relevant national professional body or institute. Institutes do not offer traineeships themselves, but may be able to offer general advice and/or give names and addresses of companies within their field. Here are a few (others can be found under ASSOCIATIONS—TRADE at www.yell.com).

> *Institute of Hospitality:* 020 8661 4900; www.hcima.org.uk
> *Institute of Chartered Accountants in England and Wales:* 01908 248040; www.icaew.co.uk/careers
> *Institute of Chartered Accountants of Scotland:* 0131 347 0100; www.icas.org.uk

Chartered Institute of Public Relations: 020 7631 6900; www.cipr.co.uk
International Federation of the Periodical Press: 020 7404 4169; www.fipp.com
Royal Institute of British Architects: 020 7580 5533; www.architecture.com

Tax and National Insurance

Income tax

Single people are entitled to a personal tax allowance, which means that you do not pay income tax until your yearly earnings exceed £6,475 (2010/11 figure). Few people are likely to earn this much over the vacation. If you earn any more than this you will have to pay tax at 20%.

To avoid paying tax you need to fill out the right form; if your employer uses the PAYE system, new employees will usually be taxed under an 'emergency code' until the Tax Office receives this form from your employer. Students working in their holidays should fill in form P38(S), and school/other students or individuals starting work for the first time should fill in a P46. A P38 allows employers to pay students without the deduction of tax. However, if you are not planning to be a student after 5 April of the next year, or if your total income (excluding student loans, scholarships and educational grants) in the tax year exceeds £6,475, you should not fill in a P38. Students who work during term time as well as during holidays are also not eligible to fill out a P38. If you pay any tax before you are put on the correct tax code, then you can claim a rebate during the year if your estimated yearly earnings do not exceed the personal allowance. If you have not been put on the right tax code by the time you leave your job, send a repayment claims form (P50) to the Tax Office together with your P45, which you will get when you finish work. If you are being paid by cash or cheque, not PAYE, then worrying about codes and rebates should not be necessary, although strictly speaking any income should be reported to your local tax office. Further information can be found at www.hmrc.gov.uk/students.

National Insurance

National Insurance contributions are compulsory for employees over 16 years of age if they earn over a certain limit. The rate you pay is calculated according to your wages. Currently, anyone who earns less than £110 a week pays nothing and then 11% of earnings above that figure.

If you require information in addition to that given above, contact your local HM Revenue and Customs, the new department responsible for the former Inland Revenue and HM Customs and Excise offices, or visit www.hmrc.gov.uk or else your local Citizens Advice Bureau.

The National Minimum Wage

The UK has a National Minimum Wage, which on 1 October 2009 was raised to £5.80 per hour for those aged 22 and over and £4.83 per hour for those aged 18–21. Most workers in the UK, including home workers, agency workers, commission workers, part-time workers, casual workers and pieceworkers, are entitled to the National Minimum Wage. The minimum wage has been extended to cover 16 (who have ceased to be of compulsory school age) and 17 years olds, at a rate of £3.57 per hour.

This is a general overview. Those wanting more detailed information, leaflets or to register a complaint should call the National Minimum Wage (NMW) Helpline on 0845 600 0678 or visit www.berr.gov.uk/employment-matters/rights/nmw.

Red tape

Before writing letters to prospective employers, **overseas applicants** should clarify the terms under which they may visit and work in Britain. Anyone arriving at UK immigration without the necessary visa, letter of invitation or other required documentation could be sent back home on the next available flight. An outline of the regulations is given below. For further information, contact the nearest British Consulate or High Commission.

The primary route for entry into the UK for the purpose of employment was previously the work permit system. Work permits were issued only where a genuine vacancy existed and where particular qualifications or skills were required that were in short supply from the resident and EEA labour force. In 2005, the government announced its intention to implement a Five Year Strategy for Immigration and Asylum. This represented a major overhaul of the work permit arrangements, as well as rules on immigration and asylum. Consequently, a new points-based system, designed to enable the UK to control immigration more effectively was introduced in March 2006 to replace the 80 different entry routes by which a non-EEA national could come to the UK to work.

Visa requirements

All those who are **not** British or EEA nationals will need a visa or entry clearance for all stays in the UK over six months. Since November 2003, nationals of 10 'phase one' countries require entry clearance for stays of over six months. These countries are: Australia, Canada, Hong Kong SAR, Japan, Malaysia, New Zealand, Singapore, South Africa, South Korea, and the USA. From November 2006, nationals of a further 55 'phase two' countries also require the same entry clearance. These include much of South America, the Caribbean island states and some African nations. Check the UK visa website at www.ukvisas.gov.uk for the latest information on visa requirements.

Entry under the points-based system for migration

Wherever relevant, entries in this book specify if the company or organisation in question welcomes applications from overseas. Unfortunately, this does not mean that all foreigners can work for them legally in this country.

EEA citizens: Nationals of the European Economic Area are free to enter the UK to seek employment without a work permit. At present this applies to citizens of EU countries, EEA member states of Norway, Iceland and Liechtenstein, and the European Free Trade Agreement (EFTA) member state of Switzerland. However EEA nationals still require a permit for the Channel Islands and the Isle of Man. Nationals from most of the new EU states who find a job in the UK are required to register with the Home Office under the new Worker Registration Scheme as soon as they find work. This scheme was set up so that the government could monitor the impact of EU accession on the UK labour market and restrict access to benefits. Nationals from Malta and Cyprus have free movement rights and are not required to obtain a workers registration certificate. EEA nationals intending to stay longer than six months may apply for a residence permit, although there is no obligation for them to do so.

Non-EEA citizens: Until the Points-Based Entry system (PBS) was introduced, the general position under the immigration rules was that overseas nationals (other than EEA nationals) coming to work in Britain should have work permits before setting out. Permits were normally issued only for specific jobs requiring a high level of skill and experience for which resident or EEA labour was not available. In other words, a UK employer could not receive a work permit for a non-EEA citizen unless it was a job for which there was no EEA National available.

The new points-based system of migration to the UK is still in the early stages of implementation. It is designed to control migration more effectively, tackle abuse and identify the most talented workers by consolidating entry clearance and work permit applications into one single-step application. The plan is to ensure that only those who benefit Britain can enter the country to work. These criteria are only for those workers from outside the EEA who wish to work or train in the UK. The system is based on five tiers:

- Tier 1: Highly skilled workers, eg scientists or entrepreneurs
- Tier 2: Skilled workers with a job offer, eg nurses, teachers or engineers
- Tier 3: Low skilled workers filling specific temporary labour shortages, eg construction workers for a particular building project
- Tier 4: Students
- Tier 5: Youth mobility workers and temporary workers, eg working holidaymakers

For each tier, applicants will need sufficient points to gain entry clearance to the UK. Points can be scored for skills or attributes which predict a worker's success in the labour market. For Tiers 3–5, under which most summer employment falls, points will be awarded depending on whether the applicant has: a valid certificate of sponsorship from an approved sponsor; adequate funds to live in the UK; proven compliance with previous immigration conditions and in some cases English language ability. A web-based self-assessment programme, which allows applicants to understand whether they meet the UK's criteria for entry can be found on the Home Office website. The system is being introduced tier by tier, so while the new scheme automatically abolishes some of the previous work permit arrangements (see below), such as the Sectors Based Scheme, others will remain in place for the foreseeable future.

Further details about the PBS are available at www.workingintheuk.gov.uk and the Home Office Immigration and Nationality Directorate (www.ind.homeoffice. gov.uk). Queries should be directed to Work Permits (UK)'s Customer Contacts Centre on 0114 207 4074.

Citizens of Commonwealth countries: Canadian students, graduates and young people should contact the Student Work Abroad Programme (SWAP), which provides support to those wishing to work in Britain. It is administered by the Canadian Universities Travel Service, which has over 40 offices in Canada. For details see www.swap.ca.

Australians and New Zealanders should contact International Exchange Programmes (IEP), a non-profit organisation specialising in sending young Australians and New Zealanders on working holidays overseas. For more details visit www.iep.org.au or www.iep.co.nz.

Seasonal Agricultural Work Scheme (SAWS): This is one of the few schemes that remains in place after the PBS has come into effect. The government plans to maintain the scheme until 2010, from when it will fall under Tiers 3 and 4.

Farm camps under this scheme are authorised by the Home Office. Although previously open to non-EEA and non-Commonwealth nationals SAWS is now restricted to Bulgarians and Romanians. Special 'Work Cards' are issued to a certain number of applicants each year. Places fill up very quickly and it is necessary to apply in November to have any chance of obtaining a card for the following year.

The recruitment for these farms is handled by nine agencies, known as SAWS operators, including Concordia. Between them they recruit pickers for over 160 farms throughout the year. An invitation to work is only valid if the work card is issued by an official operator and **not** by individual farmers. The SAWS scheme has undergone some large changes since 1 January 2004. Whereas in previous years the scheme only ran from May until November, it now runs all year long, taking in a much wider breadth of work for those involved, from daffodil picking to working with livestock. The numbers have been reduced, in the light of the addition of new EU states. The upper age limit of 25 has been removed. You can take part in the scheme for a minimum of five weeks and a maximum of six months at a time. Applicants should note that a reasonable charge may be made for the accommodation and other services provided. Applicants can participate in the scheme more than once, as long as they return to their home country for a minimum of three months before applying again.

Voluntary work: Overseas nationals seeking voluntary work in the UK will fall under Tier 5 of the new system. Overseas nationals may be admitted for up to 12 months for the purpose of voluntary work providing their sponsor is a charity or non-charitable philanthropic organisation and the applicant is receiving no remuneration other than pocket money, board and accommodation. The work which they do must be closely related to the aims of the charity, ie working with people, and they must not be engaged in purely clerical, administrative or maintenance work. Volunteers are expected to leave the UK at the end of their visit.

Vacation traineeships & internships: Again, these will fall under Tier 5 of the new system. Permission can be given for overseas nationals with pre-arranged work placements to obtain permits for professional training or managerial level work experience for a limited period of 12 months.

While many companies in this book are happy to employ overseas students as trainees since most of them run their schemes in order to try out potential employees, they may not be keen to take on anyone who cannot return to them after their studies.

Non EEA students studying in the UK: These students fall under Tier 4 of the new system. It is important to note that only institutions featured on the Tier 4 Sponsor Register allow access to the UK on a Tier 4 visa. Overseas students studying in Britain at foundation degree level or above who wish to take up vacation work no longer have to obtain permission to do so. This is on the basis that they do not pursue a career by filling a full-time vacancy or work for more than 20 hours per week during term time, except where the placement is a necessary part of their studies, with the agreement of the educational institution. Overseas students studying below foundation degree level can work part-time during term time so long as it is not more than 10 hours per week.

Au pairs: Overseas au pairs now fall under Tier 5 of the new system (previously known as the Au Pair Placement scheme). For details of regulations affecting au pairs see the chapter on *Au pair, home help and paying guests.*

Further information

Once in the UK, general information about immigration matters can be obtained from the Home Office Immigration and Nationality Directorate (0870 606 7766; www.ind.homeoffice.gov.uk) but be prepared to wait in line for your call to be answered, it will be eventually. Guidance leaflets can be downloaded from www.ukvisas.gov.uk/en/howtoapply/vafs. Further information and guidance can be found at www.ukvisas.gov.uk/en/howtoapply/infs/. Work Permits (UK) (0114 207 4074) can advise employers on the rules of the entry scheme.

THE UK

Business and industry

This category includes working as **drivers, temps, office workers, labourers** and **cashiers**, among others.

Temping: Work as a 'temp' involves providing short-term cover for staff away on holiday, sick leave, and so on, and is usually arranged by an agency. Jobs are available in virtually all corners of business and industry, though the majority are clerical/office-based and favour those with secretarial or computer skills, or experience of an office environment. Temping work is attractive as it is available at any time of the year, can offer flexible hours, and can be found at short notice. Temping can also be valuable to those looking for a more vocational experience as well as cash over the summer. You could secure a placement in a sector where internship schemes are rare, such as marketing or media, giving you vital insight as well as an edge over other candidates.

Shop work: Recent developments in retail, such as the explosion of out-of-town retail parks with huge stores and 24-hour shopping, mean that there is sizeable demand for extra staff in the summer. Those willing to work antisocial hours are in demand, and working the night shift generally ensures a significantly bigger pay packet. If you are applying for a full-time job, then be aware that many shops will favour applicants with an interest in eventually working there permanently.

Cleaning: Office and industrial cleaning is another area that offers temporary vacancies. Most cleaning companies prefer to employ staff for long periods, but they will occasionally take people on temporarily for jobs such as cleaning newly built or refurbished office blocks, or for the annual deep-clean of those factories which still shut down for a couple of weeks each summer.

Factory work: Spending the summer on a production line may not sound too thrilling, but the potential for work in this field is good. The factories most likely to require extra staff are those preparing for the Christmas rush, as they begin to increase production in August, or those that deal with the packaging and processing of seasonal food. Huge quantities of fruit and vegetables are harvested between late spring and early autumn and must be preserved by canning or freezing. The main vacancies in this business are for line workers, packers and delivery drivers. Be prepared for early mornings, shift work and high levels of boredom.

Glen Lyn Gorge

Job(s) Available: Staff required for boat crew, gardening and care of accommodation.
Duration: From April to September.
Working Hours: Dependent on the weather.
Pay: £200–£300 per week.

Head Office: Glen Lyn Gorge, Lynmouth, Devon EX35 6ER
☎ 01598 753207
🖥 www.theglenlyngorge.co.uk

Company Description: A visitor attraction with self-catering holiday accommodation.
Requirements: No experience required, just enthusiasm.
Accommodation: Available at a reasonable price.
Application Procedure: By post to Matthew Oxenham at the above address from February. Non-UK residents with suitable qualifications will be considered. An interview will be required.

Promotional Support Services

Job(s) Available: Promotional staff required nationwide.
Duration: Minimum period of work 1 day at any time of year.
Working Hours: 1, 2 or 3 day events.
Pay: £80–£150 per day, dependent on the job.

> **Head Office:** Lower Ground Floor, 11 Laura Place, Bath BA2 4BL
> ☎ 01225 443434
> ✆ info@promotionalsupport.co.uk
> 🖥 www.promotionalsupport.co.uk

Company Description: Organises roadshows, exhibitions and events and supplies promotional staff for clients such as Walkers, Robinsons, Pepsi, L'Oréal, Bounty, Great British Chicken, Wellman, Benecol, Belvoir, Wykes Farm Cheeses and other blue-chip clients.
Requirements: Applicants should have bubbly, outgoing, attractive personalities, speak good English and be reliable. No visible body piercings or tattoos.
Accommodation: Available in some areas.
Application Procedure: At any time to Promotional Support at the above address, by email, or post a CV and photograph with an s.a.e. Overseas applicants are considered. An interview is preferred, but not necessary.

Street PR

Job(s) Available: Street PR staff and Team Leaders.
Working Hours: Shifts are available every day of the week. Amount can vary from 1 shift to 20 shifts in a week. Shifts last from 2–10 hours. Shifts starting from 7am and some ending at 3am.
Pay: From £7–£10 per hour, plus commission. Team Leaders can earn up to £15 per hour.

> **Head Office:** 17 Short Gardens, Covent Garden, London WC2H 9AT
> ☎ 0207 240 1115
> ✆ jobs@streetpr.co.uk
> 🖥 www.streetpr.co.uk

Company Description: Street PR is a direct marketing and promotional company. Its client list includes clubs and bars, restaurants, gyms, festivals, the NHS, drinks and cosmetic brands.
Job Description: Promoting a range of products and businesses.
Requirements: Staff must be outgoing, positive and speak English as a first language. Staff should have a passion for entertainment, the confidence to approach strangers and be a quick learner.
Accommodation: Not provided.
Additional Information: There are team leader opportunities available for those who show aptitude.
Application Procedure: The company prefers applicants to call the number above. If applying by email, include a photo but no CV.

Tony Fresko Ice Cream Ltd

Job(s) Available: Drivers (25).
Duration: Positions are available from March to October. Minimum period of work is normally 6 weeks.
Working Hours: To work approximately 11am–9pm, 7 days of the week.
Pay: From £6 per hour.

> **Head Office:** Warren Farm, White Lane, Ash Green, Aldershot, Hampshire GU12 6HW
> ☎ 01252 315528
> ✆ tonyfresko@btconnect.com
> 🖥 www.tonyfresko.com

Company Description: Mobile ice cream outlet, with a fleet of 15 vans.
Job Description: Drivers for mobile ice cream sales at various shows and fêtes and on rounds of industrial and housing estates.
Requirements: Full driving licence required.

Accommodation: Not available.
Application Procedure: By post or phone from February onwards to Mr J Sawyer at the above address. Foreign applicants with appropriate work permits and acceptable spoken English are welcome. An interview is necessary.

Universal Extras

Job(s) Available: TV and film extras.
Duration: All year round.
Working Hours: Various.
Pay: £70 per day minimum.
Company Description: Universal Extras supply students for paid roles as extras in TV and film across the UK and Ireland. The service is free to students.
Job Description: Extras for films, television, commercials and photo shoots.
Requirements: Minimum age 16.
Additional Information: All applicants must be professional, good time keepers and able to take direction.
Application Procedure: Sign up on the above website and apply for opportunities.

> **Head Office:** Pinewood Studios, Pinewood Road, Iver Heath, Buckinghamshire SLO ONH
> ☎ 0845 009 0344
> 🖵 www.universalextras.co.uk

Wetherby Studios

Job(s) Available: Male photographic models.
Duration: Dozens needed throughout the year.
Pay: £150 cash for 2-hour sessions.
Requirements: Should be aged 18–40 years, but physique is more important than age. While more than half the models used are slim, it can be difficult to find men who have worked on their chest and arm definition, which is required if picture sessions promoting leisurewear are planned. Moustaches and beards permissible. No modelling experience necessary. Applicants must supply snapshots to show how they photograph facially and physically. Follow-ups are frequent, depending on the photographers' reactions to the first test shots.
Accommodation: Not available.
Application Procedure: By post to Mr Mike Arlen, director, Wetherby Studios. Overseas applicants are more than welcome, but must speak fluent English.

> **Head Office:** 23 Wetherby Mansions, Earls Court Square, London SW5 9BH
> ☎ 020 7373 1107
> 🖵 mikearlen@btopenworld.com

Children

This category includes opportunities as **leaders**, **playworkers**, **instructors** and even **managers**.

In response to the desperation of parents trying to occupy their children in the long summer holidays, recent years have seen a boom in American-style holiday centres, camps and playschemes for the younger generation. These have become increasingly important as more parents go out to work and private childcare costs rocket. Centres vary in size and content; some are run by big operating chains, like PGL (www.pgl.co.uk), who attend to more than 140,000 children a year, and others are run by local councils.

The main season is from around the start of April until mid-September, but longer-term work is available as PGL operate centres from February until October. The ages of the children attending these centres range from 7 to 17, so anyone aiming to be a primary or secondary school teacher could gain valuable experience.

For these jobs, applicants often will not require formal qualifications. UK legislation, however, means that most employers will require successful applicants intending to work with children to undergo a Criminal Records Bureau (CRB) check – be aware that it may be expected even if not mentioned in the job advert. Preference is likely to be given to those with experience of working with children. Trainee primary school teachers are particularly well suited.

Acorn Adventure

Job(s) Available: Catering staff, managers, qualified and non-qualified activity instructors, support staff and village managers (site reps). 300 seasonal staff positions available.

Duration: Seasonal work available from April to September. Shorter contracts also available.

Company Description: Acorn Adventure is one of the UK's leading providers of outdoor adventure activity camps for schools, youth groups and families. They operate 8 activity centres in the Lake District, the Brecon Beacons and France.

> **Head Office:** Acorn House, Prospect Road, Halesowen, West Midlands B62 8DU
> ☎ 0121 504 2066
> ✎ jobs@acornadventure.co.uk
> 🖥 www.acorn-jobs.co.uk

Job Description: *Managers:* centre admin, catering, activity and maintenance – managers of departments required at each centre. *Activity instructors:* working directly with groups of children and families providing daily multi-activity sessions such as sailing, kayaking, canoeing, climbing and abseiling. *Centre support roles:* catering, maintenance, cleaning, driving and general campsite work.

Requirements: *Managers:* experience and relevant qualifications essential. *Support staff:* no experience necessary (full training given pre-season). *Village managers:* no experience necessary (full training given pre-season). *Activity instructors:* experience of working with children, National Governing Body awards eg BCU, RYA, SPA, GNAS, BOF or MLTB. Other nationally recognised coaching awards may be considered. *Assistant instructors:* should be working towards the above qualifications/awards. Acorn runs an extensive pre-season training programme helping staff achieve these goals.

Application Procedure: For further information visit the above website or contact the recruitment department on the above email address or telephone number for a full information pack.

Adventure & Computer Holidays Ltd

Job(s) Available: Camp leaders and teachers required for day camps.

Duration: Work available every half-term and school holiday throughout the year (mostly July to August). Minimum period 1 week.

Working Hours: 9am–4.45pm.

Pay: Approximately £200–£300 per week.

> **Head Office:** PO Box 183, Dorking, Surrey RH5 6FA
> ☎ 01306 711005
> ✎ info@holiday-adventure.com
> 🖥 www.holiday-adventure.com

Company Description: A small, friendly company based at Belmont School, Holmbury St Mary, near Dorking, Surrey. The company has 28 years experience in running activity holidays for children aged 4–14.

Requirements: Minimum age 18. Qualifications or experience with children is preferred.

Accommodation: Staff must live in London or Surrey area.

Application Procedure: By post any time to Su Jones, director, at the above address. Interview required.

Barracudas Summer Activity Camps

Job(s) Available: Activity instructors (150), arts and crafts instructors (50), camp managers (27) and early years managers (27), dance and drama instructors (50), football coaches (50), group assistants (200), group coordinators (150), senior sports instructors (25), lifeguards (50).

Head Office: Bridge House, Bridge Street, St Ives, Cambridgeshire PE27 5EH
☎ 01480 497533
✆ jobs@barracudas.co.uk
🖥 www.barracudas.co.uk

Duration: Staff required from mid-July to the end of August. Minimum period of work 2 consecutive weeks.

Working Hours: All staff to work 40 hours per week.

Pay: Ranges from £208–£290 per week for general positions, dependent on age, experience and qualifications. Pay for management positions from £300–£450 per week depending on experience of individual and size of camp.

Company Description: Barracudas run activity day camps for children aged $4^1/_2$–16 years during the summer and Easter holidays.

Requirements: Experience in teaching and management required. *Group coordinators:* experience with children/sports necessary. *Group assistants:* a wish to work with children and to ensure their safety is necessary. *Activity instructors:* confidence and the ability to give clear instruction. *Football coaches:* experience in football coaching and excellent knowledge of the game needed. *Arts and crafts instructors:* experience in arts and crafts needed. *Dance and drama instructors:* drama and dance experience necessary. *Lifeguards:* should be NPLQ/NARS or American Red Cross qualified. Minimum age 17.

Accommodation: Available at some sites but is limited to qualified teachers, managers, lifeguards and instructors.

Additional Information: Training is available for all staff. Some courses lead to nationally recognised qualifications.

Application Procedure: Via the website http://recruitment.barracudas.co.uk from January onwards. Foreign applicants with fluent English who already have accommodation near to a camp are welcome to apply. Interview required and police and security checks are made.

Cross Keys, Mini Minors and Experience UK

Job(s) Available: Group leaders and group assistants (30).

Head Office: 48 Fitzalan Road, Finchley, London N3 3PE
☎ 020 8371 9686
🖥 www.xkeys.co.uk

Duration: Camps take place in all school holidays; summer camps will take place from July to August.

Working Hours: Working hours generally from 8.30am–3.30pm but may vary slightly.

Pay: £175–£225 per week depending on position and experience.

Company Description: Run both a daytime children's activity camp in north London and a residential children's activity camp (XUK) based in Norfolk.

Job Description: Staff required to work at a residential children's activity camp. Duties involve being responsible for junior or senior children aged 6–17 and includes the care of children, the planning and running of activities and the supervising of trips. Staff will work as part of a team of 3 adults per 24 children running games and activities within a school environment.

Requirements: Minimum age 18. Full in-house training will be given. Applicants for either camp should have an interest/background in childcare and must be enthusiastic team workers. Possession of lifeguard/first aid qualifications would be an advantage.

Accommodation: Includes accommodation and board.

Application Procedure: Applications to Richard on the above telephone number or go to the 'staff zone' section on the above website.

Dartington International Summer School

Job(s) Available: House Parents, Stewards, Trogs.
Duration: 5 week festival but recommended placement no longer than 2 weeks.
Cost: *House Parents/Trogs:* No cost. *Stewards:* £50 contribution.

Head Office: The Barn, Dartington Hall, Totnes, Devon TQ9 6DE
☎ 01803 847080
summerschool@dartington.org
www.dartington.org/summer-school

Company Description: Dartington Summer School takes place on the Dartington Hall Estate, Devon. It is a 5 week festival that showcases theatre, music performances and also offers specialist instrumental tuition.

Job Description: *House Parents:* to make sure all attendees are well looked after, required to be on duty and available for help at any time. *Stewards:* responsible for supervising and directing all concert and course attendees, plus hospitality following concerts. *Trogs:* general assistants of the school, recommended for those wanting experience in Arts Administration. Roles range from back-stage management to distributing post.

Requirements: *House Parents:* minimum age 21. Must have attended Dartington previously. Applicants must also have a full driving licence and a mobile phone. *Stewards:* minimum age 21. Stewarding experience, knowledge of first aid and health and safety an advantage. *Trogs:* minimum age 21. Must be physically fit with A-Level knowledge of music. Full driving licence an advantage.

Accommodation: *House Parents and Trogs:* provided. *Stewards:* provided. £50 contribution required to cover food.

Additional Information: Workers must be fluent in English. *Stewards and House Parents:* allowed to take part in courses and classes when duties permit.

Application Procedure: Apply via online form and send to above email. Closing date usually mid-April, check website for details.

Halsbury Travel

Job(s) Available: Couriers (80).
Duration: University holiday periods and term time year round. Tours usually last around 1–2 weeks.
Working Hours: 35 hours per week.
Pay: £200 per week.

Head Office: 35 Churchill Park, Nottingham NG4 2HF
☎ 0115 940 4303
workexperience@halsbury.com
www.halsbury.com

Company Description: Halsbury Travel provide group and school tours to western Europe and worldwide. They arrange sports tours, music tours, study tours, ski tours and tours for any academic theme including history, geography, media, travel and tourism, French, German, Spanish and Italian.

Job Description: Couriers, group leaders and tour guides required for coach and air groups travelling to western European destinations.

Requirements: Minimum age 21. Must speak English and either French, German or Spanish.

Accommodation: Half-board hotel accommodation, travel insurance and transportation all supplied.

Application Procedure: Applications taken in September, January and April. Apply to Meg Zanker at meg@halsbury.com.

JCA

Job(s) Available: Activity instructors (180), Centre managers (10), Senior instructors (9), Watersports instructors (6), Lifeguards (1) and Night porters (1).
Duration: Required from March to September.
Working Hours: All positions average 40 hours work per week, 5 or occasionally 6 days a week.

Head Office: The Port House, Port Solent, Portsmouth, Hampshire PO6 4TH
☎ 02392 334 600
⌖ recruitment@tuiactivity.com
🖳 www.jca-adventure.co.uk/jobs

Pay: *Activity instructors:* £255 per month. *Senior instructors:* pay to be arranged. *Centre managers:* £240-£300 per week. *Watersports/Lifeguards and Night porters:* competitive wages.
Company Description: JCA is one of the fastest growing providers of School Activity Holidays with a reputation for providing thousands of children with an unforgettable experience which promotes education, personal development and of course, fun.
Requirements: *Activity instructors:* no experience required as part of the Modern Apprenticeship scheme and full training and an NVQ 2 in Activity Leadership is provided. *Senior instructors:* minimum age 21, must be able to drive and have industry experience as will be leading a team of instructors, as well as giving necessary training. *Centre managers:* excellent communication, organisational and managerial skills necessary. Responsible for day-to-day running of the activity centre. *Watersports positions:* CC Level 1 Coach and 3 Star Certificate required.
Accommodation: Accommodation and board provided.
Application Procedure: Please apply via our website or call the JCA Recruitment Team on 02392 334 600.

The Kingswood Group

Job(s) Available: Apprentice instructors and group leaders.

Head Office: Kingswood House, Alkmaar Way, Norwich, Norfolk NR6 6BF
☎ 01603 309350
⌖ jobs@kingswood.co.uk
🖳 www.kingswoodjobs.co.uk

Duration: *Apprentice instructors:* 12 month training and development package. *Group leaders:* 6-8 week contracts from the beginning of July to the end of August.
Pay: *Apprentice instructors:* training allowance of £95 per week and food included. *Group leaders:* national minimum wage rates.
Company Description: Kingswood provides residential educational activity courses at 9 centres across the UK and northern France, covering curriculum-linked educational modules with adventure activities. Over the summer Kingswood operates Camp Beaumont Residential Camps giving children from all over the world the opportunity to have a fun-packed holiday without their parents.
Job Description: *Apprentice instructors:* deliver various educational and adventure activities which could include caving, go-karting, climbing, archery along with environmental and ICT modules. Comprehensive training is provided. *Group leaders:* will be responsible for round-the-clock welfare of a group of approximately 15 children at the Camp Beaumont Summer Camps. Must instruct and initiate games and non-specialist activities whilst monitoring the welfare needs of individual children in the group.
Requirements: *Apprentice instructors:* eligibility criteria applies. Check the above website for more details. No experience is necessary, although a friendly and outgoing personality and a passion for working with children in a must. *Group leaders:* previous experience of working with young people is desirable. Must be responsible, hardworking and extremely enthusiastic.
Accommodation: The apprentice instructor and group leader positions are residential. Accommodation is provided and for this there is a small deduction (currently £31.57 per week) from pay.

Additional Information: Apprentice instructors will work towards an Apprenticeship in Sport and Recreation which includes an NVQ Level 2 in Activity Leadership and other nationally recognised qualifications.

Application Procedure: Apply online at the above website. Telephone interviews and an assessment weekend in the UK are required as part of the recruitment process.

Lakeside YMCA National Centre

Job(s) Available: Day camp leaders (40).
Duration: Minimum period of work 8 weeks between early July and the end of August.
Working Hours: 5 days a week.
Pay: £50 per week.

Head Office: Ulverston, Cumbria LA12 8BD
☎ 01539 539000
✎ lakesidehr@fyldecoastymca.org
🖳 www.lakesideymca.co.uk

Company Description: The camp is set in 400 acres of woodland on the shores of Lake Windermere in the Lake District National Park and is one of the largest camps in Europe.

Job Description: The work involves leading groups of children aged 8–15 years in a wide range of activities, from environmental awareness to rock climbing.

Requirements: Minimum age 18. Some experience of outdoor activities is advantageous and experience of working with children necessary.

Accommodation: Free board and lodging.

Application Procedure: Application forms are available from January to May via the website or by request via email at the above addresses.

Leicester Children's Holiday Centre

Job(s) Available: Activity leaders, cook/chef and kitchen/dining room staff.
Duration: From July to the end of August.
Working Hours: *Activity leaders and kitchen/ dining room staff:* work 48-hour weeks. *Cook/chef:* to work a 6 day week.
Pay: National minimum wage rates.

Head Office: Mablethorpe, Quebec Road, Mablethorpe, Lincolnshire LN12 1QX
☎ 01507 472444
✎ helen@childrensholidaycentre.co.uk
🖳 www.childrensholidaycentre.co.uk

Company Description: A charity that provides free holidays for children from the inner city of Leicester, on the east coast of England. For anyone interested in working with children this is a fairly unique opportunity offering practical experience and an excellent grounding for a future career.

Job Description: *Activity leaders:* to organise, instruct and supervise an outdoor activities programme for children aged 7–12. Energy, enthusiasm and a good sense of humour are essential.

Requirements: Minimum age 18. No experience needed as full training is given.

Accommodation: Deduction made for board and lodging.

Application Procedure: Write or email for an application form, enclosing an s.a.e., from December to Helen Eagle-Lanzetta at the above address.

LTC English Academy London

Job(s) Available: Activity leaders for junior summer school.
Duration: To work from the end of June to the end of August.
Pay: On application.

Head Office: 16–20 New Broadway, Ealing, London W5 2XA
☎ 020 8566 2188
✎ info@ltc-london.com
🖳 www.ltc-english.com

Requirements: Minimum age 18. Some experience with children required, though no formal qualifications necessary.
Application Procedure: By post to Jane Flynn, principal, at the above address.

Mad Science

Job(s) Available: Summer camp support presenters in Nottinghamshire, Derbyshire and Leicestershire.
Working Hours: Morning (8am–1pm) or afternoon (1pm–5pm).
Pay: £6.75 per hour.
Company Description: Mad Science is the world's leader in fun science for children between the ages of 5–11. Mad Science conducts educational, entertaining and hands-on science activities.
Job Description: Camp support presenters help deliver fun, engaging, interactive and hands-on summer camp sessions.
Accommodation: Not provided.
Application Procedure: Fill out the application form at the above website.

Head Office: 12 Faraday, Nottingham Science & Technology Park, University Boulevard, Nottingham NG7 2QP
☎ 0115 922 1113
✆ enquiries@madscience-em.co.uk
🖥 www.madscience.org

PGL Travel Ltd

Job(s) Available: Activity instructors, group leaders, support staff.
Duration: Positions available from February to November, for the full season, as little as 12 weeks, or any period in between, although there are very few summer-only vacancies.
Pay: £117.50–£243.50 per week.

Head Office: Alton Court, Penyard Lane, Ross-on-Wye, Herefordshire HR9 5GL
☎ 0844 3710 123
✆ recruitment@pgl.co.uk
🖥 www.pgl.co.uk/recruitment

Company Description: PGL recruit around 2,500 staff each year to assist with the running of their children's activity centres throughout the UK, including Devon, the Isle of Wight, Lincolnshire, the south coast, Surrey, Shropshire, Perthshire and Wales. Europe's largest provider of adventure holidays for children has offered outstanding training and work opportunities to seasonal staff for more than 50 years. PGL jobs provide a break from the 9-to-5 routine. Staff need to be enthusiastic, energetic and looking for real experience and responsibility in a stimulating environment.
Job Description: *Activity instructors:* required for canoeing, sailing, windsurfing, fencing, archery, motorsports, pony trekking and more. *Group leaders:* take responsibility for groups of children, helping them to get the most out of their holiday. *Support staff:* assist the catering, domestic and maintenance teams.
Requirements: *Activity instructors:* qualifications not essential for all positions as full training will be provided. *Group leaders:* previous experience of working with children is an advantage.
Accommodation: Accommodation and meals provided.
Application Procedure: Apply online at the above website by creating your own My PGL account.

Super Camps Ltd

Job(s) Available: Activity instructors (500), senior activity instructors (400), site managers (50), swimming pool lifeguards (40), trampoline coaches (15).
Duration: Staff needed for half-terms, Christmas, Easter and summer (July and August) holidays.
Pay: *Site managers:* from £425 per week. *Senior activity instructors:* £325 per week. *Swimming pool lifeguards:* £245–£275 per week. *Trampoline coaches:* £275 per week. *Activity instructors:* from £325 per week.

Head Office: Park House, Milton Park, Abingdon, Oxfordshire OX14 4RS
☎ 01235 832222
✆ employment@supercamps.co.uk
🖳 www.supercamps.co.uk

Company Description: Runs multi-activity half-term, Christmas, Easter and summer day camps for children aged 4–14 in schools in the Midlands, south and central England. Super Camps is committed to providing safe and fun-packed activities (including art/craft and sports) for all children attending its camps.
Job Description: *Activity instructors:* required to teach a range of activities to children aged 4–14 years. First aid and relevant childcare qualifications/camp experience an advantage. Training is provided, therefore enthusiastic individuals with an interest in sports or arts and crafts and a genuine interest in working with children are welcome to apply. Good experience for those wishing to go into a teaching, childcare or a recreation/leisure profession.
Requirements: *Site managers:* qualified teachers with camp experience. *Senior activity instructors:* qualified/trainee teachers or individuals with substantial children's camp experience. *Swimming pool lifeguards:* must have experience and hold a recognised and up-to-date lifesaving/coaching qualification (NPLQ/NARS). *Trampoline coaches:* must have experience and hold a recognised and up-to-date qualification.
Application Procedure: By post to personnel at the above address or online at the above web address all year round.

Holiday centres and amusements

Tourism: The trend for short breaks and long weekends away within the UK is currently very strong, backed by industry pushes to promote such getaways. As a nation we have also shown a large leap in visits to the UK's tourist attractions, with large sites, such as Alton Towers, in Staffordshire, and the London Eye, where over 20 million people have so far enjoyed its views across the capital. Attractions such as the Eden Project in Cornwall and the Imperial War Museum in Manchester, are boosting regional tourism, while events like the Commonwealth games encouraged international interest in Britain, as will the Olympic games to be held in London in 2012. As a result, there has been an unprecedented growth in tourism and more than 2.1 million people are in employment related to UK tourism.

Holiday centres: One of the greatest recent trends in UK tourism has been the growth of holiday camps, activity centres and theme parks. These centres are some of the largest seasonal employers in the country. Not only do they take on thousands of staff between them – the largest can take on hundreds each – but they also offer a diverse range of jobs, both unskilled and skilled. As a result of the number and type of posts offered, they are often popular and competitive – the opportunity to spend a summer working with many other young people in a holiday environment can prove quite attractive. It is essential to apply as soon as possible because many of the big employers start recruitment early in the year. Although extra people are hired later in the season, to cover bank holidays and busy weeks, these are frequently contacted from a reserve list compiled from the surplus of earlier applications.

If you fail to find employment with one of the centres listed in the book, try a speculative, personal approach. Visit Britain (020 8846 9000; www.visitbritain.com) can provide information on the major theme and leisure parks throughout England. Visit Scotland (0131 332 2433; www.visitscotland.com); Visit Wales (0870 830 0306; www.visitwales.com); and Visit Northern Ireland (078 6873 4813; www.visitnorthernireland.com) provide the same information for Scotland, Wales and Northern Ireland.

The Abbey College

Job(s) Available: Activities staff/sports staff (15), administration, welfare staff (3).
Duration: Work available from the beginning of June to the end of August.
Working Hours: 6 days a week.
Pay: *Activities staff/sports staff:* £200+ per week. *Welfare and administration staff:* £170–£250 per week.

> **Head Office:** 253 Wells Road, Malvern Wells, Worcestershire WR14 4JF
> ☎ 01684 892300
> jobs@abbeycollege.co.uk
> www.abbeycollege.co.uk

Company Description: A beautiful residential campus with students from more than 30 nations.
Requirements: Minimum age 18. Sports qualifications and experience of summer schools preferred.
Accommodation: Accommodation and meals provided free of charge for all residential staff, plus free use of all sports and leisure activities and excursions.
Additional Information: Overseas applicants are welcome to work 3 weeks unpaid in exchange for a week of free English classes (or work 6 weeks and get 2 weeks of free classes). Accommodation is also free of charge, which totals around £520 per week.
Application Procedure: By post from March to the personnel department at the above address.

Allen (Parkfoot) Ltd

Job(s) Available: Bar and catering staff, cook/chef, adventure supervisor (1), secretary/receptionist (2).
Duration: Required from May to September. Period of work Easter, May bank holidays and from June to mid-September.

> **Head Office:** Howtown Road, Pooley Bridge, Penrith, Cumbria CA10 2NA
> ☎ 01768 486309
> jobs@parkfootullswater.co.uk
> www.parkfootullswater.co.uk

Working Hours: *Bar and catering staff:* to work various shifts from 8am to midnight. *Cook/chef:* to work 8am–2pm and 6pm–11pm. *Adventure supervisor:* to work 10am–5pm, Monday to Friday during school holidays. *Secretary/receptionist:* to work alternative early/evening shifts and shared weekends.
Pay: Dependent on experience.
Company Description: Family-run caravan and camping park by Lake Ullswater. Set in magnificent scenery only 6 miles from Penrith and perfect for outdoor activities.
Job Description: *Cook/chef:* to prepare cooked breakfasts, lunches and evening meals. *Adventure supervisor:* to run a children's action club from the park. Activities include archery, tennis, baseball, volleyball, football, arts and crafts and pool tournaments.
Requirements: *Bar and catering staff:* minimum age 18. *Secretary/receptionist:* must enjoy meeting people and have a pleasant telephone manner.
Accommodation: Can be arranged in shared staff caravans.
Application Procedure: Applications from Easter, enclosing colour photo, details of work experience and dates of availability, to Mrs B Allen or Mrs F Bell, Parkfoot Caravan Park.

Alton Towers Resort

Job(s) Available: Up to 1,000 fixed-term positions and a range of permanent opportunities. *Finance:* strongroom team members. *Front of house:* admissions and guest services. *Hotel:* housekeeping, restaurant and bar, conference and events, chefs, kitchen teams, reception and leisure. *Retail:* food and beverage, shops, ride photos. *Rides and shows:*

Head Office: Alton, Staffordshire ST10 4DB
☎ 0870 444 6998
💻 www.altontowers.com or www.altontowersjobs.com

operators, ride hosts and actors. *Security, medical and traffic:* security officers, nurses, traffic management, car parking, monorail operators. *Others:* Lifeguards, spa therapists and assistants, Alton Towers PCV drivers.

Duration: Positions are available from February to November in the park and year round in the hotels.

Working Hours: Full-time, 5 days a week, or part-time, including weekends and bank holidays.

Pay: Wages are £5.92 per hour and above depending on position.

Company Description: Alton Towers Resort is a large and nationally known short break destination and is part of the Merlin Entertainments Group. A theme park, two themed hotels, a Caribbean waterpark, sealife aquarium, spa and conference centre all offer excellent career opportunities for customer service-focused people.

Requirements: No specific qualifications or experience are required as training is given. Minimum age 16.

Accommodation: Help with finding accommodation can be given.

Additional Information: Employees gain use of an active social club and a range of other benefits including free entry to Merlin attractions.

Application Procedure: Applications are received all year via www.altontowersjobs.com or the employment service at the above address. Interviews and assessment centres form the recruitment process. Overseas applicants with work permits welcome.

Crealy Adventure Park

Job(s) Available: Catering supervisors and assistants (30), play supervisors, retail assistants (10), ride operators (15).

Head Office: Clyst St Mary, Exeter, Devon EX5 1DR
☎ 01395 233200
✉ fun@crealy.co.uk
💻 www.crealy.co.uk

Duration: Required for Easter and summer holiday work (from July to September). *Play supervisors, ride operators:* summer work.

Working Hours: Flexible hours.

Pay: Dependent on age and experience.

Job Description: *Retail assistants:* for the admissions and gift shops. *Catering supervisors and assistants:* for fast food outlets. *Play supervisors:* for indoor and outdoor play areas. *Ride operators:* to safely operate park rides. Staff can expect full training and benefits.

Requirements: Minimum age 16 for all jobs unless otherwise stated. *Retail assistants:* experience in till operation an advantage. *Catering assistants:* food and hygiene certificate an advantage but experience not essential. *Play supervisors and ride operators:* must have outgoing personality and be able to adhere to strict working practices to comply with health and safety best practice. Minimum age 18.

Accommodation: Not available on site but there are camping facilities nearby.

Application Procedure: Apply online at www.crealy.co.uk/careers_crealy.aspx.

Drayton Manor Park Ltd

Job(s) Available: Retail staff (30), seasonal caterers (150), seasonal ride operators (150), ticketing staff (30).

Duration: From the end of March to the end of October.

Working Hours: Hours negotiable.

Pay: To be arranged; paid at an hourly rate.

Company Description: A family-owned and run theme park of 59 years; owns a catering company.

Requirements: No experience necessary as full training is given. Minimum age 16. Foreign applicants with a work permit and able to arrange their own accommodation are welcome. Fluent English is not essential.

Accommodation: Not available.

Application Procedure: By post from 1 January to HR department at the above address. Interview is generally necessary, but applicants not expected to travel long distances.

> Head Office: Tamworth, Staffordshire B78 3TW
> ☎ 01827 287979
> info@draytonmanor.co.uk
> www.draytonmanor.co.uk

European Waterways Ltd

Job(s) Available: Boat pilots, chefs, deckhands, housekeepers, tour guides.

Duration: Applicants must be available for the whole season, which runs from early April until the end of October.

Pay: £180–£400 per week plus accommodation and meals.

Company Description: Owners and operators of luxury hotel barges cruising rivers and canals in England, Scotland and France.

Requirements: All positions require applicants to hold a valid driving license. *Chefs:* must be fully qualified and hold a valid Food Hygiene Certificate. *Boat pilots:* need to have experience on rivers. Foreign applicants with a working visa, who are able to drive in the UK and have a good level of English are welcome. Some knowledge of French is helpful.

Accommodation: All positions include on-board accommodation, meals and uniform.

Application Procedure: Apply by February sending a CV and photo to the above address or via email.

> Head Office: 35 Wharf Road, Wraysbury, Middlesex TW19 5JQ
> ☎ 01784 482439
> sales@gobarging.com
> www.gobarging.com

Fantasy Island Ingoldmells Ltd

Job(s) Available: Arcade floorwalkers (20+), cashiers (12+), cleaners (20+), ride operators (100+).

Duration: Required for seasonal work from 1 March to 31 October.

Working Hours: Required to work a 6-day week.

Pay: National minimum wage rates.

Company Description: Fantasy Island is a large indoor theme park with a large funfair.

Requirements: Full training is provided and foreign applicants who speak English are welcome.

Accommodation: Not available.

Application Procedure: By post from January onwards, including CV and 2 named photos, to the HR department at the above address.

> Head Office: Sea Lane, Ingoldmells, Skegness, Lincolnshire PE25 1RH
> ☎ 01754 874668
> rides@fantasyisland.co.uk
> www.fantasyisland.co.uk

GLL

Job(s) Available: Kids activity instructors, and lifeguards.
Duration: Positions are available from June to September. Minimum period of work 10 weeks.
Working Hours: Flexible.
Pay: Dependent on age and experience From £5.74–£6.73 hour.

> **Head Office:** Middlegate House, The Royal Arsenal, Woolwich, London SE18 6SX
> ☎ 020 8317 5000 (extension 4020)
> ✎ recruitment@gll.org
> 🖥 www.gll.org

Company Description: A leisure centre operator in London, with more than 70 centres. As a worker-owned and controlled organisation, GLL offers opportunities and benefits that exceed the rest.

Requirements: *Kids activity instructors:* coaching qualifications and experience of working with children required. *Lifeguards:* National Pool Lifeguard qualification an advantage but not essential as training is provided. Candidates must be strong swimmers. Foreign applicants with appropriate permits and a good command of the English language are welcome. Subsidised training courses are also offered to those who want to build a career in the leisure industry. All employees must undergo a CRB check.

Application Procedure: Via the website at www.gll.org/careers. Applications are only accepted online via email. Please note: lifeguard applicants will be required to complete a swimming test as part of their interview.

Hoburne Naish

Job(s) Available: Amusement arcade staff, bar staff, kitchen staff, lifeguards, receptionists and waiting staff.

> **Head Office:** Christchurch Road, New Milton, Hampshire BH25 7RE
> ☎ 01425 273586
> ✎ naish@hoburne.com
> 🖥 www.hoburne.com

Duration: Required from 1 June to mid–September.
Working Hours: To work 40 hours per week. *Bar staff, amusement arcade staff, waiting staff, kitchen staff, receptionists:* to work mainly evenings and weekends. *Lifeguards:* for daytime and weekend work.
Pay: National minimum wage rates.
Company Description: Holiday park with 1,000 units of accommodation for holidaymakers, second-home owners and residents, situated midway between Bournemouth and Southampton. Overlooks the Isle of Wight and Christchurch Bay.
Requirements: *Lifeguards:* lifesaving qualification required.
Accommodation: Not available.
Application Procedure: By post from 1 April to the general manager, at the above address. An interview is required. Foreign applicants with fluent English welcome.

LEGOLAND Windsor

Job(s) Available: Admission assistants, environmental services assistants, food and beverage assistants, retail assistants, rides and attractions assistants, security guards.

> **Head Office:** Winkfield Road, Windsor, Berkshire SL4 4AY (HR department)
> ☎ 01753 626543
> ✎ jobs@legoland.co.uk
> 🖥 www.legoland.co.uk/jobs

Duration: The operating season lasts from March to November. Minimum period of 8 weeks.
Working Hours: Average of 40 hours over 5 days (variable, including weekends). Part-time positions also available in the above areas.
Pay: Competitive rate of pay, with benefits offered.

Company Description: LEGOLAND Windsor is a theme park dedicated to the imagination and creativity of children of all ages.

Job Description: Applicants must have a passion for serving others, an exuberant personality and a natural affinity with children. To be part of the LEGOLAND team staff need to be willing to work hard and have fun whatever the weather (many positions involve working outside).

Requirements: Minimum age 17 or 18, dependent on position. No previous experience is necessary as training will be given in all departments. Fluent English is essential.

Accommodation: Help is available to find accommodation.

Application Procedure: Apply online via the above website from January onwards.

Merlin Entertainments Group

Job(s) Available: A wide variety of operational and professional roles including: customer service, aquarists, engineers and house keepers.

Duration: Fixed term and permanent roles, dependent on position.

Working Hours: Shifts vary according to the position and department.

Pay: Competitive, rates vary depending on position.

Head Office: 3 Market Close, Poole BH15 1NQ
☎ 01202 666900
info@merlinentertainments.biz
www.merlincareers.com

Company Description: The Merlin Entertainments Group has over 13,500 employees and in the UK they operate: LEGOLAND, Madame Tussauds, the London Eye, Sea Life, Dungeons, Alton Towers, Thorpe Park, Chessington World of Adventures, Warwick Castle as well as Theme Parks and family attractions worldwide.

Job Description: Merlin Entertainments look for dedicated individuals who are passionate about delivering great customer experiences. Candidates must be team focused, flexible, self-motivated and have excellent communication skills.

Requirements: Staff must have eligibility to work in the UK.

Accommodation: Not available.

Application Procedure: Apply via the website above.

Merlin Entertainments London Eye

Job(s) Available: Guest service assistants.

Duration: All positions are for the full season from the beginning of June to the end of September.

Working Hours: Approximately 40 hours, 5 days a week, on a rota basis including weekends and bank holidays.

Head Office: County Hall, Westminster Bridge Road, London SE1 7PB
☎ 020 7487 0209
human.resources@londoneye.com
www.londoneyejobs.com

Pay: From £7.50 per hour. Holidays will be paid at the end of the contract.

Company Description: The Eye is one of the tallest structures in London, standing 135m high on the south bank of the Thames, opposite Big Ben and the Houses of Parliament. It provides stunning views over central London and beyond.

Job Description: Very busy working environment with some outdoor positions.

Requirements: Minimum age 18. Applicants must have a minimum of 1 year customer service experience. No qualifications are necessary, but the right attitude is.

Application Procedure: Apply via the website from April onwards. Keep an eye on the website for more details. An interview is required for all applicants. Foreign applicants must be available for an interview, have a relevant working visa and speak fluent English.

MOTORSPORT VISION Ltd

Job(s) Available: Admission control/events stewards, catering team members, cleaning operatives, litter pickers.

Head Office: Brands Hatch, Fawkham, Longfield, Kent DA3 8NG
☎ 01474 872331
🖳 www.motorsportvision.co.uk
🖂 joanne.brown@motorsportvision.co.uk

Duration: Staff required from March to November, to work as and when required on a fixed term contract.

Working Hours: Hours worked for all positions will vary throughout the year and therefore all candidates must have a high degree of flexibility. *Admission control/events stewards, litter pickers:* weekends only. *Cleaning operatives:* full-time hours on a fixed-term contract could be available to the right applicant with mid-week and weekend positions available.

Pay: Competitive salary.

Company Description: Motorsport Vision Ltd is a large motor racing circuit operator, which owns Brands Hatch, Cadwell Park, Oulton Park, Snetterton and Bedford Autodrome and runs more than 150 racing events a year.

Job Description: *Admission control/events stewards:* work at the entrance gates during race events. This role involves cash handling and, as first point of contact for the venue, applicants must have excellent customer care skills. *Event stewards:* carry out duties such as car parking and crowd control. *Litter pickers:* venue presentation is one of the most important aspects of events and reliable, hardworking candidates are required to ensure high standards are maintained. *Catering team members:* required to work as part of the catering team within busy restaurants, bars and hospitality suites. *Cleaning operatives:* experienced cleaners to help maintain the high level of venue presentation.

Requirements: All positions require excellent customer care skills. Overseas applicants must have a valid work permit.

Application Procedure: By post to the HR administrator, from March, at the above address.

Pontins Ltd

Job(s) Available: Accommodation staff, bar staff, catering staff, cleaners/gardeners, fast food assistants, reservations staff, restaurant staff, shop staff, lifeguards, maintenance staff and Bluecoat entertainers.

HR Dept: Ainsdale House, Pontins Ltd, Shore Road, Southport, Merseyside PR8 2PZ
🖂 jointheteam@pontins.com
🖳 www.pontins.com

Duration: Staff taken on for both seasonal and permanent contracts, but positions available all year round.

Pay: National minimum wage rates and above.

Company Description: Pontins is one of the UK's leading holiday companies, entertaining over 600,000 guests every year at 6 coastal locations, and employing people throughout the UK. The centres are located in Blackpool, Lancashire; Pakefield, Suffolk; Brean Sands, Somerset; Camber Sands, Sussex; Prestatyn, north Wales; and Southport, Merseyside.

Job Description: *Fast food assistants:* to serve food and drinks, operate the tills and perform general cleaning duties in a number of fast food outlets. *Restaurant staff:* to serve meals and clean dining areas in a variety of self and waiter service restaurants, which seat up to 2,000 people. *Catering staff:* including qualified and experienced chefs, cooks and kitchen assistants. Duties include catering for large numbers, preparing and cooking fast food, taking orders, collecting money and general cleaning of the catering areas. *Bar staff:* to serve drinks, operate the tills and clean in busy bars. *Shop staff:* to be responsible for sales, operating the tills and the merchandising of stock. *Reservations staff:* to book in guests and allocate apartments. *Security:* to patrol the centre and implement and report on health and safety measures. *Lifeguards:* to supervise the heated indoor pools and the safety of guests. *Leisure staff:* to supervise and operate all leisure amenities. *Accommodation staff:* to help prepare the accommodation for the arrival of guests, including the making up of beds and cleaning of kitchens and bathrooms. *Maintenance staff:* positions are available for qualified electricians, plumbers and joiners as well as those who have experience in general maintenance. *Cleaners/gardeners:* for internal and external cleaning and maintenance of gardens. *Bluecoats:* as a Pontin's Bluecoat, you'll be experiencing every aspect of the entertainment business including production shows, cabarets and TV presenting. You get tons of on-stage experience and the chance to work alongside top celebrities, DJs and TV presenters. Daytime duties are all part of the fun whether it's karaoke for the mums and dads or fun games for the kids.

Requirements: Minimum age 18. Qualifications and experience are not always necessary, except in specialist areas, as full training is provided.

Accommodation: Limited accommodation is available. Food is subsidised.

Additional Information: Open days are held at all of the 7 coastal locations at various times throughout the year and are advertised in local newspapers and job centres. Road shows are also held across the country throughtout the year.

Application Procedure: For more information and an application form please visit www.pontins.com or email jointheteam@pontins.com.

NDSS Limited

Job(s) Available: Events stewards (300) and licensed security personnel (100).

Duration: All offers of work are based on a single event or festival.

Working Hours: Shifts are usually 12 hours and can be day or night.

Head Office: Cardiff House, Cardiff Road, Barry CF63 2AW
☎ 01446 731 280
✍ info@ndssltd.co.uk
🖳 www.ndssltd.co.uk

Pay: £5.50–£6 per hour for events stewards.

Company Description: NDSS Ltd is a provider of Licensed Security Personnel & Crowd Safety Management Services to the entertainments and leisure industry.

Requirements: Minimum age 18. You must be eligible to work in the UK and able to speak English fluently. You also need to have strong communication skills, the ability to work in a team and a lively outgoing personality. For a security position, you must be in possession of a Security Industry Authority (SIA) License.

Accommodation: Most contracts will involve camping on-site for the duration of the contract. You must provide your own camping equipment as well as your own method of transport to the events.

Additional Information: Some meals are provided. A uniform will be provided, but you will be expected to provide your own black trousers, black shoes or boots.

Application Procedure: Apply on the above website and complete an online application. Thorough background checks will be carried out.

Newlands Adventure Centre Ltd

Job(s) Available: Domestic assistants (4), kitchen assistant.

Duration: From April to October. Applicants must be able to start in April and stay until September/October.

Working Hours: To work a 44–hour week.

Head Office: Stair, Keswick, Cumbria CA12 5UF
☎ 01768 778463
✍ info@activity-centre.com
🖳 www.activity-centre.com

Pay: Further details of hours, salary and accommodation costs available on application.

Company Description: An outdoor centre located 3.5 miles outside Keswick offering multi-activity holidays in the heart of the Newlands Valley. Activities include climbing, abseiling, mountain biking, kayaking, archery and orienteering among others.

Job Description: *Domestic assistants:* to maintain a clean and hygienic environment and to assist with the preparation of meals for guests and staff. *Kitchen assistant:* to help prepare meals and to maintain a clean environment in all food preparation areas.

Requirements: Minimum age 18. No activity instructors required unless with 2 of the following UK qualifications: Summer ML, SPA, BCU Level 2 Coach Kayak, BCU Level 2 Coach Canoe.

Accommodation: Staff have their own single room with shared bathrooms and TV lounge. All meals are provided.

Additional Information: There is an opportunity to take part in the activities free of charge.

Application Procedure: Applicants to send CV and letter of introduction by email to debbie@activity-centre.com in January or February. An application form will then be sent and 2 references are required. Foreign applicants with a reasonable level of English and current visas and work permits welcome.

Pembrokeshire Coast National Park Authority

Job(s) Available: Car park attendants, coast path warden, site guide assistants, Visitor centre assistants.

Head Office: Llanion Park, Pembroke Dock, Pembrokeshire SA72 6DY
☎ 0845 345 7275
Jobs@pembrokeshirecoast.org.uk
www.pembrokeshirecoast.org.uk

Duration: Staff required from April/May to September.

Working Hours: *Visitor centre assistants, site guide assistants:* to work 2–5 days a week including weekends. *Coast path warden:* to work Monday to Friday. *Car park attendants:* working hours will vary but will include weekends and holidays.

Pay: £6.39–£6.91 per hour for all positions.

Company Description: A national park authority, responsible for building planning control, conservation and education regarding the environment within the national park.

Job Description: *Coast path warden:* main duty is maintenance of footpaths.

Requirements: *Visitor centre assistants, site guide assistants:* applicants should have good communication skills and enjoy working with the public. It may be an advantage to have knowledge of the area. *Coast path warden:* applicants should have countryside skills. *Car park attendants:* applicants should have good communication skills, experience of cash handling and practical skills for machine maintenance. Ability to speak Welsh is desirable, but not necessary for all jobs.

Accommodation: Not available.

Application Procedure: Applications should be in response to vacancy advertised on website, no speculative applications. Send to June Skilton at the above address during February and March. Information, when recruiting, will be available on the website.

Potters Leisure Resort

Job(s) Available: Food and beverage staff, housekeeping staff, kitchen and catering staff, lifeguard.

Head Office: Coast Road, Hopton-on-Sea, Norfolk NR31 9BX
☎ 01502 734812
recruitment@pottersholidays.com
www.pottersholidays.com

Duration: Positions available throughout the year.

Working Hours: *Food and beverage staff:* to work full-time and part-time positions up to 40 hours per week. *Housekeeping staff:* to work part-time, 16–20 hours over 6 days. *Lifeguards:* to work full-time and part-time positions up to 40 hours per week.

Pay: Dependent on age.

Company Description: The UK's only privately owned 5-star holiday village. Operates all year.
Job Description: *Food and beverage staff:* to work in bar, restaurant and catering positions.
Requirements: *Food and beverage staff:* minimum age 18 for bar staff. *Housekeeping staff:* minimum age 16. *Kitchen and catering staff:* minimum age 16. *Lifeguard:* minimum age 16 and must hold a NPLQ lifeguard qualification.
Accommodation: May be provided, depending on availability.
Application Procedure: By post at any time to Human Resources at the above address. Interview required. Foreign applicants with good spoken English welcome.

The Sherlock Holmes Museum

Job(s) Available: Sherlock Holmes lookalike and Victorian maids.
Duration: Period of work from July to September.
Pay: Varies according to experience.
Job Description: *Sherlock Holmes lookalike:* to dress up as Sherlock Holmes and give out promotional literature to tourists. *Victorian maids:* to receive visitors attending the museum.
Requirements: *Sherlock Holmes lookalike:* must be slim, minimum of 6ft tall and well spoken. *Victorian maids:* knowledge of other languages would be an asset.
Accommodation: Not available.
Application Procedure: Apply online at the above website.

> Head Office: 221b Baker Street, London NW1 6XE
> ☎ 020 7738 1269
> ⌨ info@sherlock-holmes.co.uk
> 🖥 www.sherlock-holmes.co.uk

Thorpe Park

Job(s) Available: Staff required for retail, food and beverage, cleaning, guest services, rides and attractions, sales, security, admissions and the medical centre.
Working Hours: Flexible hours available.
Pay: £5.85–£7.50 per hour.
Company Description: Thorpe Park is one of the UK's fastest growing theme parks and is located off junction 11/13 of the M25. It is also accessible via trains from Waterloo to Staines; a short bus ride will take you to the park.
Job Description: Enthusiastic and friendly people of all ages are required to join the teams.
Additional Information: Benefits include free uniform, free parking, staff canteen, social nights, discounted merchandise and complimentary tickets to all Merlin Entertainment Group attractions.
Application Procedure: Applications via the online form at the above website from January.

> Head Office: HR Department, Thorpe Park, Staines Road, Chertsey, Surrey KT16 8PN
> ☎ 01932 577302
> 🖥 www.thorpeparkjobs.com

Vectis Ventures Ltd

Job(s) Available: General park assistants (up to 15 per park).
Duration: Staff required from April to September/October and must work for a minimum of 6 weeks throughout July and August.
Working Hours: To work 5–6 days a week.
Pay: Dependent on age.
Company Description: Vectis Ventures Ltd are 2 visitor attractions on the Isle of Wight at Blackgang Chine and Robin Hill, with a range of family amusements. Open daily throughout the summer, attractions include a small number of rides and also activity play areas.

> Head Office: Blackgang Chine, Ventnor, Isle of Wight PO38 2HN
> ☎ 01983 730330 (Blackgang Chine) or 01983 527352 (Robin Hill)
> ⌨ info@blackgangchine.com or info@robinhill.com

Job Description: To work on rides, in retail outlets, in catering and for the gardening and car parking divisions.

Requirements: For park assistants working on rides minimum age 18. Minimum age 16 for all other positions. No experience is necessary but applicants should be friendly and outgoing.

Accommodation: Not available.

Application Procedure: By email via one of the above addresses, between January and March. An interview is necessary for all applicants. Overseas applicants are welcome but must have reasonable English.

William Grant & Sons

Job(s) Available: Tour guides.

Duration: From the end of June to the end of August.

Working Hours: 5 days a week.

Pay: Competitive salary.

> **Head Office:** The Glenfiddich Distillery, Dufftown, Banffshire AB55 4DH
> ☎ 01340 820373
> ✉ hr@wgrant.com

Job Description: Staff conduct tours of the Glenfiddich Distillery in an educational but informal manner. The distillery is fully operational. The work may particularly suit people interested in Scottish history and culture.

Requirements: Minimum age 18. Must be fluent in at least one foreign European language. Experience with the general public very desirable but not essential. Requires a bright, cheery and very outgoing personality. Only applicants with fluent English considered.

Accommodation: Limited accommodation may be available on site but local bed and breakfast costs approximately £60–£70 per week including evening meal. Self-catering accommodation can usually be found at £50–£60 per week.

Application Procedure: Between January and April to the above address in writing or by email. All applicants must be able to attend an interview at the distillery. Interviews are held before or during the Easter vacation period.

Hotels and catering

Hotels and catering establishments offer a range of jobs including work as **waiting, bar and chamber staff**, **receptionists**, **chefs and kitchen assistants**.

Many of the temporary hotel and restaurant jobs during the summer season are found in the country's main tourist resorts and beauty spots. Big hotel chains may provide the best opportunities for those based in or near cities, as they employ large numbers of staff and have a relatively fast turnover, meaning short-term vacancies can be available at any time of the year.

Working in a large and impersonal hotel in a city is likely to be more regimented and formal than spending the summer in an independent, family-run guest house on the coast, and so perhaps less friendly and enjoyable. If you choose a remote area with a lower cost of living and/or fewer opportunities to spend money, such as the Scottish Highlands or the Black Mountains, you will find it easier to save the money you earn. Many hotels start advertising for summer staff before Easter, and generally applicants who can work for the entire season are preferred.

Standard pay in bars and restaurants tends to be at the national minimum wage rate, but higher for silver service and in London, and usually lower for fast food restaurants. Hotels usually offer a similar rate, but often offer added perks like use of their leisure facilities. Often, tips can be a substantial bonus to waiting and bar staff. However, centrally pooled and divided tips may be included in the national minimum wage, and a recent European Court of Human Rights ruling set a precedent for including cheque and credit card tips as part of waiters' minimum wage.

Youth hostels: The Youth Hostels Association (www.yha.org.uk) employs seasonal assistant wardens to help run its 227 Youth Hostels in England and Wales. Work is available for varying periods between February and October.

Aviemore Highland Resort

Company Description: The Macdonald Aviemore Highland Resort is located in the heart of the Cairngorms National Park. The resort consists of 4 hotels plus luxury self-contained woodland lodges, leisure and beauty arena and a large conference facility, which encompasses both retail and food court.

Head Office: Aviemore, Inverness-shire PH22 1PN
☎ 0844 879 9152 or recruitment hotline: 01479 815 142
🖳 www.aviemorehighlandresort.com

Requirements: Applicants need to be motivated and focused, have a desire to succeed, be committed to excellence, possess excellent communication skills and wish to become part of a team.

Application Procedure: To apply, call the recruitment hotline on 01479 815142 or visit the website and apply online.

Balmer Lawn Hotel

Job(s) Available: Bar and waiting staff (2–4).
Working Hours: 45 hours per week, including weekends, serving breakfast 6.30am–11am, lunch 11am–3pm, and dinner 6pm–11pm, on a shift basis.
Pay: To be arranged, minus accommodation costs.

Head Office: Lyndhurst Road, Brockenhurst, Hampshire SO42 7ZB
☎ 01590 623116
🖅 jobs@balmerlawnhotel.com
🖳 www.balmerlawnhotel.com

Company Description: A friendly hotel situated in the heart of the New Forest with leisure facilities available. Approximately 20 minutes from Southampton and Bournemouth by train.

Requirements: Minimum age 20. Previous experience of the hotel industry preferred, though training will be given.

Accommodation: Available at £30–£35 per week.

Application Procedure: By post to Kara Birrell, general manager, at the above address or via the website.

The Balmoral Hotel

Job(s) Available: Beverage, food and housekeeping staff.
Duration: Staff required for various casual and full-time positions.
Working Hours: Usually working 5 days out of 7.
Pay: National minimum wage rates.

Head Office: 1 Princes Street, Edinburgh EH2 2EQ
☎ 0131 622 8895
🖅 hr.balmoral@roccofortecollection.com
🖳 www.roccofortecollection.com or www.thebalmoralhotel.com

Company Description: An elegant, 5-star hotel in the centre of Edinburgh. Part of the Rocco Forte Hotel group, with 188 bedrooms, Michelin-star restaurant, brasserie, Palm Court Bar and the Balmoral Bar, as well as extensive conference and banqueting facilities.

Requirements: Candidates must be flexible and motivated. Foreign applicants are welcome to apply but must be eligible to work in the UK.

Application Procedure: Applications or CVs can be submitted from April to the HR department at the above postal address or via email.

Caledonian Thistle Hotel

Job(s) Available: Food service staff for the cafe/bar or dining room.

Duration: Minimum period of work 3 months from April to October.

Working Hours: 39-hour week, split shifts.

Pay: National minimum wage rates.

Company Description: Part of the Thistle Hotel chain, the 77-bedroom Caledonian is situated in the heart of Aberdeen city centre.

Requirements: Minimum age 18. Experience preferred.

Accommodation: Board and lodging available.

Application Procedure: Email your CV and covering letter to ssc.recruitment@ northgatearinso.com or call the above phone number.

> **Head Office:** 10-14 Union Terrace, Aberdeen AB10 1WE
> ☎ 0871 376 9003
> ⌕ reservations.aberdeencaledonian@ thistle.co.uk
> ▭ www.thistlehotels.com

Camelot Castle Hotel

Job(s) Available: Bar staff, chamber staff, front-of-house staff, kitchen staff, reception and waiting staff.

Duration: Required from May to the end of October.

Working Hours: Variable.

Pay: National minimum wage rates.

Requirements: Applicants must be willing to do any aspect of hotel work.

Accommodation: Accommodation, breakfast and dinner are available. Rates to be negotiated.

Application Procedure: Applications to Katarina Scherber at the above address or by email from March. Foreign applicants with appropriate visas and sufficient English are welcome.

> **Head Office:** Atlantic Road, Tintagel, Cornwall PL34 0DQ
> ☎ 01840 770202
> ⌕ katarinascherber@camelotcastle.com
> ▭ www.camelotcastle.com

The Ceilidh Place

Job(s) Available: Bar staff (2), cooks (3), housestaff (2), waiting staff (6).

Duration: Work available between April and October, minimum period 3 months.

Pay: Wages paid monthly.

Company Description: A complex of buildings including a small hotel with 13 rooms, a bunk house, bar, café/bistro, restaurant, bookshop, gallery and venue for music and drama.

Job Description: *Waiting staff:* serving food and drink and clearing tables. *Bar staff:* serving/stocking drinks and assisting with food service.

Requirements: *Cooks:* need natural skill and enthusiasm. *Housestaff:* must be fit.

Accommodation: Full board provided with statutory deduction from wages pre-tax.

Application Procedure: Email or write to the general manager at the above address for further information and an application form. Overseas applicants eligible to work in the UK and with necessary documentation welcome.

> **Head Office:** West Argyle Street, Ullapool, Ross-shire IV26 2TY
> ☎ 01854 612103
> ⌕ effie@theceilidhplace.com
> ▭ www.theceilidhplace.com

THE UK

HOTELS AND CATERING

Crieff Hydro Ltd

Job(s) Available: Food and beverage service assistants, commis chefs, housekeeping assistants.
Duration: Positions are available year round. Minimum period of work is 6 months.
Working Hours: Approximately 39 hours per week with overtime available.

Head Office: Ferntower Road, Crieff, Perthshire PH7 3LQ
☎ 01764 65161
✆ janice.sneddon@crieffhydro.com or sarah.summers@crieffhydro.com
🖥 www.crieffhydro.com

Company Description: Crieff Hydro is a large family-run hotel and leisure resort set in 900 acres of central Perthshire countryside, approximately 20 miles north of Stirling. The hotel has 214 bedrooms and 52 self-catering units and over 55 activities on site, including a fully equipped indoor leisure club and numerous outdoor activities including archery, high and low ropes, watersports, quad biking, horse riding and golf.
Requirements: Applicants should have a good level of spoken English and excellent customer care skills. Previous hospitality experience preferred.
Accommodation: Staff accommodation including heating and lighting with meals available for approximately £32 per week. Bedding is supplied but employees need to provide their own contents insurance and towels.
Application Procedure: By post to Janice Sneddon (assistant human resources manager) or Sarah Summers (human resources manager) at the above address, or by email through the website. A phone interview is required. Overseas applicants welcome subject to valid work permits/visas and other travel documents.

Crown Hotel

Job(s) Available: General assistants.
Duration: Positions are available all year. Minimum period of work 3 months.
Working Hours: 39 hours per week.
Pay: National minimum wage rates minus board and lodgings.

Head Office: Exford, Exmoor, Somerset TA24 7PP
☎ 01643 831554
✆ info@crownhotelexmoor.co.uk
🖥 www.crownhotelexmoor.co.uk

Company Description: Award-winning 17th-century coaching inn set in the heart of beautiful Exmoor National Park.
Job Description: General assistants needed for waiting in the restaurant, bar work, cleaning rooms and washing-up duties.
Requirements: Fluent English essential. Minimum age 19.
Accommodation: Board and lodging available, cost to be arranged.
Application Procedure: By post throughout the year to Mr Chris Kirkbride at the above address. Suitably qualified foreign applicants welcome.

Dee Cooper

Job(s) Available: Live-in hotel staff.
Working Hours: Hours variable.
Pay: To be arranged.
Company Description: Agent working with more than 1,000 hotels in England, Scotland and Wales. Free service.

Head Office: Culloch Schoolhouse, Comrie, Perthshire PH6 2JG
☎ 01764 670001 or 01764 679765
✆ dee@livein-jobs.demon.co.uk
🖥 www.livein-jobs.co.uk or www.londonpubjobs.co.uk

Accommodation: All positions live-in.
Application Procedure: For a list of relevant available jobs, contact Dee Cooper using the above details. Foreign applicants with permission to work in the UK welcome.

Goodwood Food

Job(s) Available: Various catering positions available.
Duration: Casual positions from May to October.
Pay: £5.80 per hour (2010). £5.93 per hour (2011).
Company Description: Previously known as Payne and Gunter, Goodwood food is part of compass Group, the Global leader in catering
Requirements: Minimum age 16.
Accommodation: Not available.
Application Procedure: Apply online at www.compasseventsjobs.com/goodwood.

Head Office: Goodwood Racecourse, Goodwood, Chichester, West Sussex PO18 0PS
☎ 01243 774839
✆ staffing.goodwood@ compass-group.co.uk

Grange Moor Hotel

Job(s) Available: Waiting staff (10), washers up (6).
Working Hours: To work hours to suit between 1 and 23 December for lunches and evening meals. Christmas Day work available from noon to 5pm.
Pay: From £5.75 per hour. Christmas Day work at £15 per hour.
Company Description: A 50-bedroom family-run hotel with banquet room.
Job Description: Waiting staff required for plated service for Christmas dinners. Full training will be given.
Requirements: Minimum age 17. Must be friendly, helpful and polite.
Accommodation: Not available.
Application Procedure: By post to Mrs Christine Sedge at the above address.

Head Office: St Michaels Road, Maidstone, Kent ME16 8BS
☎ 01622 677623
✆ reservations@grangemoor.co.uk
🖥 www.grangemoor.co.uk

Hilton Coylumbridge

Job(s) Available: Kitchen, restaurant, waiting, bar, housekeeping staff.
Duration: Staff required from June to October. Minimum period of work 12 weeks.
Working Hours: 172 hours across a 31 day month.
Pay: Current rates for each job role displayed at www.careersathilton.com: enter Coylumbridge in the key word search.
Company Description: Hilton Coylumbridge is a family-orientated hotel situated in the heart of the Scottish Highlands. Local attractions include golf, watersports and horse riding.
Requirements: Ability to work a variety of shifts, including earlies, lates, weekends and split shifts. Applicants must have the right to work in the UK.
Accommodation: Shared en suite accommodation available at a charge of £4.51 a day.
Application Procedure: Online at www.careersathilton.com.

Head Office: Coylumbridge Hotel, Coylumbridge, Aviemore, Inverness-shire PH22 1QN
☎ 01479 813076
✆ irene.peters@hilton.com
🖥 www.hilton.co.uk

Hotel L'Horizon

Job(s) Available: Food and beverage service attendants, room attendants, kitchen porters, commis waiting staff/chef de rang.
Working Hours: 5-day week.
Company Description: A 4-star, 106-bedroom hotel, located on one of the island's beautiful beaches.

Head Office: St Brelade's Bay, Jersey, Channel Islands JE3 8EF
☎ 01534 494404
✆ sashford@handpicked.co.uk or lhorizon@handpicked.co.uk

Hotel L'Horizon offers a unique work experience for employees who prove themselves to be dedicated, responsible and efficient, with further employment prospects after the seasonal contracts terminate.

Requirements: All applicants must be presentable, have excellent customer care skills and have worked within a similar environment before. A good understanding and conversational fluency of English is essential.

Accommodation: Accommodation, uniforms and meals on duty provided.

Application Procedure: Applications should be made by application form available from the above address and website.

Jam Staffing

Job(s) Available: Bar staff and waiters/waitresses.
Duration: Positions available at all times of year.
Working Hours: Hours vary, but typically the work is during the evenings.
Pay: £5.75–£9 per hour.
Company Description: An established event staffing agency which supplies staff for the events industry at venues across London.

> **Head Office:** Tower Bridge Business Complex, 100 Clement's Road, Bermondsey, London SE16 4DG
> ☎ 0207 237 2228
> ✆ info@jamstaffing.com
> 🖥 www.jamstaffing.com

Job Description: To work at film premieres, award ceremonies and also smaller more intimate VIP occasions and private parties.

Requirements: Experience is preferred, but the most crucial attributes are immaculate presentation with a strong working attitude. Applicants must be hard working, professional and keen to be part of a team. Must be eligible to work in the UK and able to speak English fluently.

Accommodation: Not provided.

Application Procedure: Send a CV to the above email or postal address.

Kentwell Hall

Job(s) Available: Catering and retail staff (10).
Duration: June to July.
Pay: To be arranged.
Company Description: A privately owned moated Tudor mansion, situated in its own park and farmland, approximately 1.5 miles from the historic town

> **Head Office:** Long Melford, Sudbury, Suffolk CO10 9BA
> ☎ 01787 310207
> ✆ info@kentwell.co.uk
> 🖥 www.kentwell.co.uk

of Long Melford, famous for its great annual re-creations of Tudor life.

Job Description: Retail and catering staff needed to work in catering and the shop located outside of the main gates in the 21st-century area of the estate. Staff required to ensure the smooth running of the event for the public and school parties. Duties consist of serving in a temporary souvenir shop and restaurant in marquees and may also include marshalling school parties.

Requirements: Minimum age 16. Applicants need a pleasant manner and to be physically fit as they will be on their feet all day.

Accommodation: Not available.

Application Procedure: Send a CV and a letter of application by email or by post to Mrs Phillips at the above address.

Knoll House Hotel

Knoll House Hotel

Job(s) Available: Chefs (4), general assistants (2–3), housekeeping staff (6–10), kitchen assistants (2–3), waiting staff (6–10).

Head Office: Studland Bay, Swanage, Dorset BH19 3AH ☎ 01929 452233 staff@knollhouse.co.uk www.knollhouse.co.uk

Duration: Positions available for a minimum of 6 weeks between March and October. Easter and summer vacation positions also available, as well as further positions for the entire season.

Working Hours: All staff to work 38 hours.

Pay: National minimum wage rates and above paid depending on position. *Chefs:* salary dependent on experience.

Company Description: A country house holiday hotel located in a National Trust Reserve overlooking Studland Bay. Independent and family run, it has a reputation for service and care of its guests.

Job Description: *Waiting staff:* to work dining room including wine service. *General assistants:* to work in children's own restaurant. *Kitchen assistants:* washing up and helping in kitchens.

Requirements: A happy disposition and a good attitude are more important than experience. Minimum age 17. *Housekeeping staff:* no experience required. *Chefs:* 706/1 or equivalent not always necessary.

Accommodation: Deduction made for board and lodging, available in single rooms.

Application Procedure: By post or email from the start of the year to the staff manager, Knoll House Hotel. EU applicants with good spoken English welcome. Interview is not always necessary.

Land's End and John O'Groats Company

Job(s) Available: Catering personnel and retail staff for various jobs at Land's End.

Head Office: Land's End, Sennen, Penzance, Cornwall TR19 7AA ☎ 0871 720 0044 info@landsend-landmark.co.uk www.landsend-landmark.co.uk

Duration: From spring to early autumn.

Working Hours: Hours depend on the level of business.

Pay: To be arranged.

Company Description: A leading tourist attraction in Cornwall located in a spectacular setting. It comprises various exhibitions and trading units operating throughout the year. In winter the operation is reduced.

Requirements: Minimum age 16. Those with previous experience preferred.

Application Procedure: By post to personnel or via email at the above addresses.

Lochs & Glens Holidays

Job(s) Available: Kitchen, dining room, housekeeping, reception/bar team members.

Head Office: School Road, Gartocharn, Dumbartonshire G83 8RW ☎ 01389 713713 jobs@lochsandglens.com www.lochsandglens.com

Duration: Minimum period of work 12 weeks at any time of year. Dates of work are negotiable.

Working Hours: 40 hours per week.

Pay: National minimum wage rates, plus live-in terms and conditions are available.

Company Description: A hotel and tour group with 6 hotels located in beautiful and remote areas of Scotland.

Additional Information: Both temporary and permanent positions available, as well as opportunity for career development.

Application Procedure: Apply at any time to above email or link through website.

THE UK

HOTELS AND CATERING

64

LHA London Ltd

Job(s) Available: General domestic staff, voluntary jobs.

Duration: *General domestic staff:* work available all year round, long stays welcome. Minimum period of work 3 months throughout the year. *Voluntary jobs:* minimum stay 8 weeks.

Working Hours: *General domestic staff:* to work an average of 30–39 hours per week (mornings and evenings). *Voluntary jobs:* working only 20 hours per week.

Pay: Monthly wages to be arranged.

Company Description: Established in 1940, recruits residential staff for 12 London hostels run for young employed people and full-time bona fide students.

Job Description: *General domestic staff:* to do housework and help in kitchens.

Requirements: Common sense and willingness to tackle a variety of jobs required.

Accommodation: Board and lodging provided.

Additional Information: Opportunities to attend courses and improve English skills.

Application Procedure: By post 2 months before date of availability to the personnel manager, London Hostels Association, at the above address. Foreign applicants with permission to work in the UK are welcome.

> **Head Office:** 54 Eccleston Square, London SW1V 1PG
> ☎ 020 7834 1545
> ✆ ngrant@lhalondon.com
> 🖳 www.lhalondon.com

The Master Builders House Hotel

Job(s) Available: Bar staff, chamberstaff, general kitchen staff, housekeeper and waiting staff.

Duration: Positions available from the end of April/May to the end of August/September.

Pay: Above national minimum wage rates, dependent on position.

Job Description: *Bar staff:* to work in the bar to serve drinks and pub food. *Chamberstaff:* servicing guestrooms and evening turndown. *Waiting staff:* to work in the 1-rosette Riverview Restaurant. Serve at breakfast, lunch, afternoon teas, dinner and conference set-up.

Requirements: Applicants need good English, a pleasant outgoing personality, must enjoy the countryside and be good team players in an international team.

Accommodation: Accommodation may be available; single room (£50 per week), shared (£50 per week), including 2 meals a day.

Application Procedure: By post to Michael Clitheroe, general manager, at the above address or via email.

> **Head Office:** Buckler's Hard, Beaulieu, Hampshire SO42 7XB
> ☎ 01590 616253
> ✆ res@themasterbuilders.co.uk
> 🖳 www.themasterbuilders.co.uk

The National Seal Sanctuary

Job(s) Available: Positions in the catering, entertainment and retail sectors.

Duration: From April to September; preferably to work over 8 weeks.

Company Description: The Sanctuary is a well-known marine animal rescue centre.

Requirements: Minimum age 16.

Application Procedure: Enquiries by email to the above address.

> **Head Office:** Gweek nr. Helston, Cornwall TR12 6UG
> ☎ 01326 221361
> ✆ seals@sealsanctuary.co.uk
> 🖳 www.sealsanctuary.co.uk

Now and Zen

Job(s) Available: Catering assistants.
Duration: Working around Britain at summer music festivals.
Pay: On application.

☎ 07974 353 172
✆ jobs@nowandzen.co.uk
🖳 www.nowandzen.co.uk

Company Description: Now and Zen has been one of the most popular festival caterers at music festivals for the past 20 years, specialising in vegetarian world foods (including Japanese noodles, French crêpes, and Italian pastas). This is a lively, friendly, happy, and efficient organisation.

Job Description: Catering assistants needed to help in busy vegetarian world food stalls. Duties include food preparation, light cooking, cleaning, serving, packing, and so on. You will become an important part of a mainly student team.

Requirements: Applicants must be able to work happily in a team and must have lots of energy and stamina, be lively and adaptable, conscientious, and good humoured. Will not suit a person who likes a 9–5 job.

Accommodation: Opportunity for home-stay with accommodation and vegetarian food provided.

Application Procedure: Apply to Ron Zahl, proprietor, via email or on the phone number listed above.

Peppermint Events

Job(s) Available: Accounts managers, bar staff, build crew, cashiers (approximately 100), catering staff, cocktail staff, chefs/catering assistants, event managers and trained bartenders.

Duration: Required from June to September, but recruitment is ongoing.

Working Hours: Paid staff usually needed to work 8–14 hour shifts.

Head Office: 7 College Fields Business Centre, Prince Georges Road, London SW19 2PT
☎ 0845 226 7845
✆ jobs@peppermintevents.co.uk
🖳 www.peppermintevents.co.uk

Pay: Dependent on position and experience.

Company Description: An event and bar management company that caters for events and festivals such as Glade Festival, Bestival, Skandia Cowes Week and other various music festivals in London and the south-east.

Requirements: Minimum age 18. Experience of bar work is preferred, but not essential (except for trained bartender positions). Pre-1997 driver's licence required for build crew, events managers and accounts managers.

Accommodation: Camping spots may be available.

Application Procedure: By post to Tammy Vonwildenrath at the above address, or via the website. Overseas applicants are welcome to apply provided they have the relevant documentation and speak English to the same level as a native speaker.

Porth Tocyn Hotel

Jobs Available: General assistants.
Duration: Minimum period of work usually 6 weeks between March and November.
Pay: Guaranteed above national minimum wage rates.

Head Office: Abersoch, Gwynedd LL53 7BU
☎ 01758 713303
✆ bookings@porthtocyn.fsnet.co.uk
🖳 www.porthtocynhotel.co.uk

Company Description: A country house hotel by the sea, filled with antiques. The house has been in the family for 60 years, and has been in the *Good Food Guide* for more than 50 years.

Requirements: Intelligence, practical demeanour and sense of humour required. Cooking experience useful but not essential.

Accommodation: Subsidised board and lodging and use of tennis court and swimming pool.

Additional Information: Travel expenses will be paid for those able to work for short stints over Easter and the spring bank holidays.

Application Procedure: Applications from those who are able to work over Easter and/or outside the summer university vacation period especially welcome. Applications with s.a.e. to Mrs Fletcher-Brewer, at the above address or to above email or by telephone on 01758 713303.

Rufflets Country House Hotel

Job(s) Available: Housekeeping assistant, lounge service assistant, restaurant assistant.

Duration: Minimum period of work 6 months between 1 April and 30 November.

Working Hours: All staff to work hours as required, 5 days a week.

Pay: National minimum wage rates.

Head Office: Strathkinness Low Road, St Andrews KY16 9TX
☎ 01334 472594
✆ reservations@rufflets.co.uk
💻 www.rufflets.co.uk

Company Description: A privately owned 24-bedroom upmarket hotel which holds 2 AA rosettes for food quality; young and friendly staff required.

Requirements: Experience not essential. Minimum age 18.

Accommodation: Available at approximately £120 per month.

Application Procedure: See website for details on how to apply.

Tors Hotel

Job(s) Available: Chamber person, kitchen porters, waiting staff.

Duration: Season lasts from March to January. Period of work must be for the whole period from April until September, applicants only available for summer vacation need not apply.

Head Office: Lynmouth, North Devon EX35 6NA
☎ 01598 753236
✆ info@torshotellynmouth.co.uk
💻 www.torshotellynmouth.co.uk

Working Hours: All staff work 5 days a week. *Chamber person, kitchen porters:* to work 39 hours per week. *Waiting staff:* to work 39 hours, 5 days; split shifts.

Pay: National minimum wage rates plus any extra wages dependent on experience. Bonus paid on completion of season.

Company Description: A 3-star, 4-crown, 31-bedroom hotel situated on the north Devon coastline with stunning sea views across the Bristol Channel to Wales.

Requirements: Experience or the ability to learn.

Accommodation: Not available.

Application Procedure: Send applications with details of previous experience and photograph asap to the manager.

Tresco Estate

Job(s) Available: Bar staff (4), chefs (all levels) (18), cottage cleaners (6), housekeeping supervisors (2), housekeeping staff (18), kitchen assistants/porters (6), maintenance person (1), restaurant supervisors (3), retail assistants (8), receptionists (5), tractor/ transport driver (1), waiting staff (20), Leisure Spa attendant (2).

Head Office: Tresco, Isles of Scilly, Cornwall TR24 0QQ
☎ 01720 424110
✆ personnel@tresco.co.uk
🖳 www.trescojobs.co.uk

Duration: Period of work from February to November with further vacancies mid-season. Applicants will not be considered mid-season unless able to work a minimum of 10 weeks to include all of July and August.

Working Hours: 40–48 hours or more per week, generally split shifts over 5 to 5.5 days a week.

Pay: Starts at £5.80 per hour. Tips for hotel staff are split at the end of the season for all who complete their contract. Helicopter flight provided to the Isles of Scilly at beginning and end of contract period.

Company Description: Private island holiday resort, 28 miles off the Cornish coast.

Job Description: Staff needed to cover all duties in one of the Estate's 3 luxury hotels, the Flying Boat Club, the holiday cottages department, or the Abbey Garden shop and café.

Requirements: Minimum age 18. Must have a valid work permit.

Accommodation: Live-in accommodation of approximately £30 per week, meals are included in the hotels; for other departments kitchen facilities are available.

Application Procedure: At any time, by post or email (as above), stating the position you are interested in, and why you consider yourself suitable.

YHA (Youth Hostel Association)

Job(s) Available: General assistants needed to help run the YHA's youth hostels throughout England and Wales.

Head Office: Recruitment Department, Trevelyan House, Dimple Road, Matlock, Derbyshire DE4 3YH
☎ 01629 592570
✆ jobs@yha.org.uk
🖳 www.yha.org.uk

Duration: Work is available for varying periods. Minimum period of work 3 months. Recruitment starts early in the year to ensure the hostels are staffed for the summer. Vacancies reduce considerably as the year progresses.

Company Description: The YHA, a registered charity, is the largest budget accommodation provider in Britain with 200 youth hostels in diverse locations throughout England and Wales.

Job Description: Assistants undertake a variety of tasks including catering, cleaning, reception and general maintenance.

Requirements: Experience in one or more of the above areas is desirable, but customer service experience and enthusiasm are essential.

Application Procedure: For an application form call the YHA National Recruitment line on 01629 592570 between September and June. Alternatively, visit the YHA website at www.yha.careers.co.uk for details of our recruitment events. Non-EU nationals require a valid work permit. All posts are subject to an interview, usually at the hostel where the vacancy exists.

Language schools

The staff needs of language schools are principally for **EFL teachers** and **social organisers**.

Teaching English as a foreign language (TEFL), also known as TESOL (Teaching English to Speakers of Other Languages), is perhaps no longer the major growth industry it was a decade ago, but it still offers a large number of summer jobs that often pay better than average. Starting from around June, people of all nationalities and ages, though usually teenagers and students, come to Britain to learn or improve their English and absorb some British culture. The schools that cater for them proliferate along the south coast and in major university/tourist cities like Oxford, Cambridge, Edinburgh and London.

The majority of residential language schools often take on staff to work as social supervisors and organisers, both at the school outside of teaching time and on day trips. The bigger ones may also require sports and activity instructors. These positions frequently require no qualifications other than interest and an ability to work with young people.

The Abbey College

Job(s) Available: EFL teachers (20).
Duration: Work available from the beginning of June to the end of August. Minimum period of employment 3 weeks. Year round positions are also available.
Pay: £270–£350 per week.

Head Office: 253 Wells Road, Malvern Wells, Worcestershire WR14 4JF
☎ 01684 892300
jobs@abbeycollege.co.uk
www.abbeycollege.co.uk

Company Description: A 70-acre residential campus with students from more than 30 nations. Over the last 30 years, the company has developed an English course to meet every requirement alongside the main academic school. A wide range of facilities are available online.
Requirements: Must hold at least an RSA/Trinity CertTEYL. Previous summer school experience is preferred.
Accommodation: Accommodation and meals provided.
Additional Information: Free use of all sports equipment and the leisure activities and excursions are also open to all employees.
Application Procedure: By post from March to the personnel department at the above address. An interview is necessary for all applicants.

Aberystwyth University

Job(s) Available: EFL teachers (6–10).
Duration: Work involves 20 hours of teaching per week, plus 16 hours of social duties per month and 12 hours of administration per month. Minimum period of work is 1 month between mid-July and early September.
Pay: £510 per week.

Head Office: Language and Learning Centre, Llandinam Building, Penglais Campus, Aberystwyth SY23 3DB
☎ 01970 622545
tesol@aber.ac.uk
www.aber.ac.uk/tesol

Company Description: Attractive working environment in a secure seaside location between the coast of Cardigan Bay and the Cambrian Mountains. The international English centre offers courses to language learners and language teachers in a warm and welcoming academic environment.
Requirements: Applicants must have native-speaker competence in English. First degree, TEFL qualifications and 3 years of experience required.
Accommodation: Board and lodging available.
Application Procedure: By post from 1 January to Rex Berridge, director, at the above address. Interview necessary.

Briar School of English

Job(s) Available: EFL teachers, sports instructors.
Duration: Busy seasons are over the Easter period and from the beginning of June to the end of August. They also entertain out of season school parties at different times of the year. Minimum period of work 3 weeks (June to August).
Working Hours: *Sports instructors:* required to work up to 6 hours per day.

> **Head Office:** Briar School of English LTD, Aspire Centrey, Yarmouth Road, Lowestoft, Suffolk NR32 4AH
> ☎ 01502 580203
> richard@briarschool.com
> www.tiger-uk.com

Pay: *EFL teachers:* from £9 per hour. *Sports instructors:* from £6 per hour. Successful applicants for both jobs can earn extra pay by leading half/full day excursions to Norwich, Cambridge, London and other local places of interest.
Company Description: Established in 1958, the Briar School offers English courses to international students aged 12–25.
Requirements: *EFL teachers:* TEFL qualifications or experience essential. Applicants must possess either a degree or a teacher's certificate. *Sports instructors:* ideal post for physical education students.
Accommodation: Not available.
Application Procedure: By post to Richard Alan, at the above address.

Cambridge Academy of English

Job(s) Available: EFL teachers and social organisers, both residential and non-residential.
Duration: Required for 3–6 week courses between mid-June and late August.
Working Hours: Various contracts.
Pay: From £300 per week.

> **Head Office:** 65 High Street, Girton, Cambridge CB3 0QD
> ☎ 01223 277230
> cae@cambridgeacademy.co.uk
> www.cambridgeacademy.co.uk

Company Description: Situated in the leafy suburb of Girton, the Academy runs non-residential courses for teenagers and young adults, and residential courses for 9–13-year-olds and 14–16-year-olds.
Job Description: To teach teenagers and young adults.
Requirements: Must have CELTA or equivalent and relevant experience.
Application Procedure: Via email at the above address.

Concord College

Job(s) Available: Residential summer course EFL teachers (10–15), summer course outdoor education tutor(s) (1–2), summer course sports tutors (2–4).
Duration: Staff required from the end of June for July course (4 weeks) and/or August course (3 weeks).
Working Hours: Variable.
Pay: Dependent on qualifications and experience.

> **Head Office:** Acton Burnell Hall, Acton Burnell, Shrewsbury, Shropshire SY5 7PF
> ☎ 01694 731631
> summercourse@concordcollegeuk.com
> www.concordcollegeuk.com

Company Description: An independent international school.
Requirements: *Residential summer course EFL teachers:* applicants must hold as a minimum the RSA Certificate in TEFL. *Summer course sports tutors:* applicants must have the appropriate coaching qualifications. Some senior posts are available for suitably qualified applicants.
Accommodation: Available free of charge.
Application Procedure: Applications and enquiries should be sent to John Leighton, director of summer courses, at the above address at any time of year.

Concorde International Summer Schools Ltd

Job(s) Available: Centre directors, academic directors, activity managers, activity leaders, EFL teachers.

Head Office: Arnett House, Hawks Lane, Canterbury, Kent CT1 2NU
☎ 01227 453325
🖰 recruitment@concorde-int.com
🖳 www.concorde-int.com/recruitment

Duration: The centres are open in June, July and August. Minimum period of work 1 week.

Working Hours: *Centre directors:* to work up to 48 hours per week. *Academic directors:* to work up to 48 hours per week. *Activity managers:* to work up to 48 hours per week. *Activity leaders:* to work 36 or 42 hours per week. *EFL teachers:* required to teach in summer schools for full or part-time positions. An average working week consists of 17.5 hours tuition plus some activities, depending on contract and weeks vary according to individual programmes.

Pay: From £240–£500 per week. See website for more details.

Company Description: Concorde International has been organising summer schools in the south of England since 1972. They have a high return rate of international students and staff.

Job Description: *Centre directors:* to ensure the smooth running of the centre and liaise with head office, the local homestay organiser and the group leaders. *Academic directors:* duties include holding staff meetings and weekly in-house training sessions, briefing teachers and standing in for them. Both residential and non-residential positions are available depending on the centre. *Activity managers:* required to ensure the smooth running of the activity programme and take care of the students' health and welfare. Other duties include checking transfer arrangements, liaising with head office and regular staff at the centres. *EFL teachers:* both residential and non-residential positions are available.

Requirements: Fluent English is essential for all positions. *Centre directors:* applicants should have a CELTA or Trinity TESOL or equivalent and should preferably hold a qualification in EFL management although other management qualifications/experience will be considered. *Academic directors:* applicants must hold a RSA Diploma TEFL or Trinity Diploma TESOL or equivalent and have a minimum of 2 years of summer school experience. *Activity managers:* first aid and lifeguarding qualifications preferred and management experience an advantage. *Activity leaders:* experience preferred but not essential. *EFL teachers:* applicants should have a CELTA or Trinity TESOL or equivalent or PGCE in an appropriate subject and some summer school experience.

Accommodation: Available free of charge for most residential positions in return for extra activities.

Application Procedure: By email at any time of year to the director of vacation courses at the above address or by post. Interview required. EU nationals preferred but non-EU applicants with necessary work permits/visas will be considered.

Discovery Summer

Job(s) Available: Activity leaders (40).

Head Office: 33 Kensington High Street, London W8 5EA
☎ 020 7937 1199
🖰 info@discoverysummer.co.uk
🖳 www.discoverysummer.co.uk

Duration: Staff required for a minimum of 2 weeks between July and mid-August.

Working Hours: 1 day off per week.

Pay: £300 per week.

Company Description: Organises summer courses for students learning English as a foreign language.

Job Description: Activity leaders required to supervise sports, arts and craft activities, parties and excursions for students aged 9–17.

Requirements: Experience of sports coaching or teaching/supervising children is desirable. Minimum age 18.

Accommodation: On campus accommodation available free of charge.

Application Procedure: Apply between March and June to Mary Shipley, manager, via email or by post to the above address.

EF International Language Schools

Job(s) Available: EFL teachers.

Duration: Required for July and August to work full-time.

Pay: Varies according to location and experience.

Requirements: Candidates should have at least a first degree and CELTA.

> Head Office: 74 Roupell Street, London SE1 8SS
> ☎ 020 7401 8399
> ✆ Kate.williams@ef.com

Application Procedure: By post with CVs to the director of studies at the relevant address.

EF Language Travel London

Job(s) Available: Activity leaders, teachers, senior staff roles.

Duration: Minimum period of work 3 weeks between June, July and August.

Working Hours: Flexible hours, 6 days a week.

Pay: Salary varies depending on region and qualifications.

> Head Office: 22 Chelsea Manor Street, London SW3 5RL
> ☎ 020 7341 8500
> ✆ recruitment@ef.com
> 🖥 www.ef.com/summerjobs

Company Description: Language courses with free-time programmes for international students in locations throughout the UK and Ireland.

Job Description: *Activity leaders:* to work alongside a co-leader to organise and participate in a full activity programme with groups of foreign students. *Teachers:* to plan, prepare and deliver our EF English Course to groups of foreign students. *Senior staff:* responsible for the smooth running of our destinations.

Requirements: *Activity leaders:* minimum age 18. Leadership experience preferred but not essential. *Teachers:* must have a TEFL/PGCE/BEd qualification or English at degree level. *Senior staff:* previous organisational experience essential. All applicants must be fluent speakers of English.

Accommodation: Full board and lodging available for residential appointments only.

Application Procedure: Apply online or by email at the above address. All applicants must be available for interview.

EF Language Travel Oxford

Job(s) Available: Activity coordinators, EFL teachers, leaders.

Duration: From June to the end of August.

Pay: Varies depending on the role.

Job Description: Staff needed to teach English as a foreign language to students from overseas.

> Head Office: EF International Language School, Pullens Lane, Oxford OX3 0DT
> ☎ 01865 759660
> ✆ oxford.recruitment@ef.com
> 🖥 www.ef.com

Requirements: University graduate with a TEFL qualification.

Application Procedure: Apply online.

EJO

Job(s) Available: Activity staff, course directors, EFL teachers, qualified lifeguards, first aiders, senior EFL teachers.

Head Office: Eagle House, Lynchborough Road, Passfield, Hampshire GU30 7SB
☎ 01428 751549
✆ steve@ejo.co.uk
💻 www.ejo.co.uk

Duration: Staff required for Easter, June, July and August.

Working Hours: 5–6 days a week by arrangement.

Pay: Varies according to qualifications and experience.

Job Description: *Course directors, senior EFL teachers, EFL teachers:* required for residential and non-residential courses. *Qualified lifeguards, first aiders:* required for residential centres.

Requirements: *Course directors, senior teachers:* need to be TEFL qualified with a good degree (MA or TEFL/TESOL Diploma preferred) and 2 or more years of teaching experience. *Teachers:* need to have CELTA/Trinity CertTESOL qualification or QTS. *Activity staff:* should be studying towards or have graduated in a sports or arts qualification.

Accommodation: Available at residential centres.

Application Procedure: By post to the education department at the above address or via email.

Harrow House International College

Job(s) Available: Activities coordinator, drama/art leaders (2), English-language teachers (15–20), residential sports/activities teachers (19–24).

Head Office: Harrow Drive, Swanage, Dorset BH19 1PE
☎ 01929 424421
✆ info@harrowhouse.co.uk
💻 www.harrowhouse.com

Duration: Staff required for a minimum of 2 months from approximately mid-June until the end of August.

Working Hours: *Drama/art leaders, English-language teachers, residential sports/activities teachers:* to work 6 days a week.

Pay: *Activities coordinator:* £350 per week. *Residential sports/activities teachers:* £220 per week.

Company Description: A 38-year-old international language college set in the Purbecks in the heart of Dorset, which teaches English to students from more than 60 countries.

Job Description: *English-language teachers:* required to teach children from age 8 upwards. *Activities coordinator:* required to provide students with a full leisure programme. Both jobs offer residential positions.

Requirements: *Activities coordinator, drama/art leaders:* must have relevant experience and qualifications. *English-language teachers:* applicants must possess a CELTA qualification or equivalent.

Accommodation: Full board and lodging available. Where accommodation is not included as a part of the wage, it is available at a cost of approximately £80 per week.

Application Procedure: *Drama/art leaders, English-language teachers:* by post from February onwards to Sharon Patterson. *Residential sports/activities teachers:* by post to Paul Yerby at the above address. Foreign applicants are welcome to apply, but must have a level of English appropriate to the position.

International Student Club Ltd

Job(s) Available: Activity monitors.
Duration: Positions available from the first week of July to mid-August. Minimum period of work 2 weeks.
Working Hours: Variable summer school hours.
Pay: £260 per week.

> **Head Office:** 21 Park Road, Hale, Cheshire WA15 9NW
> ☎ 0161 929 9002
> ✉ jill@student-club.co.uk
> 🖥 www.student-club.co.uk

Company Description: A small, family-run organisation offering English language and activity courses to foreign students aged 10–17.
Job Description: Activity monitors required to supervise young people during sports sessions, excursions, discos and competitions.
Requirements: Minimum age 19. Preference will be given to those with sports qualifications or experience in dance and drama.
Accommodation: Board and lodging available free of charge.
Application Procedure: By email to Jill Cutting. Foreign applicants are welcome to apply but fluency in English is essential. Interview required.

Kaplan International Centres

Job(s) Available: EFL teachers (40–50), activity staff, management and administration staff.
Duration: Staff required from 3 July to 13 August. Minimum period of work 3 weeks.
Pay: Varies, depending on post.
Company Description: English-language programmes at 3 summer centre locations around the London area; also 4 year-round schools running

> **Head Office:** Kaplan International Colleges, C/O Sandra McCord, Summer Centres Coordinator, 30 Ash Hill Road, Torquay TQ1 3HZ
> ☎ 08103 210944
> ✉ Sandra.mccord@kaplan.com
> 🖥 www.kaplaninternational.com

summer English programmes for juniors in Bath, Bournemouth and Torquay. Part of Kaplan Aspect.
Requirements: Teachers must have a university degree and a minimum of a Cambridge CELTA or Trinity *Cert TESOL*.
Accommodation: Provided at residential centres.
Application Procedure: By email to the Summer Centres Coordinator at the above address from January 2011.

Kings School of English Bournemouth

Job(s) Available: Administrative assistants (10), course directors (4), director of studies (3), EFL teachers (40), residential course teachers and social and sports supervisors (20).
Duration: Positions are available between mid-June and the end of August. Most posts available for 3–12 weeks.

> **Head Office:** 58 Braidley Road, Bournemouth BH2 6LD
> ☎ 01202 293535
> ✉ info@bournemouth.kingscolleges. com

Working Hours: *Administrative assistants:* to work full-time 5–6 days a week. *Course directors:* should be available all summer to work full-time. *EFL teachers:* to give 20–40 lessons per week. *Social and sports supervisors:* to work full-time 5–6 days a week.
Pay: *Administrative assistants:* £175–£250 per week. *Course directors:* £350–£450 per week. *EFL teachers:* £200–£450 per week. *Residential course teachers and director of studies:* £350–£500 per week. *Social and sports supervisors:* £200–£275 per week.

Company Description: A private school of English for overseas students. Offers courses for all ages, but much of their work is with teenagers and children. The school is located 5 minutes from the centre of Bournemouth. It has a very busy summer period, offering a fun, vibrant but hard-working atmosphere. Also run residential summer camps in other places in the south of England.

Requirements: All applicants must be enthusiastic, versatile and enjoy working with young people. Fluent English absolutely essential for all posts. *Administrative assistants:* must have good computer, organisational and interpersonal skills. *Course directors:* must have a diploma in TEFL, university degree and considerable TEFL experience. *EFL teachers:* must have TEFL certificate or diploma, and preferably a degree and relevant experience. *Residential course teachers and director of studies:* must be qualified TEFL teacher prepared to take part in sports, social activities and excursions and act as houseparents. TEFL Diploma required for director of studies posts. Energy, enthusiasm and stamina required. *Social and sports supervisors:* must have relevant sports and social activities experience/qualifications.

Accommodation: Not usually available, but included for teachers on residential courses.

Application Procedure: By email or post from March onwards to the school principal at the above address. Interview required. Foreign applicants may be considered for positions other than teaching posts.

Kings School of English London

Job(s) Available: EFL teachers (approximately 10).
Duration: From mid-June to the end of August. Minimum 4 weeks.
Working Hours: Teachers to work 20–28 lessons per week.

Head Office: 25 Beckenham Road, Beckenham, Kent BR3 4PR
☎ 020 8650 5891
london@kingscolleges.com
www.kingscolleges.com

Company Description: The only year-round recognised EFL school in Beckenham. Welcoming 150–250 students from all over the world, they specialise in teaching English to international groups of adult learners. Established in 1966 and British Council accredited.

Job Description: Programmes for learners aged 14 and over.

Requirements: Only UCLES CELTA/DELTA qualified applicants need apply.

Application Procedure: By post from January to the director of studies at the above address.

Lal Torbay (Summer Schools)

Job(s) Available: Activity leaders, house parents, office administrators, programme coordinators, residential and non-residential teachers and welfare officers.

Head Office: Conway Road, Paignton, Devon TQ4 5LH
☎ 01803 558555
london@lalschools.com
www.lalschools.com/jobs

Duration: From July to August for a period 4–6 weeks.
Working Hours: Variable and dependent on position.
Pay: Variable and dependent on position.
Company Description: English-language school in Paignton, Torbay in Devon and summer school centres at Kelly College in Tavistock, Devon; Taunton School in Taunton, Somerset; St Swithun's School in Winchester, Hampshire and St. Mary's University College, London.
Job Description: *Activity leaders:* to assist, organise and lead activities for children aged 9–16, including leading sports, trips to theme parks, city tours, discos and transfers to and from the airport. *House parents:* to assist in all welfare aspects of residential summer school, including waking up and putting to bed of students in an accommodation house.

Office administrators: to run the office and administration aspects of a school. *Programme co-ordinators:* to organise and supervise the leisure programme. *Teachers:* to prepare and teach English as a foreign language.

Requirements: See job descriptions on website.

Accommodation: Accommodation and food available for residential positions.

Application Procedure: Download an application pack from www.lalschools.com or email torbay@lalgroup.com.

Language Link

Job(s) Available: EFL teachers (20).

Duration: To work from the end of June to the end of August, Monday to Friday.

Pay: Dependent on qualifications and experience.

Company Description: Language Link is accredited by the British Council and is a member of English UK.

Head Office: 21 Harrington Road, London SW7 3EU
☎ 020 7225 1065
✆ recruitment@languagelink.co.uk
🖥 www.languagelink.co.uk

Located in the borough of Kensington and Chelsea, it is open all year, with a friendly, family atmosphere.

Requirements: Applicants must be Cambridge, Trinity or equivalent TEFLA certified. A 4-week CELTA qualification can be taken at Language Link (email teachertraining@languagelink.co.uk).

Application Procedure: By post from May to the director of studies at the above address. An interview is required.

LTC Eastbourne

Job(s) Available: Residential EFL teachers (5), residential welfare officers (4).

Duration: Staff required from middle of June to mid-September.

Working Hours: *EFL teachers:* to teach 20 lessons per week; includes evening and some weekend social and residential duties. *Residential welfare officers:*

Head Office: Compton Park, Compton Palace Road, Eastbourne, East Sussex BN21 1EH
☎ 01323 727755
✆ info@geos-ltc.com
🖥 www.ltc-english.com

to work 40 hours per week, including evenings and weekends.

Pay: *EFL teachers:* £313 per week with full board. *Residential welfare officers:* from £263 per week with full board.

Company Description: A friendly private language school running courses for adult students and residential courses for young learners. Set in a mansion house in its own park, 20 minutes' walk from Eastbourne town centre.

Job Description: *Residential welfare officer:* position would suit a student.

Requirements: *EFL teachers:* minimum of RSA/Cambridge CELTA or Trinity CertTESOL required. *Residential welfare officers:* first aid an advantage. Overseas applicants for teaching posts must have an advanced level of English (IELTS 9 or equivalent).

Accommodation: Free board and lodging.

Application Procedure: *EFL teachers:* by email to Alisdair Goldsworthy, director of studies, alisdair@ltc-eastbourne.com; *welfare officers:* by email to Maria Bayne, student services manager, maria@ltc-eastbourne.com.

LTC London

Job(s) Available: EFL teachers (15).
Duration: To work from end of June to the end of August.
Working Hours: Full-time.
Pay: To be arranged.
Requirements: Applicants must have RSA, CTEFLA/CELTA, or Trinity CertTESOL.
Additional Information: Also has a school in Hove; email anthony@geos-brighton.com for details.
Application Procedure: By post or email to Anna Liese Agrippa, director of studies.

Head Office: 16–20 New Broadway, Ealing, London W5 2XA
☎ 020 8566 2188
✆ info@ltc-london.com
🖥 www.ltc-english.com

Manchester Academy of English

Job(s) Available: EFL teachers, EFL teachers for football programme, EFL teachers for young learners.
Duration: Positions are available between 1 July and 31 August. *EFL teachers for young learners:* positions available between 1 July and 15 August, for 2 weeks.
Working Hours: Approximately 25 hours per week.
Pay: *EFL teachers, EFL teachers for football programme:* approximately £13.50 per hour for CELTA trained teachers and £15 per hour for DELTA trained. *EFL teachers for young learners:* approximately £500 for 2 weeks.
Company Description: City centre English-language school for international students, a member of English UK, and British Council accredited.
Requirements: *EFL teachers:* applicants should have a degree and an RSA/Cambridge or Trinity CertTESOL or LTCL Diploma TESOL, in addition to 2 years of experience. Minimum age 21. *EFL teachers for football programme:* candidates should be able to participate and support the activity programme. Applicants should have a degree and an RSA/Cambridge or Trinity CertTESOL or LTCL Diploma TESOL. 1 year's experience preferred. Minimum age 20. A CRB check is necessary. *EFL teachers for young learners:* applicants should have a degree and an RSA/Cambridge or Trinity CertTESOL or LTCL Diploma TESOL. 1 year's experience preferred. Minimum age 20. A CRB check is required.
Accommodation: *EFL teachers for young learners:* available. *EFL teachers, EFL teachers for football programme:* not available.
Application Procedure: By post from February onwards to director of studies at the above address or via email. Interview required.

Head Office: St Margaret's Chambers, 5 Newton Street, Manchester M1 1HL
☎ 0161 237 5619
✆ info@manacad.co.uk
🖥 www.manacad.co.uk

Pilgrims English Language Courses

Job(s) Available: EFL teachers (25), programme staff (25).
Duration: Required to work from late June to August.
Pay: *EFL teachers:* £350 per week plus holiday pay. *Programme staff:* £270 per week plus holiday pay.
Job Description: *Programme staff:* required to lead sports, drama, art and music.
Requirements: *EFL teachers:* must have recognised TEFL qualification.
Accommodation: Full board and lodging.

Head Office: 38 Binsey Lane, Oxford OX2 0EY
☎ 01865 258336
✆ gary.luke@pilgrims.co.uk
🖥 www.pilgrims.co.uk

Additional Information: For details of working conditions see www.pilgrimsrecruitment.co.uk.

Application Procedure: By post to Gary Luke, director of training, at the above address or online at www.pilgrimsrecruitment.co.uk.

Project International

Job(s) Available: Teaching/activity staff (50). Some positions with more responsibility available.
Duration: Staff needed for up to 6 weeks from early July.
Pay: £210–£300 per week.
Job Description: Teaching/activity staff to teach English and supervise activities at residential summer school centres.
Requirements: Possession of TEFL and PGCE qualifications an advantage but not essential.
Accommodation: Full board included.
Application Procedure: Downloadable application form on the 'employment' section of the website.

Head Office: 20 Fitzroy Square, London W1T 6EJ
☎ 020 7916 2522
recruitment@projectinternational.uk.com
www.projectinternational.uk.com

Richard Language College

Job(s) Available: EFL teachers (20).
Duration: Minimum work period 2 weeks between 1 June and 30 September. Longer term year-round placements available for suitable applicants.
Working Hours: Hours 8.30am–4.30pm, Monday to Friday. Teaching 6 or 7 lessons of 45 minutes per day.
Pay: £300 per week depending on qualifications and experience.
Job Description: EFL teachers to teach adults of mixed levels and different nationalities, in classes of about 10 students.
Requirements: Must have first degree and RSA Preparatory certificate in TEFL.
Application Procedure: By post from 28 February to the academic manager at the above address.

Head Office: 43–45 Wimborne Road, Bournemouth, Dorset BH3 7AB
☎ 01202 555932
acadman@rlc.co.uk
www.rlc.co.uk

Severnvale Academy

Job(s) Available: EFL teachers (5–10).
Duration: Period of work late June to 15 August; to teach Monday to Friday daytime. Minimum period of work 4 weeks.
Pay: From £360–£400 per week.
Company Description: British Council accredited English-language school with separate adult and junior centres.
Requirements: Degree and TEFL qualification (eg CELTA/TESOL certificate) necessary. Spoken English to the standard of a native speaker required.
Accommodation: Board and lodging available for £110 per week.
Application Procedure: By email from Easter onwards to Mr JWT Rogers, principal, at the above address.

Head Office: 25 Claremont Hill, Shrewsbury, Shropshire SY1 1RD
☎ 01743 232505
enquiry@severnvale.co.uk
www.severnvale.co.uk

Southbourne School of English

Job(s) Available: EFL teachers (20), residential teachers, sports organisers/assistants (8).

Duration: Staff required from mid-June to the end of August. *EFL teachers:* to work 15–30 hours per week. *Residential teachers:* required for 4 weeks to start work in July. *Sports* organisers/assistants: to work 40–50 hours per week.

Head Office: 30 Beaufort Road, Bournemouth BH6 5AL
☎ 01202 422300
Kathryn@southbourneschool.co.uk
www.southbourneschool.co.uk

Pay: Rates of pay on application.

Company Description: A family-run school, working for more than 40 years teaching English as a foreign language. British Council accredited and a member of English UK.

Job Description: Residential teachers for junior courses.

Requirements: *EFL teachers:* must have one of the following qualifications – PGCE, BEd, Cert Ed, RSA Cert EFL, RSA Diploma EFL, TESOL, Trinity LTCL Diploma TESOL. *Sports organisers/assistants:* sports training useful. Minibus driver useful, with category D1 licence or minibus licence.

Accommodation: Free accommodation on residential courses.

Application Procedure: By post from Easter to the director of studies at kathryn@southbourneschool.co.uk.

Stafford House School of English

Job(s) Available: Activity organisers (20), EFL teachers (40).

Duration: Minimum period of work 1 week between June and September.

Pay: Rates of pay on application.

Head Office: 19 New Dover Road, Canterbury Kent CT1 3AH
☎ 01227 452250
info@staffordhouse.com
www.ceg-uk.com/english

Company Description: The summer school has mixed nationality classes with a maximum of 15 students per class. Ages 12 to adult. Emphasis is on productive skills and fluency-based activities.

Requirements: *Activity organisers:* reliability, energy and enthusiasm essential. *EFL teachers:* TEFL qualifications such as RSA/Trinity CertTESOL or RSA/Trinity LTCL Diploma TESOL required.

Application Procedure: *Activity organisers:* by email to Betty Dagistan (b.dagistan@staffordhouse.com) or at the above address. *EFL teachers:* by email from February, to Nicky Hollis (n.hollis@staffordhouse.com). An interview is required.

SUL Language Schools

Job(s) Available: EFL teachers, senior tutors and course directors.

Duration: Courses run for 2–4 weeks from April to October. Teachers required for a minimum period of 2 weeks, working mornings and possibly afternoons, supervising activities.

Head Office: 31 Southpark Road, Tywardreath, Par, Cornwall PL24 2PU
☎ 01726 814227
efl@sul-schools.com
www.sul-schools.com

Pay: Rates of pay on application.

Company Description: A well-established business that provides language holiday courses in Cornwall, Devon, Somerset, the Midlands, Scotland and Ireland for foreign teenagers.

Requirements: Applicants should be TEFL qualified or hold a teaching qualification. Applicants must be CRB checked.

Accommodation: Available at some centres.

Application Procedure: Online only via email, at www.sul-schools.com. Interview required.

Thames Valley Summer Schools

Job(s) Available: Course directors, housemasters/mistresses, recreation directors, specialised recreation teachers (arts & crafts, drama and aerobics/dance), sports instructors, EFL teachers, director of studies.

Head Office: 13 Park Street, Windsor, Berkshire SL4 1LU
☎ 01753 852001
✉ english@thamesvalleysummer.co.uk
🖥 www.thamesvalleysummer.co.uk

Duration: During the months of July and August.

Company Description: TVSS has more than 35 years of experience in providing English-language courses and activities for young learners from all over the world. Accredited by the British Council and a member of English UK, this summer school has 6 centres in locations in the south-east and Warwickshire.

Requirements: Staff should have appropriate skills, experience and qualifications relevant to the position. *Course directors:* with relevant residential experience. *Housemasters/mistresses:* with pastoral/residential experience. *Recreation directors:* with residential and recreation administration experience.

Accommodation: Free board and lodging available for residential positions.

Application Procedure: Online at www.thamesvalleysummer.co.uk. Click on 'Working for us.' Recruitment commences in February, for positions starting between the end of June and mid-July.

Medical

This category consists largely of opportunities for **nurses** and **care and support workers**.

Britain's care industry is currently suffering both from a shortage of health professionals and the pressure of an ageing population. Much of the work available is with the elderly, though some is available with the sick and disabled (applicants in these areas should be aware that UK legislation may require CRB checks on those intending to work with vulnerable adults).

Overall there should be little difficulty in finding work in this field. Often agencies do not even require experienced applicants as on-the-job training is given. Generally, though, applicants must be over 18 and having your own transport can be an advantage. In addition to the vacancies in this book, specialist nursing agencies can be found in the Yellow Pages or at www.rec.uk.com.

Apex Nursing & Care Services

Job(s) Available: Care assistants, support workers, trained/auxiliary nurses.

Head Office: Emery House, 195 Fog Lane, Didsbury, Manchester M20 6FJ
☎ 0845 600 3041
✉ hr@apex-nursing.co.uk
🖥 www.apex-nursing.co.uk

Duration: Required for all vacations and during term-time.

Pay: Rates of pay will be discussed at interview.

Job Description: To work in hospitals, nursing homes, people's own homes, and social care involving working with clients with learning disabilities and challenging behaviour.

Requirements: No experience is necessary as full free training is given. Minimum age 18.

Application Procedure: Enquiries for application forms can be made via recruitment@apex-nursing.co.uk.

Consultus

Job(s) Available: Live-in carers.
Duration: Positions are available all year to work on 2-week live-in assignments.
Pay: From £55–£82 per day (£111+ for nurses).
Company Description: Founded in 1962 by the present managing director, Consultus is one of the major providers of live-in care in Britain. Their aim is to help the elderly remain happily and safely in their own homes for as long as possible.
Job Description: Staff needed nationwide to perform domestic duties and some personal care for elderly private clients. NMC-registered nurses also welcome. Duties may include cooking, cleaning, housekeeping, driving, shopping and a varying degree of personal care of the client. Work is available across the UK.
Requirements: Minimum age 21. Some experience of care of the elderly/disabled preferred.
Accommodation: Single room and free meals in client's house while on assignment.
Application Procedure: By post at any time to the above address or through the website for overseas work. Interviews will take place in Tonbridge in the UK; in Cape Town or Johannesburg in South Africa; Harare in Zimbabwe or in Auckland, New Zealand.

> **Head Office:** 17 London Road, Tonbridge, Kent TN10 3AB
> ☎ 01732 355231
> ✆ manager@consultuscare.com
> 🖳 www.consultuscare.com

Home Comforts Community Care Ltd

Job(s) Available: Full/part-time care workers (15–20).
Duration: Positions available at all times of year.
Pay: £7 basic per hour plus travel expenses (average inclusive hourly earnings £9.25 per hour).
Company Description: Care agency/employer with clients all over Sussex. Established 1995.
Job Description: To work various shifts in nursing homes, residential homes and homes for adults with learning disabilities in East Sussex, West Sussex and Kent. Some personal care such as washing, dressing. A caring nature would be useful for this work.
Requirements: Own transport essential. Minimum age 18. Basic training will be given in first aid and manual handling.
Application Procedure: By post to Marie Ingram, HR director, at the above address. Foreign applicants with fluent English and eligibility to work in the UK welcome.

> **Head Office:** Suite 6, Quarry House, Mill Lane, Uckfield, East Sussex TN22 5AA
> ☎ 01825 762233
> ✆ wendyvennhccc@yahoo.co.uk

Options Trust Staff Recruitment

Job(s) Available: Assistant to a disabled person (10–12).
Duration: Minimum period of work 6 months at any time of year.
Pay: £150–£250 per week.
Company Description: A non-profit-making organisation, set up and run by a number of disabled people who employ personal assistants to enable them to live in their own homes, in the community.
Job Description: Personal assistants to carry out personal care, domestic duties and driving.
Requirements: Minimum age 18. Driving licence required but no previous experience necessary.
Accommodation: Free board and lodging.
Application Procedure: By post to Mrs V Mason or via email at the above addresses.

> **Head Office:** 4 Plantation Way, Whitehill, Bordon, Hampshire GU35 9HD
> ☎ 01420 474261
> ✆ optionstrust@pvm.ndo.co.uk
> 🖳 www.optionstrust.co.uk

Outdoor

The majority of vacancies in this category are for **fruit pickers**, **farm staff** and **marquee erectors**.

Agriculture: While increased mechanisation has reduced the number of pickers required at harvest time, agriculture remains the second largest source of seasonal work after tourism. The best areas for summer fruit and vegetable picking work in the summer are from the Vale of Evesham over to the River Wye (in the Midlands), Kent, Lincolnshire, East Anglia (especially the Fens) and north of the Tay in Scotland (especially Perthshire). Harvest types and times vary between regions, so raspberries may ripen two weeks later in Scotland than in the south of England. Strawberries and gooseberries are among the first fruits to ripen in southern Britain, usually in June. Processing and packing work is generally available in the Vale of Evesham after the main harvest season. Work involving harvesting outdoor salad crops is also available in the Hampshire and West Sussex area. The apple harvest runs from August until mid-October and offers traditionally more lucrative work.

The fledgling English wine industry has been growing in reputation over recent years and there are some 350 vineyards throughout England and Wales, producing around 2 million bottles a year. These vineyards, located mainly throughout the southern half of England, may require workers, though the grape harvest is unpredictable as the sugar content depends on the often elusive sun. The grape harvesting season is fairly late, usually beginning in September and finishing mid-November, although it depends largely on a number of factors such as the region, the weather and the variety of grape. For more information contact English Wine Producers (01536 772264; info@englishwineproducers.com; www.englishwineproducers.com).

While fruit picking is generally short-term, it is possible to string several jobs together by following ripening crops around the country, or by choosing a farm with several crops that will ripen in sequence. On-the-spot applications are often productive, with no interview required, and it is sometimes possible to secure employment at very short notice (note that most farmers prefer the first approach to be via telephone).

Due to the temporary nature of much accommodation offered by farmers, a comfortable night's sleep may not always follow a tiring day's work. Some provide comfortable bunkhouses and meals, but others require you to bring your own tent and cater for yourself. Some provide communal cooking facilities, but these can sometimes be in a poor state of cleanliness as upkeep is no one's direct responsibility. The Food and Farming Information Service also advises workers to take out insurance to cover personal belongings, and to visit farms in advance if possible.

Fruitfuljobs.com is a web-based agency which helps people find jobs with accommodation on UK farms; although the main season runs from March to October work is available throughout the year in the agricultural and horticultural industries – from organic farming to operating a forklift truck. You can also call 0870 0727 0050, or email info@fruitfuljobs.com, for more information. Another useful website that details agricultural jobs in both the UK and overseas is www.pickingjobs.com.

Farmers can recruit students from any part of the EU. Some farms take part in the Seasonal Agricultural Workers scheme, enabling them to recruit student pickers from outside the EU. This is done through organisations such as Concordia (YSV) Ltd. (01273 422293; www.concordia farms.org).

Pay varies according to the fruit and the difficulty involved in the picking process. Many farmers pay piecework rates, which means that you are paid according to the quantity you pick. This method can be very satisfactory when a harvest is at its peak; but when fruit is scarce, earning more than the minimum can be much more difficult. However, even if you are paid on a piecework basis, the amount you earn for each hour worked must average the rates set out in the

Agricultural Wages Order. The Agricultural Wages Board (020 7238 6523) sets minimum weekly and hourly rates for agricultural workers in England and Wales.

Removals and marquee work: While manual jobs with removal firms are available at any time of year, the summer is a real boom time for marquee erectors. During the sunny season there is a never-ending round of agricultural shows, festivals, wedding receptions and so on. And while a village fair may require just one marquee, a music festival will require a whole range of tents plus large amounts of furniture and equipment. All this has to be loaded and unloaded from lorries, as well as driven to and from a depot; for this and other driving work possession of an HGV driving license would be a useful advantage. Overtime is often available, so marquee work can be lucrative. Most employers specify a minimum height for loading work and most only take on men.

Claremont Marquees

Job(s) Available: Marquee erectors/labourers (5).
Duration: Period of work 1 April to 1 October. Minimum period of work 1 week.
Working Hours: Flexible working hours, normally approximately 8–10 hours per day.
Pay: £6–£7 per hour.
Requirements: Applicants must be fit and strong.
Accommodation: Not available.
Application Procedure: By post to Robert Atkins, owner, at the above address from the start of April.

> **Head Office:** Fishers Hill House, Hook Heath Road, Woking, Surrey GU22 0QE
> ☎ 01483 720472
> 🖂 robertatkins@tiscali.co.uk
> 🖥 www.claremontmarquees.com

D&B Grant

Job(s) Available: Fruit pickers (50).
Duration: Period of work from 10 June to 31 August.
Working Hours: To work 5 days a week. Shifts to be arranged.
Pay: To be arranged.
Job Description: Fruit pickers to pick strawberries and raspberries. Help also required to process fruit for freezing.
Accommodation: Caravan accommodation available.
Application Procedure: Apply to Colin M Grant via email. Applications must only be sent in January.

> **Head Office:** Wester Essendy, Blairgowrie, Perthshire PH10 6RA
> ☎ 01250 884389
> 🖂 cmgrant99@yahoo.com

Danco International Plc

Job(s) Available: Marquee erectors (10–15), warehouse operatives.
Duration: Period of work from April to September.
Working Hours: *Marquee erectors:* to work 50–60 hours per week. 7 day weeks are required, with days off once job is complete. *Warehouse operatives:* to work 50–60 hours per week, including weekend work.
Pay: *Marquee erectors:* starting from £6 per hour plus a £15 night-out allowance when on site. *Warehouse operatives:* starting from £6 per hour.

> **Head Office:** The Pavilion Centre, Frog Lane, Coalpit Heath, Bristol BS36 2NW
> ☎ 01454 250222
> 🖂 elisa@danco.co.uk or garyc@danco.co.uk
> 🖥 www.danco.co.uk

Job Description: *Marquee erectors:* to put up marquees around the UK. *Warehouse operatives:* to load and unload trailers and pick orders.

Requirements: Minimum age 20. Those with driving licences preferred.

Accommodation: *Marquee erectors:* basic accommodation provided but applicants need sleeping bag, pots, pans, cutlery and plates in addition to wet-weather gear and steel toe-capped boots. *Warehouse operatives:* basic accommodation provided on site.

Application Procedure: By post to Elisa Lunt, personnel manager, at the above address.

The Dorset Blueberry Company

Job(s) Available: Pickers and packers.

Duration: Positions available from July to September.

Pay: Wages are calculated by kg performance and good workers can earn high wages.

Company Description: Producers of fresh blueberries for major supermarkets.

Accommodation: Available at a cost.

Application Procedure: Applications only accepted through the above website.

> Head Office: Littlemoors Farm, Ham Lane, Hampreston, Wimborne, Dorset BH21 7LT
> ☎ 01202 891426
> info@dorset-blueberry.co.uk
> www.dorset-blueberry.com

E Oldroyd and Sons Ltd

Job(s) Available: Rhubarb and vegetable harvesters (10), strawberry harvesters (40).

Duration: Positions available from January to March and May to September. *Strawberry harvesters:* minimum period of work 1 month.

Working Hours: *Rhubarb and vegetable harvesters:* to work full/part-time, up to 8 hours per day for up to 3 months.

Pay: Piecework rates or hourly agricultural wage rates where applicable.

Company Description: 5 generations of experience with fruit and vegetables. Busy both in the winter and summer. Farms are close to Leeds city centre's shopping and nightlife and only 5 minutes from the supermarket. Email access available.

Requirements: Minimum age 17. Full training given.

Accommodation: Approved accommodation available.

Application Procedure: Early applications are recommended to avoid disappointment. Write, enclosing a CV with references, to Mrs J Oldroyd Hulme at the above address. Interview possibly required. Foreign applicants welcome.

> Head Office: Hopefield Farm, Leadwell Lane, Rothwell, Leeds, Yorkshire LS26 0ST
> ☎ 0113 282 2245
> janet@eoldroyd.co.uk
> www.yorkshirerhubarb.co.uk

Essex Outdoors

Job(s) Available: Outdoor activity instructors.

Duration: Minimum period of work 3 months, between April and October.

Working Hours: Approximately 8 hours per day, including some evenings and weekends.

Pay: To be arranged.

Company Description: Essex Outdoors is Essex County Council's outdoor education service, offering outdoor education to the young people at 5 residential and non-residential centres across Essex and 1 centre in Wales.

> Head Office: PO Box 47, County Hall, Chelmsford CM2 6WN
> ☎ 01245 430945
> essexoutdoors@essex.gov.uk
> www.essexoutdoors.org

Job Description: *Activities include:* archery, sailing, climbing, walking, canoeing, kayaking, mountain biking, caving and power boating.

Requirements: National governing body qualifications such as BCU, RYA, MLT, GNAS etc preferred.

Accommodation: Board and lodging may be available in some residential centres.

Application Procedure: Via the website.

Field and Lawn (Marquees) Ltd

Job(s) Available: Marquee erectors.
Duration: Positions are available from May to November.
Working Hours: Required to work long hours.
Pay: From £5.75 per hour.
Company Description: A young and enthusiastic company which takes a pride in its product and employees. Work-hard, play-hard atmosphere.

Head Office: Unit C, Appleton Industrial Park, Barleycastle Lane, Warrington WA4 4RG
☎ 01925 600260
lyndseyholland@fieldandlawn.com
www.fieldandlawn.com

Job Description: *Marquee erectors:* required to erect marquees throughout England and Wales. The work is very strenuous so fitness is essential.

Application Procedure: By post from 1 April through to the end of September to the operations manager at the above address or telephone number or email address above. Overseas applicants, particularly from New Zealand, South Africa and Australia welcome.

Fridaybridge International Farm Camp Ltd

Job(s) Available: Picking and packing fruit, vegetables and flowers (approximately 350).
Duration: Required from February to December.
Working Hours: Usually 40 hours per week. Some extra work available at weekends.
Pay: £5.81 per hour.

Head Office: 173 March Road, Fridaybridge, Cambridgeshire PE14 0LR
☎ 01945 860255
fbifc-contact@hotmail.com

Company Description: A unique company providing services to both workers and farmers. Offer accommodation, employment (and fun!) for people looking for work in the agricultural and food industries.

Job Description: Picking and packing.

Requirements: Minimum age 18. No qualifications or experience necessary. Fluent English not essential. Some qualifications such as tractor or forklift licenses are helpful. Applicants must be physically fit.

Accommodation: Board and lodging is available at a reasonable rate (inclusive of use of all facilities). Meals are not provided, but you can use the kitchen. There is a charge of £4 for transport to and from work.

Additional Information: Participants will have the opportunity to earn money and gain experience in the working environment; they will also be able to meet and make friends with other young people of many different nationalities. Facilities include: bar/club, swimming pool, tennis, basketball, volleyball, football, table tennis, shop, internet and TV room.

Application Procedure: Apply all year round to the bookings manager by email. No interview is necessary. Applications from all nationalities eligible to work in the UK are welcome.

Fruitgrowers Ltd

Job(s) Available: Apple and pear pickers (10).
Duration: Positions are available from 30 August to 30 September. Minimum period of work 4 weeks.
Working Hours: 8 hours per day with some overtime.
Pay: National minimum wage rates.
Company Description: A family fruit farm with a small and friendly workforce.
Requirements: Minimum age 18. Applicants must be clean, healthy and able. No previous experience necessary.
Accommodation: Available in shared caravans at £28 per week. Showers and laundry facilities are on site.
Application Procedure: By post from April onwards to Edward Newling at the above address. Foreign applicants with sufficient English to understand instructions welcome.

> **Head Office:** Turnover Farm, Decoy Road, Gorefield, Wisbech, Cambridgeshire PE13 4PD
> ☎ 01945 870749
> ⌨ p9ear@tiscali.co.uk

FW Mansfield & Son

Job(s) Available: Fruit pickers and packers (50–100).
Duration: Workers needed from May to November.
Working Hours: To work variable hours, plus overtime if desired.
Pay: National minimum wage or piecework rates.
Job Description: Fruit pickers and packers to pick and pack apples, pears, strawberries, plums and cherries.
Requirements: Minimum age 18. Must be fit and hard working.
Application Procedure: By post to the farm manager at the above postal address or via email.

> **Head Office:** Nickle Farm, Chartham, Canterbury, Kent CT4 7PE
> ☎ 01227 731441
> ⌨ rookc@mansfields.net
> 🖥 www.mansfields.net

GE Elsworth & Son

Job(s) Available: Crop thinners (6), fruit pickers (3–4).
Duration: *Crop thinners:* required during June. Possibility of pruning work from January to March also. *Fruit pickers:* to pick apples in September.
Working Hours: To work flexible hours between 9am and 5pm.
Pay: As set by the Agricultural Wage Board.
Accommodation: Available.
Application Procedure: By email to S Elsworth. Please ensure job availability before arriving unannounced.

> **Head Office:** Park Fruit Farm, Pork Lane, Great Holland, Frinton-on-Sea, Essex CO13 0ES
> ☎ 01255 674621
> ⌨ s.elsworth@farmline.com

GL Events Snowden's

Job(s) Available: Marquee erectors.
Duration: From 1 April to 30 September.
Working Hours: To work an average of 10 hours per day, 6 days a week (extra hours are available).
Pay: Average £300 per week, dependent on hours worked.

> **Head Office:** Second Drove Eastern Industry, Fengate, Peterborough PE1 5XA
> ☎ 01733 294615
> ⌨ adrian.west@snowdens.co.uk

Company Description: Snowden's is a subsidiary of GL Events, a leading marquee hirer in the show and hospitality market.
Requirements: Minimum age 18. Applicants must be physically fit and able.
Accommodation: Only provided when working away on site.
Additional Information: Successful applicants may visit some prestigious sporting locations, eg Ascot, Newmarket and Silverstone.
Application Procedure: By post from 1 March to Adrian West at the above address or via email. Foreign applicants with all relevant work permits and acceptable level of spoken English are welcome.

The Granta Boat and Punt Company

Job(s) Available: Ice cream servers (2), punt chauffeurs (10).
Duration: Staff required for a minimum period of 3 months from March to October.
Working Hours: Various hours are available for both positions. Applicants must be flexible as the hours will include weekend and evening work.
Pay: Competitive hourly rates.
Company Description: Boat and punt hire company situated on the River Cam.
Job Description: *Punt chauffeurs:* applicants must be able to provide informative verbal tours to guests, which will include memorising historical facts.
Requirements: *Ice cream servers:* minimum age 16. *Punt chauffeurs:* Minimum age 16. Applicants must be outgoing, confident and physically fit. Previous experience of working in a customer service environment and knowledge of a foreign language are preferable, but not essential.
Accommodation: Not available.
Application Procedure: By post from the end of February to Sarah Austen, director, at the above address. Overseas applicants are welcome to apply but must be able to speak English to the same standard as a native speaker.

Head Office: Newnham Mill Pond, Newnham Road, Cambridge CB3 9EX
☎ 01223 301845
www.puntingincambridge.com

Harold Corrigall

Job(s) Available: Fruit pickers (10), managerial posts.
Duration: *Fruit pickers:* staff required for a minimum of 4 weeks between June and September. *Managerial posts:* for approximately 5 months from May to September.
Working Hours: Required to work 6am–3pm per day, 6 days a week.
Pay: Approximately £40–£60 per day.
Company Description: A small farm growing 40 acres of strawberries under tunnels and 5 acres of raspberries.
Requirements: Minimum age 18. *Managerial posts:* must speak a good level of English.
Accommodation: Available at a charge of £4 per day.
Application Procedure: By post from February to Harold Corrigall at the above address. The farm takes many European students with appropriate permits or authorisation.

Head Office: Leadketty Farm, Dunning, Perthshire PH2 0QP
☎ 01764 684532
haroldcorrigall@btconnect.com

Hill Farm Orchards

Job(s) Available: Fruit packers (10), fruit pickers (10), pruners (10).
Duration: *Fruit packers:* to work from October to March. *Fruit pickers:* to work from September to October. *Pruners:* to work from January to April. The minimum period of work is 1 month.
Working Hours: 8am–4.30pm, Monday to Friday, with occasional weekends.
Pay: As set by Agricultural Wages Board and piecework rates at the height of the seasons.
Company Description: Pleasantly situated between Portsmouth and Southampton, with shops and pubs nearby.
Job Description: *Fruit pickers:* packing apples and pears for high-class outlets.
Requirements: Minimum age 20. Applicants must be eligible to work in the UK and have a moderate level of English.
Accommodation: Available at a reasonable rate.
Application Procedure: Apply by email or post to Mr Paul Roberts, farm manager, at the above address.

Head Office: Droxford Road, Swanmore, Hampshire SO32 2PY
☎ 01489 878616
farm@hillfarmorchards.co.uk
www.hillfarmorchards.co.uk

HR Philpot & Son Ltd

Job(s) Available: Experienced machine operators, general farm workers.
Duration: Required to work the harvesting season from the end of June until October.
Company Description: Highly mechanised progressive large arable farming company based in Essex and Suffolk.
Job Description: Working on a farm with modern equipment, CAT 85, Fastrac, Vaderstat Cultivators, Drills/FC, Combine Harvesters, modern potato harvesting and grading equipment.
Requirements: Must be adaptable to take on any job when asked. Must have full UK driving licence, valid work permit and be able to understand and speak English.
Accommodation: Provided for single persons.
Application Procedure: By post to Sue Nash at the above address or via email from December onwards.

Head Office: Barleylands Farm, Barleylands Road, Billericay, Essex CM11 2UD
☎ 01268 290215
sue@barleylands.co.uk
www.barleylands.co.uk

Jersey Cycletours

Job(s) Available: Cycle mechanic, bike issuer.
Duration: From July to the end of September.
Working Hours: 20–40 hours per week.
Pay: Wages according to age and experience
Company Description: The company's bikes (Trek, Giant, Dawes) are some of the best maintained and equipped hire bikes in Jersey. Require staff who are keen and able to maintain their standards.
Requirements: *Cycle mechanic:* must have experience in bike building and repair. *Bike issuer:* should be clear-headed and enjoy cycling and helping people.
Application Procedure: Contact Paul Bell or Bob Vincent at the above address.

Head Office: Old German Tunnels, Railway Walk, Le Mont Les Vaux, St Brelade, Jersey JE3 8AF
☎ 01534 746780
jerseycycletours@yahoo.co.uk

John Brownlee

Job(s) Available: Fruit pickers (4–6).
Duration: Period of work is usually from the end of September to the end of October depending upon the crop.
Pay: Piecework rates.

> **Head Office:** Knockmakagan, Newtownbutler, County Fermanagh BT92 6JP
> ☎ 028 6773 8275 or 079894320131
> ✉ john518brownlee@btopcnworld.com

Company Description: 5 apple orchards situated half an hour from Enniskillen, on the border with the Republic of Ireland. Many tourist attractions in the area.
Job Description: Fruit pickers required for apple orchard work, either hand-picking or shaking.
Requirements: Applicants must be in good physical condition as work is heavy manual labour.
Accommodation: No accommodation, but workers can camp at farm.
Application Procedure: By post to Mr John Brownlee at the above address, or by phone on the above phone number, from July onwards. Overseas applicants, preferably from EU countries, welcome.

L Wheeler & Sons (East Peckham) Ltd

Job(s) Available: Apple and hop pickers (20).
Duration: Minimum period of work 5 weeks between 24 August and 30 September.
Working Hours: Required to work 8–9 hours per day for 5.5 days a week.

> **Head Office:** Bullen Farm, East Peckham, Tonbridge, Kent TN12 5LX
> ☎ 01622 871225
> ✉ lwheelerandsons@yahoo.co.uk

Pay: Approximately £5.93 per hour with the possibility of bonuses.
Company Description: A hop and fruit farm within an hour's journey to London. Local facilities such as shops and pubs are available.
Accommodation: Available with only a charge for electricity.
Application Procedure: By post or email from June to the manager at the above address. Overseas applicants authorised to work in the UK welcome.

Leapfrog International Ltd

Job(s) Available: Events crew (up to 100).
Duration: Period of work between May and September.
Pay: Set figure per event. Hours of work vary from day to day.

> **Head Office:** Riding Court Farm, Datchet, Berkshire SL3 9JU
> ☎ 01753 580 880
> ✉ enq@leapfrog-int.co.uk
> 🖥 www.leapfrog-int.co.uk

Job Description: Events crew needed to help set up and run outdoor activities such as team-building challenges, family fun days and 'It's a Knockout' tournaments. Events take place all around the UK. Travel to events is organised by Leapfrog International from their headquarters in Datchet.
Requirements: Applicants should be aged 18–40, enthusiastic and outgoing and should enjoy working with people. A clean driving licence is an advantage. Previous experience is not essential as training will be given.
Application Procedure: Please complete an online application form via the website or call the event management team on 01753 589305 for a form. Please mark enquiries FAO Andy Walton.

Man of Ross Ltd

Job(s) Available: Fruit harvesters (60).
Duration: Minimum period of work 3 months between June and October.
Working Hours: Hours vary according to crop needs, approximately 6–8 hours per day, 5–6 days a week.

Head Office: Glewstone, Ross-on-Wye, Herefordshire HR9 6AU
☎ 01989 562853
✆ office@manofross.co.uk

Pay: Hourly and/or piecework rates.
Company Description: Situated in the Wye Valley, Man of Ross is a family-run, 250-hectare farm, which supplies mainly to supermarkets.
Job Description: Fruit harvesters to work in cherry, plum, apple and pear orchards.
Requirements: Minimum age 18.
Application Procedure: By post from January to Roger Green at the above postal address or via email. Applicants from EU countries welcome.

Mobenn Hire Services

Job(s) Available: Marquee erectors for work all over the country.
Duration: Period of work by arrangement.
Pay: £50–£60 per day; same daily rate paid for long and short days. Students must complete P38; all others to produce CIS card and submit invoices for payment by Friday each week.

Head Office: Mobenn House, Naunton Parade, Cheltenham, Gloucestershire GL51 7NP
☎ 01242 584515
✆ enquiries@mobenn.co.uk
🖳 www.mobennmarquees.co.uk

Company Description: Company is for those who like outdoor work. Hard days, good days and a great team spirit are all part of the job.
Requirements: Applicants need a clean driving licence. The work is quite strenuous so it is necessary to be fit and active.
Accommodation: Not available.
Application Procedure: By post to Matt Dean, manager, at the above address.

Peter Marshall & Co

Job(s) Available: Farm assistants, fruit pickers (250), raspberry field supervisors.
Duration: Minimum period of work 1 month between June and August.
Working Hours: To work 7 hours per day.
Pay: *Fruit pickers:* £45, piecework rates. New pickers

Head Office: Muirton, Alyth, Blairgowrie, Perthshire PH11 8JF
☎ 01828 632227
✆ meg@petermarshallfarms.com or muirton@petermarshallfarms.co.uk

often earn below average in their first week, while more experienced pickers earn far more. *Farm assistants, raspberry field supervisors:* national minimum wage rates.
Company Description: Farm growing 200 acres of raspberries over extended season.
Job Description: Farm assistants, raspberry field supervisors to work on raspberry machines and tunnel building.
Requirements: Minimum age 18. Fluent English not essential. No experience necessary but it is an advantage.
Accommodation: Available at a very reasonable rate.
Application Procedure: By post or email to the above addresses. Foreign applicants welcome.

R & JM Place Ltd

Job(s) Available: Fruit picking.
Duration: From May to late September.
Company Description: Large soft-fruit growers in the centre of the Broadland National Park.
Job Description: Fruit picking, weather permitting. Details on application.

Head Office: Church Farm, Tunstead, Norwich NR12 8RQ
☎ 01692 536337
✆ info@ifctunstead.co.uk
💻 www.ifctunstead.co.uk

Requirements: Must be in good health. No previous experience necessary.
Accommodation: Available for £60.20 per week, including breakfast, in purpose-built dormitory blocks. Tents and caravans are not permitted.
Additional Information: Social activities in camp include tennis, volleyball, badminton, basketball, football, pool and many more.
Application Procedure: Application form available to download on website. By post, enclosing an s.a.e. to the administrator, or by email at the address above. Overseas applicants welcome.

Roustabout Ltd

Job(s) Available: Tent crew.
Duration: From May to September.
Job Description: Tent crew for setting up and dismantling tents at events all over the UK and expanding to mainland Europe. Long, unsocial hours and lots of travel to be expected.

Head Office: Frongoch Boatyard, Smugglers Cove, nr Aberdovey, Gwynedd LL35 0RG
☎ 01654 767177
✆ info@roustabout.ltd.uk

Requirements: Driving licence useful, but not essential. Applicants must be physically fit.
Accommodation: Stay in own tents at events.
Application Procedure: By post to Geoffrey Hill, managing director, at the above postal address or via email.

S&A Produce (UK) Ltd

Job(s) Available: Strawberry pickers (1,000).
Duration: Workers are required from 15 May.
Working Hours: Pickers are expected to work around 39 hours per week.
Pay: National minimum wage rates. Overtime paid in accordance to the Agricultural Wages Order.

Head Office: Brook Farm, Marden, Hereford, Herefordshire HR1 3ET
☎ 01432 880235
✆ saproduceukltd@sagroup.co.uk
💻 www.sagroup.co.uk

Company Description: S&A Produce is an independent strawberry grower supplying UK supermarkets. The company is managed and operated by a young dynamic team with a wealth of experience in growing and other related industries, who are able to cope with a fast moving and profitable business.
Requirements: No experience necessary, but applicants must be in good physical health. Fluent English is not essential as they have a number of interpreters on site.
Accommodation: Available.
Application Procedure: Applications received via the website. All applicants are registered on an internal system and receive a reply to their application within 1–3 working days. Overseas applicants are welcome.

Sentance Marquees

Job(s) Available: Marquee erectors (2–6).
Duration: Required between April and the end of September. Minimum period of work 2–3 months.
Working Hours: To work 5–6 days a week for 8–10 hours per day.
Pay: National minimum wage rates.
Company Description: A total event hire company.

> **Head Office:** Hilltop Farm, Caythorpe Heath, nr Grantham, Lincolnshire NG32 3EU
> ☎ 01400 275165
> ✆ info@sentancemarquees.co.uk
> 🖳 www.eventsandtents.co.uk

Requirements: Minimum age 18. Must be strong and fit with a driver's licence or reliable transport to premises. Spoken English is an advantage.
Application Procedure: By post to Andrew Beamish at the above address, phone or email at any time. Non-UK citizens will be considered.

Stuart Line Cruises

Job(s) Available: Boat crew (2).
Duration: Positions available for the summer.
Working Hours: Flexible.
Pay: £100–£150 per week.
Company Description: Passenger boat operator in Devon.

> **Head Office:** 5 Camperdown Terrace, Exmouth, Devon EX8 1EJ
> ☎ 01395 279693
> ✆ info@stuartlinecruises.co.uk
> 🖳 www.stuartlinecruises.co.uk

Requirements: Fluent English helpful. No experience necessary as full training is given. Minimum age 16.
Accommodation: Not available.
Application Procedure: By post to Ian Stuart at the above address. Interview required.

Vibert Marquees Ltd

Job(s) Available: Marquee erectors (10).
Duration: Period of work runs from April to September; minimum period of work from June to August.
Working Hours: Required to work from 8am to finish, varied hours including overtime and weekends, approximately 40 hours per week.
Pay: From £7 per hour.

> **Head Office:** The Shed, Beaupre Farm, Ruede Creux, Baillot JE3 2DR
> ☎ 01534 482970
> ✆ vibmarq@localdial.com
> 🖳 www.vibertmarquees.com

Company Description: Long-established, family-run business with 4 full-time and 20 seasonal workers.
Requirements: Minimum age 17. Applicants must be hard working.
Accommodation: Not provided, but there is a campsite within walking distance.
Additional Information: Working shirts are provided free; shorts are recommended.
Application Procedure: By post or email from January onwards to Nigel Vautier at the above address. Foreign applicants who speak good English are welcome.

Wallings Nursery Ltd

Job(s) Available: Strawberry pickers.
Duration: Positions available from April to October.
Company Description: 3 hectares of glasshouses and 2 hectares of polytunnels, growing tabletop strawberries off the ground.

> **Head Office:** 38 Harwich Road, Lawford, Manningtree, Essex CO11 2LS
> ☎ 01206 230163
> ✆ C.batchelor@wallingsnursery.com

Accommodation: Board and lodging available in communal converted barns.
Requirements: Fluent English is essential.
Application Procedure: By post from February/March onwards to Christopher Batchelor at the above address. EU and Commonwealth citizens with permission to work in the UK welcome.

Wilkin & Sons Ltd

Job(s) Available: Fruit pickers (20–30).
Duration: Required from 10 June to 15 July (approximately). Minimum period of work 5 weeks.
Working Hours: 8–10 hours per day, 7 days a week.
Pay: £2 per kilo of fruit picked.

> Head Office: Tiptree, Essex CO5 ORF
> ☎ 01621 815407
> ✆ tiptree@tiptree.com
> 🖥 www.tiptree.com

Company Description: Wilkin & Sons is a world-famous maker of the finest quality preserves at the Tiptree factory since 1885. The company own a freehold estate of about 1,000 acres and grows many choice varieties of fruit selected for their fine flavour.
Job Description: Strawberry picking.
Requirements: Minimum age 18. Fluent English not essential.
Accommodation: £30 per person per week to stay on site. Free pitch if they choose to camp.
Additional Information: Programmes offered in Bulgaria and Romania through SAWS programme.
Application Procedure: FAO Stephen Cook at above email or address. No interview necessary. Overseas students welcome to apply.

Sport

The range of jobs under this category includes, among others, **instructors**, **coaches**, **boat crew**, **stable staff**, and **walk leaders**.

Sports holiday centres often specialise in sea, river or mountain activities and as such are often found in remote and beautiful places such as Scotland and the Lake District. They almost always need to recruit live-in workers. While there are opportunities for unskilled staff, most vacancies are for sports instructors, teachers and camp managers. Applicants will normally require governing-body qualifications and a reasonable amount of experience; growing concern about insufficient supervision and instruction at activity centres in the past has resulted in new, tougher controls.

Teaching centres along the south and west coasts particularly are keen to recruit windsurfing, sailing and canoeing instructors in ever-increasing numbers. Several lake centres also advertise in this book. Anyone with life-saving qualifications could consider working as a lifeguard at a leisure centre.

Riding: Riding schools and trekking centres (which are particularly common in Wales) may take on experienced riders. Since a lot of the work is dealing with groups, the ability to get on well with people is also important. There might be a riding school or holiday centre in your area where you could ask about the possibility of a temporary job. The British Horse Society (0870 120 2244; www.bhs.org.uk) publishes a list of more than 900 approved establishments, available on the above website. The Association of British Riding Schools (01736 369440; www.abrs-info.org) provides a free directory of its members on their website. You should also contact them for information about trekking holidays and centres. Employment can also be found with racing stables, which sometimes require stable staff. If you are looking for employment as a sports coach, it is advisable to check the listings for children's camps as they often also require qualified instructors.

Alston Training & Adventure Centre

Job(s) Available: Assistant outdoor activity instructors and domestic staff.

Requirements: Should have current driving licence. MLC or canoe qualification useful. Training provided.

Application Procedure: For further details and applications contact Dave Simpson, head of centre, at the above address.

> **Head Office:** Alston, Cumbria CA9 3DD
> ☎ 01434 381886
> ✍ alstontraining@btconnect.com
> 🖥 www.alstontraining.co.uk

Cairnwell Mountain Sports

Job(s) Available: Activity instructors (2), lodge worker (1), ski instructors (2).

Duration: *Activity instructors:* required from April to end of August for a minimum of 4 weeks. *Lodge worker:* required from December to the end of May and July to the end of September. *Ski instructors:* required from January to March for 5–10 weeks.

> **Head Office:** Gulabin Lodge,
> Spittal of Glenshee, Blairgowrie,
> Perthshire PH10 7QE
> ☎ 01250 885255
> ✍ info@gulabinlodge.co.uk
> 🖥 www.gulabinlodge.co.uk

Working Hours: *Activity instructors:* to work 5 days a week. *Ski instructors:* to work 6 days a week.

Pay: *Activity instructors:* £250 per week. *Lodge worker:* £200 per week. *Ski instructors:* £300 per week.

Company Description: A multi-activity centre and hostel for 35 persons. Winter activities include ski school, snowboard school and Nordic skiing; summer activities include climbing, walking, archery, zip wire, gorge ascents and more.

Requirements: *Activity instructors and ski instructors:* must have a national qualification. *Lodge worker:* no experience necessary.

Accommodation: Available at a cost of £50 per week.

Application Procedure: By post to Darren Morgan at the above address throughout the year. Interview and references are necessary. Overseas applicants are welcome for the posts of lodge worker and ski instructor.

Caledonian Discovery Ltd

Job(s) Available: Mate/instructor, bosun, cook.

Duration: To work from March to the end of October. Staff must be available for the whole season to qualify for a bonus, with the exception of the assistant cook whose minimum period is 1 week.

> **Head Office:** The Slipway, Corpach,
> Fort William PH33 7NB
> ☎ 01397 772167
> ✍ info@fingal-cruising.co.uk
> 🖥 www.fingal-cruising.co.uk

Working Hours: All full-time staff to work 6.5 days a week and all crew live on board the barge.

Pay: *Mate/Instructor:* Up to £1,350 per calendar month. *Bosun:* Up to £950 per calendar month. *Cook:* Up to £ 1,350 per calendar month. No live-in deductions for any positions.

Company Description: Organises activity holidays based on a barge cruising the Caledonian Canal/Loch Ness. The 12 guests take part in various outdoor activities at numerous stops along the way. Activities include sailing, canoeing, windsurfing, walking, and biking, with other specialist weeks available. The work is hard, but varied and great fun.

Job Description: *Mate/Instructor:* responsible for teaching canoeing, sailing, guiding cycle tours and walks and barge duties. *Bosun:* boat maintenance, safety boat, barge duties. *Cook:* to prepare food for 18 people.

Requirements: *Mate/instructor:* Open Canoe qualification, Level 2 Coach qualification, Mountain Leader Qualification, First Aid certificate and outdoor experience an advantage. *Bosun:* training provided. Personal experience of outdoor sports an advantage. *Cook:* must have experience in good cooking.

Application Procedure: Send a covering letter along with CV to above email or address before the end of January.

Clyne Farm Activity Centre

Job(s) Available: Activity instructor, riding instructor.
Duration: Minimum period of 1 month between May and September.
Working Hours: 40 hours per week.
Pay: From £200 per week depending on qualifications and experience.

Head Office: Westport Avenue, Mayals, Swansea SA3 5AR
☎ 01792 403333
info@clynefarm.com
www.clynefarm.com

Company Description: Multi-activity centre in converted stone buildings with a wide range of client groups from school and youth groups to adults and families. Activities include everything from archery to windsurfing.

Accommodation: Not available.

Application Procedure: By post to Geoff Haden at the above address from January. Interview required. Foreign applicants with recognised qualifications and good English welcome.

Contessa Riding Centre

Job(s) Available: Stable helpers.
Duration: Minimum period of work 2.5 months.
Working Hours: To work 8am–5pm (beginning at 8.30am on 2 days), 5.5 days a week, throughout the year, especially around the holiday periods.

Head Office: Willow Tree Farm, Colliers End, Ware, Hertfordshire SG11 1EN
☎ 01920 821792
contessariding@aol.com
www.contessa-riding.com

Company Description: Riding school and competition yard with a particular interest in dressage. Set rurally 30 miles north of London with easy access to Cambridge and Stansted Airport.

Job Description: Stable helpers to perform general yard duties including mucking out, grooming, tack cleaning and horse handling. Horses range from novice to grand prix standard.

Requirements: Minimum age 17. Qualifications and experience preferred.

Accommodation: Self-catering accommodation available.

Additional Information: Riding is provided; brochures available.

Application Procedure: Applicants should ideally be available for an interview and must apply with CV and references. Applications are welcome year-round by post to Tina Layton BHSI at the above address.

HF Holidays Ltd

Job(s) Available: Walk leaders.

Duration: Applicants may choose where, how often and when they want to lead week-long walking holidays (2–30 weeks per year).

Company Description: A walking holiday company (founded in 1913) which is a non-profit-seeking organisation. Owns 17 country house hotels based in some of the most scenic parts of Britain.

Head Office: Leader Recruitment Manager, Redhills, Penrith, Cumbria CA11 0DT
☎ 01768 890091
walkleaders@hfholidays.co.uk
www.walkleaders.co.uk

Job Description: Walk leaders required to lead walks catering for all levels of walker. Travel expenses and training opportunities will be provided.

Requirements: Applicants should be UK residents, experienced walkers with leadership potential, fully competent in the use of map and compass, considerate and tactful.

Accommodation: Full board and lodging is provided.

Application Procedure: Via the website.

James Given Racing Ltd

Job(s) Available: Stable staff.

Duration: To work from March until November or by arrangement.

Pay: Dependent on experience.

Working Hours: To work 7.00am–1.30pm and 4.30pm–6pm, with overtime available.

Head Office: Mount House Stables, Long Lane, Willoughton, Gainsborough DN21 5SQ
☎ 01427 667618
www.jamesgivenracing.com

Job Description: Duties including riding out, mucking out and all yard duties.

Requirements: Applicants must have previous experience of riding racehorses.

Additional Information: Staff will be able to take horses racing.

Application Procedure: By post to Suzanne Maclennan, secretary, at the above address. An interview will be necessary.

Loch Insh Watersports & Skiing Centre

Job(s) Available: Watersports instructors, skiing instructors, restaurant staff.

Duration: Minimum period of work 4 months, with work available all year round.

Pay: Dependent on qualifications.

Company Description: Loch Insh Watersports and

Head Office: Insh Hall, Kincraig, Inverness-shire PH21 1NU
☎ 01540 651272
office@lochinsh.com
www.lochinsh.com

Skiing Centre is nestled in the foothills of the Cairngorm Mountains in the scenic Spey Valley. The centre also has a loch-side restaurant. Skiing from December to April.

Requirements: *Watersports instructors:* RYA and BCU qualified, or trainee instructor standard. *Skiing instructors:* BASI-qualified, or trainee instructor standard. *Restaurant staff:* non-smokers with experience are preferred.

Accommodation: Bed and breakfast en suite accommodation and self-catering log chalets on site. Board and lodging provided at a charge of £60 per week.

Additional Information: Free watersports and skiing for staff.

Application Procedure: By post to Mr Clive Freshwater, at the above address. Overseas applicants with good spoken English welcome.

Northfield Farm

Job(s) Available: Trek leaders (2).
Duration: Work available from April to September; minimum work period from June to August.
Working Hours: To work 8am–5pm, 5.5 days a week.
Pay: Dependent on age and qualifications.

Head Office: Flash, nr Buxton, Derbyshire SK17 0SW
☎ 01298 22543
🖉 info@northfieldfarm.co.uk
🖥 www.northfieldfarm.co.uk

Company Description: BHS-approved riding centre and working farm, situated in a small village. There is a post office and a pub under 100m away. 30 horses are used, including an Andalusian stallion at stud, a few breeding mares and young stock.

Requirements: Applicants should be enthusiastic, experienced riders used to hacking out. They should also have good people skills and preferably possess a driving licence. Riding and road safety test and first aid qualification(s) are also preferred. Applicants must be fluent in English.

Accommodation: Free accommodation provided (for females only).

Application Procedure: By post between March and June only (no applications before March) to Mrs E Andrews, Northfield Farm, at the above address. Interview required if possible.

Peak District Hang Gliding Centre

Job(s) Available: Hang gliding instructor (1–2), telesales assistant/secretary.
Duration: *Hang gliding instructor:* to work from July to September. *Telesales assistant/secretary:* period of work by arrangement.

Head Office: 8 Whitfield Street, Leek, North Staffordshire ST13 5PH
☎ 07000 426445
🖉 mike@peakhanggliding.co.uk
🖥 www.peakhanggliding.co.uk

Working Hours: *Hang gliding instructor:* hours by arrangement.
Pay: *Hang gliding instructor:* £80 per day. *Telesales assistant/secretary:* wages by arrangement.
Company Description: The longest established hang gliding school in the UK, based in the Peak District National Park.
Requirements: *Hang gliding instructor:* must be experienced. *Telesales assistant/secretary:* must have a good telephone manner.
Application Procedure: By post or email to Mike Orr.

Rookin House Equestrian & Activity Centre

Job(s) Available: Activity instructor, trek leaders (2).
Duration: Staff are required from June to September and must work July and August.
Working Hours: 40 hours per week.
Pay: From £220 per week.
Company Description: Situated on a hill farm,

Head Office: Troutbeck, Penrith, Cumbria CA11 0SS
☎ 01768 483561
🖉 deborah@rookinhouse.co.uk
🖥 www.rookinhouse.co.uk

Rookin House is a multi-activity centre offering quad biking, go-karting and archery as well as an equestrian centre with 38 horses offering trekking, hacking and lessons.

Job Description: For both positions, work will involve taking clients on activities and the maintenance of equipment and surroundings. There is also a self-catering unit which will require cleaning.

Requirements: *Activity instructor:* minimum age 18. Will preferably hold GNAS for Archery Leader Award, first aid certificate and ATV qualification. In-house training can be provided if applicant does not hold the above. *Trek leaders:* minimum age 18. Must hold riding and road safety qualifications and be able to ride well.

Accommodation: Available at a charge of £30 per week.
Application Procedure: By post to Deborah Hogg at the above address from March. Overseas applicants are welcome but must have a work permit and speak good English.

Snowdonia Riding Stables

Job(s) Available: Trek leaders (2).
Duration: Staff required during the summer months.
Working Hours: Approximately 40 hours per week.
Pay: To be arranged.
Company Description: A trekking centre/riding school with 25 horses.

Head Office: Waunfawr, Caernarfon, Gwynedd LL55 4PQ
☎ 01286 650342
📧 snowdonia.riding@btconnect.com
💻 www.snowdonia2000.fsnet.co.uk

Job Description: Work includes care of horses, yard work, trek leading and light maintenance work.
Accommodation: Available in self-catering caravans free of charge.
Requirements: Minimum age 18. Applicants must have good riding ability.
Application Procedure: By post to Mrs R Thomas or via email at the above addresses from spring onwards. Overseas applicants are welcome.

South Wales Carriage Driving Centre

Job(s) Available: Carriage driving horse assistants (maximum 2 at any one time), volunteer stable staff.
Working Hours: Hours to suit individual.
Company Description: Small company teaching people how to drive a horse and carriage for commercial work and just for fun.

Head Office: Llwyn Mawr Farm, Gowerton, Swansea SA4 3RB
☎ 01792 874299
📧 rowena@rowena-moyse.com
💻 www.rowena-moyse.com

Requirements: Minimum age 16. Fluent English is essential.
Accommodation: Could be provided.
Application Procedure: By post to Rowena Moyse at the above address at anytime.

Vacation traineeships and internships

Listed below are placements and schemes that aim to provide young people with an opportunity to gain on-the-job training during their holidays. They are variously referred to by firms as 'work placements', 'internships', 'vacation schemes' and 'training schemes', as well as a myriad of other names. They are generally short-term placements for students lasting from two weeks to the whole summer holiday.

Traineeships and internships may not appeal to those wanting a summer job just to have fun or to earn enough money for a holiday or to repay an overdraft. Some employers offer fantastic remuneration, with some City internships paying up to £650 a week. Others see the reward as the experience itself and just pay expenses. In the long run though, a work placement can prove to have been the most valuable investment of your vacations.

The content and style of traineeships and internships varies from one firm to another. Some, especially large banks, accountants and consultancies, will put you into a position of real responsibility so you can learn the ropes of the business from its centre. Others operate more of a 'work-shadow' scheme where you are expected to follow and observe a member of staff, and perhaps help them with their work.

Advertised traineeships and internships tend to be most numerous in areas of science, technology and engineering, since these industries have seen a serious decrease in numbers of students coming into them. In other areas, like finance and law, competition is likely to be strong. Traineeships and internships in oversubscribed areas tend to be the unpaid ones; media and marketing among others.

The advantages of vacation training and internships: Many schemes pay impressive salaries, but the value of the experience gained far outweighs that of the salary. Traineeships/internships can give you a valuable insight into potential careers. It is an incredible advantage, when looking for permanent jobs, to have had a taste of various industries without having had to make a commitment to any, and perhaps more importantly to have it listed on your CV. Employers are far more likely to value a candidate who spent a summer gaining experience and skills, and probably cultivating a more mature approach to work, than one who worked sporadically at a local pub.

In addition, when it comes round to interview time for permanent jobs, you will have already been able to practice and will be better prepared as a result. Having done a traineeship/internship will also provide a good source of interview conversation. Employers frequently say that they are looking for work experience, practical business skills, personality and initiative, and if you are able to demonstrate these on your CV, a minimum degree requirement for the job may be waived.

Many companies also treat their schemes as extended assessment periods: while you are getting an insight into them, they can assess your suitability for a permanent position. Some interns leave with a permanent job offer in the bag and even sponsorship for their final year. Even if the company does not make you a job offer, a good reference from them can help you find work elsewhere. Experience in sectors where placements are rare, like media or the arts, can enable you to build up a bank of contacts that would help enormously in future job-hunts. Further guidance and advice on work placements and internships can be obtained from the National Council for Work Experience (www.work-experience.org).

Accountancy, banking and insurance
Financial Services Authority _____

Job(s) Available: Internships (40–60) and work placements (5).
Duration: The internships last for 10 weeks throughout the year. Placements are for 12 months.
Pay: Approximately £450 per week.
Company Description: The FSA ensures integrity in the UK financial markets and protects consumer interests.

Head Office: 25, The North Colonnade, Canary Wharf, London E14 5HS
☎ 020 7066 3568
fsa.graduates@fsa.gov.uk
www.fsagraduates.com

Job Description: The FSA summer internship is available to students in any year of study at university. Interns spend their time getting to know how the FSA upholds the highest standards and how that impacts on the world of business. Through project-based work in 1 department, interns will have the chance to gain a unique insight into the UK financial system.

Requirements: Applicants should be on track for a 2:1 degree but students not meeting this criteria will be considered. International students welcome.

Application Procedure: Applications should be made online via the FSA website. An interview and assessment centre test will be required.

PricewaterhouseCoopers LLP (PwC)

Job(s) Available: Summer internship programme (The INS1GHT Internship Programme). Approximately 150 positions throughout the country.

Duration: 6-10 weeks from the first week of July.

Pay: Competitive rates of pay.

> Head Office: Offices nationwide
> ☎ 0808 100 1500
> 🖳 www.pwc.com/uk/careers

Company Description: As one of the largest professional services firms in the world, PricewaterhouseCoopers LLP (PwC) provides industry-focused assurance, tax, advisory, actuarial and consulting services to a significant range of clients.

Job Description: The INS1GHT Internship Programmes are open to penultimate-year students, and run for 6-10 weeks during the summer and throughout the UK. After a 1-week induction, you'll join your chosen business area, work alongside specialists, and do the same kind of work and make the same kind of contribution as our graduate recruits. The INS1GHT International Internship also helps penultimate-year undergraduates develop the skills the company needs in their future talent.

Requirements: PwC are looking for outstanding penultimate year undergraduates of any degree discipline. As competition for places is fierce you will need a strong academic record, expecting at least a 2:1, with a minimum of 300 UCAS points or equivalent, and should be able to demonstrate excellent communication and interpersonal skills.

Application Procedure: Apply online at pwc.com/careers before 31 March 2011. Early applicants stand a better chance of gaining a position in their area of preference.

Charity Work

Barnardo's

Job(s) Available: Volunteer internships are available around the UK.

Duration: 12 weeks from June to September. The scheme also runs in autumn and spring. There is some flexibility regarding the duration of internships.

> Head Office: Tanners Lane, Barkingside, Ilford, Essex IG6 1QG
> ☎ 020 8550 8822
> 🖂 info@barnardos.org.uk
> 🖳 www.barnardos.org.uk

Working Hours: Full-time and part-time internships are available.

Pay: Internships are unpaid, but full travel expenses and lunch expenses of up to £4 each day are reimbursed.

Company Description: One of the UK's leading charities dedicated to helping children and young people in crisis.

Job Description: Opportunities are available in fundraising, marketing, communications, retail as well as the corporate audit and inspection unit and the children's services finance and information operations. Each internship has its own role description. Interns will work on real projects that make a significant contribution to the charity. Training will be provided for each role, as well as a session covering interview and CV techniques. Visits will be organised to different schemes run by Barnardo's and interns can volunteer at events like project launches. These internships are aimed at school leavers, university students, graduates and those changing their career path.

Requirements: Minimum age 18. Candidates must be educated to at least A level standard or equivalent, have good ICT skills and be committed to Barnardo's goals. Any previous charity or office work would be a bonus.

Accommodation: Not available.

Additional Information: If you have any queries, telephone Kelly Butler on 020 8498 7314 or send an email to internships@barnardos.org.uk.

Application Procedure: Search online for vacancies in your area. Download an application form from the above website and email it to internships@barnardos.org.uk. Interviews are necessary. Certain internships also require a CRB check.

British Red Cross

Job(s) Available: Up to 40 summer internships at central London office and around the UK and up to 150 internships the rest of the year.

Duration: 8–12 weeks from July to September and throughout the year.

Working Hours: Interns typically work for 2–3 days a week.

Head Office: 44 Moorfields,
London EC2Y 9AL
☎ 020 7877 7552
📧 kappleby@redcross.org.uk
🖥 www.redcross.org.uk

Pay: The internships are unpaid but reasonable travel expenses are reimbursed and lunch is provided.

Company Description: The British Red Cross helps people in crisis, whoever and wherever they are. They are part of a global network of volunteers, responding to natural disasters, conflicts and individual emergencies.

Job Description: Each internship has its own role description. All interns should be enthusiastic, committed and interested in pursuing a career in the voluntary sector. The internships are aimed at university students, school leavers, people in further education, those changing career path or anyone interested in the charity sector.

Application Procedure: Applications should be made via the above website. Interview necessary. Overseas applicants are welcome to apply, provided they have the relevant documentation and funding.

Cancer Research UK

Job(s) Available: Internship programme.

Duration: Period of 12 weeks from July to September.

Working Hours: Applicants are required to work normal office hours.

Head Office: 61 Lincolns' Inn Fields,
London WC2A 3PX
☎ 0845 009 4290
📧 internships@cancer.org.uk
🖥 www.cancerresearchuk.org.uk
/internships

Pay: Internships are unpaid, but travel and lunch expenses are provided.

Company Description: Cancer Research UK is a world-renowned charity dedicated to beating cancer through research. Their research work has saved millions of lives.

Job Description: Cancer Research UK is seeking high-calibre individuals looking to gain work experience in the fields of fundraising, marketing, retail, communications and campaigning for their internship programme. Interns work on real projects that will make a difference to the charity. They are also provided with a thorough induction to the charity, as well as given mid-internship training on CV writing and interview techniques. Applicants are usually undergraduates, graduates or professionals looking for a career change.

Accommodation: Not available.

Application Procedure: For more information and to download an application form visit the website from May. Selection process includes a written application form and an interview. Overseas applicants are welcome to apply provided they have the correct documentation to work in the UK and speak English to a very high standard.

Fashion

Bordelle

Job(s) Available: Studio internships.
Duration: Minimum period 4 weeks.
Working Hours: 37 hours per week, 5 days per week.
Pay: Travel expenses only up to £8 per day.
Company Description: Bordelle is a high-end

> **Head Office:** Atelier Bordelle Ltd, Unit 16, 2-4 Exmoor Street, London W10 6BD
> ☎ 0208 968 4488
> Camilla@bordelle.co.uk
> www.bordelle.co.uk

lingerie label offering high fashion, future-minded pieces that can be worn as under- or outerwear. Their collections have received a vast press interest and are stocked in Selfridges, Liberty and Coco de Mer.
Job Description: Assist production team with cutting and sewing.
Requirements: No formal requirements but an interest in womenswear, contour and fashion is necessary.
Application Procedure: Email Camilla at the above address. For general enquiries email info@bordelle.co.uk.

Law

Ashurst

Job(s) Available: 55–60 placements in the summer and 25–30 at Easter.
Pay: £275 per week.
Company Description: International city law firm with 223 partners, around 780 solicitors and a total staff of 1,900. Main areas of practice are in:

> **Head Office:** Broadwalk House, 5 Appold Street, London EC2A 2HA
> ☎ 020 7638 1111
> gradrec@ashurst.com
> www.ashurst.com

corporate; employment; incentives and pensions; energy, transport and infrastructure; EU and competition; international finance; litigation; real estate; tax; and technology and commercial.
Job Description: During the schemes, students sit with a solicitor in his or her office. The main aim is that students become involved in the solicitor's daily workload by completing 'real' tasks such as letter writing, drafting, legal research and attending client meetings. In addition, a series of lectures, workshops and social activities are arranged and visiting students are regularly encouraged to participate.
Requirements: Penultimate year law degree students and final year non-law degree students are eligible.
Accommodation: Not provided but help in finding accommodation can be given.
Application Procedure: Applications should be made online to Stephen Trowbridge, graduate recruitment and development manager, by 31 January 2011. Foreign applicants who speak fluent English are welcome.

Burges Salmon Solicitors

Job(s) Available: 40 summer placements for 2011 and 25 training contracts for September 2013.
Duration: 2 weeks.
Pay: Remuneration £250 per week.

Head Office: One Glass Wharf, Bristol BS2 0ZX
☎ 0117 939 2000
✎ nataliebyarc@burges-salmon.com
🖥 www.burges-salmon.com

Company Description: Based in Bristol, Burges Salmon is one of the UK's leading commercial law firms, offering an exceptional quality of life combined with a concentration of legal talent unsurpassed by any other firm in the country. Burges Salmon provides national and international clients such as Orange, Virgin and Thomson Reuters with a full commercial service through 5 main departments: corporate and financial institutions (CFI); commercial; property; private client and wealth structuring; and disputes, environment and planning. Specialist areas include: banking; competition; corporate finance; employment; IP and IT; and transport. The firm is ranked top tier by Chambers and Partners for 15 of its practice areas.

Application Procedure: Applications can be made online via website. Queries to Natalie, recruitment officer, at the above address. Closing date for applications 31 January 2011.

Charles Russell LLP

Jobs Available: 24 Summer placements in 2011.
Duration: 1 week during June or July.
Working Hours: 35 hours per week.
Pay: £210 per week.

Head Office: 5 Fleet Place, London EC44 7RD
☎ 0207 203 5353
✎ graduate.recruitment@charlesrussell.co.uk
🖥 www.charlesrussell.co.uk

Company Description: Charles Russell is a top 50 full service law firm. Clients range from international FTSE and AIM businesses to private companies, governments and private individuals.

Job Description: Attendees on our Summer Placement Programme will gain a good insight into what life is like at Charles Russell. By spending one week in a particular service area the individual can expect to get involved in 'real' client work, attend meetings/court and be part of the team. Attendees will also be able to gain an insight into other areas of law on offer at Charles Russell and meet a variety of people from across the Practice and be able to piece together a full picture. During the week attendees will also participate in assessment centre exercises which could lead to an offer of a training contract without the need to attend the full assessment centre day. A mentor is allocated to each attendee to answer any questions, to ensure the attendee has a full and varied week and to generally provide support and guidance.

Requirements: Candidates with good GCSE and A-Level results (or equivalent); have achieved, or are expected to achieve a 2:1 degree. Training to commence in 2012 or 2013.

Application Procedure: Applications to be completed via the website, the application process lasts from 1 December to 31 January.

Clifford Chance

Job(s) Available: Vacation placements and workshops.
Duration: During the winter, spring and summer breaks.

Head Office: 10 Upper Bank Street, Canary Wharf, London E14 5JJ
☎ 020 7006 3003
✎ Recruitment.London@CliffordChance.com
🖥 www.cliffordchance.com/gradsuk

Company Description: Clifford Chance's goal is to be at the forefront of the elite group of international law firms that is emerging. The practice is broad and far reaching, engaging with the issues and decisions that underpin our clients' success. Clifford Chance advises its clients internationally and domestically; under common law and civil law systems; in local and cross-border transactions and disputes; on day-to-day operations and on 'game-changing' transformational deals and issues. Setting the pace in the legal sector, Clifford Chance has more tier-one international practices than any other law firm. The business is organised into six global practices – Corporate, Capital Markets, Banking and Finance, Real Estate, Litigation and Dispute resolution, and Tax, Pensions and Employment. As a Clifford Chance trainee you will work in at least three of these practices, learning from professionals at the leading edge of our profession.

Job Description: The Clifford Chance training programme will give you the skills and experience to begin contributing to your team immediately and to lay the foundations for a long-term, rewarding legal career. You will gain experience of working in at least three different practice areas, including the required level of exposure to contentious work. You will also enjoy the prospect of secondments to our overseas offices and major client organisations. Clifford Chance offer work experience programmes to give you an insight into the type of work and culture Clifford Chance are involved in and to help you make an informed decision about a possible career with Clifford Chance. The summer vacation scheme is a structured four-week programme featuring workshops, seminars and the opportunity to work alongside a trainee lawyer or associate to gain first-hand experience of the work they do. The winter and spring workshops provide a shorter, condensed version of the summer vacation scheme, offering many of the same features during your winter or spring breaks.

Requirements: Clifford Chance is a firm of lawyers drawn from a wide range of backgrounds – there is no one 'type' here. A lot is asked of trainees – focus and dedication are taken as read, but you'll also need to be flexible and willing to adapt to new challenges and a lot of responsibility. Counterbalancing this is a level of investment in your career development which is only offered by a handful of professional services firms.

Application Procedure: For more information about working with Clifford Chance visit www.cliffordchance.com/gradsuk.

CMS Cameron McKenna

Job(s) Available: Training contracts, Easter and summer schemes.

Duration: Training contracts will have 4 6-month seats, gaining experience in various practice areas.

Company Description: CMS is the leading organisation of European law firms which includes CMS Cameron McKenna, a firm famed for being client-focused with excellent training and overseas opportunities.

Head Office: Mitre House, 160 Aldersgate Street, London EC1A 4DD
☎ 0845 300 0491
gradrec@cms-cmck.com
www.cmstalklaw.com

Job Description: Trainee solicitors are being recruited for their London, Bristol and Scottish offices.

Requirements: Students who apply must have a minimum of 320 UCAS points (or equivalent) and have achieved (or be on line for) a 2:1 at degree level.

Application Procedure: All applicants must apply online at the above address. The closing date for the spring and summer schemes is 31 January 2011. All training contract applications must be received by 31 July 2011.

Mills & Reeve LLP

Job(s) Available: Formal placement scheme (25–30 placements).
Duration: Throughout June or July for 2 weeks.
Pay: £250.
Company Description: Mills & Reeve is a leading law firm based in Norwich, Cambridge and Birmingham who offer a full range of corporate, commercial, property, litigation, and private client services to a mix of regional businesses and national household names.

Head Office: 112 Hills Road, Cambridge CB2 1PH
☎ 01223 222336
graduate.recruitment@mills-reeve.com
www.mills-reeve.com

Job Description: Mills & Reeve offer a formal placement scheme at each of their offices. Students gain experience in 4 main departments, attend seminars and take part in extra curricular events.
Requirements: Preference is given to penultimate-year law students, final-year non-law students and all those who have already graduated and are interested in a legal career.
Application Procedure: Applications should be made online via the firm's website and should be submitted before 31 January 2011.

Nabarro

Job(s) Available: Summer 2011 vacation placements: London (50 places), Sheffield (8 places).
Duration: Period of 3 weeks.
Company Description: Nabarro is one of the country's leading commercial law firms, offering a broad range of legal services to major national and international clients across a range of practice areas. Offices are in London, Sheffield and Brussels.

Head Office: Lacon House, 84 Theobalds Road, London WC1X 8RW
☎ 020 7524 6000
graduateinfo@nabarro.com
www.nabarro.com/graduates

Requirements: Applicants must be in at least their penultimate year of a law degree or final year of a non-law degree (Mature Graduates, Graduate Diploma in Law and Legal Practice Course students are also welcome to apply).
Application Procedure: Apply online at www.nabarro.com/graduates. Students should submit an application form between 1 November 2010 and 31 January 2011.

Pannone LLP Solicitors

Job(s) Available: 120 vacation placements in Manchester.
Duration: Placements last for 1 week, at Easter and over the summer vacation.
Company Description: A high-profile full service firm.

Head Office: 123 Deansgate, Manchester M3 2BU
☎ 0161 909 3000
graduaterecruitment@pannone.co.uk
www.pannone.com

Job Description: Students are given a real experience of the kind of work that trainee solicitors do – drafting correspondence or documents, researching, and spending time with trainees, fee-earners and partners. In 2011 placements are aimed at those seeking a training contract in 2013, mainly second-year law and third-year non-law undergraduates. Non-UK applicants will be considered as long as they are planning a career as a solicitor in Manchester.
Accommodation: Not available.

Application Procedure: Applications online on above website. For enquiries email graduate recruitment (main contact: Amy Bell, training manager) at the above address. Closing dates vary for placements. Full graduate recruitment information is available at the above website.

Pinsent Masons LLP

Job(s) Available: 100 summer vacation placements.
Duration: 2 week summer placement between mid-June and the end of July.
Company Description: Pinsent Masons is a top 15 UK law firm and top 100 law firm internationally, that is committed to sector focused growth through its core sector approach.

> **Head Office:** City Point, 1 Ropemaker Street, London EC2Y 9AH
> ☎ 020 7418 7000
> ✆ graduate@pinsentmasons.com
> 🖳 www.pinsentmasons.com/graduate

Job Description: The firm offers depth, scope and opportunity for its trainees in a culture of early responsibility and high quality work. As a member of a creative, resourceful and supportive team, trainees can expect a constant flow of stimulating assignments – developing legal expertise, market knowledge and commercial vision to deliver commercial legal solutions.
Requirements: Applications from all degree backgrounds are welcome. In addition to a strong academic background, the firm is looking for people who can combine a sharp mind with commercial acumen and strong people skills to work in partnership with their clients' businesses. The minimum academic requirements are 300 UCAS points and 2:1 in any discipline.
Additional Information: Pinsent Masons is also offering 65 training contracts to commence in 2012 and 2013. Please see the website for more details.
Application Procedure: Applications should be made online via the graduate website www.pinsentmasons.com/graduate.

Pritchard Englefield

Job(s) Available: Student placements (20).
Duration: 2 weeks between the end of June and the end of August.
Company Description: Pritchard Englefield is a full-service City law firm, with international capabilities and credentials.

> **Head Office:** 14 New Street, London EC2M 4HE
> ☎ 020 7972 9720
> ✆ isilverblatt@pe-legal.com
> 🖳 www.pe-legal.com

Job Description: Student placements are based in the London office and involve assisting legal advisers in a variety of tasks.
Requirements: Applicants should be undergraduates who have completed at least 1 year of an English law degree course, English law graduates, or non-law graduates who have completed at least the Graduate Diploma in Law (or similar), as well as being fluent in German and/or French.
Additional Information: Travel expenses will be paid.
Application Procedure: Apply to Mr Ian Silverblatt between 1 January and 31 March 2011.

Reed Smith

Job(s) Available: 20 vacation placements.
Duration: 2 weeks each.
Pay: £250 per week.
Company Description: Reed Smith is an international law firm with its largest office in the City of London and 22 other offices worldwide.

> **Head Office:** The Broadgate Tower, 20 Primrose Street, London EC2A 2RS
> ☎ 020 3116 3000
> ✆ graduate.recruitment@reedsmith.com
> 🖳 www.reedsmith.com

Job Description: Reed Smith offer students the chance to sample the working environment, students partake in skills training, social events, presentations and 2 mini-seats. The schemes are aimed at 2nd year law students and 3rd year non-law students.

Application Procedure: Applications open in November and should be submitted online via the website by 31 January 2011.

Simmons & Simmons

Job(s) Available: Summer vacation schemes.
Duration: 3 weeks from mid-June or mid-July.
Pay: £250 per week.
Company Description: Simmons & Simmons lawyers provide high-quality advice and a positive working atmosphere in their 20 international

Head Office: CityPoint, One Ropemaker Street, London EC2Y 9SS
☎ 020 7628 2020
✆ recruitment@simmons-simmons.com
💻 www.simmons-simmons.com/traineelawyers.

offices. The firm offers their clients a full range of legal services across numerous industry sectors. They have a particular focus on the world's fastest growing sectors that include: financial institutions; energy and infrastructure; and technology. They provide a wide choice of service areas in which their lawyers can specialise. These include corporate and commercial; information, communications and technology; commercial litigation; financial litigation; employment and benefits; EU, competition and regulatory; financial markets; IP; projects; real estate; taxation and pensions.

Job Description: Simmons & Simmons' summer vacation scheme is one of their primary means of selecting candidates for a career at the firm. Candidates spend time in 2 practice areas and work alongside a partner or associate who will provide mentorship. Candidates are also involved in researching, drafting, minute taking and working directly with clients. You will also be assigned a project which will be presented to the firm at the end of your stay.

Application Procedure: Applications should be marked for the attention of Anna King, graduate recruitment officer, from 1 November 2010.

Stephenson Harwood

Job(s) Available: 40 vacation placements.
Duration: 1-2 weeks.
Pay: £260 per week.
Company Description: Stephenson Harwood is an international City law firm with 5 overseas offices across Europe and Asia. A medium-sized law firm

Head Office: 1, St Paul's Churchyard, London EC4M 8SH
☎ 0207 809 2812
✆ graduate.recruitment@shlegal.com
💻 www.shlegal.com/graduate

based in a spectacular location opposite St Paul's Cathedral, with a friendly culture and international practice. Their main areas of work are: corporate; employment and pensions; finance group, dry and wet shipping litigation; commercial litigation and real estate.

Job Description: Stephenson Harwood offer students the opportunity to spend 1-2 weeks work-shadowing solicitors. Students spend 1 week each in 2 different departments.

Requirements: Applicants must be second year law undergraduates or third year non-law undergraduates. They also offer placements to graduates and mature students.

Accommodation: Not available.

Application Procedure: Applications by online application form only at www.Apply4Law.com/SH/. Use the same application form as training contracts. If you are offered a vacation placement you will automatically be considered for a training contract with the firm.

Trowers and Hamlins

Job(s) Available: 30 vacation placements.
Duration: 2 weeks.
Pay: £225 per week in London or £180 per week in Manchester.
Company Description: Trowers and Hamlins offers vacation placements for candidates seeking to start training in September 2012.

Head Office: Sceptre Court, 40 Tower Hill, London EC3N 4DX
☎ 020 7423 8000
✆ hking@trowers.com
🖥 www.trowers.com

Job Description: Candidates assist solicitors and trainee solicitors for a period of 2 weeks, during which time they spend a week in 2 different departments. The focus is real work, attending court and client meetings. Placements will take place in the firm's head offices in London, Manchester and Exeter.
Requirements: Successful applicants should have a minimum of 320 UCAS points and a 2:1 or above at degree level (predicted or obtained).
Accommodation: Cannot be provided.
Application Procedure: Apply online at the above address by 1 March 2011.

White & Case LLP

Job(s) Available: Vacation placement programme for 1 week at Easter and 2 weeks during the summer. 48 placements available in total.
Pay: £350 per week.
Company Description: White & Case is a leading global law firm with more than 2,000 lawyers in 35

Head Office: 5 Old Broad Street, London EC2N 1DW
☎ 020 7532 1000
✆ trainee@whitecase.com
🖥 www.whitecase.com/trainee

offices in 23 countries. The firm works with international businesses, financial institutions and governments worldwide on corporate and financial transactions and dispute resolution proceedings. Clients range from some of the world's longest established and most respected names to many start-up visionaries.
Job Description: The programmes provide an opportunity to discover what working in a global law firm is really like. Students will work with lawyers on a daily basis and attend organised presentations, training events and social activities.
Application Procedure: To apply for a placement in 2011, complete the online application form available on the website and submit it by 31 January 2011.

Media

Birds Eye View Film Festival

Job(s) Available: A number of internships.
Duration: Staff required all year round.
Working Hours: Hours are flexible, but interns must commit to a minimum of 2 days a week over 2 months.
Pay: All internships are voluntary.

Head Office: Unit 306 Aberdeen Centre, 22-24 Highbury Grove, London N5 2EA
☎ 020 7704 9435
✆ info@birds-eye-view.co.uk
🖥 www.birds-eye-view.co.uk

Company Description: Birds Eye View presents the new generation of talented women filmmakers from across the globe. Through London-based festivals and UK touring programmes, they entertain audiences with innovative films, including short features and documentaries.

Job Description: A number of internships are available across the office, including project assistant, office management, research assistant and marketing assistant positions.
Requirements: Minimum age 18. Office experience is preferred.
Accommodation: Not available.
Additional Information: Travel expenses are paid.
Application Procedure: By email to the Managing Director and via the above address. Overseas applicants are welcome, but must speak good English.

Meridian Records

Job(s) Available: 1 candidate at a time.
Duration: The placements run for a varying number of weeks during any of the 3 main vacations.
Pay: Unpaid.
Company Description: Meridian Records is a small record company specialising in the recording and production of classical records.

Head Office: PO Box 317, Eltham, London SE9 4SF
☎ 020 8857 3213
✆ mail@meridian-records.co.uk
✉ www.meridian-records.co.uk

Job Description: In 2011 the company will be seeking candidates who can demonstrate motivation and a keen interest in music. The successful candidate(s) will participate in a wide variety of tasks including the preparation of artwork, accounting, recording, editing and the maintenance of machines, buildings and grounds.
Requirements: No particular qualifications are required, although applicants should have a general interest in all aspects of running a record company. An ability to read music is useful but not essential. It is the policy of Meridian Records to employ only non-smokers.
Application Procedure: By post to Mr Richard Hughes, director, at the above address. Overseas applicants will be considered.

Now Magazine

Job(s) Available: Unpaid work experience placements in editorial, fashion, *Now Online* or sub-editing/art.
Duration: 4 weeks.
Working Hours: 10am–6pm, Monday to Friday, for placements in editorial, fashion or sub-editing/art.

Head Office: 5th Floor, Blue Fin Building, 110 Southwark Street, London SE1 0SU
☎ 020 3148 5000
✉ www.nowmagazine.co.uk

9am–5pm or 8am/8.30am–4pm/4.30pm, Monday to Friday, for placements at Now Online.
Company Description: *Now Magazine* is one of the UK's best-loved celebrity magazines. Now is part of the major media corporation IPC Media.
Job Description: Tasks involve the day-to-day running of *Now Magazine* or Nowmagazine.co.uk, shadowing to learn new skills. Duties will include administrative tasks, research and sub-editing. Candidates who prove they are conscientious, thorough and efficient, may also be given the chance to both interview and write.
Requirements: Minimum age 21 for *Now Magazine* and 20 for Now Online. A sound understanding of grammar, punctuation and spelling is essential. Must be a hard worker, punctual and reliable. For *Now Magazine* previous editorial experience, at a local newspaper for example, is preferable. For Now Online, you must have good ICT skills. Familiarity with Apple Macs is helpful and a basic understanding of Photoshop is a plus.
Accommodation: Not provided.

Application Procedure: For placements in editorial, fashion or sub-editing/art, applications must be sent only by post to WORK EXPERIENCE, Now Magazine at the above address. Send a covering letter and CV at least 4 months before your preferred start date. For Now Online, email nowfriends@ipcmedia.com. Indicate availability dates first, then website work experience in the subject field. For immediate availability, say NOW until when - and also how much notice will be needed. Include a concise personal statement about yourself, your experience and your aspirations as part of the email body text (no more than 250 words in total.) Include details of any other work experience, past or future, with IPC Media. Include a mobile phone number. You may be contacted at short notice if NOW has a cancellation. CVs can be submitted, but don't add large attachments. Applicants who follow these instructions with the most care will be given priority. Applicants under consideration will be given a quick task to complete. You will only be contacted if your application is successful.

Public sector
Government Economic Service

Job(s) Available: 50 economist summer vacation placements.
Duration: Placements last for 6–12 weeks between July and September.
Working Hours: 36-hour week.
Pay: £17,000–£22,000 pro rata.

> **Head Office:** HM Treasury, 1 Horse Guards Road, London SW1A 2HQ
> ☎ 020 7270 4577
> ✆ ges.int@hmtreasury.gsi.gov.uk
> 🖳 www.civilservice.gov.uk/ges

Company Description: The Government Economic Service is the UK's largest recruiter of economists with over 1,500 professionals in more than 30 departments. The GES gives you access to a wide range of economist career options.
Job Description: Interns are expected to provide support to professional economists dealing with a range of issues affecting government policy. Placements are usually available in a number of government departments.
Requirements: Applicants must be studying for a degree in economics, or, if it is a joint degree, economics must comprise at least 50% of the total course (including macro and micro economics). They should also be either UK nationals, Commonwealth citizens, Swiss nationals or members of the European Economic Area.
Application Procedure: Applications available for 2011 from the GES website from early December 2010 and should be sent to ges.int@hmtreasury.gsi.gov.uk.

Science, construction and engineering
AECOM

Job(s) Available: Summer vacation placements/ sponsorships/industrial placements.
Pay: Competitive.
Company Description: A global provider of professional design, technical and management support to a broad range of markets including transportation,

> **Head Office:** AECOM House, 63-77 Victoria Street, St Albans AL1 3EK
> ☎ 01727 535000
> ✆ applications.europe@aecom.com
> 🖳 www.aecom.com

buildings engineering, environmental, water, energy, design and planning and programme management. Operating in over 100 countries with 45,000 employees.
Job Description: Open to students looking to pursue a career within the industry.
Application Procedure: Applications online at http://graduates.aecom.com.

Gifford

Job(s) Available: Summer placements.
Duration: A summer placement which usually lasts between 8–10 weeks.
Pay: Competitive.
Company Description: Gifford is an award-winning consultancy, offering a comprehensive service in engineering and design. Prime disciplines cover civil, structural and building services engineering, together with complementary support from geotechnical, environmental, survey, transportation and archaeological departments. With more than 50 years in the industry, 670 staff worldwide and 8 UK offices, Gifford values creativity, clarity and the ability to appreciate the problem from the client's perspective, and pride themselves on their reputation for providing technically innovative engineering solutions.

Head Office: Carlton House, Ringwood Road, Woodlands, Southampton SO40 7HT
☎ 023 8081 7500
✆ recruitment@gifford.uk.com
🖳 www.gifford.uk.com

Job Description: Summer placements for students to work at offices located in Southampton, Chester, Leeds, London, Oxford, Manchester, and Birmingham. Student engineers and Environmental Scientists will support you to become a fully integrated member of the team and hopefully develop a working relationship that will continue throughout your degree.
Requirements: Gifford welcomes applications from students studying any of the above disciplines.
Application Procedure: Apply online via the graduate website from January 2010.

Niab

Job(s) Available: Vacation work (approximately 30).
Pay: National minimum wage rates.
Job Description: Vacation work involving working in fields and laboratories at regional trial centres and the head office.

Head Office: Huntingdon Road, Cambridge CB3 0LF
☎ 01223 342282
✆ jobs@niab.com
🖳 www.niab.com

Accommodation: Not provided although lists of accommodation are available.
Application Procedure: Applications from April 2011 for summer work to the personnel office at the above address.

Rolls Royce Plc

Job(s) Available: Summer internships and full internships.
Duration: Summer internships are 10-week placements. Full internships are placements that last anywhere from 4 to 12 months, usually as part of a degree course. Typically they run from mid-June and

Head Office: 65 Buckingham Gate, London SW1E 6AT
☎ 01332 33 33 33
✆ HRSharedservicecentre@rolls-royce.com
🖳 www.rolls-royce.com/university

last for 1 year, although it is possible to accommodate both shorter and longer placements.
Pay: £17,500 pro rata.
Company Description: A global company operating in 4 dynamic markets: civil and defence aerospace, energy and marine.
Job Description: Rolls Royce offer Summer internships in engineering, commercial, customer management, finance, HR, supply chain planning and control, purchasing and operations management.
Requirements: Applicants must be in their second year of undergraduate study to apply and be expecting to achieve a minimum of a 2:1 degree. Please visit the website for specific details on each scheme.
Accommodation: Help may be given in finding accommodation locally.
Application Procedure: To apply, visit the website listed above.

Shell Step Classic Programme

Job(s) Available: Work experience placements.
Duration: 8–12 weeks over the summer.
Pay: Approximately £210 per week (tax and national insurance free).
Job Description: The Shell Step Classic programme offers work experience placements to undergraduates in small to medium-sized businesses and community organisations throughout the UK.

Head Office: Step Enterprise House, 14-16 Bridgford Road, West Bridgford, Nottingham NG2 6AB
☎ 0844 248 8242
✎ employers@step.org.uk
🖥 www.step.org.uk

Requirements: Applicants must be second/penultimate year undergraduates registered on a full-time UK university degree course.
Application Procedure: To apply visit www.step.org.uk.

Sir Robert McAlpine Ltd

Job(s) Available: Summer placements (35).
Duration: Minimum 8 weeks.
Pay: Dependent on experience and qualifications.
Company Description: Sir Robert McAlpine Ltd is one of the UK's major building and civil engineering contractors, undertaking projects such as industrial plants, marine works, power stations, hospitals, offices, theatres, leisure and retail complexes.

Head Office: Eaton Court, Maylands Avenue, Hemel Hempstead, Hertfordshire HP2 7TR
☎ 01442 233444
✎ careers@sir-robert-mcalpine.com
🖥 www.sir-robert-mcalpine.com

Job Description: University students reading degrees in construction-related subjects, or 'A' Level students considering such degrees, are offered summer placements. Students assist site engineers and quantity surveyors working on various major construction sites throughout the country.
Accommodation: Assistance in finding lodgings is provided.
Application Procedure: Applications should be made to the HR department, at the above address, or via the above website.

Tata Steel (Corus group)

Job(s) Available: Summer placements and 12-month placements.
Pay: £14,500 per year pro rata.
Company Description: Tata Steel is one of the largest steel producers, with a combined presence in nearly 50 countries.
Job Description: Every year Corus offers summer

Head Office: Corus Group HR, Ashorne Hill, Leamington Spa, Warwickshire CV33 9PY
☎ 01926 488025
✎ recruitment@corusgroup.com
🖥 www.corusgroupcareers.com

placements and 12-month placements around the UK in the following areas: engineering; manufacturing and operations management; metallurgical and technical services; research development and technology; commercial (sales and marketing); supplies; logistics; finance and HR. These positions are suitable for students in their first or second year at university.
Accommodation: Help can be given in finding accommodation.
Application Procedure: All applications are online at www.corusgroupcareers.com.

Voluntary work

The category of voluntary work encompasses a large range of activities including **archaeology, children, conservation and the environment**, heritage, **physically/mentally disabled, social and community schemes** and **work camps**.

Many organisations throughout the UK need volunteers to help with a host of different types of work, from caring for people with disabilities or the elderly to taking part in conservation and archaeological projects. Festivals and events are also a good source of temporary voluntary work, though very short-term. The Cheltenham Festival of Literature is one of the larger examples here – you can apply personally to smaller local events, particularly in university or historical towns. You might be paid travel and other expenses and will usually get free entrance to all the events of the festival.

If you are interested in becoming involved in local issues in your area, contact Millennium Volunteers through the Department for Education and Skills (millennium.volunteers@dfes.gsi.gov.uk; www.mvonline.gov.uk). Millennium Volunteers is a UK-wide, government-funded initiative providing 130 volunteering opportunities for young people aged between 16 and 24. Volunteers contribute to a range of voluntary organisations from their local Citizens Advice Bureau, to joining a conservation project organised by BTCV, to projects such as sports coaching and music and dance. A national online database of voluntary work is available at www.do-it.org.uk. Those completing 200 hours of voluntary activity in a year receive an award of excellence signed by the secretary of state. Most UK universities also have thriving community Action groups offering a range of volunteering opportunities in the local area.

Sources of information: *The International Directory of Voluntary Work* (Victoria Pybus, Vacation Work, £12.95) includes information on both short- and long-term opportunities. It is available from www.crimsonpublishing.co.uk. The National Council for Voluntary Organisations (0800279 8798; www.ncvo-vol.org.uk) publishes the *Voluntary Agencies Directory*, priced £35 plus £5.50 postage and packing for non-members, which lists more than 2,000 organisations countrywide.

Volunteering England (0845 305 6979; www.volunteering.org.uk) produces information sheets on finding out about volunteering opportunities. The website details voluntary organisations, ideas about the types of volunteering available and where to find your nearest Volunteer Centre for local volunteering opportunities. Information on voluntary work in Wales can be obtained from Wales Council for Voluntary Action (0870 607 1666; www.wcva.org.uk).

Archaeology
Arbeia Roman Fort

Job(s) Available: Volunteers (5 per week).
Duration: Needed from June to end of September.
Working Hours: 8.45am–4.45pm, Monday to Friday.
Company Description: Part of the Tyne & Wear Archives and Museums service and within easy reach of Newcastle by metro. South Shields has good parks and beaches and is an ideal base from which to visit the nearby cities or countryside.

Head Office: Tyne and Wear Museums Service, Baring Street, South Shields, Tyne and Wear NE33 2BB
☎ 01914 544093
📧 liz.elliott@twmuseums.org.uk

Job Description: Volunteers to excavate the site, record and process finds, draw the site and take photographs.
Requirements: Minimum age 16. Disabled people may find access to the site difficult.
Accommodation: Volunteers are responsible for their own travel, board and other costs.
Application Procedure: By post to Elizabeth Elliott, office manager, at the above address.

Archaeolink Prehistory Park

Job(s) Available: Volunteers are needed to work in reconstruction and living history.
Duration: From April to October.
Working Hours: 20–37 hours per week.
Company Description: Archaeolink was started in 1997 to introduce the public to Aberdeenshire's rich

Head Office: Oyne, Insch, Aberdeenshire AB52 6QP
☎ 01464 851500
🖰 info@archaeolink.co.uk
🖳 www.archaeolink.co.uk

archaeological heritage. It operates reconstructions including Stone Age camps, a Roman marching camp, a Bronze Age metal-smith workshop and an Iron Age farm based on archaeological evidence from north-east Scotland.
Requirements: No experience is necessary and volunteers may be as young as 14 if they are accompanied by a guardian.
Accommodation: Available at a local bed and breakfast. Volunteers must pay for travel, food and accommodation; however, lunch is provided by the company on days of volunteering.
Application Procedure: Contact the park, at the above address, for further information.

Bamburgh Research Project

Job(s) Available: Volunteers (22 per week).
Duration: From June to the end of July.
Company Description: A project centred on Bamburgh Castle dedicated to using the most modern field techniques to provide training for both students and volunteers. The castle is located 50 miles north of Newcastle on the coast.

Head Office: 23 Kingsdale Avenue, Blyth NE24 4EN
☎ 01670 352100
🖰 graemeyoung@bamburghresearch project.co.uk
🖳 www.bamburghresearchproject.co.uk

Job Description: Volunteers needed for excavation, training, field walking, test pitting and media. There are many sites being excavated, including an early medieval gatehouse and a medieval metalworking site, within the castle. There is also a comprehensive survey programme and a media department dedicated to filming the archaeological process. The sites excavated range in period from prehistoric, medieval to modern.
Requirements: Volunteers of all ages and levels of experience are welcome.
Accommodation: Accommodation is provided at a fully equipped campsite but volunteers must bring their own camping equipment. There is also a £5 per night camping fee.
Additional Information: The nearest railway station is Berwick-on-Tweed and there is a regular bus service to Bamburgh, or pick up in Newcastle if arranged in advance. The cost is approximately £155 per week which includes tuition; travel to and from the site; food; and space for camping. Please check website for up-to-date campsite details.
Application Procedure: Via email or by writing to the above address.

Council for British Archaeology (CBA)

Job(s) Available: Working on excavations and fieldwork projects.
Company Description: The CBA is an educational charity working throughout the UK to involve people in archaeology and to promote the appreciation and care of the historic environment for the benefit

Head Office: St Mary's House, 66 Bootham, York YO30 7BZ
☎ 01904 671417
🖰 info@britarch.ac.uk
🖳 www.britarch.ac.uk

of present and future generations. Details of excavations and other fieldwork projects are given on the Council's website and in the Council's publication *British Archaeology*.

Additional Information: The magazine is published 6 times a year. An annual subscription costs £28 (£19 for the first year); however, it also forms part of an individual membership package which is available for £32 per year and brings extra benefits.

Application Procedure: Having studied the magazine you should make applications to the director of the projects which interest you.

Silchester Roman Town Life Project

Job(s) Available: Volunteers.

Duration: Required for July and August to work on the excavation.

Company Description: Situated midway between Reading and Basingstoke, a major long-term excavation of the industrial and commercial area of a Roman town.

Job Description: The project is suitable for both beginners and those with more experience.

Requirements: Minimum age 16.

Head Office: Reading University, Department of Archaeology, Whiteknights, PO Box 227, Reading, Berkshire RG6 6AB
☎ 01183 788132
✆ archaeology@rdg.ac.uk
🖳 www.silchester.rdg.ac.uk

Accommodation: Cost is approximately £250 per 6 day week, which includes food, campsite facilities and hot showers. Volunteers must provide their own camping equipment.

Application Procedure: Visit the above website for further information, or contact Amanda Clarke at the above address.

Conservation and the Environment

Bardsey Island Bird and Field Observatory

Job(s) Available. Volunteer programme for assistant wardens.

Company Description: Situated on a bird island 2 miles off the tip of the Llyn Peninsula.

Additional Information: On account of the location, postal mail can often be delayed due to bad weather, as can normal ferry service. Only Orange and Vodafone mobiles work.

Head Office: Cristin, Bardsey off Aberdaron via Pwllheli Gwynedd LL53 8DE
☎ 07855 264 151
✆ warden@bbfo.org.uk
🖳 www.bbfo.org.uk

Application Procedure: For further details contact the warden.

British Trust for Ornithology (BTO)

Job(s) Available: Volunteer bird surveyors.

Duration: Surveys run by the BTO range from extremely long to short-term schemes.

Company Description: An organisation set up to promote the appreciation and conservation of birds.

Head Office: The Nunnery, Thetford, Norfolk IP24 2PU
☎ 01842 750050
✆ info@bto.org
🖳 www.bto.org

Job Description: Volunteers needed to participate in surveys run by the BTO. Some training sessions are organised through the summer.

Application Procedure: By post to the above address at any time. Check the website for details.

Conservation Volunteers Northern Ireland

Job(s) Available: Volunteers.

Duration: For those who wish to take on extra responsibility, a commitment of at least 6 months is requested.

Company Description: Conservation Volunteers Northern Ireland is part of BTCV, which involves more than 70,000 volunteers each year in environmental projects throughout Northern Ireland, England, Wales and Scotland, making it the largest practical conservation charity in the country.

Head Office: 159 Ravenhill Road, Belfast BT6 0BP
☎ 028 9064 5169
CVNI@btcv.org.uk
www.btcv.org.uk

Job Description: Volunteers to participate in projects to inspire people to improve the places they live in throughout Northern Ireland. These include community development work, biodiversity projects, health initiatives and the use of practical skills etc. There are opportunities to suit all levels of commitment.

Requirements: All training, protective clothing and tools are provided according to the role the volunteer takes on. No experience is necessary. Minimum age 16.

Accommodation: Limited amount of accommodation is available at the tree nursery site for volunteer officers.

Application Procedure: By post to Kate Holohan, at the above address, at any time of the year.

Hessilhead Wildlife Rescue Trust

Job(s) Available: Volunteers (40 annually).

Duration: Minimum period of work 2 weeks, maximum 6 months in the period between April and October.

Company Description: A wildlife rescue and rehabilitation centre in Scotland.

Head Office: Gateside, Beith, Ayrshire KA15 1HT
☎ 01505 502415
info@hessilhead.org.uk
www.hessilheadwildlife.org.uk

Job Description: Volunteers help with a range of jobs involving rescue, daily care and cleaning of wild birds and animals, as well as treatment and hand-rearing, assessment for release and post-release monitoring.

Requirements: Experience with animals is advantageous, but not necessary, as full training is given.

Accommodation: Provided with heating and cooking facilities at a cost of £15 per week.

Application Procedure: For further details, contact Gay Christie at the above address.

Marine Conservation Society (MCS)

Job(s) Available: Volunteers.

Duration: At certain periods of the year, large amounts of data need to be entered into databases; volunteers with computer skills are particularly welcome at these times.

Head Office: Unit 3 Wolf Business Park, Alton Road, Ross-on-Wye, Hereford HR9 5NB
☎ 01989 566017
info@mcsuk.org
www.mcsuk.org

Company Description: The MCS is the only charity in the UK devoted solely to protecting the marine environment.

Job Description: Volunteers are sometimes needed in the society's offices and for participation in campaigns and surveys.

Additional Information: Unfortunately, the society is unable to provide any financial payment, accommodation or transport. There are several other campaigns in which volunteers can participate. Check the website for further details.

Application Procedure: For further information, contact the society at the above address.

Merryweather's

Job(s) Available: Gardeners (2).
Duration: Minimum period of work 4 weeks.
Working Hours: To work 9am–5pm, 2 days a week (normally Wednesday and Thursday).
Company Description: Garden development and wildlife project extending to nearly 6 acres and incorporating a small nursery, situated in the beautiful Sussex High Weald. Whole project managed organically.

> **Head Office:** Merryweather's Farm, Chilsham Lane, Herstmonceux, East Sussex BN27 4QH
> ☎ 01323 831726 or 07884 293417
> ✆ info@morethanjustagarden.co.uk
> 🖥 www.morethanjustagarden.co.uk

Job Description: Volunteer gardeners to perform general garden maintenance and development, fruit and vegetable growing and wildlife habitat management, as well as some nursery propagation.
Requirements: Training will be given but some experience preferred. Non-smokers only.
Accommodation: No accommodation available.
Application Procedure: By post or email to Liz O'Halloran, proprietor, at the above address. References required. Foreign applicants with good spoken English welcome.

National Trust

Job(s) Available: Volunteers needed for working holidays in the countryside or coastal locations (400).
Duration: Minimum period of work 2–3 days.
Cost: From £90 a week, including food and hostel-type accommodation.

> **Head Office:** The National Trust, PO Box 39, Warrington WA5 7WD
> ☎ 0844 800 1895
> ✆ enquiries@nationaltrust.org.uk
> 🖥 www.nationaltrust.org.uk

Company Description: The National Trust is a charity which works to preserve and protect the buildings, countryside and coastline of England, Wales and Northern Ireland through practical conservation and learning and discovery.
Job Description: Volunteers are needed for the following categories of work: active events, archaeology, construction, education, family, gardening, green living, historic houses, rural skills and survey. Some holidays allow you to combine activities such as surfing, horse riding and digital photography with conservation tasks for a really varied week.
Requirements: Minimum age 18. No previous experience is necessary as you will be led by trained volunteer leaders and staff. Must be team-spirited, enjoy being outdoors and ready to get your hands dirty.
Accommodation: Most holidays are based in a National Trust base camp. Large, comfortable, basic self-catering accommodation is provided for groups. A few of the holidays spend some nights camping or have higher grade facilities. The details of location can be found in the holiday descriptions. Food is made fresh every evening by the volunteers.
Application Procedure: Search online for a suitable opportunity at www.nationaltrust.org.uk/main/w-trust/w-volunteering/w-workingholidays.htm or call the booking office on 0844 800 3099.

WDCS (Moray Firth Wildlife Centre)

Job(s) Available: Volunteers.
Duration: Seasonal.
Company Description: The Whale and Dolphin Conservation Society takes on seasonal volunteers to work at the Moray Firth Wildlife Centre.

> **Head Office:** WDCS, Brookfield House, 38 St Paul Street, Chippenham, Wiltshire SN15 1LJ
> ☎ 01249 449500
> ✆ volunteering@wdcs.org
> 🖥 www.wdcs.org

Job Description: The work is varied and includes research, interpretation, and awareness-raising events around Scotland.

Accommodation: Provided and a contribution is made towards expenses.

Application Procedure: For more information send an email to the above address.

RSPB Residential Volunteering Scheme

Job(s) Available: Volunteers.

Duration: Bookings start and finish on a Saturday and can be for a week or more.

Company Description: If you are interested in birds and conservation, here is an ideal opportunity to help conservation work at RSPB, gain practical

Head Office: The Lodge, Potton Road, Sandy, Bedfordshire SG19 2DL
☎ 01767 680551
✆ volunteers@rspb.org.uk
🖥 www.rspb.org.uk/residentialvolunteering

work experience, meet new people, explore new areas, enjoy a working holiday and simply make good use of spare time while keeping fit in the great outdoors. Nationally, the RSPB has more than 14,500 volunteers. There are currently 41 reserves within the scheme and the work varies from season to season and from reserve to reserve but physical management tasks are an important aspect of the RSPB's work on most sites. Visitor work is also available, especially from April to September.

Job Description: A willingness to help with even mundane jobs and to work as part of a team is essential. At sites where work is (mainly) helping visitors to the reserve, you must feel comfortable communicating with others.

Requirements: No special skills needed for most of the volunteering opportunities but a genuine interest in and enthusiasm for nature is essential. Volunteers from overseas must have good conversational English. Minimum age 16 (18 on some reserves).

Accommodation: Volunteers need to organise and pay for their own travel to and from the reserve and to provide and cover the cost of their own food during their stay. The RSPB will provide self-catering accommodation free of charge.

Application Procedure: For a brochure on residential volunteering, *Do Something Different*, and an application form visit the website or write to The Volunteering Development Department (Residential), at the above address.

Suffolk Wildlife Trust

Job(s) Available: Volunteer education assistants and youth project volunteers.

Duration: Hours vary but may include weekdays and weekends.

Company Description: Promotes and protects Suffolk wildlife through education, including out-door lessons and activities, games, crafts, events, family and adult talks and walks.

Head Office: Carlton Marshes, Burnt Hill Lane, Carlton Colville, Lowestoft NR33 8HU
☎ 01502 564250
✆ carlton.education@suffolkwildlifetrust.org
or yoe.project@suffolkwildlifetrust.org
(for youth outdoor experience project)

Job Description: *Volunteer education assistants:* environmental education for all ages, including assisting with preparation of resources and assisting with wildlife and conservation themed activities. Help with clubs (young wardens and watch clubs). *Youth project volunteers:* helping with the youth outdoor experience project for 11–18 year olds, which includes assisting with the preparation of resources, with wildlife and with conservation themed activities.

Requirements: Minimum age 18.

Accommodation: Not available.

Application Procedure: By post or to the education officer or via email at the relevant above address. An informal 'trial' day is required. Foreign applicants with some English welcome.

The Centre for Alternative Technology

Job(s) Available: Short- and long-term volunteer programme.

Duration: *Short-term programme:* runs from March to September inclusive, for stays of 1 or 2 weeks. *Long-term programme:* runs for 6 months.

Head Office: Machynlleth, Powys SY20 9AZ
☎ 0165 705955
✆ joni.pickering@cat.org.uk
💻 www.cat.org.uk/volunteers

Company Description: Established in 1974, the Centre for Alternative Technology is an internationally renowned display and education centre promoting practical ideas and information on technologies, which sustain rather than damage the environment.

Job Description: *Short-term volunteers:* could help with gardening, landscaping, site maintenance and preparation for courses and engineering. *Long-term volunteer programme:* for individuals to help in specific work departments. Jobs include the following departments: biology, engineering, gardening, information, media and site maintenance.

Requirements: Minimum age 18. Foreign applicants are welcome to apply. *Long-term volunteer programme:* applicants should have relevant experience.

Accommodation: Cooked lunches and hot drinks are provided for all. *Short-term volunteers:* accommodation is basic, youth hostel-style, shared with other volunteers. *Long-term volunteer programme:* volunteers need to make other arrangements; they would need to be self-supporting, for example by claiming state benefits payments if eligible.

Application Procedure: *Long-term volunteer programme:* to apply send a full CV and covering letter (giving details about yourself and stating which department you would like to work with) to Joni Pickering on 01654 705955 or email barbara.wallace@cat.org.uk.

The Monkey Sanctuary Trust

Job(s) Available: Volunteers.

Duration: Open to the public between April and September and during the closed season (October to March).

Head Office: Looe, Cornwall PL13 1NZ
☎ 01503 262532
✆ volunteer@monkeysanctuary.org
💻 www.monkeysanctuary.org

Working Hours: 40 hours per week.

Company Description: Home to a colony of Woolly Monkeys and a rescue centre for ex-pet Capuchins, the sanctuary is a community dedicated to conservation, sustainable living and animal welfare. Education of the public in these areas is their main summer activity.

Job Description: Volunteers are required in the sanctuary and are essential in allowing the team of keepers to care for the colony. Help is needed in the kiosk, and with cleaning while the sanctuary is open to the public. In the closed season volunteers assist with general maintenance work and cleaning.

Requirements: No qualifications are necessary but workers must have an interest in animal welfare and conservation. Minimum age 18.

Accommodation: Food and accommodation are provided and volunteers are asked to make a voluntary donation to the Monkey Sanctuary Trust (suggested £45 per week waged, £35 per week students/unwaged).

Application Procedure: By post, 4 or 5 months in advance, to the volunteer coordinator at the above address, enclosing an s.a.e. or international reply coupon. Overseas applicants with a good standard of English welcome.

The National Seal Sanctuary

Job(s) Available: Volunteers.
Duration: Taken all year round; to work for over 2 weeks.
Company Description: The sanctuary is a well-known marine animal rescue centre.
Job Description: Volunteers are to help with the sanctuary's work, including caring for seals and sea lions.
Requirements: Minimum age 18.
Application Procedure: By email via the above address. Volunteer information on website.

Head Office: Gweek nr Helston, Cornwall TR12 6UG
☎ 01326 221361
seals@sealsanctuary.co.uk
www.sealsanctuary.co.uk

The Wildlife Trust of South and West Wales

Job(s) Available: Voluntary assistant wardens.
Duration: Island volunteers will work for a full week (Saturday to Saturday) or a maximum of 2 weeks between March and October.
Company Description: The 4th largest wildlife trust in the UK, covering more than 100 nature reserves. The organisation is concerned with educating people about the Welsh environment and its protection and potential.

Head Office: The Welsh Wildlife Centre, Cilgerran, Pembrokeshire SA43 2TB
☎ 01239 621212 or 01239 621600
islands@welshwildlife.org
for Skomer Island
or wwc@welshwildlife.org
for other enquiries
www.welshwildlife.org

Job Description: Voluntary assistant wardens required for Skomer Island, a national nature reserve off the Welsh coast. Work involves greeting visitors, census work, general reserve maintenance and wildlife recording.
Requirements: Minimum age 16. Applicants should have an interest in natural history.
Accommodation: Self-catering accommodation is available at £35 per week but food is not included.
Application Procedure: Please phone first to check availability and make a provisional booking. Application forms available from Island Bookings or website; apply via email if overseas. Overseas applicants welcome. Booking office for 2011 opens 27 September for Friends of the Islands. Open 11 October to all public.

Trees for Life

Job(s) Available: Conservation Work Week volunteers (10 per week, over 500 annually).
Duration: Volunteers needed for a week at a time. Work Weeks run from midday Saturday to midday Saturday, including 5 working days and 1 day off. The Work Weeks run in 2 seasons every year - spring (March–May) and autumn (September–November). See the website for a full list of dates and locations. Volunteers can do as many work weeks as they like but bookings are not accepted for more than 2 consecutive weeks due to the physical work involved and group dynamics.

Head Office: The Park, Findhorn Bay, Forres, Moray IV36 3TZ
☎ 0845 602 7386
rosie@treesforlife.org.uk
www.treesforlife.org.uk

Company Description: Scottish charity dedicated to the restoration of the Caledonian Forest to a 900 square mile target area in the Highlands.
Job Description: To carry out vital practical forest restoration work including tree planting, fence removal, removing small non-native trees, wetland restoration, tree nursery work, stock-fencing and seed collecting.

Requirements: Minimum age 18. Applicants must understand English and be reasonably fit, as the work is of a physical nature.

Accommodation: All food, accommodation and transport from Inverness provided. Prices start at £130 (£70 for concessions).

Application Procedure: Book online at the above website. Foreign applicants are welcome providing they have a good understanding of English and the relevant paperwork to volunteer in the UK.

Wildfowl & Wetlands Trust (WWT)

Job(s) Available: Volunteers.

Duration: Full-time and part-time opportunities are available but some placements do require volunteers to commit to a minimum of 2 months at the centre to allow time for training.

> **Head Office:** Volunteer Opportunities, Slimbridge, Gloucester GJ2 7BT
> ☎ 01453 891137
> volunteers@wwt.org.uk
> www.wwt.org.uk

Company Description: WWT is a charity aiming to promote the conservation of wildfowl and their wetland habitats as well as increasing the public's knowledge of these birds. The centre has the world's largest collection of wildfowl.

Job Description: WWT depends on help from volunteers to assist the teams at all 9 centres. At Slimbridge, volunteers assist throughout the grounds and centre including the visitor services, education, aviculture and horticulture departments. Grounds and reserve volunteers assist the wardens in their daily duties and gain practical conservation knowledge and experience. Duties for volunteers working in visitor services include manning the information desk, meeting and greeting groups, selling grain to visitors that want to feed the birds and generally being a friendly and helpful face for the public. Education volunteers assist with the development of educational material and help run teaching and informal learning sessions such as pond dipping and story telling. Other areas where volunteers assist are within marketing, administration and maintenance. Volunteers in all areas will have the opportunity to help with a number of exciting new developments including Crane School (where cranes are being reared for release into the wild) and Toad Hall (a collection of amphibians from the UK and overseas) through helping project development, interpretation and giving talks and presentations to visitors and our Canoe Safari.

Requirements: Minimum age 16. No previous experience or qualifications are required, only plenty of enthusiasm, a willingness to help and a capacity to learn.

Accommodation: Limited on-site accommodation is available.

Application Procedure: For further details contact Kate Barker or Sarah Aspden on the above phone number or at kate.barker@wwt.org.uk or sarah.aspden@wwt.org.uk. Other WWT centres also welcome the assistance of volunteers. Please see the website for contact details of the centre you are interested in working at.

Festivals and Special Events

Oxfam Stewards

Job(s) Available: Festival stewards (up to 5,000).

Duration: The festivals run from June to September.

Working Hours: Minimum of 3 shifts per festival. Shifts last 8 hours and 15 minutes.

> **Head Office:** Brunswick Court, Brunswick Square, Bristol BS2 8PE
> ☎ 0300 200 1266
> stewards@oxfam.org.uk
> www.oxfam.org.uk/festival

Pay: Applicants are asked to pay a deposit at the beginning of the summer, which is returned once all stewarding duties are completed. One deposit can cover as many festivals as you'd like to apply for. In return, stewards receive free entrance to the festival, a meal ticket for every shift worked and a separate camping area with toilets and showers.

Company Description: Oxfam has been providing volunteer stewards for music festivals since 1993 and now offer stewarding places at 14 festivals. This service forms part of the Oxfam Events team.

Job Description: Stewarding is about providing a safe environment for everyone at a festival. It usually involves giving directions, checking tickets, monitoring crowd build-up, talking to people and answering general enquiries. On occasions, you may be called upon to deal with serious incidents or emergencies.

Requirements: Minimum Age 18. No previous experience necessary, only common sense and good team work required. Visa restrictions apply to non-UK nationals

Application Procedure: Applications should be made from February/March. Please visit the website for an online application form and further details.

Peppermint Events

Duration: Required from June to September, but recruitment is ongoing.

Working Hours: Volunteer staff work 6–9 hour shifts.

Pay: Volunteers are reimbursed with free entry tickets to festivals, public camping, plus a free meal and 2 free drinks per shift in exchange for 2 shifts per event.

Head Office: 7 College Fields Business Park, 19 Prince Georges Rd, London SW19 2PT
☎ 0845 226 7845
jobs@peppermintevents.co.uk
🖥 www.festivalvolunteer.co.uk

Company Description: An event and bar management company that caters for events and festivals such as Glade Festival, Bestival, Skandia Cowes Week and other various music festivals in London and the south-east.

Accommodation: Camping available.

Application Procedure: By post to Tammy Vonwildenrath at the above address, or via the website. Overseas applicants are welcome to apply provided they have the relevant documentation and speak English to the same level as a native speaker.

The Times Cheltenham Festival of Literature

Job(s) Available: Festival volunteers (30).

Duration: The work is for 13 days from 5 to 17 October (the festival runs from 7 to 16 October).

Working Hours: The hours at the festival are fairly long; a typical festival day runs from 10am–midnight.

Head Office: Cheltenham Festivals, 109–111 Bath Road, Cheltenham, Gloucestershire GL53 7LS
☎ 01242 775861
clair.greenaway@cheltenhamfestivals.com

Company Description: The Times Cheltenham Literature Festival will be in its 62nd year in 2011 and is one of the largest and most popular of its kind in Europe. There is a wide range of events including talks and lectures, poetry readings, novelists in conversation, creative writing workshops, exhibitions, discussions and a literary festival for children.

Job Description: Festival volunteers are required to look after both the authors and the audience as well as helping with the setting up of events, front of house duties, in the office and assisting the sound crew.

Requirements: Applicants should be graduates over 18 with an interest in literature, arts administration or events management.

Accommodation: Volunteers are given free accommodation, travel expenses and food and drink. Free entry to all events is also provided.

Application Procedure: By post to Clair Greenaway, festival executive director, from February onwards to the above address. Overseas applicants are welcome but must be over 21 and must have a very high standard of spoken and written English.

Fundraising and office work

Oxfam

Job(s) Available: Volunteering programmes.
Pay: Oxfam reimburses reasonable local travel and lunch expenses.
Company Description: Oxfam runs a number of different programmes including volunteering in the shop network.

Head Office: Oxfam House, John Smith Drive, Oxford OX4 2JY
☎ 01865 473259
givetime@oxfam.org.uk
www.oxfam.org.uk/get_involved/volunteer/index.html

Job Description: For those interested in a career with Oxfam, volunteering is an excellent way to gain relevant experience and to get to know the organisation.
Additional Information: Call into your local shop for more details. Oxfam also advertises more specialised volunteer vacancies on its website at www.oxfam.org.uk/get_involved/volunteer/latest all of which are UK based, and many of which are at its head office in Oxford. Follow the instructions from recruiting managers. Email the above address with any general questions or queries. See www.oxfam.org.uk/interns for more information.
Application Procedure: Further information is available from www.oxfam.org.uk/interns or call into your local Oxfam shop.

Heritage

Alexander Fleming Laboratory Museum

Job(s) Available: Volunteer guides. The museum also offers a summer placement working as a volunteer in the archives of St Mary's Hospital and as a guide, offering experience in archives and museums.

Head Office: St Mary's Hospital, Praed Street, London W2 1NY
☎ 020 331 26 528
kevin.brown@imperial.nhs.uk

Duration: *Volunteer guides:* needed all year round. *Summer placement candidates:* during the summer.
Working Hours: *Volunteer guides:* hours 10am–1pm, Monday to Thursday. *Summer placement candidates:* hours 10am–5pm, Monday to Friday.
Company Description: The museum, which is situated close to Paddington station, has been designated an International Historic Chemical Landmark and visitors come from all over the world.
Job Description: *Volunteer guides:* needed to conduct visitors around the Alexander Fleming Laboratory Museum, which is based on a reconstruction of the laboratory in which Fleming discovered penicillin. The job includes making a short presentation as well as carrying out retail duties in a small museum shop.
Requirements: Full training will be supplied and knowledge of the subject matter is not required. Minimum age 16.
Additional Information: The museum lacks disabled access.
Application Procedure: By post to Kevin Brown, trust archivist and museum curator, at the above address.

Ffestiniog Railway Company

Job(s) Available: Volunteers.
Duration: Throughout the year.
Job Description: Hundreds of volunteers are needed to help in the operation and maintenance of a 150-year-old narrow gauge railway between Porthmadog and Blaenau Ffestiniog. The work done

Head Office: Harbour Station, Porthmadog, Gwynedd LL49 9NF
☎ 01766 516035
✆ tricia.doyle@festrail.co.uk
🖳 www.festrail.co.uk

by individual volunteers depends on their skills, many of which are built up over a period of regular commitment to the railway which provides on-the-job training. The railway is divided into various diverse departments, and so jobs range from selling tickets and souvenirs to the 'elite' task of driving the engines.
Requirements: Railway enthusiasts and non-enthusiasts of any nationality may apply provided they speak a good standard of English. Minimum age 16.
Accommodation: Limited self-catering accommodation is provided for regular volunteers, for which a small charge is made. Food is extra. Camping space and a list of local accommodation is also available.
Application Procedure: Further information may be obtained from the volunteers resource manager, Ffestiniog Railway Company.

House of Dun

Job(s) Available: Volunteers.
Duration: From April to October.
Company Description: Beautiful Georgian mansion dating from 1730 and designed by William Adam.
Job Description: Volunteers required to conduct guided tours, gardening and handyman duties.

Head Office: House of Dun by Montrose, Angus DD10 9LQ
☎ 01674 810264
✆ gmckenna@nts.org.uk
🖳 www.nts.org.uk

Accommodation: Free accommodation may be available.
Application Procedure: By post to the property manager, at the above address or via email.

Kentwell Hall

Job(s) Available: Volunteer Tudors (700).
Duration: Annual recreation of Tudor life takes place for 3 weeks during June and July. Most volunteers stay 1 or 2 weeks from May/June to August/September.
Working Hours: 6 days a week.

Head Office: Live as a Tudor, Long Melford, Sudbury, Suffolk CO10 9BA
☎ 01787 310207
✆ info@kentwell.co.uk
🖳 www.kentwell.co.uk

Company Description: A privately owned Tudor mansion, situated in park and farmland, approximately 1.5 miles from the historic town of Long Melford. Up to 1,500 schoolchildren visit on weekdays and the public at weekends.
Job Description: Volunteer Tudors needed for historical re-creations and for other smaller events throughout the year. Duties consist of demonstrating 16th-century life and activities to visiting schoolchildren and the public.
Requirements: An interest in the 16th century would be helpful; staff should have knowledge of 16th-century skills or can learn them there. All ages and nationalities are welcome and applicants can be of any age.
Accommodation: All meals, evening entertainment and space on campsite provided for volunteers.

Applications Procedure: If interested in applying, applicants should write to the above address and include a large, stamped, self-addressed envelope. Potential applicants will then be sent full details of how to apply in January/February.

Mid Hants Railway (Watercress Line)

Job(s) Available: Volunteers.
Duration: Staff are required from May to September for a minimum of 2 months. Both full-time and part-time positions are available.
Company Description: A preserved steam railway running trains between Alresford and Alton.

> **Head Office:** Railway Station, Alresford, Hampshire SO24 9JG
> ☎ 01962 733810
> info@watercressline.co.uk
> 🖥 www.watercressline.co.uk

Job Description: Tourism students are particularly encouraged to apply and there is the possibility of work for engineering students.
Application Procedure: By post to volunteer recruitment at the above address from the beginning of February.

River Stour Trust

Job(s) Available: Volunteer tea room helpers, volunteer event helpers, working party volunteers, volunteer marketing/fund-raising advisors, boat crew volunteers, volunteer boat maintenance and engineers.

> **Head Office:** The Granary, Quay Lane, Sudbury, Suffolk CO10 2AN
> ☎ 01787 313199
> administrator@riverstourtrust.org
> 🖥 www.riverstourtrust.org

Duration: Voluntary positions available from Easter to October, although there may be some available in the winter. *Volunteer boat maintenance and engineers:* needed all year round.
Working Hours: *Volunteer tea room helpers:* to work Sundays and bank holidays. *Volunteer event helpers:* to work mainly on weekends. *Working party volunteers:* to work weekdays and weekends as required. *Volunteer marketing/fund-raising advisors:* to work when required. *Boat crew volunteers:* to work weekdays and weekends.
Company Description: The River Stour Trust is a charity dedicated to restoring and conserving the Essex/Suffolk River Stour navigation, by raising funds to rebuild locks, provide other navigation enhancements.
Job Description: *Volunteer boat maintenance and engineers:* to help with electric launches.
Requirements: *Volunteer tea room helpers:* minimum age 18. *Volunteer event helpers:* full training given for each situation. *Working party volunteers:* skilled and unskilled applicants required. Full training given for each situation. *Volunteer marketing/fund-raising advisors:* must have successful track record in these areas. *Boat crew volunteers:* will be trained by charity and must meet appropriate standards. *Volunteer boat maintenance and engineers:* volunteers must have knowledge of electric boat engines and design. All volunteers welcome but fluent English is essential for dealing with the public.
Application Procedure: By post to the Trust administrator at the above address. Interview required.

Special Olympics Great Britain

Job(s) Available: Media monitoring/researcher intern, picture desk intern, website intern, events volunteers.
Duration: *Interns:* minimum 6 weeks. *Volunteers:* to be arranged.
Pay: Internships and volunteer positions are unpaid but travelling and lunch expenses up to £5 per day will be covered.

Head Office: Corinthian House, 1st floor, 6-8 Great Eastern Street, London EC2A 3NT
☎ 020 7247 8891 (ext. 204)
✆ andrea.zapata@sogb.org.uk
🖳 www.sogb.org.uk

Company Description: To provide year-round sports training and competition in a variety of Olympic-type sports for people with learning disabilities giving them the continuing opportunities to develop physical fitness, demonstrate courage, experience joy and participate in a sharing of skills, gifts and friendship with their families, other Special Olympics athletes and the community.

Job Description: *Media monitoring/researcher intern:* follow up media monitoring services, collect and record press cuttings. *Picture desk intern:* organise and improve efficiency of the picture desk, deal with AV library. *Website intern:* update web content, draft and upload news stories, update calendar of events, update facebook and twitter pages. *Events volunteers:* assist with a variety of functions at Special Olympics events and games.

Requirements: *Media monitoring/researcher intern:* must have a good attention to detail, excellent organisational skills and an interest in print and online media. *Picture desk intern:* must have knowledge of editing and transferring videos to different AV formats, an interest in photography and good attention to detail. *Website intern:* must have knowledge of HTML, Photoshop and CMS and social media. *Events volunteers:* must be enthusiastic and committed.

Application Procedure: To apply send a covering letter and CV to Andrea at the above email address.

The Alice Trust

Job(s) Available: Volunteer gardeners. Other volunteers positions can include: aviary assistants, warehouse assistants, event assistants, garden guides, raffle ticket sellers, room wardens, retail assistants, plant centre assistants, land train drivers, car park attendants, caterers and collection department assistants.

Head Office: Waddesdon Manor, Aylesbury, Buckinghamshire HP18 0JH
☎ 01296 653307
✆ liz.wilkinson@nationaltrust.org.uk
🖳 www.waddesdon.org.uk

Duration: Each role varies so please see website for full details. Full-time garden volunteers are needed for a minimum of 3 months.

Company Description: Waddesdon Manor, a National Trust property, is a magnificent French Renaissance-style chateau, home to the Rothschild Collection of 18th-century French furniture and decorative arts, with acclaimed Victorian gardens.

Job Description: *Volunteer gardeners:* required for a diverse range of maintenance tasks, alongside the team of professional gardeners including weeding, planting out bedding and deheading. See website for all job descriptions.

Requirements: Commitment and reasonable fitness are required and experience is preferred but not essential. Volunteers should have an interest in fine arts, gardening, exotic birds and be keen to be involved in a lively environment. See the website for more specific requirements.

Accommodation: Rent-free accommodation and some assistance with food expenses may be available.

Application Procedure: By post with CV and references to Liz Wilkinson at the above address. Overseas applicants with a good level of English are considered.

The Cleveland Ironstone Mining Museum

Job(s) Available: Collection care workers (2+), museum guides (6+), visitor receptionists (2+).

Working Hours: Museum is open Monday to Saturday. Minimum period of work is 4 hours per week.

Pay: Expenses only are paid.

Head Office: Deepdale, Skinningrove, Saltburn, Cleveland TS13 4AP
☎ 01287 642877
✒ visits@ironstonemuseum.co.uk
🖥 www.ironstonemuseum.co.uk

Company Description: The Cleveland Ironstone Mining Museum preserves and interprets the ironstone mining heritage of Cleveland and North Yorkshire. This is a unique, award-winning, small, independent museum run by volunteers on a day-to-day basis.

Requirements: Applicants should be interested in local history and heritage. Minimum age 16.

Accommodation: Not available.

Application Procedure: By post all year round to the museum manager or via email at the above addresses. Interview preferred.

Waterway Recovery Group

Job(s) Available: Volunteers.

Duration: Work is available year-round; minimum period of work 1 day.

Working Hours: To work either on weekends or week-long canal camps.

Head Office: Island House, Moor Road, Chesham HP5 1WA
☎ 01494 783453
✒ enquiries@wrg.org.uk
🖥 www.wrg.org.uk

Company Description: The national coordinating body for voluntary labour on the inland waterways of Great Britain.

Job Description: Volunteers needed to restore Britain's derelict canals: work may involve restoring industrial archaeology, demolishing old brickwork, driving a dumper truck, clearing mud and vegetation and helping at a National Waterways festival.

Requirements: No experience or qualifications are necessary but volunteers should be between the ages of 18 and 70.

Accommodation: Accommodation and food provided for £56 per week/£8 per day for food and basic accommodation.

Application Procedure: By post to the enquiries officer at the above address. Overseas applicants welcome, but must be over 21.

Wirksworth Heritage Centre

Job(s) Available: Voluntary general museum assistant.

Duration: Minimum period of work 1 month. Positions are available all year.

Working Hours: To be arranged.

Head Office: Crown Yard, Wirksworth, Derbyshire DE4 4ET
☎ 01629 825225
✒ enquiries@storyofwirksworth.co.uk
🖥 www.storyofwirksworth.co.uk

Company Description: The Centre is a small registered museum telling the story of a small, formerly very important town in Derbyshire. The 'Wirksworth Story' in a former silk mill offers information about local customs and social history. The museum is family friendly and there are some 'hands-on' exhibits. There is also a small gallery which exhibits and sells the work of local artists, ceramicists, sculptors and photographers.

Job Description: Ideal post for a museum studies student.

Requirements: Must be able to communicate confidently with the public, be proactive and enthusiastic and able to help with all aspects of running a small museum.

Accommodation: Not available.

Application Procedure: By post at the above address. Interview necessary.

Physically/mentally disabled

Beannachar

Job(s) Available: Volunteers.
Pay: Pocket money provided.
Duration: Minimum work period 2 months between June and September, 1 year for long-term volunteers.
Working Hours: To work long hours, 6 days a week.
Company Description: Beannachar is one of the

> **Head Office:** Banchory-Devenick, Aberdeen AB12 5YL
> ☎ 01224 861200
> ✍ elisabeth@beannachar.org
> 🖳 www.beannachar.co.uk

Camphill communities in which vulnerable children and adults can live, learn and work with others in healthy social relationships based on mutual care and respect. Beannachar is a training community for teenagers and young adults with learning disabilities.
Job Description: Volunteers are needed for household, workshop, garden and farm duties.
Requirements: Minimum age 19. Must have lots of enthusiasm and a positive attitude. Overseas applicants must speak fluent English.
Accommodation: Free board and lodging.
Application Procedure: Applications by post or email.

Independent Living Alternatives

Job(s) Available: Volunteers.
Duration: Vacancies arise all year round.
Pay: Volunteers receive £63.50 per week.
Job Description: Volunteers required to provide support for people with disabilities, to enable them to live independently in their own homes. The work

> **Head Office:** Trafalgar House, Grenville Place, London NW7 3SA
> ☎ 020 8906 9265
> ✍ enquiry@ILAnet.co.uk
> 🖳 www.ILAnet.co.uk

involves helping them get dressed, go to the toilet, drive, do the housework, and so on. ILA offers a chance to learn about disability issues and see London at the same time.
Requirements: No qualifications required, except good English.
Accommodation: Free accommodation, usually in the London area or in Cumbria.
Application Procedure: By post to Tracey Jannaway at the above address.

Kith & Kids

Job(s) Available: Volunteers.
Duration: Minimum period of work 2 consecutive weeks in late July/early August or a week at Christmas/ Easter. There is also a 3-day training course before each project.
Working Hours: 9.30am–5:30pm daily.

> **Head Office:** The Irish Centre, Pretoria Road, London N17 8DX
> ☎ 020 8801 7432
> ✍ projects@kithandkids.org.uk
> 🖳 www.kithandkids.org.uk

Company Description: A self-help organisation that provides support for families of children with a physical or learning disability.
Job Description: Volunteers needed to take part in social development schemes working with disabled children and young people, helping them with everyday skills and community integration.
Requirements: Minimum age 16. No experience necessary, but lots of enthusiasm essential.
Accommodation: Not available. Lunch and travel expenses within Greater London provided.
Additional Information: The organisation also runs a 1-week camping holiday in the second half of August with accommodation for volunteers.
Application Procedure: For further details contact the volunteer organiser at the above address.

The 3H Fund

Job(s) Available: Volunteers (approximately 60).
Duration: Holidays are usually for 1 week and take place between May and September.
Company Description: The fund organises subsidised group holidays for physically disabled children and adults with the support of volunteer carers, thus affording a period of respite for regular carers.

> **Head Office:** B2 Speldhurst Business Park Langton Road, Tunbridge Wells, Kent TN3 0AQ
> ☎ 01892 860207
> 🖰 info@3hfund.org.uk
> 🖳 www.3hfund.org.uk

Job Description: Volunteers are asked to provide as much help as they feel comfortable with. This could range from assisting with cutting up a guest's food, to helping with lifting and pushing a wheelchair. Full training is provided. Each holiday has an experienced leader, co-leader and nurse as well as other supportive volunteers.
Requirements: A caring nature, the willingness to ensure that a disabled guest has an enjoyable holiday and the ability to cooperate as a team member are essential qualities. Minimum age 17. Applicants must have a reasonable level of physical fitness.
Accommodation: Board and lodging are provided in venues such as holiday centres but a financial contribution (50% for students) is requested. Advice can be given on raising this by sponsorship.
Application Procedure: By post to Lynne Loving at the above address throughout the year for further information.

Vitalise

Job(s) Available: Volunteers.
Duration: Needed for 1 or 2 weeks at a time.
Company Description: Vitalise is a leading UK charity providing holidays for disabled people and breaks for carers.

> **Head Office:** Shap Road, Kendal, Cumbria LA9 6NZ
> ☎ 01539 814682
> 🖰 volunteer@vitalise.org.uk
> 🖳 www.vitalise.org.uk

Job Description: Volunteers to help trained staff enhance the holiday atmosphere for the guests. Holidays are available at purpose-built centres in Essex, Nottingham, Cornwall, Southport and Southampton, where guests can enjoy a break with or without their regular carer.
Accommodation: Volunteers are provided with free accommodation and meals in exchange for their time.
Application Procedure: For an application form please contact the team at the above address. Overseas applicants with good English welcome. Non-EU applicants must apply via an agency.

Woodlarks Camp Site Trust

Job(s) Available: Volunteer carers/enablers.
Duration: Camps are held weekly from May to September. Volunteers are normally taken on for 1 camp lasting a week, though some help on more.
Company Description: Woodlarks Camp Site Trust provides a setting for people of all ages with disabil-

> **Head Office:** Kathleen Marshall House, Tilford Road, Farnham, Surrey GU10 3RN
> ☎ 01252 716279
> 🖰 woodlarks103@btinternet.com
> 🖳 www.woodlarks.org.uk

ities to expand their capabilities and have fun. This small-scale camping site and woodland activity area has facilities including a heated outdoor swimming pool, an aerial runway, a trampoline, archery and more. A dining/recreation room, disabled-friendly toilet block and some indoor sleeping accommodation are alongside the camping area. A new building provides up-to-date moving, handling and showering facilities. Woodlarks is staffed and maintained entirely by volunteers.

Job Description: 8 open camps accept individual disabled campers and require volunteer carers/enablers.

Accommodation: Tent accommodation provided. Helpers and disabled campers pay a modest fee to cover the cost of food, outings.

Application Procedure: Applications via email or phone for details. Duke of Edinburgh Awards candidates welcome.

Social and community schemes

Concordia

Job(s) Available: Volunteers working on community-based projects.

Duration: Last for 2–4 weeks with a main season running from June to September, although there are some spring and autumn projects. Volunteers can also apply for long-term volunteer projects through the EVS programme.

> **Head Office:** 19 North Street, Portslade, Brighton, East Sussex BN41 1DH
> ☎ 01273 422 218
> ✉ info@concordiavolunteers.org.uk
> 🖥 www.concordiavolunteers.org.uk

Cost: Volunteers pay a registration fee of approximately £180 for UK projects and must fund their own travel and insurance. For projects in Africa, Asia and Latin America only there is an additional preparation weekend fee of £40 and an extra fee payable to the in-country host of approximately £80–£150.

Company Description: Concordia is a small not-for-profit charity committed to international youth exchange. Its International Volunteer Programme offers young people the opportunity to join an international team of volunteers working on community-based projects ranging from nature conservation, restoration and construction to more socially based schemes.

Requirements: In general no special skills or experience are required but real motivation and commitment are essential. Applicants must be over 19 to participate on a project in Latin America, Africa and Asia. Concordia can only place volunteers who are resident in the UK.

Accommodation: Food and basic accommodation are available free of charge for all projects in Europe, North America, Russia, Japan and South Korea. For projects in Africa, Asia and Latin America only, food and accommodation are provided by the host and covered by the in-country extra fee mentioned in the cost section above.

Additional Information: Concordia also recruits volunteers (20+) to act as Group Coordinators on UK-based projects, for which training is provided and all expenses are paid. This training takes place in spring each year. Early application is advised.

Application Procedure: Applications should normally be made to the above address. Details of all projects can be found on the website. Please note that overseas applicants must apply through a voluntary organisation in their own country; if necessary Concordia can pass on details of partner organisations.

Hilt

Job(s) Available: Independent living support volunteers (20).

Duration: Minimum period of work 6 months at any time of the year.

Company Description: Hilt supports adults with learning disabilities to live independently in the community. Work across East London.

> **Head Office:** 65 Dalston Lane, London E8 2NG
> ☎ 020 7014 7444
> ✉ info@hilt.org.uk
> 🖥 www.hilt.org.uk

Job Description: Volunteers live with and support adults with learning disabilities with household tasks, such as shopping, cooking and cleaning, as well as with social and leisure activities, for example going to the pub, cooking and cleaning, playing sport or visiting a museum. Volunteers support people on an individual basis to achieve their personal goals and develop their living skills. Induction, training and ongoing supervision are provided.

Requirements: Volunteers must speak a good level of conversational English, be reliable, responsible and punctual, enjoy working with people and have an understanding of Hilt's aims and values. Minimum age 18.

Accommodation: Volunteers are provided with furnished accommodation either living with other volunteers or with the people they support. They receive a weekly living allowance to cover the cost of food, socialising etc and are reimbursed for a weekly Zones 1 and 2 travel card.

Application Procedure: Contact the Volunteer Co-ordinator on the above details for an application form. Interview, references and criminal record check necessary. Apply at least 6–10 weeks in advance of intended start date.

The Black-E

Job(s) Available: Volunteering opportunities.

Duration: Minimum period of work 4 weeks. Volunteers are welcome throughout the year and particularly over the summer, winter and spring holiday periods.

> **Head Office:** 1 Great George Street, Liverpool L1 SEW
> ☎ 0151 709 5109
> 🖥 www.theblack-e.co.uk

Working Hours: 40+ hours per week.

Company Desceription: The Black-E re-opened in 2008 and is a community and arts project which aims to provide opportunities to socialise and experience contemporary arts.

Job Descripton: Diverse volunteering. Opportunities including youth work; crafts and games; workshops with local youngster staging exhibitions and events; and administration, fundraising and maintenance work.

Requirements: Minimum age 18. Volunteers are expected to provide their own food costs.

Accommodation: Provided.

Application Procedure: For further information write to the above address.

Iona Community

Job(s) Available: Volunteers.

Duration: Between 6 and 12 weeks between March and November.

Working Hours: 5.5 days a week.

Pay: Pocket money of approximately £30 per week.

> **Head Office:** Iona Abbey, Isle of Iona, Argyll PA76 6SN
> ☎ 01681 700404
> ✉ staffing@iona.org.uk
> 🖥 www.iona.org.uk

Company Description: An ecumenical Christian community sharing work, worship and meals with guests visiting the Macleod and Abbey centres on Iona and at Camas, the more basic outdoor centre on nearby Mull. Guests come and stay for a week to take part in the common life of work, worship and the programme.

Job Description: Volunteers work in the kitchen, shop and office, help with driving, maintenance and housekeeping.

Requirements: Volunteers should be in sympathy with the Christian faith and the ideals of the Iona community. Minimum age 18.

Accommodation: Full board and lodging and travelling expenses within the UK.

Application Procedure: For details and applications, email the volunteer coordinator at the above address. Overseas applicants with a working knowledge of English are welcome and please note non-EU applicants need to apply for a visa. Recruitment begins in the autumn.

L'Arche

Job(s) Available: Volunteer assistants.
Duration: Assistants required all year, usually for 12 months.
Pay: Minimum £43 per week.
Company Description: Seeks to reveal the particular gifts of people with learning disabilities who

Head Office: 10 Briggate Silsden, Keighley, West Yorkshire BD20 9JT
☎ 01535 656186
✆ info@larche.org.uk
🖥 www.larche.org.uk

belong at the very heart of their communities and who call others to share their lives. There are L'Arche communities in Kent, Inverness, Ipswich, Liverpool, Lambeth, Bognor, Brecon, Edinburgh and Preston, where people with and without learning disabilities share life in ordinary houses.
Job Description: Volunteer assistants required to share life and work with people with learning disabilities in an ecumenical Christian-based community.
Requirements: Minimum age 18.
Accommodation: Free board and lodging.
Application Procedure: By post or email to the above address. After completing the application form candidates are invited to visit the community and interviews are held. Overseas applicants with fluent English are welcome.

Lee Abbey Community

Job(s) Available: Volunteers.
Duration: Minimum stay 3 months. June to end of August.
Pay: Pocket money provided.
Company Description: A Christian conference, retreat and holiday centre on the north Devon coast,

Head Office: Personnel, Lee Abbey, Lynton, Devon EX35 6JJ
☎ 01598 754250
✆ personnel@leeabbey.org.uk
🖥 www.leeabbey.org.uk

run by a 90-stong international community with a vision to renew and serve the church.
Requirements: Volunteers must be committed Christians. Minimum age 18.
Accommodation: Board and lodging provided.
Application Procedure: Applications should be made using the application form obtainable from the above address. Foreign applicants with fluent English welcome.

The Lilias Graham Trust

Job(s) Available: Volunteers.
Duration: Required throughout the year to work for a minimum of 6 months.
Working Hours: 35 hour week.
Pay: £40 pocket money per week.
Job Description: Volunteers required at a

Head Office: Braendam Family House, Thornhill, Stirling FK8 3QH
☎ 01786 850259
✆ cathmorrison@thelgt.org.uk
🖥 www.thelgt.org.uk

short-stay family house for families experiencing disadvantage and poverty. Tasks include: offering direct support to families; participating in trips and outings; helping with domestic chores; driving; organising children's activities and play; and generally responding to the needs of families.
Requirements: Minimum age 18. Applicants must be willing to work long days and to carry out domestic chores and maintain enthusiasm and energy for supporting families in need. A clean driving licence would be an advantage.
Accommodation: Full board provided. Most accommodation is in a single room although it may be necessary to share.

Additional Information: Volunteers are entitled to holidays, use of house car and bicycles and access to internet/email. Volunteers will also have the opportunity to explore Scotland on days off.

Application Procedure: Applications to Cath Morrison, chief executive, at the above postal or email address.

The Prince's Trust

Job(s) Available: Volunteers.
Duration: 12 week course.
Company Description: The Prince's Trust is the UK's leading youth charity. It helps young people overcome barriers and get their lives working.
Job Description: Volunteers for the team pro-

Head Office: 18 Park Square East, London NW1 4LH
☎ 020 7543 1234
✆ generalse@princes-trust.org.uk
🖳 www.princes-trust.org.uk

gramme, enabling young people to develop essential life skills of benefit to future employment. Some 10,000 people take part each year. The programme involves team building activities, an outdoor residential week away, work experience and projects in the community. They take place in over 300 different locations throughout the UK.

Application Procedure: For further information call the above number or visit the website.

Work camps
ATD Fourth World

Job(s) Available: Work camp and street workshop.
Duration: Take place from July to September. Most last 2 weeks.
Company Description: ATD Fourth World is an international voluntary organisation which adopts a human rights approach to overcome extreme

Head Office: 48 Addington Square, London SE5 7LB
☎ 020 7703 3231
✆ atd@atd-uk.org
🖳 www.atd-uk.org

poverty. It supports the efforts of very disadvantaged and excluded families in fighting poverty and taking an active role in the community. Founded in a shanty town on the out-skirts of Paris in 1957, it now works in 27 countries on 5 continents.

Job Description: ATD Fourth World organises work camps, street workshops and family stays in the UK and in other European countries. *Work camps:* a combination of manual work, in and around ATD's buildings; conservation; and reflection on the lives of families living in poverty. *Street workshops:* bring a festival atmosphere to underprivileged areas. Voluntary artists, craftsmen and others share their skills with the children and their parents. Street workshops take place in the streets of deprived areas and make it possible to break down bar-riers between people from different cultures and backgrounds. They also encourage freedom of expression and help build confidence.

Accommodation: Participants pay their own travel costs plus a contribution to the cost of food and accommodation.

Application Procedure: For UK opportunities, contact the above address.

THE UK

WEBSITES

International Voluntary Service (IVS)

Job(s) Available: Volunteers.

Duration: Most projects are short-term, lasting 2–4 weeks in some 60 countries around the world. IVS also offers longer-term opportunities of 2–12 months.

> Head Office: IVS-GB, Thorn House,
> 5 Rose Street, Edinburgh EH2 2PR
> ☎ 0131 243 2745
> 🖱 info@ivsgb.org
> 🖳 www.ivsgb.org

Company Description: IVS is the British branch of Service Civil International (SCI), a peace organisation working for international understanding and cooperation through voluntary work. IVS organises some 20 projects in Britain each year, as well as sending volunteers to some 1,000 projects in 60 countries abroad.

Job Description: Volunteers work in an international team of between 6 and 20 people. They live and work together in order to contribute to the sustainable development of a local community organisation. Types of project work include working with children; with the disadvantaged and disabled; on peace, anti-racism and environmental campaigns; and in arts and culture.

Requirements: Minimum age 18 if going abroad, or 16 for projects in the UK. Volunteers pay their own travel costs and a registration fee (abroad £195/£150, in UK £105/£55), which includes annual membership.

Accommodation: Accommodation and food are provided by the project. Ranges from sharing a twin room, to sleeping in a dormitory or camping. Any available accommodation will be clearly stated in each project description.

Application Procedure: Application forms are available online or from an office. For more information, visit the above website (IVS Menu – How to apply) or contact the office. The brochure is available from April and all up-to-date project information is on the website. Applicants resident outside the UK should apply for IVS projects through partner organisations in their own country or country of residence, see www.sciint.org for a full list of offices.

Websites

www.fruitfuljobs.com

Job(s) Available: Seasonal work for backpackers and permanent positions for those looking to develop a career in the UK (anything from farm managers to logistics assistants).

> ☎ 01989 500 130
> 🖱 info@fruitfuljobs.com
> 🖳 www.fruitfuljobs.com

Duration: Jobs can last from a few weeks to 12 months. Peak employment is from March until October, but work is available throughout the year.

Job Description: The seasonal work Fruitful can offer on UK farms and within the produce industry includes: working as field, packhouse and camp supervisors; quality controllers; drivers; pickers; packers; production operatives and tractor drivers.

Accommodation: The majority of seasonal jobs have cheap accommodation available; they are out of the city and in the countryside, giving the opportunity to earn some money.

Additional Information: The workforces are multi-national which gives employees the opportunity to mix with different cultures and also means that the growers have plenty of experience employing overseas travellers.

Application Procedure: Please see www.fruitfuljobs.com or call 01989 500 130.

www.seasonal-jobs.com

Job(s) Available: Seasonal jobs, cruise ships and yachts, sports jobs, ski resort and winter jobs, gap years, hospitality and leisure.

Duration: *Summer jobs:* from April to October. *Cruise ships and yachts:* available year round. Varied contracts available. *Winter jobs:* November to April. Football, rugby, cricket, tennis, golf and other sports jobs all year round.

Working Hours: *Summer jobs:* usually work a 6 day week. *Ski resort and winter jobs:* to work a 6 day week.

Pay: *Summer jobs:* start at £50 per week. *Cruise ships and yachts:* from £500 a month. *Ski resort and winter jobs:* start at £50 per week. Sports jobs from £100 per week.

Company Description: A seasonal recruitment website.

Job Description: Positions are available in the UK and Ireland, across Europe and around the globe. *Summer jobs:* available in beach resorts, camp sites, activity centres, lake and mountain regions and on barges and flotillas. Include positions as instructors; nannies; couriers; chefs; bar and hotel staff. *Ski resort and winter jobs:* include work in chalets; hotels; bars; ski and snowboard hire; and retail shops. There are also positions available for ski technicians; ski instructors; reps; ski guides; nannies; resort administrators; and accounts, sales, resort and area managers.

Requirements: Minimum age 18.

Accommodation: *Summer jobs:* accommodation and transport provided. *Ski resort and winter jobs:* ski pass, transport to resort and accommodation/food provided.

Additional Information: The website also includes gap year job ideas for around the globe, from voluntary to TEFL, in addition to useful information and links on gap year activities. Other jobs on offer include hotel, restaurant and bar work; theme park jobs; TEFL and fruit picking.

Application Procedure: For further details see www.seasonal-jobs.com.

www.sportingjobs.net

Job(s) Available: Coaches, events and match day staff, sports staff for professional clubs, governing bodies, local clubs and other sporting organisations, stewards.

Duration: Varied contracts available including year-round, temporary, part-time, full-time and internships.

Pay: From £100 per week.

Company Description: A network of websites specialising in jobs in sport including rugby, football (soccer), golf, cricket, hockey, tennis, equine and motorsports.

Job Description: Positions are available in the UK, Ireland, across Europe and around the globe. Most common jobs are for football, rugby, tennis and cricket coaches.

Requirements: Minimum age 18.

Application Procedure: For further details see www.sportingjobs.net.

Au pair, home help and paying guest agencies

Among the types of job to be found in this category are positions for **au pairs**, **mother's helps**, **playscheme leaders** and **paying guests**.

Playschemes: Most local authorities organise playschemes for children during the summer holidays, as a cheaper alternative to private childcare. Throughout the country dozens of playleaders and assistants are needed to run activities for children of all ages. Cash limits mean that some councils ask specifically for volunteers. Councils will usually advertise in local newspapers a few months before the end of the school term, or you can contact their education or leisure departments to find out what they will be offering.

Domestic work: Anyone preferring closer contact with children should consider working in a family as a mother's help or (for applicants from overseas) as an au pair. This work usually requires some experience and involves light housework and looking after children. Mother's helps and au pairs work to assist the mother, not replace her as a nanny might, and therefore qualifications are not usually necessary. There are many agencies in the UK which specialise in placing home helps. If you prefer to find work independently, job advertisements appear in *The Lady* magazine and occasionally in *Horse and Hound*, both available from newsagents.

A2Z Aupairs

Job(s) Available: Au pairs, au pair plus, mother's helps.
Duration: Required in May/June/July for up to 3 months.
Working Hours: To work 25–40 hours per week.
Pay: Pocket money of £70–£200 per week.

> **Head Office:** Catwell House, Catwell, Williton, Taunton TA4 4PF
> ☎ 01984 632422
> ✆ enquiries@a2zaupairs.com
> 🖥 www.a2zaupairs.com

Job Description: Working with children and covering domestic duties.
Requirements: Minimum age 18.
Accommodation: Provided.
Application Procedure: By post to Rebecca Haworth-Wood at the above address or via the above website.

Abbey Au Pairs

Job(s) Available: Au pair placements.
Duration: Minimum period of work 2 months. Positions are available all year round.
Working Hours: 2–3 evenings per week babysitting and 25 hour week.
Pay: £65 per week.

> **Head Office:** 55 Howard Rd, Queens Park, Bournemouth BH8 9EA
> ☎ 01202 549549
> ✆ abbeyaupairs@aol.com
> 🖥 www.abbey/aupairs.co.uk

Company Description: Established in 1988, the agency places girls with families mainly in Dorset. Regular coffee mornings are held and advice is given on language classes and activities.
Job Description: Normal housework and childcare duties.
Accommodation: Full board and lodging available.
Application Procedure: By post at any time to Mrs Ursula Foyle at the above address.

Angels International Au Pairs

Job(s) Available: Au pairs.
Duration: Placements can be anywhere in length from 3 months to 2 years.
Working Hours: To work 25–40 hours per week.
Pay: Pocket money between £55–£150 per week.
Company Description: An au pair agency specialising in placements within the UK and Europe. Angels International offers full support for both families and au pairs.
Requirements: Childcare experience necessary. Applicants from abroad pay no fees; applicants wishing to go abroad pay £100 in fees.
Application Procedure: To apply, email the above address or via the website.

Head Office: Bristol & West House, Post Office Road, Bournemouth, Dorset BH1 1BL
☎ 01202 313653
✉ earnot@btinternet.com
🖥 www.aupair1.com

Au Pair Connections

Job(s) Available: Au pairs and mother's helps (300).
Duration: Minimum period of work 6 weeks. Placements available all year round.
Working Hours: 25 hours per week.
Pay: Approximately £80 per week.
Cost: £50 for outgoing aupairs.
Company Description: An au pair agency operating in southern England since 1986.
Requirements: Must have a minimum of 2 years of childcare experience. Minimum age 18.
Accommodation: Available free of charge.
Additional Information: There is a big demand from mainland Europe during the summer vacation for au pairs.
Application Procedure: By post from January to mid-June to Denise Blighe at the above address. Note that all applicants must enclose either an international reply coupon or an s.a.e.

Head Office: 39 Tamarisk Road, Hedge End, Hampshire SO30 4TN
☎ 01489 780438
✉ apconnect@ntlworld.com
🖥 www.aupairconnections.co.uk

County Nannies (incorporating Au Pair International and The Nanny Agency)

Job(s) Available: Au pairs, au pair plus.
Duration: Placements in the UK throughout the year. Minimum stay 6–12 months, but summer stays of 2–3 months also available.
Working Hours: *Au pair:* 25 hours per week. *Au pair plus:* up to 37 hours per week.
Pay: *Au pair:* pocket money is £60–£65 per week. *Au pair plus:* £80 per week.
Job Description: European au pairs placed in the UK. The families in the UK are mostly in London, London suburbs and the southern counties and south coast.
Requirements: Applicants should be aged 17–27 years old, with some childcare experience and childcare references. All nationalities that are within the British au pair scheme can be accepted. Male applicants can also be placed.
Additional Information: County Nannies also provides fully qualified nannies, maternity nurses and mother's helps. County Nannies covers Kent, London, south-east England and the home counties.
Application Procedure: By post or email to Benedicte Speed, managing director. Include 2 to 3 childcare references, 2 character references, police check and medical certificate with application. Personal interview held wherever possible for candidates in the UK.

Head Office: Cherry Gardens, Nouds Lane, Lynsted, Kent ME9 0ES
☎ 01795 522544 (au pair division)
✉ info@countynannies.co.uk
🖥 www.countynannies.co.uk

Euro Pair Agency

Job(s) Available: Au pairs (100+).
Duration: Minimum period of work 6 months in the UK, 2 months for summer positions in France.
Working Hours: 5 hours per day, 5 days a week.
Pay: £70 per week.

> **Head Office:** 28 Derwent Avenue, Pinner, Middlesex HA5 4QJ
> ☎ 020 8421 2100
> ✆ info@europair.net
> 🖳 www.euro-pair.co.uk

Company Description: The agency supplies French-speaking au pairs to British families in Great Britain and British au pairs to families in France. Takes great care in the selection of posts available and has a back-up service if things do not work out.
Requirements: Minimum age 18. Childcare experience and driving licence helpful.
Accommodation: Live-in positions.
Application Procedure: By email or phone.

Jolaine Au Pair & Domestic Agency

Job(s) Available: Au pair/plus and mother's help.
Duration: Minimum stay is 6 months. Shorter stay for summer months only. Positions in the UK throughout the year.
Pay: *Au pair:* £70 per week. *Au pair plus:* £90 per week. *Mother's help:* from £120 per week. *General helpers:* £200 per week

> **Head Office:** 18 Escot Way, Barnet, Hertfordshire EN5 3AN
> ☎ 020 8449 1334
> ✆ jolaine@talktalk.net
> 🖳 www.jolaineagency.co.uk

Company Description: Jolaine Agency has been successfully placing applicants in the UK and abroad since 1975 and operates a follow-up system to ensure that all applicants are happy with their stay.
Accommodation: Available for individuals or groups of any size. Discounts given to groups and extended stays. Visits, excursions, activities and classes arranged on request.
Additional Information: Also arranges paying guest family stays in the London suburbs throughout the year, from £100 per week. Also place applicants in Italy and Spain as au pair and mother's help, both short and long term contracts.
Application Procedure: For further information telephone, write or preferably email with your details to the above address.

Nanny & Aupair Connection

Job(s) Available: Au pairs, au pair plus, mother's helps, foreign housekeepers, nannies.
Duration: From 2 months to 2 years.
Working Hours: *Au pairs:* up to 5 hours per day with 2 days off per week. *Au pair plus:* 35 hours per week plus babysitting 2–3 evenings a week. 2 days free each week. *Nannies:* 8–9 hours per day.

> **Head Office:** 435 Chorley New Road, Horwich, Bolton BL6 6EJ
> ☎ 0845 166 22 16
> ✆ info@aupairs-nannies.co.uk
> 🖳 www.aupairs-nannies.co.uk

Pay: *Au pair:* £65 per week. *Au pair:* £80 per week. *Mother's helps:* £150 per week. *Foreign housekeepers:* £200 per week. *Nannies:* £350 per week.
Company Description: Specialist au pairs agency, established since 1989, with opportunities to work with families in Britain and learn languages at a local college or university.
Requirements: All positions open for girls and boys aged 17–27 years old. *Au pair plus:* EC Nationals only. *Nannies:* minimum age 18; must have NNEB qualification or similar.
Accommodation: *Au pairs:* own room and meals provided. *Au pair plus:* room and meals provided.

Additional Information: *Au pairs:* opportunity to have English classes. *Au pair plus:* can sometimes attend English classes.

Application Procedure: Applications welcome from all EC Nationals and Andorra, Bosnia-Herzegovina, Croatia, Cyprus, Faroe Islands, Greenland, Liechtenstein, Macedonia, Malta, Monaco, San Marino, Slovenia, Switzerland and Turkey.

UK Nannies and Au Pairs

Job(s) Available: Au pairs and nannies.
Duration: From 1 month to 2 years.
Working Hours: Between 25 and 60 hours per week.
Pay: £100–£400 per week; overtime is paid. Applicants are not charged any fees.

Head Office: 19, The Severals,
Newmarket CB8 7YW
☎ 01638 560812
✆ help@uknanniesandaupairs.com
🖥 www.uknanniesandaupairs.com

Company Description: Support for the au pair/nanny is offered by the company.
Job Description: Live-in and live-out au pair, nanny and domestic placements in the UK, Ireland, Europe and the USA.
Requirements: Minimum age 18.
Application Procedure: Apply via the website.

PART 2: EUROPE

ORGANISATIONS WITH VACANCIES ACROSS EUROPE

General

Jobcentre Plus

Company Description: Jobcentre Plus handles vacancies for work in the UK and overseas, which can be accessed through the job search facility on the Jobcentre Plus website, or via touch-point screens called Jobpoints, available in all Jobcentre Plus offices and Jobcentres, or by calling Jobseeker Direct on 0845 606 0234. Jobcentre Plus also publishes a series of fact sheets for each of the EEA countries.

> **Head Office:** International Jobsearch Advice Team, Unit 3 Innovation Way, Europarc, Grimsby, North East Lincolnshire DN37 9TT
> 🖳 www.jobcentreplus.gov.uk

Additional Information: EURES Website (www.eures-jobs.com): as part of the European Employment Services (EURES) network, Jobcentre Plus receives new jobs from Europe on a daily basis. To find out more about the EURES network and to get information about living and working in EEA countries visit the EURES job mobility portal www.europa.eu.int/eures. This site has a job bank of vacancies based in Europe and a facility to post CVs so that employers throughout Europe may view them.

Application Procedure: Check website, or call 0845 606 0234 or visit your nearest Jobcentre Plus office or Jobcentre.

InterExchange

Job(s) Available: Cultural exchange programmes including work and travel, camp USA, work abroad, career traning and language school programmes within the USA and around the world. In the USA they offer J-1 Visa programs for au pair, seasonal work, internship, camp counselor and staff positions.

> **Head Office:** 161 Sixth Avenue, New York, NY 10013, USA
> ☎ +1 212 924 0446
> 🖰 info@interexchange.org
> 🖳 www.interexchange.org

InterExchange also offers working abroad placements for US residents to travel to Australia, Costa Rica, France, Germany, Chile, China, India, Namibia, Netherlands, South Africa, Spain, New Zealand and Thailand. InterExchange also offer H-2B Visa programmes for seasonal work.

Company Description: InterExchange is a non-profit organisation dedicated to promoting cultural awareness.

Additional Information: Most InterExchange programmes include placements.

Application Procedure: For further details contact InterExchange at the above address.

Boats

European Waterways

Job(s) Available: Master chefs, deckhand mechanics, tour guides, stewards/stewardesses.

Duration: Period of work is from April to October.

Pay: *Master chefs:* £1,200–£1,400 per month. *Deckhand mechanics:* £850 per month. *Tour guides:* £850 per month. *Stewards/stewardesses:* £800 per month.

Head Office: 35 Wharf Road, Wraysbury, Staines, Middlesex TW19 5JQ, UK
sales@gobarging.com
www.gobarging.com

Company Description: Owners and operators of luxury hotel barges cruising rivers and canals in England, Scotland and France.

Job Description: *Master chefs:* preparing all meals on board for between 8 and 12 guests and crew. *Deckhand mechanics:* assisting captain in maintenance of vessel, bicycles, some tour guiding. *Stewards/stewardesses:* duties include cleaning, ironing and waiting on.

Requirements: A knowledge of French is useful for all positions in France. *Master chefs:* experience in hospitality preferred and applicants must hold a driving licence. Non-smokers. *Deckhand mechanics:* must have a driving licence and some mechanical experience. *Tour guides:* full, clean driving licence required and an interest in culture and history. Some experience in hospitality is also necessary. *Stewards/stewardesses:* must be hard working and have some experience in hospitality.

Accommodation: All positions include on-board accommodation, meals and uniform.

Application Procedure: Apply by February sending a CV and photo to the above address or via email.

Hotel work and catering

Scott Dunn

Job(s) Available: Beauty therapists (5), chalet and villa chefs/cooks (33), chalet and villa hosts (35), drivers/maintenance people (15), nannies (20), resort managers (12).

Duration: Work is available during the winter and summer season. *Resort managers:* summer only. *Drivers/maintenance people:* winter only.

Head Office: Fovant Mews, 12 Noyna Rd, London SW17 7PH, UK
020 8682 5005
recruitment@scottdunn.com
www.scottdunn.com

Working Hours: To be discussed at interview.

Pay: To be discussed at interview.

Company Description: A small, professional company, which provides villas and chalets in locations all over Europe. Scott Dunn expect the attitude that 'nothing is too much trouble' from their teams. Doing a season for Scott Dunn is hard work but also good fun and they offer a competitive package to the right applicants.

Job Description: *Beauty therapists:* required to provide mobile beauty services to guests. *Chalet and villa chefs/cooks:* required to plan the menu and cook to a very high standard for the clients in their exclusive villas and chalets. *Drivers/maintenance people:* required to transport people and goods within resort, to manage and maintain all Scott Dunn properties and equipment and to carry out any repairs or maintenance as and when necessary. *Nannies:* required to care for the younger guests. *Resort managers:* required to run all aspects of the resort operations in Moilets, France required to assist the chef, look after the guests and maintain a high level of service.

Requirements: Knowledge of French, Spanish, Italian or Portuguese is useful but not mandatory. *Beauty therapists:* applicants must have a recognised qualification, at least one year's experience and be organised, flexible and proactive. *Chalet and villa chefs/cooks:* applicants should be organised and outgoing and must have completed a 6-month cooking course, or have extensive experience and flair. *Chalet and villa hosts:* no formal qualifications necessary, although hospitality experience is essential. Applicants must be outgoing, organised and have excellent customer service skills. *Drivers/maintenance people:* applicants must be flexible and have a practical mind. Must have a clean driving licence and/or a qualification in plumbing, carpentry or electrical matters. Previous hospitality experience is desirable. *Nannies:* must have a recognised childcare qualification, at least one year's childcare experience and be organised, confident and outgoing. If applying for the summer, must be a confident swimmer. *Resort managers:* applicants must have previous management and hospitality experience, as well as fluency in the local language (French for summer positions). Bookkeeping and computer literacy are essential.

Accommodation: Board and accommodation are provided free of charge.

Application Procedure: For summer positions apply in January, or for winter positions apply from June. Application forms are available to download from the above website. Email the form and a CV to the above email address.

Sports, couriers and camping

Acorn Adventure

Job(s) Available: Managers, qualified and non-qualified activity instructors, village managers (site reps), catering staff and support staff. 300 seasonal staff positions available.

Duration: Seasonal work available from April until September. Shorter contracts also available.

Pay: Seasonal rates of pay, plus supplements subject to position.

Head Office: Acorn House, Prospect Road, Halesowen, West Midlands B62 8DU, UK
☎ 0121 504 2066
✆ jobs@acornadventure.co.uk
💻 www.acorn-jobs.co.uk

Company Description: Acorn Adventure is one of the UK's leading providers of outdoor adventure activity camps for schools, youth groups and families. They operate 8 activity camps in the Lake District, the Brecon Beacons and France.

Job Description: *Managers:* centre admin, catering, activity and maintenance. *Activity instructors:* working directly with groups of children and families providing daily multi-activity sessions such as sailing, kayaking, canoeing, climbing and abseiling. *Centre support roles:* catering, maintenance, cleaning, driving and general campsite work.

Accommodation: Pay includes free tented accommodation and all meals overseas.

Application Procedure: For further information go to www.acorn-jobs.co.uk or contact the recruitment department on the above email address or telephone number for a full information pack.

Alan Rogers Guides Ltd

Job(s) Available: Campsite inspectors.
Duration: From May to September.
Pay: An inspection fee and expenses are paid.
Company Description: Alan Rogers Guides are one of Britain's leading camping and caravanning guides.
Requirements: Must have a thorough knowledge and experience of camping and/or caravanning in Europe. Knowledge of a foreign language would be useful.

Head Office: Spelmonden Old Oast, Spelmonden Road, Goudhurst, Kent TN17 1HE, UK
☎ 01580 214000
✆ contact@alanrogers.com
💻 www.alanrogers.com

145

Accommodation: Must have own caravan or motorhome.

Application Procedure: Applications should be made to the campsites director at the above address.

American Council for International Studies (ACIS)

Job(s) Available: Tour managers (100).

Duration: Busiest periods are March–April and June–July. Tour managers for both short and long periods are needed. Minimum period of work 10 days.

Working Hours: Flexible.

Pay: Dependent on experience. Generous tips.

> **Head Office:** 38 Queen's Gate, London SW7 5HR, UK
> ☎ 020 7590 7474
> ✉ tm_dept@acis.com
> 🖥 www.acis.com

Company Description: ACIS has been offering quality educational travel for over 30 years. Tour managers are vital to the success of the company, and are given unequalled training and support.

Job Description: Tour managers to lead American high school teachers and students on educational trips through Europe. Tour managers meet groups on arrival, travel with them, act as commentators and guides, keep accounts, direct bus drivers, troubleshoot etc.

Requirements: Fluency in French, Italian, German or Spanish is essential. Minimum age 21. Applicants must either have or be studying for a university degree.

Accommodation: Provided with the groups in 3 or 4-star hotels.

Application Procedure: Apply online in November 2010 via the website where there is an application form.

Bombard Balloon Adventures

Job(s) Available: Ground crew (12).

Duration: During the summer season (May–October), the team travels to France, Tuscany, Switzerland, Austria, and to the Swiss Alps in winter (January–February). Period of work by arrangement.

> **Head Office:** 9, Avenue 8 Septembre, 21200 Beaune, France
> ✉ jobs2011@bombardsociety.org
> 🖥 www.bombardsociety.org/jobs

Company Description: Since 1977, Bombard Balloon Adventures has provided complete luxury travel programmes built around hot-air ballooning.

Job Description: Ground crew to assist in preparation and packing of ballooning equipment, driving, and general household chores.

Requirements: Requires a clean driving licence, excellent physical fitness, a cheerful personality, responsible driving skills, the ability to live with others and a neat, clean-cut appearance. Language skills are a plus but not a requirement.

Additional Information: Complete job description can be found on www.bombardsociety. org/jobs.

Application Procedure: Applicants should send a CV including height, weight and nationality; a scanned ID photo and copy of driving licence; and dates of availability to Michael Lincicome by email (preferred) at the address above. Please include the letters 'SRO' in the subject line of inquiries.

Canvas Holidays

Job(s) Available: Campsite courier, children's courier.

Duration: Full season positions start in March, April or May and end in September/October. Minimum period of work 6 weeks.

Pay: Package includes competitive salary.

Head Office: Canvas Holidays Recruitment & Welfare, East Port House, Dunfermline KY12 7JG, UK
☎ 01383 629012
📧 campingrecruitment@canvasholidays.com
🖥 www.canvasholidaysrecriutment.com

Company Description: Canvas Holidays provide luxury mobile home and tent holidays at over 100 campsites throughout Europe.

Job Description: *Campsite courier:* involves cleaning accommodation, welcoming families to the site and showing them to their accommodation. Visiting customers, providing local information and basic maintenance are very important parts of the job. *Children's courier:* needed to work at Hoopi's Club.

Requirements: Minimum age 18. *Children's courier:* applicants must have formal experience of working with children. Children's couriers should be energetic, enthusiastic and have good communication skills. A tent is provided as a Club venue and for equipment storage; this has to be kept safe, clean and tidy. Visiting new arrivals on site is an important and fun part of the job. Children's couriers also help with other campsite duties as needed. All staff receive comprehensive training.

Accommodation: Package includes tent accommodation, medical insurance, uniform and a contribution to return travel from a UK port of entry.

Application Procedure: Please call the recruitment department for more information and an application form, or apply online at www.canvasholidaysrecruitment.com.

Club Europe Holidays Ltd

Job(s) Available: Concert tour manager.

Duration: Tour length varies from 3 to 8 days.

Pay: Increases with experience but starts at £60 per day.

Head Office: Fairway House, 53 Dartmouth Road, London SE23 3HN, UK
☎ 020 8699 7788
📧 fiona.j@club-europe.co.uk or travel@club-europe.co.uk
🖥 www.club-europe.co.uk

Company Description: Club Europe Holidays employ concert tour managers on a freelance basis, to accompany school and youth ensembles on tour in Europe. The nature of their business means that most of the work is on offer during the spring and summer school holidays, making the positions ideal for students and teachers. Tours are to France, Germany, Italy, Austria, Spain, Holland and Belgium.

Job Description: Duties include reconfirming booked excursions and concerts; introducing the group at the venues; interpreting and communicating the client's needs with regards to accommodation and local agents; coordinating any minor alterations to the itinerary with the coach drivers; and accompanying the group at all times including all concerts and excursions.

Requirements: Friendly, confident staff with excellent organisational and communication skills. Applicants should be fluent in English and at least one other European language.

Accommodation: Provided with the same board and accommodation as the client.

Application Procedure: Applications are ongoing.

Crystal Finest

Job(s) Available: Resort representatives, chalet chefs, chalet hosts, childcare, hotel hosts, and for the winter ski season.

Duration: November–April.

Company Description: Crystal Finest is part of TUI UK, and is one of the top ski specialists in the UK. They offer a selection of catered chalet and hotel holidays on their winter ski programme featured in 140 resorts worldwide.

Head Office: Crystal Ski Recruitment, King's Place, 12–42 Wood Street, Kingston-upon-thames, Surrey KT1 1JY, UK
☎ 020 8541 2223
✆ sla.recruitment@tuiski.com
🖥 www.jobsinwinter.co.uk/crystal

Requirements: Representatives need to be independent and have a thorough understanding of customer requirements, be able to ski or snowboard at solid intermediate level or above and be able to ski/ride confidently on Black and Red runs. They must also have strong group leadership skills. Chalet hosts need to be customer focused with excellent catering and housekeeping skills. Childcare requires qualifications and a passion for working with children.

Application Procedure: Apply online at www.jobsinwinter.co.uk/crystal.

Esprit Holidays Ltd

Job(s) Available: Hotel/chalets assistants, managers, child carers and chefs/cooks.

Duration: All staff must be available from mid-June to mid-September.

Pay: Weekly wage and living package.

Company Description: Esprit Family Adventures

Head Office: 185 Fleet Road, Fleet, Hants GU51 3BL, UK
☎ 01252 618318
✆ recruitment@esprit-holidays.co.uk
🖥 www.esprit-holidays.co.uk

run alpine holidays in France, Switzerland and Austria, for families in catered chalets and hotels providing childcare in nurseries and alpine adventure clubs for children aged 4 months to 12 years old.

Job Description: Ideal for anyone who has an interest in alpine activities, ie mountain walking and biking, white-water rafting etc. All staff have to assist with chalet cleaning, babysitting and hosting guests. Staff to run chalet hotels and chalets. *Nannies:* needed to run Esprit Nurseries and Alpies Club and required to take care of babies and toddlers in Esprit's nurseries. *Alpies rangers:* required to run adventure activity clubs for children aged 3–12 years.

Requirements: All staff must be EU passport holders. Staff need to have friendly and outgoing personalities and previous experience. *Manager:* good command of spoken French or German, hospitality and customer service experience, management and supervisory skills and a full, clean driving licence. *Nannies:* dedicated, fun-loving and enthusiastic. Should have a DCE NNEB, NVQ3, BTEC or NVQ level 3. *Alpies rangers:* experience as play scheme leaders, children's sports coaches or as a trained teacher. Should have a mature and fun-loving personality.

Accommodation: Food and accommodation, uniform, medical insurance, and transport provided.

Application Procedure: Further information can be obtained regarding vacancies on the website or by calling 01252 618318. Applications available on the website above.

Eurocamp

Job(s) Available: Campsite courier, children's courier, courier team leaders, children's courier team leaders, *montage/demontage*.

Duration: *Campsite courier:* applicants should be available to work from March/April to September/ October or mid-July to mid-September. *Children's courier:* applicants should be available from early May to September or June to September. *Courier team leaders:* applicants should be available from April to mid-September. *Children's courier team leaders:* applicants should be available from early May until September. *Montage/demontage:* applicants should be available from February to May or August to October.

Head Office: Overseas Recruitment and Training Department, Holidaybreak Hartford Manor, Greenbank Lane, Northwich CW8 1HW, UK
☎ 01606 787525
🖳 www.holidaybreakjobs.com/camping

Pay: Competitive salary, comprehensive training, return travel to and from an agreed meeting point, accommodation, medical and luggage insurance and uniform.

Company Description: Part of the Holidaybreak Camping Group Eurocamp is a leading tour operator in self-drive camping and mobile home holidays in Europe. Offers customers a wide range of holiday accommodation on over 200 premier campsites. Each year the company seeks to recruit enthusiastic people to work the summer season in a variety of roles.

Job Description: *Campsite courier:* a courier's responsibility begins by ensuring that the customer's accommodation is both inviting and cleaned to the highest of standards. Courier will welcome new arrivals, be the customers' main point of contact and provide local and general information, give assistance and act as interpreter if required. Part of the role will involve helping out with minor repairs to accommodation and equipment and will also involve basic administration and accounts. *Children's courier:* responsible for planning and delivering a fun, safe, daily activity programme to customers' children. The age of the children attending the club will range from 4 to 12 years old. *Courier team leaders:* must be able to deliver first-class customer service and organise the daily workload of the courier team. Role also includes all the duties of a campsite courier and you will be expected to lead by example. There are a variety of team leader roles available, dependent on team size; courier in charge, senior courier and site manager. *Children's courier team leaders:* role will involve the management, motivation and development of the children's couriers to ensure they provide a varied range of quality activities. Your role includes all the duties of a children's courier. *Montage/ demontage: montage* and *demontage* assistants are employed to either help set up for the season or close down at the end of the season. This involves putting up or taking down tents, moving/distributing equipment and cleaning/preparing accommodation.

Requirements: Applicants must hold a UK/EU passport. A good working knowledge of the English language and basic numeracy are also required. Applicants must also have a UK or Irish bank account, address and a National Insurance number. *Campsite courier:* you should have lots of energy, basic common sense and a genuine desire to help people. *Children's courier:* previous childcare experience is essential. Successful candidates will be asked to apply for an Enhanced Disclosure. *Courier team leaders:* you must have previous experience of leading a team. *Children's courier team leaders:* previous experience with children and leading a team necessary. The successful candidate will be asked to apply for an Enhanced Disclosure. *Montage/demontage:* previous experience of physical and repetitive work.

Accommodation: Provided.

Application Procedure: Applicants should apply online at www.holidaybreakjobs.com/ camping or telephone 01606 787525 for an application pack.

Freewheel Holidays

Job(s) Available: Freewheel hosts.

Duration: Mid-May to mid-September. Minimum period of work 4 weeks.

Working Hours: Approximately 30–35 hours per week, approximately 6 days a week (depending on guest numbers).

Pay: £200 per week.

> **Head Office:** 11, de Montfort Street, Leicester LE1 7GE, UK
> ☎ 01162 558417
> info@freewheelholidays.com
> www.freewheelholidays.com

Company Description: Freewheel Holidays is a successful independent tour operator whose guests enjoy cycling through wonderful landscapes in Austria, Holland, Ireland, Italy, Sardinia, Sicily and Spain, experiencing sights, sounds and cultures of different regions (little or no traffic, hills going down not up!) – while their hosts manage the luggage and logistics.

Job Description: Freewheel are looking for mature, outgoing, resourceful people with a full driving licence and knowledge of bicycle maintenance to be Freewheel hosts. Hosts provide information and support to guests, meet them at airports and stations, transfer luggage and liaise with hotels.

Requirements: All applicants must speak either native or fluent English as well as another appropriate language. Applicants should possess a full driver's licence and first aid qualification and have knowledge of bicycle maintenance. Must be aged 21 or over.

Accommodation: Accommodation and training provided free of charge.

Application Procedure: Apply online at www.freewheelholidays.com/careers.

Halsbury Travel

Job(s) Available: Couriers, group leaders and tour guides required for coach and air groups travelling to western European destinations (80).

Duration: University holiday periods and term time year round. Tours usually last around 1–2 weeks. Minimum period of work 1 week.

Working Hours: 35 hours per week.

Pay: £200 per week.

> **Head Office:** 35 Churchill Park, Nottingham NG4 2HF, UK
> ☎ 0115 940 4303
> workexperience@halsbury.com
> www.halsbury.com

Company Description: Halsbury Travel provide group and school tours to western Europe and worldwide. They arrange sports tours, music tours, study tours, ski tours, and tours for any academic theme including history, geography, media, travel and tourism, French, German, Spanish and Italian.

Requirements: Minimum age 21. Must speak English and either French, German, Italian or Spanish.

Accommodation: Half-board hotel accommodation, travel insurance and transportation all supplied.

Application Procedure: Applications taken in September, January and April. Apply to Meg Zanker at meg@halsbury.com. EU applicants with fluent English and a western European language are welcome to apply.

Halsbury Travel

Job(s) Available: Group leaders (100), language tutors (20), couriers (50), ski reps (10) required for coach and air groups travelling to western European destinations.

Head Office: 35 Churchill Park, Nottingham NG4 2HF, UK
☎ 0115 9404303
✎ workexperience@halsbury.com
🖳 www.halsbury.com

Duration: University holiday periods and term time year round. Tours usually last around 1-2 weeks. Minimum period of work 1 week.

Working Hours: 8 hours per day, 6 days a week. *Language tutors:* 3-4 hours work a day.

Pay: *Group leaders:* £200 per week. *Language tutors:* pay on application. *Couriers:* £200 per week. *Ski reps:* £200 per week. Discount offered on ski-pass. (Please note that it is not a ski-ing holiday! Applicants should be customer focused.)

Company Description: Halsbury Travel is an ABTA/ATOL Bonded Tour Operator, specialising in school group, European and worldwide tours. Established in 1986, they are one of the leading UK student group tour operators.

Job Description: *Group leaders:* required to work with touring groups in France, Germany or Spain. *Language tutors:* required to work with touring groups in France, Germany and Spain. *Couriers:* required to accompany history, geography, art, business studies, sports, travel and leisure/tourism groups. *Ski reps:* required to accompany ski groups to French resorts, liaise with local partners, organise evening activities or assist the groups as required.

Requirements: All applicants should be fluent in the language or a native of the country they wish to work in.

Accommodation: Accommodation and meals included in pay. *Ski reps:* ski equipment included.

Application Procedure: Applications for skiing related jobs are taken from July to December and should be directed to audrey@halsbury.com. All other applicants should be sent to Meg Zanker at meg@halsbury.com.

Headwater Holidays

Job(s) Available: Overseas representatives, canoeing instructors, walking guides.

Head Office: The Old School House, Chester Road, Castle, Northwich, Cheshire CW8 1LE, UK
☎ 01606 720006
✎ mike.wheeler@headwater.com
🖳 www.headwater.com

Duration: Staff required for full season from April to October.

Working Hours: To work hours as required. Must be on call 24 hours a day.

Pay: From £140 per week.

Company Description: Headwater offers relaxed discovery and adventure holidays. Headwater guides and information packs help clients make their own discoveries off the beaten track.

Job Description: *Overseas representatives:* to work in France, Italy, Spain and Austria. Duties include meeting clients at airports and stations, supervising local transportation for them and their luggage, hotel and client liaison, bike maintenance and on-the-spot problem solving. *Canoeing instructors:* duties as for overseas representatives but also include giving canoe instruction. *Walking guides:* to work in France, Spain and Italy.

Requirements: *Overseas representatives:* good, working knowledge of the language and full, clean driving licence required. Organisational skills, resourcefulness and cheerfulness essential. *Walking guides:* must have experience leading and interacting with small groups and be confident working independently. A good working knowledge of the language

EUROPE

SPORTS, COURIERS AND CAMPING

is useful. Full, clean driving licence and 3 years' driving experience is required in all locations except for Greece.

Accommodation: Provided. Return travel to country of work is also provided.

Application Procedure: Further information and an online application form can be found on the website, or contact Mike Wheeler, operations manager, on the above email address.

Inghams Travel

Job(s) Available: Representatives (approximately 160). Extensive Ski Programme in North America and Europe for Overseas Representatives and Chalet Staff (Europe only).

Duration: From May to September. From December to April (Europe only).

Working Hours: 6 days a week.

Pay: £900–£1,300 per month including commission.

> **Head Office:** 10–18 Putney Hill, London SW15 6AX, UK
> ☎ 020 8780 4400
> ⌂ RepsRecruitment@inghams.co.uk
> 🖳 www.inghams.co.uk

Company Description: Inghams Travel is the largest independent operator of lakes and mountains holidays in the UK with an excellent reputation built up over the last 75 years. They offer quality lake and mountain holidays to Europe and aim to attract the best staff in the industry and the offered salaries and conditions of employment reflect this policy.

Job Description: Representatives for client service, administration, sales, guiding of excursions and general problem solving.

Requirements: Knowledge of French, German, Italian or Spanish is required. Applicants must be friendly, outgoing and flexible team players with enthusiasm and a good sense of humour. They must also be customer care-orientated and have a liking for the country and culture.

Accommodation: Accommodation provided, plus some meals are provided.

Application Procedure: Applications all year round to the above address.

Sport & Educational Travel LTD

Job(s) Available: Couriers.

Duration: All durations of visits are organised from day trips to week-long stays.

Pay: From £120 for a day trip. Longer trips: £110 for first day and £65 for every subsequent day.

> **Head Office:** 47 Church Lane, Gorleston, Great Yarmouth, Norfolk NR31 7BG, UK
> ☎ 01493 665965
> ⌂ info@set-uk.com
> 🖳 www.set-uk.com

Company Description: Sport & Educational Travel Ltd was established in 1991 and organises group travel for school parties consisting of students aged 11–17 years old. Trips are organised to France, Belgium, Germany and Spain, and range from an introduction to northern France and visits to Paris (including Disneyland) to First and Second World War tours.

Job Description: Couriers accompany groups, provide factual information during the trip in both English and the local language and manage checking-in procedures, visits and general timings throughout the visit.

Requirements: Must speak French or German fluently. Knowledge of the area would be an advantage but is not essential as full training is given.

Accommodation: For overnight visits or longer, accommodation and meals are provided on the same basis as the groups accompanied.

Application Procedure: Applications for this post to Mrs M Savage, at the above email address.

STG Travel

Job(s) Available: Representatives to work with school groups on cookery, language or sports tours in France, Germany, Italy and Spain.

Duration: Positions are available for periods varying from 2 days to 1 week between February and October.

Pay: £35 per day.

Head Office: 1 Jubilee Street, Brighton, East Sussex BN1 1GE, UK
☎ 01273 648255
✆ recruitment@equity.co.uk
🖥 www.equityski.co.uk/employment

Company Description: STG Travel is part of the Educational Travel Group and is one of the leading tour operators. STG are made up of Equity, Pavilion, STS, Skiplan and UK connections.

Job Description: Reps have a briefing from the Brighton office before travelling and a day in resort to set up prior to the group's arrival. Duties include liaising between the group, hotelier and coach driver; organisation of pre-booked, course-related excursions and interviews; translating during demonstrations and helping pupils with course-related work.

Requirements: Applicants must be fluent in French, German, Italian or Spanish, well organised and able to work on their own initiative. They must be able to relate to children and will ideally have some experience of working with school groups or in a public service industry. A driving licence is required for most tours.

Accommodation: Full board, accommodation, travel expenses, insurance and uniform provided.

Additional Information: We also have winter positions, both full and peak season.

Application Procedure: By post with a CV and a covering letter to Sue Lloyd at the above address.

Tracks Travel Ltd

Job(s) Available: Cooks, drivers and tour managers.

Duration: Work is available throughout the year, but all applicants should be prepared to work for a minimum of 2 full seasons.

Head Office: The Flots, Brookland, Romney Marsh, Kent TN29 9TG, UK
☎ 0845 1300 936
✆ info@tracks-travel.com
🖥 www.tracks-travel.com

Working Hours: Hours vary, depending on the nature of the tour.

Pay: To be confirmed.

Company Description: Tracks Travel is a coach tour operator operating throughout the UK and Europe.

Requirements: Knowledge of languages other than English is not required. *Drivers:* valid UK PCV licence required. *Tour managers:* must be good with a microphone, and confident in dealing with large groups. *Cooks:* must be able to cook for large groups. Relevant experience preferred.

Accommodation: Board and accommodation are available.

Application Procedure: Applications should be made to the above address at any time of year.

Venue Holidays

Job(s) Available: Supervisors, campsite representatives, *montage/demontage* assistants.

Duration: *Supervisors:* required from March to October. *Campsite representatives:* minimum period of work 2 months; the complete season runs from April to October. *Montage and demontage assistants:* required from March to May and September/October.

Head Office: 1 Norwood Street, Ashford, Kent TN23 1QU, UK
☎ 01233 629950
✆ info@venueholidays.co.uk
🖥 www.venueholidays.co.uk

EUROPE

SPORTS, COURIERS AND CAMPING

Working Hours: To work hours as required.

Pay: Competitive salary paid monthly.

Company Description: Venue Holidays is a family-run independent tour operator offering self-drive family holidays to first class camping resorts in France, Italy and Spain. Offer clients a choice of fully equipped tent or mobile home accommodation with a range of travel, hotel and insurance services. Over 25 years of experience within the camping industry and employ around 40 staff for overseas operation.

Job Description: *Campsite representatives:* duties to include cleaning and maintaining holiday units, welcoming clients and looking after them during their stay, sorting out any problems, and liaising between the campsite's management and the UK office. *Assistants:* jobs include setting up tents, preparing the campsite units for occupation and cleaning accommodation prior to the season. In September/October the process must be done in reverse.

Requirements: *Supervisors:* must possess a clean driver's licence. Minimum age 21. *Campsite representatives* and *assistants:* minimum age 18.

Application Procedure: Apply online at www.venueholidays.co.uk/UK/Jobs/application form.htm.

Village Camps

Job(s) Available: *Spring and autumn residential camps:* outdoor education and specialist instructors. *Summer programmes:* chefs, domestic and kitchen assistants, house counsellors, nurses, receptionists, French/TEFL/German teachers. *Winter season:* domestic and kitchen assistants.

> **Head Office:** Recruitment Office, Rue de la Morache, 1260 Nyon, Switzerland
> ☎ +41 2 2990 9405
> ✎ personnel@villagecamps.com
> 🖥 www.villagecamps.com

Duration: *Outdoor, Education:* April–June (Switzerland and France), August–October (Switzerland). *Summer Camps:* June–August.

Pay: Generous allowance provided, paid in local currency.

Company Description: Village Camps has been organising educational and activity camps for children from all over the globe for over 38 years with a serious commitment to client and staff alike. Camps are in Austria, England, France, Switzerland.

Requirements: Minimum age 21. A second language is desirable. A valid first aid and CPR certificate is required while at camp. *Domestic/kitchen and facilities assistants:* must have relevant experience and/or qualifications.

Accommodation: Room and board, accident and liability insurance and a weekly allowance provided.

Application Procedure: There is no deadline to submit applications but positions are limited. Interviews are by telephone. For information on dates, locations, positions available and to download an application form, visit www.villagecamps.com/personnel/index.html or contact the organisation at the above address.

Voluntary work

ATD Fourth World

Job(s) Available: Work camp and street workshop.

Duration: Take place from July to September. Most last 2 weeks.

Company Description: ATD Fourth World is an international voluntary organisation which adopts a

> **Head Office:** 107 Avenue du General Leclerc, 95480 Pierrelaye, France
> ☎ +33 1 34 30 46 10
> 🖥 www.atd-fourthworld.org

human rights approach to overcome extreme poverty. It supports the effort of very disadvantaged and excluded families in fighting poverty and taking an active role in the community.

Founded in a shanty town on the outskirts of Paris in 1957, it now works in 27 countries on 5 continents.

Job Description: ATD Fourth World organises work camps, street workshops and family stays in the UK and in other European countries. *Work camps:* a combination of manual work in and around ATD's buildings; conversation; and reflection on the lives of families living in poverty. *Street workshops:* bring a festival atmosphere to underprivileged areas. Voluntary artists, craftsmen and others share their skills with the children and their parents. Street workshops take place in the streets of deprived areas and make it possible to break down barriers between people from different cultures and backgrounds. They also encourage freedom of expression and help build confidence.

Accommodation: Participants pay their own travel costs plus a contribution to the cost of food and accommodation.

Application Procedure: For international opportunities please see the website above or contact our summer activities team at the above address.

Bridges for Education Inc

Job(s) Available: Volunteer English teachers. About 100 volunteers are placed each year.

Duration: Volunteers teach for 3 weeks together as a team in the summer.

Cost: $960 for Europe, $990 for China.

Pay: Board and lodging and a modest stipend are provided by the host country.

> **Head Office:** 94 Lamarck Drive, Buffalo, New York, NY 14226, USA
> ☎ +1 716 839 0180
> ⌖ jbc@bridges4edu.org
> 🖳 www.bridges4edu.org

Company Description: The purpose of Bridges for Education (BFE) is to promote tolerance and understanding using English as a bridge. BFE sends Canadian and American volunteer teachers, educated adults and college students to teach conversational English in the summer in eastern and central Europe and China. Since 1994, BFE has organised 86 camps in 10 countries serving 12,000 students from 38 countries. High school students whose parents or teachers are participants may also join a BFE team. BFE is not a religious or ethnic organisation.

Requirements: Those skilled in teaching English as a second language are preferred but teachers who are certified in any area are welcome. American high school students whose parents or teachers are participants may also join a BFE team. The team is prepared in basic ESL prior to departure. Applicants must be in good health.

Accommodation: Receive free room and board while teaching and an additional week of travel within the host country.

Application Procedure: Applications from US or Canadian citizens only should be sent to the above address or made online. Programmes are posted on our website in December and January.

The Disaway Trust

Job(s) Available: Volunteers (about 40).

Duration: 8–14-day periods during the year. The organisation usually arranges 2–3 holidays a year which take place between May and October.

Cost: A £100 deposit is required toward cost of travel, accommodation, board and entertainment.

> **Head Office:** 51 Sunningdale Road, Worthing, West Sussex BN13 2NQ, UK
> ☎ 01903 830796
> ⌖ nicki.sunni@btinternet.com
> 🖳 www.disaway.co.uk

Company Description: The Disaway Trust provides group holidays with physically disabled adults. Disaway Trust relies on helpers to enable them to provide holidays for adults who would otherwise be unable to have a holiday.

Job Description: Volunteers are required to help disabled people on holiday. The holiday venues are in the UK and many other countries.

Requirements: No special qualifications or experience are required. Minimum age 18.

Application Procedure: Apply to Nicki Green for further details including information on dates and locations. The information pack for 2011 will be available mid-January 2011.

EIL Cultural Learning

Job(s) Available: Voluntary work.

Duration: 2–12 months.

Pay: Pocket money provided.

Company Description: EIL is a registered charity and approved sending organisation for the European Voluntary Service programme.

> Head Office: EVS Unit, EIL Cultural and Educational Travel, 287 Worcester Road, Malvern WR14 1AB, UK
> ☎ 0800 018 4015 or 01684 562 577
> ✉ k.morris@eiluk.org
> 🖥 www.volunteering18-30.org.uk

Job Description: EVS is for young people aged 18–30 who want to work in a community-based project in another country.

Accommodation: Travel, food, accommodation and medical insurance are provided free of charge.

Application Procedure: For more details contact the above address.

L'APARE

Job(s) Available: Volunteers for Euro-Mediterranean campuses and international voluntary work camps in Provence and the Mediterranean region.

Duration: *Euro-Mediterranean campuses:* 3–5 weeks during the students' summer holidays. *International voluntary work camps:* last 2–3 weeks.

> Head Office: 25 Boulevard Paul Pons, 84800 L'Isle sur la Sorgue, France
> ☎ +33 4 90 27 21 20
> ✉ apare@apare-gec.org
> 🖥 www.apare-gec.org

Company Description: L'APARE is an NGO which promotes transnational cooperation by bringing together professionals, local participants and young volunteers from around Europe and the Mediterranean region. Its objective is to carry out projects that contribute to the protection and enhancement of the environment and local heritage. L'APARE develops voluntary efforts in favour of the environment and heritage preservation across Europe and the Mediterranean regions.

Job Description: *Euro-Mediterranean campuses:* the campuses are intended for students from Europe and Mediterranean countries. They take the form of workshops with about 15 participants working in multi-disciplinary international groups. They include field studies and surveys that use professional skills in the areas of heritage preservation and the environment (in the widest possible sense), architecture, history of art, regional development, sociology, law etc. *International voluntary work camps:* (carried out in the context of the European Voluntary Service) allow participants to invest their skills in voluntary projects abroad, to the benefit of local communities. They can be held in urban or rural settings. 10–15 participants in each group.

Requirements: *International voluntary work camps:* this programme is designed for people who are 16 and above of whatever nationality or professional training, as long as they reside in a participating country of Europe. Preferably from different disciplines and cultural backgrounds.

Application Procedure: Applications to the above address.

Service Civil International (SCI)

Job(s) Available: Volunteers.
Duration: *Workcamps:* 2–4 weeks. *Placements:* 3–12 months.
Working Hours: *Workcamps:* 35 hours per week, weekends are generally free. *Placements:* Some weekend work but time is given in lieu.
Cost: Registration fee between £50–£180.

Head Office: International Secretariat Antwerpen, St-Jacobsmarkt 82, B-2000 Antwerpen, Belgium
☎ +32 322 65727
✆ info@sciint.org
🖳 www.sciint.org

Company Description: SCI is a peace organisation that co-ordinates international voluntary projects across 5 continents.

Job Description: These projects aim to give volunteers the opportunity to experience and demonstrate peaceful living with people from different cultures, at the same time as contributing in a positive way to other communities.

Requirements: Minimum age 18.

Accommodation: Food and accommodation are provided by the workcamp.

Application Procedure: Apply under the country you reside in, all details can be found on the website.

TEJO (Tutmonda Esperantista Junulara Organizo)

Job(s) Available: Volunteer (1).
Duration: Normally from 6 to 18 months.
Pay: Pocket money is provided.

Head Office: Nieuwe Binnenweg 176, 3015 BJ Rotterdam, The Netherlands
☎ +31 10 436 1044
✆ oficejo@tejo.org
🖳 www.tejo.org

Company Description: TEJO is the World Organisation of Young Esperantists. It is an international, non-governmental youth organisation founded in 1938, which aims to foster peace and instil intercultural understanding among young people around the world through Esperanto.

Job Description: To carry out administrative tasks in the central office in Rotterdam. To be a representative of the organisation.

Requirements: Applicants should be aged between 18 and 30. Must have knowledge of Esperanto and English. Must be a citizen of the European Union.

Accommodation: Provided.

Application Procedure: For details contact the above address.

Au pairs, nannies, family helps and exchanges

The Au Pair Agency

Job(s) Available: Au pairs and mother's helps.
Duration: Summer stays of 12 weeks possible, early applicants receive priority. At all other times, a minimum commitment of 9–12 months is required.
Working Hours: Approximately 25 hours per week.
Pay: Pocket money of approximately £70 per week for Au-Pairs, £90 per week for Au-Pair Plus and £150 per week for mother's helps.

Head Office: 231 Hale Lane, Edgware, Middlesex HA8 9QF, UK
☎ 020 8958 1750
✆ elaine@aupairagency.com
🖳 www.aupairagency.com

Requirements: Au pairs should be aged between 17 and 25. Non-smokers preferred; drivers always welcomed. A reasonable knowledge of the language of the chosen country is needed. Mother's helps must speak good English, have excellent childcare references and be non-smokers. Minimum age 21. All applicants must be EU citizens.

Accommodation: Full board and lodging.

Application Procedure: Apply online at www.aupairagency.com/applicants. For further details contact Mrs Newman on the above number at least 12 weeks before preferred starting date.

Au Pair Agency Bournemouth

Job(s) Available: Au pair: 20 summer placements and 70 long-term placements.

Duration: *Long-term placements:* from end of August/beginning of September for 6–12 months. *Summer Placements:* from June/July to end of August/beginning of September.

> Head Office: 45 Strouden Road, Bournemouth BH9 1QL, UK
> ☎ 01202 532600
> 🖂 andrea.rose@virgin.net

Working Hours: 25–30 hours per week, 5 days a week.

Pay: Approximately £70 per week.

Company Description: Au Pair Agency Bournemouth, established in 1976, offers placements with fully vetted host families for British applicants throughout western Europe.

Job Description: Expected to help out with children, plus some light domestic duties around the home.

Requirements: Applicants must have a genuine liking of children and have some previous experience in childcare (eg babysitting, at summer camps) and a basic knowledge of the language of the country they would like to visit.

Accommodation: Free board and accommodation provided.

Additional Information: A 24-hour emergency mobile number is provided for au pairs during the placement.

Application Procedure: Apply to Andrea Rose. See above for contact details.

Au Pair Connections

Job(s) Available: Au pairs, mother's helps.

Duration: Minimum stays normally 6 months, but some summer stays of 10 weeks.

> Head Office: 39 Tamarisk Road, Wildern Gate, Hedge End, Southhampshire SO30 4TN, UK
> ☎ 01489 780438
> 🖂 apconnect@ntlworld.com
> 🖳 www.aupairconnections.co.uk

Working Hours: 25 hours per week.

Pay: Pocket money approximately £80 per week.

Cost: £50 for outgoing au pairs.

Company Description: Established in 1986, the agency specialises in placing au pairs and mother's helps mainly in France, Spain including the Balearic Islands, Italy, Austria and sometimes elsewhere in Europe. Applicants from overseas are also placed in the UK.

Requirements: Applicants must have experience of childcare and a good knowledge of English is also useful as some families want their children tutored in English.

Additional Information: The agency places au pairs all year round, but there is a big demand from mainland Europe for the summer vacation.

Application Procedure: For further details apply to Denise Blighe at the above address or email.

En Famille Overseas

Job(s) Available: Paying guest stays and homestays.
Job Description: *Paying guest stays:* arranged in France, Germany, Italy and Spain. Families in England are found for non-English speakers too. *Homestays:* arranged with small private schools.
Application Procedure: Applications to the above address.

Head Office: 58 Abbey Close, Peacehaven, East Sussex BN10 7SD, UK
☎ 01273 588636
✆ info@enfamilleoverseas.co.uk
🖳 www.enfamilleoverseas.co.uk

Other

www.natives.co.uk

Job(s) Available: A season workers website.
Company Description: A season workers website where jobs across Europe are listed, as well as advice on how to get one. Search by job (campsite manager, bar staff, chefs, lifeguards and so on) and country.
Accommodation: Usually available.
Requirements: Fluent English necessary.
Application Procedure: Apply all year round to the email above or via the website.

Head Office: 263 Putney Bridge Road, Putney, London SW15 2LJ, UK
☎ 020 8788 4271
✆ vicky@natives.co.uk
🖳 www.natives.co.uk or www.resortjobs.co.uk

EUROPE

OTHER

WESTERN EUROPE

ANDORRA

Once governed jointly by France and Spain, Andorra has been a sovereign country in its own right since 1993. Only limited opportunities for finding temporary employment exist in Andorra, because of its small size. Opportunities are best in the tourist industry – particularly in the winter ski season. There is a chapter on Andorra in *Working in Ski Resorts – Europe & North America* (Victoria Pybus, Vacation Work 2006).You might be able to get leads on hotel work in the summer through the Andorra Hoteliers Association (Antic Carrer Major, 18 Andorra la Valla, AD500, Andorra; uhotelera@uha.ad).

Red tape

ADDRESS: EMBASSY OF THE PRINCIPALITY OF ANDORRA
63 Westover Road, London SW18 2RF
andorra.embassyuk@btopenworld.com
☎ 020 8874 4806
💻 www.andorra.ad

Visa information: While it straddles the borders of France and Spain, Andorra is not itself a member of the European Union. This means that all foreigners, including nationals of EU countries, need work permits before they can take up employment. Applicants from neighbouring countries and then EU countries are usually given precedence over other nationalities. Permits for temporary and seasonal work have to be obtained by the employer and are non-renewable. No visas are needed by EU nationals for tourist purposes.

For up-to-date information about visa requirements check with the embassy before travel.

Centre Andorrà De Llengües

Job(s) Available: Teachers (1–2) of English as a foreign language.

Duration: Minimum period of work 9 months between September/October and June. Renewable contract.

Working Hours: 27 hours a day, 5 day week. Must be willing to work between 8am and 10pm.

Head Office: 17 F/G 1st Floor, Av del Fener, Andorra la Vella
☎ +376 804 030
centrandorra.lang@andorra.ad
💻 www.call.ad

Pay: €1,650 per month.

Company Description: A small family-run language school established in 1976 in the very centre of Andorra La Vella. Students range from 6-year-old children to professional adult employees. All levels from beginners to British Council exam preparations.

Requirements: A university degree, plus TEFL qualification, plus at least 3 years of experience is requested. Applicants should be between 23 and 70. Non-smokers preferred. A good knowledge of French or Spanish is favourable. The posts would be ideal for a teaching couple.

Accommodation: Board and lodging available from €350 per month.

Application Procedure: Applications in the first instance can be made by email.

AUSTRIA

There is an English-language magazine for Austria on the internet – *Austria Today* (www.austriatoday.at). It and the Austrian Embassy's website – www.bmeia.gv.at/london – are excellent sources of information on jobs and the social, cultural and economic conditions of Austria; in particular, the living and working in Austria section of the website contains details of immigration, work and residence permits and social security procedures as well as information for jobseekers about Austrian Employment offices.

For many years Austria has offered seasonal work in its summer and winter tourist industries. Eastern Europeans, especially from the countries newly acceded to the EU, take an estimated 25% of jobs in the tourist industry. Some knowledge of German will normally be necessary unless you are working for a foreign tour operator with English-speaking clients.

During the summer, fruit is grown along the banks of the Danube, and in the early autumn chances of finding a job grape picking are best in the Wachau area around Durnstein west of Vienna, or Burgenland on the Hungarian border around the Neusiedler See. As well as this, Austria offers many jobs in the winter and summer tourist industries and ski resorts include Montafon, Saalbach-Hinterglemm, Zell-am-See, Kaprun, Carinthia, Mayrhofen, Bad Gastein, Ischgl, Arlberg, Otztal, Solden, Kitzbuhel and Schladming.

The public employment service of Austria, the Arbeitsmarktservice (AMS), publishes its vacancies on its website – www.ams.or.at – (or at its local office) but you must be able to speak German. For hotel and catering vacancies in the South Tyrol Region try a season work bureau, such as the BerufsInfoZentren (BIZ). Private employment agencies operate in Austria, but most of these specialise in executive positions or seasonal positions in the tourist industry for German speakers. It may be possible to find employment by placing an advertisement in daily newspapers: try *Salzburger Nachrichten* (Salzburg; +43 662 8373-223; www.salzburg.com), *Kurier* (Vienna; +43 1 521000; www.kurier.at) and *Die Presse* (Vienna; +43 151414 281; www.diepresse.com). *Die Presse* also organises an annual initiative to get leading Austrian companies to take on students for summer traineeships. These papers advertise job vacancies as well on Fridays, Saturdays and Sundays. See also *Der Standard* (www.derstandard.at), one of the biggest newspapers concerning job vacancies.

There are opportunities for voluntary work in Austria arranged by UNA Exchange.

Red tape

ADDRESS: AUSTRIAN EMBASSY
18 Belgrave Mews West,
London SW1X 8HU
☎ 020 7344 3250
✆ london-ob@bmeia.gv.at
🖥 www.bmeia.gv.at/london

Visa requirements: Certain nationals do not require a visa providing their stay in Austria does not exceed three months. Citizens of original EU countries have the right to live and work in Austria without a work permit or residence permit, however citizens of newer member states may require working visas.

Residence permits: EWR Lichtbildausweis is an ID card which EU nationals can apply for within three months of arrival, though it is not compulsory. Non-EU nationals wishing to work or live in Austria must apply for a residence permit (Aufenthaltsgesetz). Once a work permit is granted, it must be presented together with an application for residence permit. The form can be obtained from the embassy. As a rule, first application for a residence permit must be submitted from abroad either directly to the relevant authority or by means of the Austrian Diplomatic Mission (not Honorary Consulates). A residence permit is also required if you intend to take up seasonal work in Austria. It will normally be valid for six months.

Work permits: British and Irish citizens and nationals of other original EU countries do not need work permits. Owing to its proximity to many of the newer members of the EU (Estonia, Latvia, Lithuania, Poland, the Czech Republic, Slovakia, Hungary, Slovenia, Bulgaria and Romania), a seven-year transition phase has been set up between Austria and these countries to prevent a flooding of the national labour market and newer EU members are subject to the same regulations as non-EU countries. Non-EU nationals require work (Sicherungs bescheinigung) and residence permits for all types of employment. Work permits have to be applied for by the future employer in Austria and must be obtained prior to departure from the country of residence. Work permits are not granted while on a visit to Austria.

Work permits are also required by non-EU nationals for work with recognised voluntary organisations. The website www.help.gv.at gives useful details of all aspects of working in Austria.

For up-to-date information about visa requirements check with the embassy before travel.

Agriculture work

WWOOF Austria

Job(s) Available: Volunteers.
Cost: A year's membership for WWOOF Austria costs approximately €25 per person but €37 for a couple, plus €2 for postage. Membership includes a list of Austrian organic farmers looking for work-for-keep volunteer helpers.

> **Head Office:** Pichling 277/9,
> A 8510 Stainz
> ☎ +43 4 3633 2096 or +32 676 505639 (mobile)
> ✆ wwoof.welcome@utanet.at
> 🖥 www.wwoof.at

Job Description: Volunteers required to take part in a form of cultural exchange where you live with and help a farming family, learning about organic farming methods in the process. Work is available on more than 200 farms. Movement between farms is possible.
Accommodation: Board and accommodation provided.
Additional Information: Applicants from outside the EU must secure their own travel insurance and all WWOOFers pay for their own travel. In Austria they are covered by an insurance against accidents. Volunteers are unpaid.
Application Procedure: For more information contact Hildegard Gottlieb at the above address.

Sports, Couriers and Camping

Bents Bicycle & Walking Tours

Job(s) Available: Company representatives (5–6).
Duration: Minimum period of work 8 weeks between the end of May and the end of September.
Working Hours: To work varied hours as needs of work dictate. Generally around 40 hours over a 7-day week.
Pay: Around £600 per month.

> **Head Office:** The Blue Cross, Orleton, Ludlow, Shropshire SY8 4HN, UK
> ☎ 01568 780800
> ✍ info@bentstours.com
> 🖥 www.bentstours.com

Job Description: Company representatives for a tour operator offering cycling and walking holidays in the following countries: Czech Republic, France, Germany, Switzerland, Italy and Austria. Duties to include meeting clients at the airport, maintaining bicycles, transporting luggage between hotels and generally taking care of the needs of clients.
Requirements: Applicants should be fluent in English and have a reasonable grasp of one of the following languages: Czech, German, French, Italian. They must also possess a full valid driving licence.
Accommodation: Board and accommodation provided.
Application Procedure: By post with a photograph, to Stephen Bent, at the above address from January.

Teaching and Language Schools

English for Children – Summer Camp

Job(s) Available: Camp counsellors.
Duration: Day camp Mondays–Fridays over 4 weeks. Week 1 is orientation week for counsellors only, where camp is set up, to cement the team and go through the programmes. Weeks 2, 3 and 4 comprise of the ELDC itself where counsellors and campers are present. It is necessary that the counsellors attend the entire 4-week camp.

> **Head Office:** Weichselweg 4, 1220 Vienna
> ☎ +43 1 958 19720
> ✍ scott.matthews@englishforchildren.com
> 🖥 www.englishforchildren.com

Job Description: To work in a total immersion summer camp, motivating children to speak English through different activities: sports, English-language classes, arts and crafts, music, and to acquaint children with the different cultures of the English-speaking world through games and songs etc.
Requirements: Applicants must have experience of working with children (aged 5–15), and of camps, be versatile, conscientious, oriented towards children and safety and have an outgoing personality. Experience in more than 1 subject area is preferable. All applicants must be native English speakers. All applicants must also be able to work within the EU. Knowledge of the German language not necessary but preferable. Minimum age 18.
Accommodation: Not available. Help with finding accommodation is available. Lunch is included in the working day.
Application Procedure: Applications with photos from English speakers invited from March onwards to English language day camp, at the above address or by email.

English for Kids

Job(s) Available: Camp counsellors, TEFL teachers (8–10) for residential summer camps and day camps.
Duration: *Residential summer camps:* minimum period of work 3 weeks in August. *Day camps:* minimum period of work 4 weeks in July and August.
Pay: Varies depending on position held at camp; starting at €1,000 net for 4 weeks. Full insurance also provided.

Head Office: Postgasse 11/19, A-1010 Vienna
☎ +43 166 74579
✍ magik@e4kids.co.at
🖳 www.e4kids.at

Company Description: EU accredited language school offering full-immersion programmes since 1989.

Job Description: *Residential summer camps:* take place in Upper Austria in a renovated 17th century, 4-square building surrounded by 40 hectares of meadows and woods. Pupils' age range is from 5–15. *Day camps:* take place in Vienna. Pupils' age range is from 5–10. The teaching style is full immersion with in-house methods, following carefully planned syllabus and teachers' manual, supplemented with CD-Roms etc.

Requirements: *TEFL teachers:* with CELTA or Trinity CertTESOL (minimum grade B) and some formal teaching experience. Must hold EU passport.

Accommodation: Full board and accommodation plus travel expenses within Austria included in pay.

Application Procedure: By post or email to Irena Köstenbauer, principal, at the above address. Further information can be found at www.e4kids.at/txt/jobs/apply/job_opportunity.html.

Au pairs, nannies, family helps and exchanges

Au Pair Austria

Job(s) Available: Incoming au pairs (200), outgoing au pairs (30).
Duration: Minimum stay of 8 weeks for summer au pairs. For 6–12 months for the academic year.
Company Description: In business since 2001 and a member of IAPA.

Head Office: Ignaz Kock Str: 10, A-1210 Wien
☎ +43 1 405 4050
+436 7641 40150 (24/7 hotline)
✍ office@aupairaustria.com
🖳 www.aupairaustria.com

Application Procedure: Candidates submit a written application and must undergo an interview. Contact Jana Varga-Steininger.

BELGIUM

Unemployment in Belgium is at 8% but there are work opportunities.

Although small in area, Belgium is densely populated and can seem complicated to the outsider, as three languages are spoken within the country's federal states. These languages are Flemish, French and German. In broad terms Flemish is spoken in the north (Flanders) and French in the south (Wallonia), with both being spoken in Brussels in the centre of the country; German is spoken mainly in the Eastern Cantons. With its coastal resorts Belgium has an active hotel and tourism industry in the north which makes seasonal work in Belgium a viable prospect. Adecco, a group of temporary jobs agencies, has information for local employment agencies at www.adecco.be.

EU nationals looking for work can get help from the Belgian employment services, which are organised on a regional basis. They cover three main areas: in the Flemish region the services are known as the Vlaamse Dienst voor Arbeidsbemiddeling en Beroepsopleiding (VDAB) (0800 30 700 or 32 2508 1938 1911 from abroad; info@vdab.be; www.vdab.be); in the French region they are Office Wallon de la Formation Professionnelle et de l'Emploi (FOREM) (0800 93 947; www.leforem.be); and in the Brussels region they are known as Office Régional Bruxellois de l'Emploi (ORBEM)/Brusselse Gewestelijke Dienst voor Arbeidsbemiddeling (BGDA) (02 800 42 42; www.actiris.be). There are local employment offices in most towns.

There are also some employment offices specialising in temporary work, known as the T-Interim, which are operated as Dutch and French-speaking offices under the aegis of VDAB and FOREM; as may be expected the VDAB T-Interim offices are in Flanders and the French T-Interim offices are found in Wallonia, with ORBEM/BGDA running the T-Interim offices for Brussels. These offices can only help people who visit them in person, and the staff are multi-lingual in most cases. They can assist in finding secretarial work, especially in Brussels where there are a large number of multinational companies needing bilingual staff. Other opportunities they may have available consist of manual work in supermarkets and warehouses or engineering and computing. They are most likely to be able to help you during the summer, when companies need to replace their permanent staff who are away on holiday. T-Interims can be found on the internet at www.t-interim.be.

You could also try advertising yourself as being available for work. One of the main newspapers published in Belgium is *Le Soir* (French) (+32 2 2255500/5432; journal@lesoir. be; www.lesoir.be). The daily newspaper *De Standaard* (0800 155 11 or 02 467 2255; www.standaard.be) is for Flemish speakers. There is a weekly English-language magazine called *The Bulletin* (classifieds@ackroyd.be; www.thebulletin.be); it comes out on Thursdays and is available from newsstands. *The Bulletin* lists offers of work on their website www.xpats.com. Twice a year they publish a very useful magazine-type supplement called *Newcomer* aimed at new arrivals in Belgium.

Those looking for work on Belgian farms should be warned that most conventional Belgian farms are highly mechanised and thus offer little scope for casual work.

The Fédération Infor Jeunes Wallonie-Bruxelles (www.inforjeunes.be) is a non-profit organisation which coordinates 11 youth information offices plus 28 local points of contacts in French-speaking Belgium. These can give advice on work as well as leisure, youth rights, accommodation, etc. A leaflet listing the addresses is available from the Fédération Infor Jeunes can be found on their website. Among Infor Jeunes' services, they operate holiday job placement offices (*Service Job Vacances*) between March and September.

Americans can apply through Interexchange in New York to be placed in a summer job, internship or teaching position in Belgium. CIEE in New York helps to place Americans in short term voluntary positions in this country, as does Service Civil International.

Voluntary work in Belgium can be arranged for UK nationals by Concordia, International Voluntary Service, or UNA Exchange (entries for these organisations can be found in the *Worldwide* chapter).

For yet further information consult the free booklet *Working in Belgium* published by the Employment Service (see *Useful publications*) or for jobs abroad you can contact the European Employment Service (EURES; http://ec.europa.eu/eures).

Red tape

ADDRESS: BELGIAN EMBASSY
17 Grosvenor Crescent, London SW1X 7EE
☎ 020 7470 3700
✆ london@diplobel.be
🖳 www.diplomatie.be/london

Visa requirements: Visas are not required by EU citizens, or those of many other countries (including the USA, Canada, Japan, Australia and New Zealand and those listed at www.ufs-be-uk.com) provided they have a valid passport and that the visit is for less than three months. Other nationalities will have to obtain an entry permit, which should be applied for at a Belgian embassy or consulate in advance of travel in the applicant's country of residence, see www.vfs-be-uk.com for more information.

Belgium is a member of the Schengen countries and those with a Schengen visa may travel freely in the Schengen zone.

Residence Permits: All non-Belgians must register at the local town hall within eight days of arrival to obtain a residence permit. EU nationals should take documents proving that they have sufficient funds and a valid passport.

Work Permits: These are not required by EU nationals. Others must first arrange a job, then the prospective employer should apply for a work permit at the regional ministry of employment. There are some exceptions to work permit requirements according to the employment to be taken up; consult embassies and consulates for details. It is not normally necessary to obtain permits for short-term voluntary work with recognised organisations.

For up-to-date information about visa requirements check with the embassy before travel.

Hotel work and catering

Hotel Lido

Job(s) Available: Waiting staff.
Duration: Minimum period of work 1 or 2 months between June and September.
Working Hours: *Kitchen assistants:* to work 9am–12am, 1pm–3pm and 6.30pm–9.30pm.
Pay: £750 net per month.
Requirements: *Waiting staff:* basic French required.
Accommodation: Provided.
Application Procedure: Applications with a CV and recent photograph to A Simoens at the above address or by email.

Head Office: Zwaluwenlaan,
18 Albert Plage, 8300 Knokke-Heist
☎ +32 5 060 1925
✆ info@lido-hotel.be

Sports, couriers and camping

Ski Ten International

Job(s) Available: English teacher, sports teacher and tennis teacher.
Duration: Summer camp in July and August.
Working Hours: 6 hours per day.
Pay: Approximately £600.

Head Office: Château d'Émines, 5080 Émines
☎ +32 8 121 3051
📧 martine@ski-ten.be
💻 www.ski-ten.be

Company Description: Ski Ten offers the experience of working a month in an international team at the Château d'Émines which has 14 hectares of grounds with lakes, swimming pool etc.
Job Description: Duties of teachers will include looking after, eating with and arranging games for the children in their care.
Requirements: Some knowledge of French and previous experience working with children would be useful.
Accommodation: Provided.
Application Procedure: Applications should be sent in writing, with a photograph, to the above address.

Venture Abroad

Job(s) Available: Resort representatives (2–3).
Duration: Minimum period of work 5 weeks from June to August.
Working Hours: Flexible hours, 6 days a week.

Head Office: 37 Brunel Parkway, Pride Park, Derby DE24 8HR, UK
☎ 01332 342050
📧 jo.porteor@ventureabroad.co.uk
💻 www.ventureabroad.co.uk

Company Description: Venture Abroad organise package holidays for scout and guide groups to the continent. They arrange travel and accommodation and provide representatives in the resort.
Job Description: Resort representatives to work in Belgium and Switzerland; checking in groups, dealing with accommodation enquiries, organising and accompanying local excursions etc.
Requirements: Applicants should be practical, resourceful and calm under pressure. Speaking German an advantage.
Application Procedure: Applications to the above address.

DENMARK

Denmark's low level of unemployment (currently around 4%), and very high standard of living would appear to provide a big incentive for jobseekers to look for work there. However English-speaking jobs in Denmark are becoming more and more common as Denmark's large companies such as Carlsberg, Novo and Nordea, and increasingly smaller companies too, adopt English as their corporate language. Normally, non-EU citizens will only get a residence permit if they are offered a job under the Job Card Scheme. However, there is also a Green Card Scheme in effect that makes it possible for highly qualifield individuals to seek work in Denmark.

The Ministry of Science, Technology and Innovation website, www.workindenmark.dk, is a useful information resource.

Despite the increasing mechanisation of farming there is still a need for fruit pickers during the summer; up to 1,000 people are needed each year for the strawberry harvest. Be warned, however, that the hours can be very long when you are paid by the kilo with picking taking place between 6am and noon. The main harvests are strawberries in June/July, cherries in July/August, apples in September/October and tomatoes throughout the summer. Fruit producing areas are scattered around the country: some of the most important are to be found to the north of Copenhagen, around Arhus, and to the east and west of Odense.

You may be able to obtain a job on a farm or other work by contacting the pan-European agency EURES through your local job centre; vacancies for the fruit harvest and other seasonal work are announced in the spring on the Danish EURES website www.eures.dk where an online application can be made. Another method is to advertise in the farming magazine *Landbrugs Avisen* (+45 33394700; www.landbrugsavisen.dk).

It is also possible to arrange unpaid work on an organic farm. Another possibility is to contact VHH (the Danish WWOOF) to obtain a list of their 25–30 member farmers, most of whom speak English. In return for three or four hours of work per day, you get free food and lodging. Always phone or write before arriving. The list can be obtained online. To obtain a copy of the list you must register at the Danish WWOOF website and then pay €10 using visa, Mastercard or Paypal. (http://wwoof.gbuteus.sel).

The Danish state employment service is obliged to help Britons and other EU nationals who call at their offices to find a job. The administrative headquarters of the employment service – the National Labour Market Authority (Arbejdsmarkedsstyrelsen) – is at Holmen Channel 2D, 1060 Copenhagen K (+45 35288100; ams@ams.dk; www.ams.dk). When you are actually in Denmark, you can find the address of your nearest employment office under Arbejdsformidlingen in the local telephone directory.

There are also opportunities for voluntary work in Denmark, arranged by International Voluntary Service, UNA Exchange and Concordia for British applicants and CIEE and Service Civil International for Americans (see the *Worldwide* chapter for details). It is also possible to work as a volunteer at the mid-June Roskilde Festival (+45 46 36 66 13; www.roskilde-festival.dk). Volunteers are expected to be self-funding. A camping ground is provided and shifts last 8 hours.

There are a number of private employment agencies in Denmark, but most are looking for trained secretarial staff who speak fluent Danish. An advertisement in a Danish paper may bring an offer of employment. Crane Media Partners Ltd, St Edmunds House, 13 Quarry Street, Guildford, Surrey GU1 3OY (+441483461770) are advertising agents for Berlingske Tidende. *Morgenavisen-Jyllands-Posten* (+45 87383838; http://jp.dk) is one of the more important papers for job advertisements; visit their website for details.

Red tape

ADDRESS: ROYAL DANISH EMBASSY
55 Sloane Street, London SW1X 9SR
☎ 020 7333 0200
✆ lonamb@um.dk
🖳 www.amblondon.um.dk/en _____

Visa requirements: Visas are not required by citizens of EU countries.
Denmark is a member of the Schengen countries and those with a Schengen visa may travel freely in the Schengen zone.

Residence permits: A residence permit (Opholdsbevis) should be applied for through Kobenhavns Overpraesidium at Hammerensgade 1, 1267 Copenhagen K, Denmark (+45 33122380). EU nationals wishing to stay in Denmark for longer than three months and all visitors from non-EU countries must gain a residence permit. Non-EU nationals planning to stay for more than three months in Denmark must apply for a residence permit at the Danish embassy or consulate.

Work permits: The Royal Danish Embassy has indicated that nationals of countries not in the EU or Scandinavia will not be granted work permits except where the employer can prove that the applicant has a unique skill. The exceptions are Australian and New Zealand nationals aged 18–30, who are entitled to apply for a working holiday visa, which entitles them to work in Denmark for up to six months. Further details can be obtained from the Danish Immigration Service website (www.newtodenmark.dk). EU, Australian and New Zealand nationals who wish to take up employment in Denmark may stay there for a period not exceeding three months from the date of arrival in order to seek employment provided they have sufficient funds to support themselves. All work, paid and unpaid, is subject to the above regulations.

For up-to-date information about visa requirements check with the embassy before travel.

Voluntary work

Mellemfolkeligt Samvirke (MS)

Job(s) Available: Volunteers to work in international work camps around the world.
Duration: The camps last from 2 to 3 weeks between July and August.
Cost: Most work camps cost £150. Participants must provide their own travelling expenses.

Head Office: Faelledvej 12, 2200 Copenhagen
☎ +45 7 731 0022
🖂 globalcontact@ms.dk
🖥 www.globalcontact.dk

Job Description: The camps normally involve community projects such as conservation of playgrounds, renovation, conservation, archaeological work, nature protection, reconditioning of used tools to be later sent to Africa, etc.
Requirements: Minimum age 18.
Accommodation: Board and accommodation are provided.
Application Procedure: British applicants should apply through Concordia (Second Floor, 19 North Street, Portslade BN41 1DH; www.concordia-iye.org.uk) and the UNA Exchange (Temple of Peace, Cathays Park, Cardiff CF10 3AP; www.unaexchange.org). Applications to the above address.

Roskilde Festival

Job(s) Available: Volunteers.
Duration: All year round (400). 8 days in June and July for the festival (25,000).
Working Hours: Between 24 and 100 hours, job depending.
Pay: No wage but free entry to festival.

Head Office: Havsteensvej 11, DK-4000, Roskilde
☎ +45 4 636 6613
🖂 info@roskilde-festival.dk
🖥 www.roskilde-festival.dk

Company Description: Roskilde is the most extensive music festival in northern Europe, running for almost 40 years. 160 bands take part in the festival. It is a non-profit organisation, with a humanitarian focus.

Job Description: Volunteers work in different areas of the festival. As a reward, volunteers not only receive a free ticket to the festival but also free camping. There are social events and a field trip is organised.

Accommodation: Camping provided free of charge.

Application Procedure: See website for more details.

FRANCE

France has long been one of the most popular destinations for British and Irish people looking for summer work. This is due to its physical proximity, the fact that French is the first (and often only) foreign language learned at school, and, possibly most important of all, because during the summer France still needs many extra temporary workers for both its vibrant tourist trade and farm work, even though there is currently high unemployment of about 10%, mainly amongst young people. Theme parks like Disneyland Paris or Parc Asterix need extra staff through peak times such as the summer holidays. Disneyland Paris alone employs many thousands of seasonal workers.

This chapter contains details of many jobs in the tourist industry: you can find others in the *Worldwide* chapter and in the weekly hotel trade magazine *L'Hotellerie* (+33 1 45 48 64 64; www.lhotellerie.fr) where you can check out the classified jobs section (arranged by region) at any time online.

British and Irish citizens, along with other EU nationals, are allowed to use the French national employment service (Pôle emploi; 01 5302 25 50; eei.anaem@pole-emploi.fr; www.pole-emploi.fr/accueil), although the offices in towns throughout France will know more about vacancies in their region. There is a comprehensive website detailing the services provided by Pôle emploi in both French and English. British citizens can apply for work through the service by visiting any of almost 600 local offices around the country, see the website for details.

There are also a number of private employment agencies such as Manpower, Kelly, Bis, Select France, and Ecco in large cities which can help people who speak reasonable French to find temporary jobs in offices, private houses, warehouses, etc. They can be found in the *Yellow Pages* (*Les Pages Jaunes;* www.pagesjaunes.fr) under *Agences de Travail Temporaire*. These can normally only find jobs for people who visit in person. For further information relevant to British citizens consult the free booklet *Working in France* published by the UK's national Jobcentre Plus (see *Useful publications*).

Seasonal farm work can be difficult to obtain from outside France. If you cannot arrange a job in advance using the information in this chapter, it is best to be on the spot and approach farmers in person, or ask at the local employment offices, town halls (*mairies*) or youth hostels. A word of warning: if you arrange to go grape picking with an organisation not mentioned in this chapter, read the small print carefully – you may be buying just a journey out to France, with no guarantee of a job at the end. For help in finding temporary work during the grape picking season, you could contact Pôle emploi. Pôle emploi have offices in most large towns in France's main agricultural regions. Each office can offer around 1,000 jobs to those who wish to work on farms up to 50km from the town, apple picking and grape picking being the most prevalent jobs available and within a month or so, they will be able to inform you of the approximate date of the beginning of the harvest.

Workers are needed to help harvest the following fruits (among others), especially in the valleys of the Loire and the Rhône and the south-east and south-west of the country. The exact dates of harvests can vary considerably from year to year and from region to region: bear in mind that harvests tend to begin first in the south of the country.

- *Strawberries:* May to mid-June
- *Cherries:* mid-May to early July
- *Peaches:* June to September
- *Pears:* mid-July to mid-November
- *Apples:* mid-August (but chiefly from mid-September) to mid-October

French farmers employ over 100,000 foreigners for seasonal work during the summer. Many of these are skilled 'professional' seasonal workers from Spain, Poland, Portugal and Morocco who return to the same regions every year: if there is a choice of applicants for a job, a farmer will prefer an experienced worker to a total beginner. In recent years there has also been an influx of people from eastern Europe who are desperate for work and prepared to work for less than the minimum wage (*le SMIC*, approximately €8.86), for any farmer who will employ them illegally. Anyone going to France to look for farm work should be prepared to move from area to area in the search for a job; it would also be wise to take enough money to cover the cost of returning home in case of failure. Also be warned that payment is generally by piecework, so there are no wages if picking is suspended because of bad weather.

You could track down vineyards ahead of time using a detailed wine guide, and remove some of the uncertainty of the job-hunt by visiting farmers to arrange a job before their harvests start: by doing so you should also be given an informed estimate of when the harvest will start. Note that although vineyard owners normally provide accommodation for grape pickers, workers on other harvests will normally need camping equipment. The increasing sophistication of Pôle emploi means that grape picking and fruit picking jobs are advertised on their website (www.pole-emploi.fr/accueil) in English.

France is rich in opportunities for voluntary work, as the entries in this chapter will testify. The CEI in Paris and Service Civil International (see the IVS entry) can assist Americans. International Voluntary Service (IVS), UNA Exchange and Concordia can help can UK residents to find short-term voluntary work; their entries can be found in the *Worldwide* chapter.

A great many archaeological digs and building restoration projects are carried out each year. The French Ministry of Culture focuses on archaelogy and the restoration of monuments: Ministère de la Culture, 3 rue de Valois, 75033 Paris Cedex 01; +33 140 1580 00. Each year the ministry publishes a list of these archaeological fieldwork projects throughout France in a brochure and on the internet (www.culture.gouv.fr/fouilles) requiring up to 5,000 volunteers. Another brochure, *Chantiers de benevoles,* published by Rempart (see entry under Voluntary Work), lists projects relating to building restoration.

Advertising for a job in France can be arranged in the Paris edition of the *International Herald Tribune.* For further information visit http://classads.nytimes.com or call (212) 556 3900 or 1800 458 5522.

Red tape

ADDRESS: EMBASSY OF FRANCE
58 Knightsbridge, London SW1X 7JT
☎ 020 7073 1000
✆ consulat.londres-fslt@diplomatie.fr
🖥 www.ambafrance-uk.org

Visa requirements: Visas are not required for visits to France by EU, American, Canadian, Australian or New Zealand nationals. Others should check with their nearest French consulate.

France is a member of the Schengen countries and those with a Schengen visa may travel freely in the Schengen zone.

Residence permits: EU citizens are not obliged to have a *carte de séjour* (residence permit) for stays of any length. You can apply for one voluntarily as it can be a useful proof of ID for long-term foreign residents, but as the paperwork involved is so cumbersome, it is likely that most long-stayers will not bother. If you decide you want one, application for this permit should be made on a special form available from the *Prefecture de Police* in Paris, or the local *Prefecture* or *Mairie* (town hall) elsewhere. The following documents are required: passport, birth certificate, proof of accommodation, proof of payment of contributions to the French Social Security, three passport photos, a contract of employment, pension receipts or student status documents. Non-EU nationals need to possess a long stay visa before applying for a *carte de séjour*, and a work permit before obtaining either. Application for a long stay visa should be lodged with a French consulate in the applicant's country of residence.

Work permits: Members of the EU do not need work permits to work in France. The standard procedure for non-EU nationals is that the prospective employer in France must apply to the Office des Migrations Internationales, 14 rue de Bargue, 75015 Paris. A work permit is required even for voluntary work.

Work abroad schemes for US citizens: There is a special scheme allowing American students to work in France run by the Centre d'Echanges Internationaux (CIE; +33 1 40511186; wif@cei4vents.com; www.cei4vents.com). To participate applicants must be in full-time higher education and have at least intermediate French skills (tests are available on request). Two types of scheme are available through the 'Work in France' department, the Job Placement and the Internship Placement.

Internship placement: Offers an internship covered by a written work placement agreement, which must be signed by the student, the employer and the university. The work placement may not last longer than a year. The placement assigned to a student should have a direct link to the subject they are studying.

Job placement: This programme allows candidates to get a temporary work permit for a three month period for a paid job during school holidays. For more information please visit or contact the CEI French Centre.

For up-to-date information about visa requirements check with the Embassy before travel.

Agriculture work

Appellation Controllee

Job(s) Available: Grapepicking.
Duration: 1 to 4 weeks. Workers are able to choose
the amount of weeks they work.
Working Hours: 8 hours per day, 7 days a week.
Pay: Hourly rate. Approximately £55 per day.
Company Description: An organisation that
organises working holidays in France and England.

> **Head Office:** Neutronstraat 10, 9743 AM
> Groningen, The Netherlands
> ☎ +31 5 0549 2434
> 📧 info@apcon.nl
> 🖥 www.apcon.nl

Job Description: Working in a mixed group (15–50 pickers) grapepicking, this takes place
in the Beaujolais, Maconais and Bourgogne regions during September.
Requirements: Minimum age 18.
Accommodation: Board and lodging. Accommodation will be either camping or the farmer
may provide clean, basic accommodation.
Application Procedure: By post to the above address.

Boats

Croisieres Touristiques Francaises

Job(s) Available: Chefs, deckhands, drivers/guides,
pilots, stewardesses.
Duration: Must be available for work from April to
early November.
Working Hours: Long hours, over 5–6 days a week.

> **Head Office:** 2 Route de Semur, F-21150
> Venarey-les-Laumes
> ☎ +33 3 80 96 17 10
> 📧 ctf.boat@club-internet.fr

Pay: *Chefs:* from £1,300 per month. *Deckhands:* from £900 per month. *Drivers/guides:* from
£1,100 per month. *Pilots:* from £1,300 per month. *Stewardesses:* from £900 per month.
Salaries quoted are for inexperienced crew members. Gratuities are divided equally amongst
crew members.
Company Description: Croisieres Touristiques Francaises owns and operates 5 ultra-deluxe
hotel barges, offering 6-night cruises in 5 regions of central France. The clientele is principally North American.
Job Description: *Chefs:* required to plan menus and prepare gourmet cuisine. Must have a
working knowledge of French. *Deckhands:* to assist the pilot during navigation and mooring
and to carry out exterior maintenance of the barge. *Drivers/guides:* applicants must have a
French permit. *Stewardesses:* work involves cleaning cabins, general housekeeping, food/bar
service and care of passengers.
Requirements: Crew members must be EU nationals, or possess appropriate visas permitting work in France. Minimum age 21. Applicants must be energetic, sociable, and able to
provide a consistently high standard of service. *Chefs:* professional training and experience
in haute cuisine establishments are essential, some knowledge of French useful. Cordon Bleu
standard. *Deckhands:* some knowledge of French useful. *Drivers/guides:* applicants must
have a PSV licence, should speak fluent French and have a concise knowledge of French heritage and culture. *Pilots:* must have French Inland Waterways Permit to drive 38m hotel
Barge and have mechanical experience. Some knowledge of French useful. *Stewardesses:*
Must speak basic French and have a good knowledge of French history, culture and customs.
Accommodation: Salaries include accommodation, full board and uniform.
Additional Information: Social security coverage is taken care of by the company.
Application Procedure: Apply with CV, contact telephone number and recent photo to
Mme Severine at the above address.

Holiday centres

Disneyland Paris

Job(s) Available: Permanent or seasonal staff.
Duration: Temporary contracts lasting 2–8 months from March (minimum availability July and August) or permanent contracts starting at any time.
Working Hours: 35-hour working week.

> **Head Office:** Casting, BP110, F-77777 Marne La Vallée cedex 4
> 🖳 www.disneylandparis-casting.com/en

Job Description: Permanent or seasonal staff to work in the restaurants, on counter service or reception, in sales, for the attractions, sports and leisure attractions of the Disneyland Paris Resort situated 30km east of Paris.
Requirements: Minimum age 18. Must have a good working knowledge of French and be customer-service orientated. Experience not essential.
Application Procedure: Apply online at www.disneylandparis-casting.com/en/apply.

Hotel work and catering

Alpine Elements

Job(s) Available: Chalet hosts, hotel chefs, maintenance, resort managers, and UK-based accounts staff, sales staff.
Duration: 4 months.
Company Description: Alpine Elements arrange ski/snowboard and activity holidays as well as ski

> **Head Office:** 3–9 Wigton, London SE11 4AN, UK
> ☎ 0870 011 1360
> 🖉 info@alpineelements.co.uk
> 🖳 www.alpineelements.co.uk

weekends from catered chalets and hotels in Chamonix, Morzine, Les Gets, Meribel, Alpe d'Huez, Val d'Isere, Les Arcs Courchevel and Tignes in France.
Requirements: Minimum age 18. Staff should be British passport-holders. Staff receive preseason training in France. *Reps:* must hold a clean driving licence.
Accommodation: Provided.
Application Procedure: Applicants should send their CV and a covering letter to the above address or email for the attention of Vikki Barker.

Alpine Tracks

Job(s) Available: Bar person, chef, cleaners (3), minibus driver, mountain bike and ski guides.
Duration: *Summer season:* 1 June to 30 September. *Winter season:* 1 December to end of April. Minimum period of work 2 months.
Working Hours: 7am–10am and 5pm–9pm, 7 days a week.

> **Head Office:** Kestrel Court, Waterwells Business Park, Waterwells Lane, Quedgely, Gloucester GL2 2AT, UK
> ☎ 0800 028 2546
> 🖉 sales@alpinetracks.com or info@alpinetracks.com
> 🖳 www.alpinetracks.com

Pay: £350–£500.
Company Description: Alpine Tracks are a friendly, informal, small, professional holiday company operating chalets. They offer a personal service of a high standard in the French and Swiss Alps for skiers and mountain bikers.
Job Description: *Chef and bar person:* dining and bar work, catering for up to 30 people.

Requirements: Applicants should be friendly, outgoing, preferably French speakers and hold relevant qualifications.
Accommodation: Board and lodging provided free of charge.
Application Procedure: By post to the above address.

Hostellerie Le Beffroi

Job(s) Available: Bar, kitchen and restaurant staff, reception assistant.
Duration: Minimum period of work 3 months between April and the end of September.
Working Hours: 8 hours per day, 5 days per week, sometimes 6 days per week.
Pay: By arrangement.

Head Office: BP 85, F-84110 Vaison la Romaine, Provence
☎ +33 4 90 36 04 71
✆ ychristiansen@wanadoo.fr
🖳 www.le-beffroi.com

Job Description: Duties by arrangement according to jobs.
Requirements: Applicants should speak French (and German if possible) and must have experience of hotel or restaurant work. Minimum age 18.
Accommodation: Board and accommodation provided.
Application Procedure: Applications to Yann Christiansen at ychristiansen@wanadoo.fr. Send a cover letter (written in French) with CV and include a recent photo.

Hotel Belle Isle Sur Risle

Job(s) Available: Receptionist (1), waiter (1).
Duration: Minimum period of work 1–2 months during the summer vacation, July and August.
Working Hours: 35 hours per week.
Pay: National minimum wage rates.
Requirements: Experience necessary. Good English and some French required.

Head Office: 112 Route de Rouen, 27500 Pont-Audemer
☎ +33 2 32 56 96 22
✆ hotelbelle-isle@wanadoo.fr or hotel@bellile.com
🖳 www.bellile.com

Accommodation: Not available.
Application Procedure: Send a CV and photo by email.

Restaurant Cruaud

Job(s) Available: Summer staff to work in a hotel and restaurant. (Catering and service.)
Duration: From April to October.
Working Hours: 186 hours per month, 5 days a week.

Head Office: 30, Avenue du Maréchal Joffre, 84300 Cavaillon
☎ +33 6 80 26 69 98

Pay: National minimum wage rates.
Company Description: François Cruaud is a Conseiller Culinaire and Officier du Mérite Agricole and offers cookery courses and classes for hotel and restaurant trainees. In 2005, he created the Association des Conseilles Alimentaires Français et Europeens.
Requirements: Applicants must speak French and English.
Accommodation: Board and lodging provided.
Application Procedure: By post to Mr and Mrs Cruaud at the above address from January.

Domaine Saint Clair Le Donjon

Job(s) Available: Dining room, kitchen positions, receptionist, and service.
Duration: Available all year.
Working Hours: 39 hours per week.
Pay: By arrangement.
Company Description: Hotel and restaurant in Normandy with 21 rooms including jacuzzi. The restaurant is of a high standard.

Head Office: Chemin de Saint Clair, 76790 Etretat
☎ +33 2 35 27 08 23
📠 direction@hoteletretat.com or info@hoteletretat.com
🖥 www.hoteletretat.com

Job Description: Staff required for a 2-part organisation. *Hotel and restaurant:* reception and room cleaning. *Restaurant:* service, bar, kitchen staff.
Requirements: *Dining room staff:* should speak French and English. *Kitchen positions:* require experience. *Receptionist:* must be fluent in French and English and have experience.
Accommodation: Board and lodging provided.
Application Procedure: Send CV and photo by post to the director at the above address.

Hotel Edouard VII

Job(s) Available: Chamber maid, luggage porter, receptionist, waiter/waitress.
Duration: Between June and September. Minimum period of work 2 months.
Working Hours: 39 hours per week, 5 days a week.
Pay: National minimum wage rates, dependent on job and experience.

Head Office: 39 Avenue de l'Opéra, 75002 Paris
☎ +33 1 42 61 56 90
📠 info@edouard7hotel.com
🖥 www.edouard7hotel.com

Company Description: The Edouard VII Hotel is a well-known, stylish, 4-star, family-run establishment that takes pride in the impeccable service offered to clients.
Job Description: *Chamber maid:* required for thorough cleaning of the rooms and bathrooms, bed making, stock taking and replacing. This can be a very physical job. Must have enthusiasm and professionalism. *Luggage porter:* required to welcome clients and transport their baggage, to run occasional errands and supervise the lobby. Need to be physically fit as this can be very physical work. Must be friendly, have a professional outlook and excellent people skills. *Waiter/waitress:* required to prepare, serve and tidy away after breakfast. Involves a lot of client interaction.
Requirements: Minimum age 18. Good knowledge of English and French is essential. Other languages especially Spanish, Russian or Japanese an advantage.
Accommodation: Can be arranged.
Application Procedure: Email CV and cover letter to info@edouard7hotel.com to Mr Peter Nocker. Applications by April.

Hotel-Restaurant Le Fleuray

Job(s) Available: Gardeners, housekeeping staff, porters, restaurant service.
Duration: March to October.
Working Hours: 5 days a week.
Pay: By arrangement.
Company Description: Boutique country house

Head Office: F-37530 Cangey, Amboise
☎ +33 2 47 56 09 25
📠 contact@lefleurayhotel.com
🖥 www.lefleurayhotel.com

hotel of the highest standard with 23 rooms, heated swimming pool, tennis courts, jacuzzi and a gastronomic restaurant. Close to Amboise, Tours and Blois as well as the chateaux and vineyards of the Loire valley. 55 minutes by train from Paris.

Job Description: Hotel staff required for all aspects of work in the hotel, including restaurant service, housekeeping, kitchen work and gardening. Male and female staff required.

Requirements: Candidates must be outgoing, friendly and prepared to work hard. Knowledge of French is useful but not essential. Applicants will ideally be students, although those taking time off or who have graduated will be considered.

Accommodation: Travel ticket, full board and accommodation provided.

Application Procedure: Applications by post or email to above address.

Hotel Imperial Garoupe

Job(s) Available: Chambermaids, chef de rang, commis chef.

Duration: Minimum period of work 4 months between April and October.

Working Hours: 8 hours per day, 5 days a week.

Pay: Varies.

Head Office: 770 Chemin de la Garoupe, 06600 Le Cap d'Antibes
☎ +33 4 92 93 31 61
✆ cap@imperial-garoupe.com
💻 www.imperial-garoupe.com

Job Description: *Chambermaids:* required to clean and prepare bedrooms for guests. *Chef de rang, commis chef:* to prepare food in the restaurant.

Requirements: Applicants should be able to speak both French and English confidently.

Accommodation: Board and accommodation provided.

Application Procedure: Check the above website for vacancies. Applications with CV, a photo and a cover letter should be sent to the above email address.

Chateau De Rochecotte

Job(s) Available: Maitre d'hotel, chef de rang, receptionist, commis de salle.

Duration: Positions available from May to October.

Working Hours: 35 hours, 5 days a week.

Pay: *Maitre d'Hotel:* €1,700 per month. *Chef de*

Head Office: 37130 St Patrice
☎ +33 2 47 96 16 16
✆ chateau.rochecotte@wanadoo.fr
💻 www.chateau-de-rochecotte.fr

rang: €1,400 per month. *Receptionist:* €1,200 per month. *Serveur:* €1,150 per month.

Company Description: A chateau hotel in the Val de Loire with 34 rooms and gastronomic cuisine.

Job Description: *Maitre d'hotel:* in charge of the hotel. *Chef de rang:* to run the restaurant/dining room.

Requirements: *Maitre d'hotel:* minimum of 3 years of experience. Must speak English and French. *Chef de rang:* minimum of 2 years of experience. Must speak English and French. *Receptionist:* minimum of 2 years experience. Good presentation. Must speak English and French.

Accommodation: Can be arranged.

Application Procedure: Applications should be made to Mme Brosset by email with CV.

Simon Butler Skiing

Job(s) Available: Chalet people (4), chef (1), maintenance man (1).

Duration: Minimum period of work 3 months between June and September.

Working Hours: 7–8 hours per days, 6 days a week.

Pay: To be agreed on application.

Head Office: Portsmouth Road, Ripley, Surrey GU23 6EY, UK
☎ 01483 212726
✆ info@simonbutlerskiing.co.uk
💻 www.chalet-antoine.co.uk
or www.simonbutlerskiing.co.uk

Company Description: Simon Butler Skiing is a small independent company operating in Megève for the last 22 years and has many returning staff each year. The company also runs a summer activities programme with hotel accommodation.

Job Description: All jobs are in Megève, French Alps. *Chalet hosts/hostesses:* required to clean to a high standard, serve evening meals and breakfasts, maybe a small amount of reception work. *Maintenance man:* required to have plumbing, electrical and carpentry skills to a competent level.

Requirements: *Chalet hosts/hostesses:* should be confident and hard working. Must be able to speak French. *Maintenance man:* should be confident and hard working. Speaking French makes life easier but is not essential.

Accommodation: Accommodation and travel included.

Application Procedure: Applications invited from March 2011.

Simply Morzine

Job(s) Available: Chalet hosts (3), chalet chef (1–2), guide driver, representative (3).

Duration: Mid/late June until mid-September.

Working Hours: *Chalet hosts:* approximately 7.30am–11am and 6pm–10pm, 6 days a week. *Chalet chef:* similar hours and days as chalet hosts (see above). *Guide, driver, representative:* approximately 8.30am–6pm, 5–6 days a week.

> **Head Office:** 118 Redwood Avenue, Melton Mowbray, Leicestershire LE13 1UT, UK
> ☎ 01664 568902
> ✆ info@simply-morzine.co.uk
> 🖥 www.simply-morzine.co.uk

Pay: *Chalet hosts:* £450 per month (approximately) plus excellent package. *Chalet chef:* £650 (approximately) per month plus excellent package. *Guide driver, representative:* £550 per month (approximately) plus excellent package.

Company Description: Simply Morzine is a family-run company who have been offering alpine holidays for over 15 years. Morzine is one of the world's premier ski, snowboard and summer alpine resorts. Simply Morzine's main clientele in late June and early September are artists, golfers and walkers enjoying special interest holidays while from July to August they operate family activity/adventure holidays.

Job Description: Positions with Simply Morzine are an excellent summer opportunity. The work is demanding and tiring; yet alongside hard work it is fun, sociable and gives free time to enjoy the mountains. You will be expected to be flexible and very much 'hands-on', working as part of a closely-knit multi-functional team. The roles are an ideal opportunity to become involved with a progressive and forward-thinking company, either for a short career break post-university gap year, or for longer-term employment. If the summer season were successful, there would be a possibility of extending employment to the following winter and perhaps in the longer-term to an annual position such as a future resort manager or assistant manager. *Chalet hosts:* serve and clear meals, assist in the kitchen and generally have professional contact with guests. *Chalet chef:* responsible for breakfast, afternoon tea and 4-course evening meal 6 days a week. Needs to plan menus, budget, shop alone and maintain impeccable hygiene standards. *Guide driver representatives:* varied roles as follows. *Repping and coordinating:* welcoming clients, acting as a source of information and advice, booking activities, taking payments and solving problems to ensure the smooth running of their holiday. *Guiding:* to lead mountain biking, mountain walks and excursions. *Driving:* transporting guests in resort minibuses including airport transfers, excursions, to/from activities and general chauffeuring around the resort. *General maintenance:* basic upkeep of properties and vehicles.

Requirements: Minimum age 21. EU nationals only. Must be able to demonstrate a 'can-do' service-orientated professional approach, dedication, self-motivation, physical and mental toughness and team working skills. *Chalet hosts:* must have experience of working in restaurants, pubs or hotels, general customer service and cleaning. *Chalet chef:* must have minimum 1 year of experience with catering qualifications or 3 years of experience without a qualification. *Guide/driver/representative:* must be a good all-rounder including being physically strong, have basic DIY skills, be an experienced driver and ideally possess some working knowledge of French. Must have a keen interest in outdoor pursuits with a good level of fitness.

Accommodation: Full board and lodging included, in a private staff chalet. Also provide return flights, comprehensive insurance, full area lift pass, company clothing, free or discounted alpine sports and a generous end of season bonus.

Application Procedure: For a job description and further information please send a CV and covering letter to the above email address. Applications are invited from March 2011.

Travelbound

Job(s) Available: Activity instructor, assistant managers, chefs, general assistants, kitchen porter/night porters, handypersons and lifeguards.

Duration: From February to October. Shorter contracts available.

Company Description: Part of the TUI Travel Group, TravelBound is a tour operator specialising in group travel for schools and adults. As well as an extensive worldwide hotel programme, TravelBound operate a chateau in Normandy, north-west France. The chateau is situated in 38 acres of land and is located near the village of Molay Littry. The chateau has 40 bedrooms (can sleep up to 200 people) with meeting rooms, library, games room, lounge area and bar. There is an outdoor heated swimming pool (open from May), tennis court, crazy golf, mini golf, grade A rugby and football pitch and access to mountain bikes.

Requirements: Applicants must have a national insurance number and either an EU passport or relevant EU visa/permit. Minimum age 18.

Accommodation: Travel to and from France, emergency medical insurance, uniform, food and accommodation provided.

Application Procedure: Visit the website.

> **Head Office:** TravelBound Recruitment Team, TUI Travel Activity, The Port House, Port Solent, Hants PO6 4TH, UK
> ☎ 02392 334600
> 📠 recruitment@tuiactivity.com
> 🖥 www.travelbound.co.uk

Hotel 3 Colombes

Job(s) Available: Chambermaids, restaurant staff.

Duration: Period of work from May to August.

Company Description: A 3-star hotel restaurant in the heart of Provence.

Job Description: *Restaurant staff:* for waiting service, place-setting, taking orders and washing up.

Requirements: Applicants must be smartly dressed, well-groomed non-smokers, and preferably good English speakers with some knowledge of French. *Restaurant staff:* preferably with 2–3 years of experience in restaurant work.

Accommodation: Provided for €50 per month.

Application Procedure: Send CV, cover letter and photo by email or to the above address.

> **Head Office:** 148 avenue des Garrigues, 84210 Saint-Didier-les-Bains, Provence
> ☎ +33 4 90 66 07 01
> 📠 contact@hotel3colombes.com
> 🖥 www.hotel3colombes.com

UK Overseas Handling (UKOH) International Recruitment __

Job(s) Available: UKOH recruit all kinds of resort/hotel staff for clients in France, but also offers a number of management trainee and student placement roles involved in all aspects of the resort and hotel management. Positions include gardeners and maintenance/handy staff, housekeeping, management trainee, night audit, pool cleaners, reception, restaurant staff.

Head Office: Third Floor, Link Line House, 65 Church Road, Hove, East Sussex BN3 2BD, UK
☎ 0870 220 2148
✍ ukoh@ukoh.co.uk

Duration: Staff required between May and October, various contract available. 1 June–1 September is the shortest contract available. Winter season also available.

Job Description: To work in holiday residences, apartments and villas in the south and south-west coasts of France, and also in the Alps Pyrenees and the city of Montpellier.

Requirements: Successful candidates must be EU passport holders with a permanent British national insurance number. Must be bright, flexible, keen and prepared for hard work. Experience and an excellent standard of French essential for reception and restaurant positions. Some knowledge of French is useful for other posts.

Accommodation: Package includes accommodation.

Application Procedure: Applications to the above address. Interviews are necessary.

Industrial and office work

The Automobile Association

Job(s) Available: Customer advisors (up to 50).
Duration: Minimum period of work 8 weeks, (July and August essential) between March and September.
Working Hours: 35 hours per week on shifts.
Pay: Approximately €1,185 per month, overtime available.

Head Office: European Operations, Fanum House, Basing View, Basingstoke RG21 4EA, UK
☎ 01256 492398
✍ elaine.badham@theaa.com
🖥 www.theaa.com

Job Description: To work in the AA's multilingual European call centre in Limonest, north of Lyon. The centre provides 24-hour assistance to AA customers who have broken down or become involved in a road traffic accident in Europe.

Requirements: Applicants must be fluent in English and French and preferably have one other European language. You will need to be efficient, responsible, compassionate and able to work under pressure.

Accommodation: Local accommodation can be arranged.

Application Procedure: Applications with CV to Elaine Badham by email.

Sports, couriers and camping

Balloon Flights – France Montgolfieres

Job(s) Available: Balloon chase crew.
Duration: April to November.
Working Hours: Variable.
Pay: £600–£700 per month. National minimum wage rates.

Head Office: 24 rue Nationale, 41400 Montrichard
☎ +33 2 54 32 20 48
✍ jane@franceballoons.com
🖥 www.franceballoons.com

Company Description: A government licensed company in France registered to carry passengers. Over 20 years of experience. Various sites throughout France.

Job Description: Balloon crew to work for passenger-carrying operation with bases in the Burgundy and Loire Valley regions. Duties include maintaining and cleaning of vehicles and balloon equipment, driving and navigation of balloon chase vans, helping out in a balloon repair workshop, passenger liaison and secretarial work, etc. Farm work is also available.

Requirements: Knowledge of French preferred. Minimum age 21. Driving licence and own car essential.

Application Procedure: Please send a CV, a photo, a cover letter and a copy of your driving licence. Applicants should be EU nationals or possess correct working permits.

Carisma Holidays

Job(s) Available: Children's couriers, site managers, couriers.

Duration: April to September.

Working Hours: Varied.

Pay: £135–£180 per week.

> **Head Office:** Bethel House, Heronsgate Road, Chorleywood WD3 5BB, UK
> ☎ 01923 287339
> ✎ jobs@carisma.co.uk
> 🖥 www.carismaholidayjobs.co.uk

Company Description: Specialises in self-drive, family holidays in mobile homes on private sandy beaches in the sunny south-west of France. All campsites are family run and located on or very near to the beach.

Requirements: Minimum age 18. Full training is given on-site in France at the start of the season. Spoken French is preferable but not essential for all positions. *Children's couriers:* Minimum age 18.

Accommodation: Self-catering accommodation provided. Travel costs to and from the resort are paid.

Application Procedure: See website for online application form.

In2Camping

Job(s) Available: Area controllers, *montage/ demontage*, representatives/couriers.

Duration: *Area controllers:* period of employment may cover: start season Easter to July, and/or high season July to September. *Representatives/couriers:* period of employment may cover any or all of: start

> **Head Office:** Office 4, 321 Resbank Road, Bispham, Blackpool, Lancs FY2 0HJ, UK
> ☎ 01253 593333
> ✎ admin@in2camping.com
> 🖥 www.in2camping.com

season Easter to July; mid-season Easter to July; mid-season May to July; or high season July to September. *Montage/demontage:* period of employment: 6–8 weeks from March to May and/or 6–8 weeks in September and October.

Pay: *Area controllers:* approximately £650 per month, plus £14 per week bonus paid on completion of contract, dependent on service. *Representatives/couriers:* approximatley £130 per week.

Company Description: A company that offers mobile homes and holidays on quality sites in France, chosen for ambience.

Job Description: *Area controllers:* required to cover groups of campsites to ensure couriers are performing to the required standards. *Montage/demontage:* required to assist in the preparation of mobile homes at the start of the season and/or the closing of mobile homes at the end of the season. *Representatives/couriers:* required to meet clients at reception, prepare tents, organise social events and children's clubs. Each vacancy is an all round position with responsibility for the clients together with In2Camping's representation at the campsite.

Requirements: *Area controllers:* previous courier experience is essential. Vehicle provided or mileage allowance given. Experience of working within the service industry would be an advantage. Basic French required. Minimum age 18. *Montage/demontage:* applicants should and be physically fit and motivated. *Representatives/couriers:* basic French an advantage. Experience of working within the service industry would be an advantage. Minimum age 18.

Accommodation: Provided.

Application Procedure: For all positions, please send a full CV and covering letter with head and shoulders photograph, stating the exact dates that you are available to the above address. Alternatively, request an application form from the personnel manager.

Keycamp Holidays

Job(s) Available: Campsite courier, children's courier, courier team leaders, children's courier team leaders, *montage/demontage.*

Duration: *Campsite courier:* applicants should be available to work from March/April to September/October or mid-July to mid-September. *Children's courier:* applicants should be available from early

Head Office: Overseas Recruitment and Training Department Holidaybreak Hartford Manor, Greenbank Lane, Northwich CW8 1HW, UK
☎ 01606 787525
🖥 www.holidaybreakjobs.com/camping

May to September or June to September. *Courier team leaders:* applicants should be available from April to mid-September. *Children's courier team leaders:* applicants should be available from early May until September. *Montage/demontage:* applicants should be available from February to May or August to October.

Pay: Receive a competitive salary, comprehensive training, return travel to and from an agreed meeting point, accommodation, medical and luggage insurance and uniform.

Company Description: Part of the Holidaybreak Camping Group Keycamp is a leading tour operator in self-drive camping and mobile home holidays in Europe. Offers customers a wide range of holiday accommodation on over 200 premier campsites. Each year the company seeks to recruit enthusiastic people to work the summer season in a variety of roles.

Job Description: *Campsite courier:* a courier's responsibility begins by ensuring that the customer's accommodation is both inviting and cleaned to the highest of standards. Courier will welcome new arrivals, be the customers main point of contact and will be expected to provide local and general information, give assistance and even act as interpreter if required. Part of the role will involve helping out with minor repairs to accommodation and equipment and will also involve basic administration and accounts. *Children's courier:* responsible for planning and delivering a fun, safe, daily activity programme to customers' children. The age of the children attending the club will range from 4–12 years old. *Courier team leaders:* must be able to deliver first-class customer service and organise the daily workload of the courier team. Your role also includes all the duties of a campsite courier and you will be expected to lead by example. There are a variety of team leader roles available, dependent on team size; courier in charge, senior courier and site manager. *Children's courier team leaders:* role will involve the management, motivation and development of the children's couriers to ensure they provide a varied range of quality activities. Your role includes all the duties of a children's courier. *Montage/demontage: montage* and *demontage* assistants are employed to either help set up for the season or close down at the end of the season. This involves putting up or taking down tents, moving/distributing equipment and cleaning/preparing accommodation.

Requirements: Applicants must hold a UK/EU passport. A good working knowledge of the English language and basic numeracy are also required. Applicants must also have a UK or Irish bank account, address and a National Insurance number. *Campsite couriers:* lots of energy, basic common sense and a genuine desire to help people. *Children's courier:* previous childcare experience is essential. Successful candidates will be asked to apply for an Enhanced Disclosure. *Courier team leaders:* must have previous experience of leading a team. *Children's courier team leaders:* previous experience with children and leading a team. The successful candidates will be asked to apply for an Enhanced Disclosure. *Montage/demontage:* previous experience of physical and repetitive work.

Accommodation: Provided.

Application Procedure: Applicants should apply online at www.holidaybreakjobs.com/camping or telephone 01606 787 525 for an application pack.

Matthews Holidays

Job(s) Available: Campsite/couriers representatives.
Duration: Period of work from April or May until mid/late September.
Working Hours: 5 day week.
Pay: £170 per week.

Head Office: 8 Bishopsmead Parade, East Horsley, Surrey KT24 6RP, UK
☎ 01483 284044
✆ information@matthewsholidays.co.uk
🖳 www.matthewsfrance.co.uk

Job Description: To receive clients and maintain and clean mobile homes in western France, Brittany, the Vendée and south of France.
Requirements: Knowledge of French essential. Minimum age 21.
Accommodation: Accommodation and board provided at the rate of £50 per week, deducted from wages.
Application Procedure: Applications to the above email or postal address. If applying by post enclose an s.a.e. Please give details of age, present occupation and other relevant experience, and date available to commence work.

Orangerie De Lanniron

Job(s) Available: Seasonal jobs or more. *Animateur*, coordinators, bar person, host/hostess, shop attendant/cook.
Duration: 2–3 months. 6 months maximum.
Working Hours: 35 hours per week.
Pay: National minimum wage rates depending on experience.

Head Office: Château de Lanniron, F-29336 Quimper
☎ +33 2 98 90 62 02
✆ camping@lanniron.com
🖳 www.lanniron.com

Company Description: A 10-acre campsite set in amongst 42 acres of woodland. Orangerie de Lanniron has holiday cottages, static caravans and space for touring caravans. 10 minutes' drive away from Benodet and Quimper.
Job Description: *Animateur:* responsible for entertaining both the young and older clients and organising garden parties and theme parties. Required to give information to guests about the entertainment programme. *Bar person:* required to run the bar, restock the bar and deal with money. Responsible for bar terrace and lounge. *Host/hostess:* to care for the camping guests, register arrivals and departures, make telephone calls, handle money and show the guests their pitches. *Shop attendant/cook:* responsible for tending and restocking the grocery shop and preparation of takeaway food.
Requirements: Applicants for all the posts must speak English and French (at least 2 languages) and a third language such as Dutch or German would be useful. Applicants should be well-educated, honest, and punctual and be able to endure stress. Applicants must also have previous experience in hotel or restaurant work and good references. Minimum age 18.
Accommodation: In tents.
Application Procedure: Send CV with photo and a cover letter by email to camping@lanniron.com.

PGL Travel

Job(s) Available: Children's group leaders, general positions in catering, administration, driving (car or D1 towing), stores, site cleaning, children's activity instructors.
Duration: Vacancies available for the full season (February to October) or shorter periods between April and September.

Head Office: Alton Court, Penyard Lane, Ross-on-Wye, Herefordshire HR9 5GL, UK
☎ 0844 3710 123
✆ recruitment@pgl.co.uk
🖳 www.pgl.co.uk/recruitment

Pay: £117.50–£243.50 per week.

Company Description: With 36 activity centres located in the UK, France and Spain, PGL Travel provides adventure holidays and courses for children. Each year over 2,500 people are needed to help run these adventure centres.

Job Description: *Children's group leaders:* required to take responsibility for groups, helping them to get the most out of their holiday.

Requirements: *Children's group leaders:* previous experience of working with children is essential. *Children's activity instructors:* qualified or personally competent in canoeing, sailing, windsurfing or multi-activities.

Accommodation: Full board and lodging.

Application Procedure: Apply online at the above website by creating your own My PGL account.

Richmond Christian Holidays

Job(s) Available: Assistant managers, chefs and assistant chefs, children's and teen's workers, hosts, resort managers, resort representatives, waterfront managers.

Duration: Varying between May to October, depending on position. Also ski season positions available between December and April.

Working Hours: Various, depending on role.

Head Office: Sunrise House, Coombe Lane West, Kingston KT2 7DB, UK
☎ 020 3004 2661
✆ jobs@richmond-holidays.com
🖥 www.richmond-holidays.com

Company Description: Richmond Holidays is a holiday provider offering sun and ski holidays with a Christian emphasis.

Accommodation: Contractual accommodation and travel is included.

Application Procedure: Download an application form from the website, email or apply in writing to above addresses.

Rockley Watersports

Job(s) Available: Couriers/entertainments team (45), watersports instructors (over 100).

Duration: March to October.

Working Hours: Approximately 40 hours per week.

Pay: Competitive rates.

Head Office: Enefco House, Strand Street, Poole, Dorset BH15 1HJ, UK
☎ 01202 677272
✆ info@rockleywatersports.com
🖥 www.rockleywatersports.com

Company Description: Based in the Poole harbour and south-west France, Rockley teach water sports to all abilities and ages. It is a highly regarded water sports centre, where around 150 seasonal staff are employed at any one time.

Job Description: *Couriers/entertainments team:* for duties including evening entertainments, aiding water based sessions and general site duties. *Watersports instructors:* experienced RYA sailing, windsurfing, BCU kayaking instructors are required to work in south-west France at 5 of the largest RYA recognised water sports centres in Europe. The positions offer the opportunity to gain water sports experience and use all the facilities of the centres.

Requirements: *Watersports instructors:* RYA or BCU qualifications.

Accommodation: Full board and lodging in France. Optional at UK centres.

Application Procedure: Application forms available at www.rockleywatersports.com/wiw/how_to_apply.

Snowcrazy Ltd

Job(s) Available: Chalet hosts.
Duration: 5–14 weeks between July–September.
Working Hours: 6 days, approximately 6 hours per day.
Pay: £100 per week.

Head Office: 55 Lancaster Drive, East Grinstead, West Sussex RH19 3XJ, UK
☎ 01342 302910
✆ mike@snowcrazy.co.uk
▣ www.snowcrazy.co.uk

Company Description: The Alpine Fit Club, a 1 week course aimed at women who want to get fit in the Alps.

Job Description: Hosts are required to serve and prepare breakfast, lunch and dinner. The menu will be a nutritionally based diet. General cleaning and housekeeping duties also required.

Requirements: Preferably over 25. Experience running a catered chalet (min. 12 bed) essential. No training provided.

Accommodation: Full board and lodging provided.

Application Procedure: Applications to Mike Kew at mike@snowcrazy.co.uk.

Susi Madron's Cycling for Softies

Job(s) Available: Company assistants.
Duration: Minimum period of work 2 months between May and September.
Pay: Fixed wage plus bonus.

Head Office: 2–4 Birch Polygon, Rusholme, Manchester M14 5HX, UK
☎ 01612 488282
✆ info@cycling-for-softies.co.uk
▣ www.cycling-for-softies.co.uk

Job Description: Company assistants to work for a company offering cycling holidays in France. Full training in bicycle maintenance is given.

Requirements: Must be a keen cyclist, non-smoker, aged over 25 and speak French.

Application Procedure: Application forms can be found on the website.

TJM Travel

Job(s) Available: Beach lifeguards, holiday reps, hotel staff, mountain leaders, water sports instructors.
Duration: Summer season: May to August. Winter season: December to April.

Head Office: PO Box 74, Redruth, Cornwall TR16 6WY, UK
☎ 01209 860002
✆ schools@tjmtravel.com
▣ www.tjmtravel.com

Working Hours: Varies as to when required to work, usually 6 days a week.

Pay: Dependent on job and experience.

Company Description: TJM run hotels and activity centres in France, Spain and the UK in the summer months, and they operate ski holidays from French alpine hotels in the winter.

Requirements: Ideally 18 or over and available to work full or part season between May and September at adventure centres or December to April at ski centres. Applicants must have a British national insurance number and a British bank account. First aid qualification required (except hotel staff and reps). *Sailors and windsurf instructors:* RYA power boat level 2 or above. *Water sports instructors:* need to be either fully qualified RYA dinghy instructors, fully qualified RYA windsurfing instructors, or fully qualified BCU instructors.

Accommodation: Board and lodging provided.

Application Procedure: Apply online at www.tjmtravel.com/tjm_jobs.

185

Teaching and language schools

Centre International d'Antibes/Institut Prevert _____

Job(s) Available: Work experience programmes in France.

Company Description: The Centre is situated on the French Riviera between Cannes and Nice and teaches French to more than 5,000 foreign students a year.

Head Office: 38 Bd d'Aguillon 06600 Antibes, France
☎ +33 4 92 90 71 70
🖐 info@cia-France.com
💻 www.cia-france.com

Requirements: Applicants must be students from the European Union.

Application Procedure: For more details on work experience programme see website.

Mrs Julie Legree _____

Job(s) Available: TEFL teachers (4) to teach English to 9–11-year-old pupils. TEFL teacher to teach 14–21-year-olds.

Duration: Contracts run from 15 September to 31 May.

Head Office: Syndicat Mixte Montaigu-Rocheserviere, 23 Avenue Villebois Mareuil, F-85607 Montaigu Cedex
💻 www.gapyear-france.com

Working Hours: All posts require 20 hours per week teaching, per 4-day week, with no work on Wednesdays, weekends or school holidays.

Company Description: This is a local government scheme which has been running for 15 years. They are looking for Francophiles who wish to develop their social and professional skills.

Job Description: *TEFL teachers to teach 9–11-year-old pupils:* to teach in 19 different primary schools in the Vendée. *TEFL teacher to teach 14–21-year-olds:* to teach in a college and lycée as an assistant.

Requirements: Minimum age 18. Full training is given. Applicants should be outgoing, independent, organised and mature enough to act on their own initiative, as well as having a love of France and children. Candidates will need the maturity and self-confidence to deal with teenagers, and be able to relate to a large teaching staff.

Accommodation: Included in the remuneration package is free board and lodging with local families and an allowance of approximately €180 per month, after national insurance contributions.

Application Procedure: Send application form with a cover letter, a photo and a CV by post to Mrs Julie Legree at the above address or by email.

Voluntary work

Association Chantiers Histoire & Architecture Médiévales _

Job(s) Available: Volunteers.

Duration: Placements are available from April, July and August and sometimes at other times of the year, with a minimum recommended stay of 2 weeks.

Head Office: 5 et 7 rue Guilleminot, 75014 Paris
☎ +33 1 43 35 15 51
💻 www.cham.asso.fr

Working Hours: Approximately 6–8 hours per day.

Cost: Volunteers pay their own travel and health insurance. *Historic monument session (stage):* €110 for the whole period. *Volunteer and teenage camps (chantier):* €12 per day, plus €30 membership. Require an extra €15 for registration payments from other countries than France to cover bank charges.

Company description: The association aims to preserve local cultural heritage. Volunteers take part in the restoration of historic, medieval monuments.

Job Description: Volunteers required for conservation work camps at various locations in France. The work includes restoration and repair of historic monuments, châteaux and churches. Receive on-the-job training under qualified supervisors.

Requirements: Minimum age 16. Volunteers must be in good health.

Accommodation: Tent accommodation and cooking facilities are provided, but volunteers need to bring their own bedding and work clothes.

Application Procedure: For full details of the work camps write to CHAM at the above address, or visit www.cham.asso.fr.

Associations Des Paralyses De France

Job(s) Available: Assistants required for work in holiday centres for physically disabled adults.

Duration: Period of work 15–21 days during the summer break.

Pay: Expenses provided plus travel within France.

Company Description: Paralyses de France is a national association.

Requirements: Minimum age 18. Applicants should be able to speak French.

Accommodation: Board and accommodation provided.

Application Provided: Applications to APF Evasion at the above address.

> Head Office: 17 Boulevard Auguste-Blanqui, F-75013 Paris
> ☎ +33 1 40 78 69 00
> 🖥 www.apf.asso.fr

Club Du Vieux Manoir

Job(s) Available: Volunteers.

Duration: Minimum trial period of 15 days.

Working Hours: No set hours to work but everyone is expected to lend a hand when the group decides to work on a project. Approximately 5 hours a day.

Pay: Work is unpaid.

Cost: Volunteers are expected to contribute around £12 per day and £12.80 for subscription and insurance per year.

Company Description: Since 1952 the organisation has welcomed over 100,000 volunteers from all over the world. They have restored and saved more than 240 buildings, such as castles, churches and fortresses.

Job Description: The volunteers share in the day-to-day organisation of the camp and site. The centres are at the Château Fort de Guise (Aisne), the Abbey Royale du Moncel à Pontpoint (Oise) and the Château d'Argy (Indre). Volunteers required for work on the restoration of ancient monuments and similar tasks. There are also about 25 sites open 15 days to 1 month during the summer. Volunteers carve stone or work on masonry or wood.

Requirements: Minimum age 14. Training organised for participants of 16 years and over.

Accommodation: Usually in tents during summer season and in temporary construction for winter time.

Additional Information: Long-term stays are a possibility for volunteers at the Château Fort de Guise and the Abbey de Moncel (Oise).

Application Procedure: By post to the above address.

> Head Office: Abbaye du Moncel à Pontpoint, F-60700 Pont Ste Maxence
> ☎ +33 3 44 72 33 98
> 🖥 contact@clubduvieuxmanoir.fr
> 🖥 www.clubduvieuxmanoir.fr

Etudes Et Chantiers Espace Central Pole International (UNAREC)

Job(s) Available: Voluntary work in France and abroad. The organisation sometimes recruits camp leaders.

Duration: Work camps lasting for 2-3 weeks for adults and 10–12 days for teenagers.

Cost: Application fees (including membership and insurance).

Head Office: 33 rue Campagne Premiere, 75014 Paris
☎ +3301 45 389626
✆ unarec@wanadoo.fr
🖳 www.unarec.org

Company Description: NGO that organises volunteer exchanges for international work camps.

Job Description: Working in areas of environmental conservation, heritage, renovation, cultural festivals, and social issues. Tasks vary and include such activities as river cleaning, the preservation of old buildings and districts in small towns, organising local cultural festivals.

Requirements: Teenagers between 11 and 17. Adults must be over 18.

Application Procedure: For further details by email contact unarec@wanadoo.fr.
For residents in France an application form is available on www.unarec.org. For other countries, applications accepted through local organisations. British volunteers must apply through Concordia or another UK organisation. An annual programme is produced in March.

Jeunesse Et Reconstruction

Job(s) Available: Volunteers needed for work camps throughout France and abroad.

Duration: Most camps last for 3 weeks.

Working Hours: Projects consist of 4 hours work in the morning and activities in the afternoons with weekends off.

Head Office: 10 rue de Trévise, Paris 75009
☎ +33 1 47 70 15 88
✆ info@volontariat.org
🖳 www.volontariat.org

Pay: Unpaid.

Company Description: The national and international volunteer organisation Jeunesse et Reconstruction organises work camps in France in the Auvergne, Basse Normandie, Pays de La Loire, Midi-Pyrénées, Rhône Alpes, Languedoc-Rouissillon and PACA. It is an association called Education Populaire et Tourisme.

Job Description: Type of work varies from camp to camp. Includes sharing the daily lives and activities of disabled adults, laying out an orientation course and helping to organise a festival of music. Volunteers are likely to come from all over the world.

Requirements: Minimum age 18. A training period is given to French coordinators (April to June). French people could be accepted as an internship.

Accommodation: Free board and accommodation provided (camping, family, youth hostel).

Additional Information: There is also the possibility of voluntary work lasting for 3 months, which provides pocket money. Longer-term projects (about 1 year) available through ICYE (International Cultural Youth Exchange; www.icye.org).

Application Procedure: Applications should be made online at www.volontariat.org.

Les Amis De Chevreaux – Chatel

Job(s) Available: Volunteers.

Duration: Usually about 3 weeks.

Working Hours: Approximately 30 hours per week.

Cost: A fee of €65 is required.

Company Description: The château of Chevreaux is situated in a hilltop village above the Bresse Plains.

Head Office: 2 Rue du Château, 39190 Chevreaux
☎ +33 3 84 85 95 77
✆ accjura@free.fr
🖳 www.accjura.fr

Les Amis de Chevreaux is a place where young people of different nationalities can meet and spend time together.

Job Description: The work site requires willing volunteers to help with the restoration of the 12th-century castle of Chevreaux. Duties involve cleaning, reconstruction of the ruins, stone working, carpentry, masonry, archaeology.

Requirements: Volunteers aged 16–25.

Accommodation: Volunteers will be lodged on site (at the castle) in tents with camp beds; all sanitary and kitchen equipment provided.

Application Procedure: Application forms online at www.accjura.fr/inscription_chantiers.htm, with a covering letter.

Neige Et Merveilles

Job(s) Available: Volunteers (4) to take part in international work camps.
Duration: 2–3 weeks. Opportunities for some longer-term programmes.
Working Hours: 6 hours per day.
Cost: €120.
Requirements: Minimum age 18.
Accommodation: Provided.
Application Procedure: Apply by email or post with CV and cover letter by April.

> **Head Office:** Association Neige at Merveilles, Miniere de Vallauria, 06430 Saint Dalmas de Tende
> ☎ +33 4 93 04 62 40
> 🖥 www.neige-merveilles.com

Rempart

Job(s) Available: Volunteer restorers and preservers.
Duration: Most stays are for 2 or 3 weeks.
Working Hours: 35 hours per week
Cost: Application fees about €38 (including membership and insurance).
Job Description: Volunteer restorers and preservers for various castles, fortresses, churches, chapels, abbeys, monasteries, farms, ancient villages, Gallo-Roman sites, etc on the 170 sites organised by REMPART every year, during holidays. Work includes masonry, woodwork, carpentry, coating, restoration and clearance work.

> **Head Office:** 1 rue des Guillemites, F-75004 Paris
> ☎ +33 1 42 71 96 55
> ⌁ contact@rempart.com or lefrant@rempart.com
> 🖥 www.rempart.com

Requirements: Most participants are 18–25 year olds. Some knowledge of French is needed. Previous experience is not necessary.

Accommodation: Board and accommodation are provided at a cost.

Application Procedure: Application details available online from 1 March.

Au pairs, nannies, family helps and exchanges

Butterfly Et Papillon School of International Languages & Au Pair Agency

Job(s) Available: Au pairs.
Duration: Most positions last 6–12 months. 3 month positions are available during the summer.
Working Hours: 30 hours per week, plus 2 evenings babysitting. 1 day off.

> **Head Office:** 8, Av de Genève, F-74000 Annecy
> ☎ +33 4 50 67 01 33
> ⌁ aupair.france@wanadoo.fr
> 🖥 www.butterfly-papillon.com

Pay: €65–€95 per week.

Requirements: 18–26 years old. Basic French required. Driving licence and experience with children preferred.

Accommodation: Board available.

Additional Information: Butterfly et Papillon also run a work exchange programme. Under the auspices of the EU's Leonardo scheme, this programme offers foreign students the unique opportunity to live and work in France for up to 13 weeks.

Application Procedure: Applications to the above address. Application forms available online.

Other employment in France

Centre D'Echanges Internationaux

Job(s) Available: Jobs in hotels, restaurants, catering for foreign students. Coordinator for French applicants.

Head Office: 1 rue Gozlin, F-75006 Paris
☎ +33 1 43 29 60 20
info@cei4vents.com
www.cei4vents.com

Duration: Period of work covers university holidays, June to September and also December to March.

Pay: Varies.

Job Description: Jobs are in France, however for French applicants the work could be found elsewhere.

Requirements: Applicants must have an intermediate level of French. Minimum age 18. BAFA for french applicants is required.

Application Procedure: Application form available from April. French applicants must send their application form to Mouna Dixon at mouna@cei4vents.com. For foreign applicants send application to wif@cei4vents.com.

Centre D'Information Et De Documentation Jeunesse

Job(s) Available: Various.

Company Description: Advertises temporary jobs on a daily basis, mainly in Paris and the surrounding area. It also gives information on cheap places to stay, on French university courses for foreigners and practical advice on the regulations as part of its gen-

Head Office: 101 quai Branly, F-75740 Paris Cedex 15
☎ +33 1 44 49 12 00 or
+33 8 25 09 06 30 (information line)
www.cidj.com

eral information serviced for young people. CIDJ also publishes booklets on a range of subjects for young people.

Application Procedure: To get details of the jobs you must visit the centre personally; the CIDJ does not send out information on this subject. Opening hours are 10am–6pm Monday, Tuesday, Wednesday and Friday, 1pm–6pm on Thursdays and 9.30am–1pm on Saturdays.

Sejours Internationaux Linguistiques Et Culturels

Job(s) Available: Unpaid internship in a French company, work experience in a French company.

Duration: Minimum period of work 4 weeks.

Working Hours: 30–35 hours per week.

Cost: From €460.

Head Office: 32 Rempart de l'Est, F-16022 Angoulême Cedex
☎ +33 545 974125
volodia.m@silc.fr
www.silc-international.com

Requirements: Minimum age 18. Upper-intermediate level of French (possibility to take French course prior to work placement).

Accommodation: Homestay or residence.

Additional Information: Also offers a variety of language study courses, international summer centres, individual homestays and private tuition.

Application Procedure: 12 weeks prior to the beginning of the work placement. For application contact email address above.

GERMANY

Over the last couple of years German hotels have turned to eastern Europe for their seasonal staff that now arrive by the busload delivered straight to the employer's door. It is reported that unemployment is very high depending on the season, fluctuating between 8%–10%. However, although it requires great perseverance, it is not impossible for the truly determined with a grasp of German to get a job. The main opportunities are in the western and southern regions.

Many of the seasonal jobs available are in hotels, especially in tourist areas such as the Bavarian Alps, the Black Forest and resorts on the North Sea Coast. People going to work in a German hotel should note that managers may demand extra hours of work from their employees, and some will not always give extra time off or pay overtime as compensation. They may also ask workers to do jobs that are not specified in their contract by asking them to fill in for other members of staff. Anyone who feels that their contract is being breached and who cannot come to any agreement with their employer should appeal to the local Arbeitsamt (see below) for arbitration. Jobs in other sectors in the tourist industry can be found in this chapter and in the *Worldwide* chapter.

Ski resorts also offer jobs in the winter from December until April. Ski resorts in Germany include Garmisch-Partenkirchen, Mittenwald, Oberstaufen, Oberstdorf and Reit im Winkl. There are also fruit picking jobs available, although not nearly as many as in France. During the summer the best region to try is the Altes Land which stretches between Stade and Hamburg in north Germany and includes the towns of Steinkirchen, Jork and Horneburg. The work there consists of picking cherries in July and August, and apples in September. Try also the Bergstrasse south of Frankfurt where apples and many other fruits are grown. Germany's vineyards also provide a source of work, particularly because in recent years, German winemakers have found it increasingly difficult to find workers to help with the grape harvest. The harvest begins in October and continues into November. The vineyards are concentrated in the south-west of the country, especially along the valleys of the Rhine to the south of Bonn and Moselle.

Au pair agencies in Germany no longer have to be licensed so there are now lots of private agencies. Agencies in Germany include IN VIA Germany (+49 761 200206; aupair.invia@caritas.de; www.aupair-invia.de) with 40 branches, and Verein für Internationale Jugendarbeit (+49 69 469 39 700; au-pair@vij.de; www.au-pair-vij.org). The German YWCA (VIJ) has more than 20 offices in Germany and places both male and female au pairs for a preferred minimum stay of one year. Pocket money is paid. Au pairs must be between 18 and 24 years of age.

On arrival in Germany, EU nationals may go the Arbeitsamt (employment office) in the area in which they wish to work and obtain information on job opportunities – the address will be in the local telephone directory. The system is computerised nationally and is highly efficient so it is not necessary to arrange a job in advance. However, if you prefer to have a job already arranged you can try to arrange a job through the EURES contact in your local employment office or through the Bundesagentur für Arbeit; (Federal Employment Agency, Regensburg StraBe 104, 90478 Nürnberg; 01801 555 111; www.arbeitsagentur.de) which is the largest employment agency in Germany. For further information about the official German employment service and other aspects of work there consult the free fact sheet *Working in Germany* published by Jobcentre Plus.

This is available from the European and International Jobsearch Advice Team (0113 3078090; international-jobsearch-advice@jobcentreplus.gsi.gov.uk) and Jobcentre Plus offices throughout the UK.

In addition to those jobs listed in this chapter there are opportunities for voluntary work in Germany. British applicants can apply through International Voluntary Service, UNA Exchange and Concordia; CIEE and Service Civil International (see the SCI entry) can help US residents; their entries can be found in the *Worldwide* chapter.

An advertisement in a German newspaper may bring an offer of a job such as *Rheinische Post* (01802 115050; www.rp-online.de). The following weekly newspapers might also be of interest: *The Süddeutsche Zeitung* (01805 3 55 900; www.sueddeutsch.de); the *Bayernkurier* (contact point on the website; www.bayernkurier.de); *Die Welt* (www.welt.de); or the *Frankfurter Allgemeine Zeitung* (www.faz.net).

Red tape

ADDRESS: EMBASSY OF THE FEDERAL REPUBLIC OF GERMANY
23 Belgrave Square, Chesham Place, London SW1X 8PZ
☎ 020 7824 1300
🖱 info@london.diplo.de
🖥 www.london.diplo.de

Visa requirements: A visa is not required by citizens of EU nations. Members of other countries who wish to go to Germany to do paid work need a visa/residence permit before entering Germany.

Germany is a member of the Schengen countries and those with a Schengen visa may travel freely in the Schengen zone. As of 5 April 2010 only passports that have been issued during the past 10 years can be endorsed with a visa.

Residence permit: Within a week of finding permanent (ie not hotel accommodation) you should register your address (and any subsequent change of address) with the registration office (Einwohnermeldeamt), usually found in the town hall. A permit is required for any visit of more than three months or where employment is intended. Applications should be made to the visa section of the nearest embassy or consulate general of the Federal Republic of Germany. Or in the case of EU Nationals already in Germany, and the Foreign Nationals of the USA, Australia, Canada, Israel, Japan, New Zealand, and Switzerland it is possible to apply for residence and a work permit while remaining in Germany as visitors. Citizens of these countries, however, are not allowed to work in Germany until after their work and residence permit application is approved. A residence permit is usually provided within two to four weeks of application and is provided free of charge.

Working holiday visas: Germany has working holiday agreements with Australia, New Zealand, Japan, the Republic of Korea and Hong Kong. Under the working holiday programme visa holders will be able to stay in Germany for up to 12 months. Contact the embassy to check for eligibility.

Work permits: To find work in Germany it is essential to speak some German. The regulations for work permits are the same as for visas. EU nationals intending to look for work for more than three months might have to show the local authority that they are self-supporting while conducting a job-hunt. There are no restrictions on voluntary work.

For up-to-date information about visa requirements check with the embassy before travel.

Hotel Work and Catering

Hotel Bayerischer Hof/Hotel Reutemann/Hotel Seegarten

Job(s) Available: Chambermaids, waiting staff.
Duration: Minimum period of work 3 months.
Working Hours: 8 hours work per day, 5 days a week.
Pay: Approximately €1,000 net per month.
Requirements: Applicants must be students.
Chambermaids: knowledge of German not essential. *Waiting staff:* must speak reasonable German.
Accommodation: Board and accommodation available at a price.
Application Procedure: Applications to the above address.

> Head Office: Seepromenade, D-88131 Lindau
> ☎ +49 8 382 9150
> ✆ hotel@bayerischerhof-lindau.de
> 🖥 www.bayerischerhof-lindau.de

Hotel Brudermuhle Bamberg

Job(s) Available: Waitresses (2).
Duration: Minimum period of work 3 months.
Working Hours: 5 days a week, 8–10 hours per day at varying times during the day.
Job Description: Those working in the restaurant will serve food, drinks and wine.
Requirements: Knowledge of German is necessary.
Accommodation: Not provided.
Application Procedure: Applications are invited at any time by email or post to the above address.

> Head Office: Schranne 1, D-96049 Bamberg
> ☎ +49 9 5195 5220
> ✆ info@brudermuehle.de
> 🖥 www.brudermuehle.de

Familotel Allgauer Berghof

Job(s) Available: Chambermaids, kitchen assistants.
Working Hours: 40 hours per week.
Duration: Minimum period of work 3 months.
Pay: Varies according to role.
Company Description: A 280-bed hotel with 50 staff situated in a hill-top ski resort, with access to world-cup races, hiking, tennis and mountain biking.
Requirements: Knowledge of German required. No previous hotel experience required. Minimum age 18.
Application Procedure: Enquiries to Mrs Neusch at the above address.

>
> Head Office: D-87544 Alpe Eck, über Sonthofen, Gunzesried-Ofterschlang
> ☎ +49 8 321 8060
> ✆ m.neusch@allgaeuer-berghof.de
> 🖥 www.allgaeuer-berghof.de

Hotel Jakob

Job(s) Available: General assistants.
Duration: Period of work from mid-May to mid-October.
Working Hours: 5 days a week.
Pay: Around €900 per month.
Requirements: A basic knowledge of German is necessary.
Accommodation: Free board and lodging provided.
Application Procedure: Applications to Frau G Jakob at the above address.

> Head Office: Schwarzeweg 6, D-87629 Fussen-Bad Faulenbach
> ✆ info@kurhotel-jakob.de
> 🖥 www.kurhotel-jakob.de

Kloster Hornbach

Job(s) Available: Apprentices and hospitality staff.
Working Hours: 40 hours per week.
Pay: Varies depending on role.
Company Description: Kloster Hornbach is a former monastery, founded in 742, and rebuilt over the last 8 years into a 4-star hotel with 34 rooms, 2 restaurants, a large garden restaurant and several banqueting rooms.

Head Office: Kloster Hornbach, Loesch GmbH Im Klosterbezirk, D-66500 Hornbach
☎ +49 6 3389 10100
🖰 hotel@kloster-hornbach.de
🖳 www.kloster-hornbach.de

Requirements: Good level of German and hotel experience. Minimum age 18. Must be EU citizens.
Application Procedure: Applications by email with CV and cover letter to Christiane and Edelbert Loesch at the above address.

Hotel-Weinhaus-Oster

Job(s) Available: Waiting assistant, general assistant.
Duration: Minimum period of work 3 months between July and October.
Working Hours: 7 hours per day, 5 days a week.
Pay: Approximately €400 per month plus tips.

Head Office: Moselweinstrasse 61, D-56814 Ediger-Eller 2
☎ +49 2 675 232
🖰 hotel-oster@t-online.de
🖳 www.hotel-oster.de

Company Description: A family-owned hotel facing the magnificent river Mosel, with many attractions including the local wine festivals and wine-tastings arranged by the owner's brother.
Requirements: Applicants must speak German.
Accommodation: Free board and accommodation.
Application Procedure: Applications to Mrs ML Meyer-Schenk at the above address from January.

Voluntary work

IJGD Internationale Jugendgemeinschaftsdienste EV

Job(s) Available: Volunteers.
Duration: Period of work 3 weeks at Easter or between May and October.
Working Hours: 25 hours per week.
Company Description: An independent non-profit organisation active in the field of international

Head Office: Kasernen Street 48, 53111 Bonn
☎ +49 2 2822 80011
🖰 workcamps@ijgd.de
🖳 www.ijgd.de

youth work. A large work camp organisation which encourages intercultural understanding as a main focus. IJGD enable people to actively create community life while giving them the opportunity to broaden their horizons.
Job Description: Volunteers to work on summer projects such as environmental protection, the restoration of educational centres and to assist with city fringe recreational activities.
Requirements: Applicants should be aged 14–26. Knowledge of German required on some social projects, but the majority are English-speaking camps.
Accommodation: Free board and accommodation provided.
Application Procedure: Applications should be made to the above address as early as possible. British volunteers should apply through Concordia, VAP or UNA exchange.

Open Houses Network

Job(s) Available: Restoration work.
Duration: 2 or 3 weeks (building weeks) to any length of time (open houses). July to September for building weeks. Open houses run all year round.
Cost: Contribution of €25–€40 per week depending on individual means. Includes all food, accommodation, insurance and seminars but participants must pay for their own travel costs.

Head Office: Offene Hauer (Open Houses), Gortheplatz 9B D 99423 Weimar
☎ +49 3 6435 02390 (only German speaking) or +49 3 6435 02879 (English speaking)
✍ incoming@openhouses.de
🖥 www.openhouses.de

Company Description: Formed in the mid-1980s when a group of young people voluntarily undertook to restore village churches in danger of decay, the network currently runs 6 historic buildings in the eastern part of Germany.
Job Description: Anybody can help out with restoration work in return for board and lodging. Anybody can walk into an 'open house' and stay as long as they are prepared to work there. However, the project has grown to include building weeks, art workshops, work camps and practical training for students. Building weeks allow participants to gain real restoration experience, working under the guidance of trained professionals.
Requirements: Minimum age 18.
Accommodation: Basic lodgings provided in exchange for work. Meals are prepared by the group and are part of community life.
Application Procedure: See website for details.

Au pairs, nannies, family helps and exchanges

In VIA

Job(s) Available: Au pair positions in Germany.
Duration: Minimum length of stay 6 months, but stays of 1 year preferred.
Company Description: With regional offices in 26 cities IN VIA can arrange to place au pairs with German families.
Requirements: Aged 18–24.
Application Procedure: For further information please contact the above address.

Head Office: Katholischer Verband fur Maedchen- und Frauensozialarbeit Deutschland e.V., Karlstrasse 40, 79104 Freiburg
☎ +49 7 6120 0206
✍ au-pair.invia@caritas.de
🖥 www.aupair-invia.de

Verein Für Internationale Jugendarbeit

Job(s) Available: Au pairs.
Duration: Length of stay varies from 6 months to 1 year.
Pay: Pocket money of around €200–€300 per month, at host family's discretion.
Job Description: Au pairs are placed with families in Germany.

Head Office: Burgstr. 106, 60389 Frankfurt
☎ +49 6 9469 39701
✍ au-pair@vij.de
🖥 www.au-pair-vij.org

Requirements: Girls and boys between 18 and 24 years. Applicants should have a high understanding of German (A Level standard).
Additional Information: Season ticket for local transport also provided. Au pairs have 1½ days off a week and get 2 paid holidays every month.
Application Procedure: Those interested should contact the above address.

GREECE

Every year Greece receives around 10 million foreign tourists, and it is the tourist trade with employers such as those listed in this chapter that offer the best chances of finding temporary work to the foreigner. One reason for this is that in the tourist industry, having a native language other than Greek is an asset rather than a liability. Such work is best found by making opportunistic enquiries once at the main tourist destinations. Even so, most Greek proprietors, in defiance of EU guidelines on male/female parity in the workplace, prefer to employ girls.

Other opportunities for foreigners involve domestic work with Greek families, helping with the housework and perhaps improving the family's English. Wages in Greece are generally low, but are enough to permit an extended stay. In recent years wage levels for unskilled work have been depressed in some areas because of the large number of immigrants – legal and otherwise – from Albania and other countries in eastern Europe who are willing to work for low rates. However, Greece has severe economic problems and the unemployment rate is currently around 12%.

British, Irish and other EU nationals are permitted to use the Greek national employment service: local branches are called offices of the Organisimos Apasholisseos Ergatikou Dynamikou, or OAED (the Manpower Employment Organisation: 210 99 89 215; www.oaed.gr). For further information consult the free booklet *Working in Greece* published by the UK Employment Service. Jobs are also advertised in the local major newspapers such as *Ta Nea* (www.tanea.gr), *Eleftheros Typos* (www.e-tipos.com), *Eleftherotypia* (www.enet.gr) and *Apogevmatini* (www. apogevmatini.gr).

Although people have succeeded in finding casual farm work, such as picking oranges and olives, it is almost impossible to arrange this from outside Greece. The large number of foreigners from eastern Europe who are already present in Greece usually fill these jobs, so it is just as difficult to arrange this kind of work on arrival. Oranges are picked between Christmas and March, especially south of Corinth. Grapes are grown all over the mainland and islands, and growers often need casual help during the September harvest. Those who are prepared to take a chance on finding casual work in Greece will find further information on harvests in the book *Work Your Way Around the World* by Susan Griffith (Vacation Work 2009; see *Useful publications*).

There are opportunities for voluntary work in Greece arranged by International Voluntary Service, Concordia and UNA Exchange for British applicants and Service Civil International and for other nationalities: see the *Worldwide* chapter for details.

It may be possible to obtain a job by means of an advertisement in one of the English language newspapers in Athens. The *Athens News* is a weekly newspaper published every Friday whose classified department is at 181 Doiranis Str, Kallithea, Athens, 176 73; classified @athensnews.eu.

Red tape

ADDRESS: EMBASSY OF GREECE
1A Holland Park, London W11 3TP
☎ 020 7229 3850
🖥 www.greekembassy.org.uk

Visa requirements: Citizens of the EU, Australia, Canada, New Zealand, Japan, Israel and the USA do not require a visa to travel to Greece providing that they stay no more than 90 days. If you intend to visit Greece for more than 90 days to take up employment, you have to apply in person in the consulate general of Greece for a national visa.

Greece is a member of the Schengen countries and those with a Schengen visa may travel freely in the Schengen zone.

Residence permits: Non-EU citizens wishing to stay in Greece for longer than three months require permission to do so from the Aliens Department (*Grafeio Tmimatos Allodapon*) or Tourist Police in the area along with your passport and a letter from your employer. The permit is normally granted on the spot.

According to EU regulations EU citizens do not need to apply for a residence permit, just to register with the relevant authorities once they arrive.

Work permits: A permit must be obtained by a prospective employer on behalf of a non-EU national prior to arrival in Greece. Failure to follow this procedure may result in refusal of entry to the country. EU nationals do not require a work permit to work in Greece. For more information see the Greek Embassy in London's website: www.greekembassy.org.uk. The residence permit also serves as a work permit.

For up-to-date information about visa requirements check with the Embassy before travel.

Hotel work and catering

Hotel Eri

Job(s) Available: Bar staff and couriers.
Job Description: Bar staff and couriers needed to work in this hotel in the Cyclades, on the Island of Paros.
Application Procedure: Applications to the above address.

Head Office: Parikia Paros Island
☎ +30 2 2840 23360
rivolli1@otenet.gr
www.erihotel.gr

Rizos Resorts

Job(s) Available: Cooks (4), Thai massage therapist and spa attendant (1).
Duration: Minimum period of work 4 months between 15 May and 1 October.
Working Hours: 8 hours per day, 6 days a week.
Pay: From €750 per month.
Company Description: Hotel Paleokastritsa, Palace Mon Repos, Corfu, Greece.
Job Description: *Cooks:* to prepare food for around 400 people daily. *Thai massage therapist:* to treat guests and administrate small spa facility on hotel premises.
Requirements: *Cooks:* should have previous experience of professional cooking of international specialities, with an emphasis on Italian cooking. *Thai massage therapist:* must have Thai Education Ministry Certification in Thai massage and previous experience in a spa/health club environment.
Accommodation: Not available.
Application Procedure: Applications to Dr Paul Rizos, manager, at above address or email (Subject line: ATTN HR – Dr Paul Rizos).

Head Office: Rizos hotels, PO Box 188, Corfu 49100
rizosresorts@sympnia.com

Sports, couriers and camping

Olympic Holidays

Job(s) Available: Overseas administrators, overseas resort representatives, transfer and guiding representatives.

Duration: The season begins in March/April until October, but high season positions from June to September are also available.

Head Office: 1 Torrington Park, Finchley, London N12 9TB
☎ 0208 492 6742
✆ julian.pearl@olympicholidays.com
🖳 www.olympicholidays.com

Working Hours: *Overseas administrators:* hours are variable, 6 days a week.

Overseas resort representatives: hours are variable, 6 days a week and may be on call 24 hours a day, 7 days a week. *Overseas transfer and guiding representatives:* hours are variable, 6 days a week.

Pay: *Overseas administrators:* approximately £600 per month (tax free) and flights and insurance are provided. *Overseas resort representatives:* approximately £110 per week (tax free), plus generous commission (tax free), return flights, and insurance. *Overseas transfer and guiding representatives:* approximately £350 per month (tax free), return flights and insurance.

Company Description: Olympic Holidays was one of the first tour operators in Greece over 40 years ago. They are now one of the leading independently owned tour operators to both Greece and Cyprus. They cover a variety of resorts. In recent years they have added Bulgaria, Tunisia and Turkey to their portfolio. They also feature a range of more exotic destinations such as Egypt, The Gambia and Goa.

Job Description: *Overseas administrators:* office-based administration work includes arranging flights and transfers, accommodation allocation and guest related reports, along with accompanying guests on transfers. *Overseas resort representatives:* acting as front-line ambassadors of the company, applicants must be professional, hardworking and possess unlimited stamina. Duties involve airport transfers, hotel visits, guiding excursions, administration, health and safety checks, complaint handling and welcome meetings. *Overseas transfer and guiding representatives:* applicants will be responsible for accompanying guests to and from the airport and their holiday accommodation. They will also guide day and evening resort excursions and assist the representatives whenever required.

Requirements: Greek language skills are an advantage, but not essential. *Overseas administrators:* applicants should be able to use Word, Excel, and possess advanced PC skills along with good organisational skills. *Overseas resort representatives:* applicants should have at least 12 months' customer service experience. Sales experience is preferable. Maturity, a calm manner and good organisation are all necessary skills. *Overseas transfer and guiding representatives:* applicants should have at least 6 months customer service experience.

Accommodation: Provided, meals not included.

Application Procedure: Applications should be made via the online application form on the Olympic website http://www.olympicholidays.com/information/job-overseas.htm. Interviews will take place from November 2010 to April 2011.

Richmond Christian Holidays

Job(s) Available: Assistant managers, chefs and assistant chefs, children's and teen's workers, hosts, resort managers, resort representatives, waterfront managers.

Duration: Varying between May and October, depending on position. Also ski season positions available between December and April.

Head Office: Sunrise House, Coombe Lane West, Kingston KT2 7DB, UK
☎ 020 3004 2661
✆ jobs@richmond-holidays.com
🖳 www.richmond-holidays.com

Working Hours: Various, depending on role.

Company Description: Richmond Holidays is a holiday provider offering sun and ski holidays with a Christian emphasis.

Accommodation: Contractual accommodation and travel included.

Application Procedure: Download an application form from the website, email or apply in writing to above addresses.

Skyros

Job(s) Available: Work scholars.

Duration: Period of work about 3 months; either April to July or July to October.

Head Office: 9 Eastcliff Road, Shankin, Isle of Wight PO37 6AA, UK
☎ 01983 865566
✆ office@skyros.com

Working Hours: Variable working hours, but normally 6–8 hours per day, 6 days a week.

Pay: Allowance of around £50 per week plus full board and accommodation.

Company Description: Skyros offer holistic holidays: combine a holiday in a Greek island with the chance to participate in over 200 courses from yoga to sailing and cooking.

Job Description: Work scholars to assist in the smooth running of Atsitsa, a holistic holiday centre on Skyros island. Duties include cleaning, bar work, laundry, gardening and general maintenance. Work scholars live as part of the community; in exchange for their hard work they may participate in the courses (such as yoga, dance and windsurfing) where their duties allow.

Requirements: Minimum age 21. Qualified nurses, chefs and Greek speakers preferred.

Application Procedure: Applications should be sent to the above address between January and February.

Voluntary work

Archelon Sea Turtle Protection Society of Greece

Job(s) Available: Volunteers.

Duration: Minimum period of work 4 weeks. Projects run from mid-May to mid-October. There are greater needs for volunteers at each end of the project (May, June, September, October).

Head Office: Archelon Solomou, Solomou 57 Street, GR-104 32 ATHENS, Greece
☎ +30 210 5231342
✆ volunteers@archelon.gr
🖳 www.archelon.gr

Cost: Once approved, an applicant will have to pay a non-refundable participation fee of €250. This covers administration costs, annual subscription to ARCHELON, an exclusive 'volunteer' t-shirt and a turtle biology book (both received upon arrival). However fees vary during certain periods: from May to 15 June €150, 16 June to 20 August €250 and 21 August to mid-October

€150. Archelon cannot provide any financial assistance. Volunteers cover both travel and food expenses. A minimum of €15 per day should suffice to cover basic food needs. Applicants arriving at the rescue centre will have to pay the fee of €150 all year round.

Company Description: Archelon is a non-profit-making NGO founded in 1983 to study and protect sea turtles and their habitats as well as raising public awareness. Each year over 300 volunteers participate in STPS projects.

Job Description: Volunteers are required for summer fieldwork on the islands of Zakynthos, Crete and Peloponnesus, where the Mediterranean's most important loggerhead nesting beaches are to be found. Volunteers will participate in all aspects of the projects including tagging turtles and public relations, and will receive on-site training. The work can involve long nights in the cold or long days in the heat, so a resilient, positive and friendly attitude is essential, especially as the society's work requires constructive co-existence with local communities. Volunteers are also required to work at the Sea Turtle Rescue Centre. This is a new centre set up on the coast 20km from Athens to help treat and rehabilitate turtles caught in fishing nets or injured by speedboats. Volunteers will help in the treatment of injured turtles, assisting the ongoing construction of the site and carry out public relations work with visitors.

Requirements: A basic knowledge of animal care is helpful but not essential. Minimum age 18. Volunteers must be willing to work in teams with people from other nationalities and backgrounds. Volunteers should be able to communicate in English and have their own health insurance.

Accommodation: *Islands of Zakynthos, Crete and Peloponnesus:* provided at basic camp-sites. Volunteers will need to provide their own tents and sleeping bags; warm clothing will be required for night work as the temperature can get quite cold. Smart clothes are needed when working in hotels and information stations. *Sea Turtle Rescue Centre:* free accommodation is provided in converted railway carriages.

Application Procedure: Application forms can be obtained by contacting the above address including an International Reply Coupon. Successful applicants will be informed within one month of application.

Elix-Conservation Volunteers Greece

Job(s) Available: Volunteers.
Duration: Minimum period of work 2 weeks.
Working Hours: 5–6 hours per day, 6 days a week.
Company Description: Since 1987 Elix-Conservation Volunteers Greece through its activities promotes the creative cooperation among young people from all over the world.

Head Office: Veranzerou 15, 106 77 Athens
☎ +30 2 1038 25506
🖥 www.elix.org.gr
✉ communication@elix.org.gr

Job Description: Volunteers will be working on projects that have a strong emphasis on Greek culture and the protection of the Greek environment and take place in several areas of the country from remote villages to big cities.

Accommodation: ELIX-CVG provides food, shared accommodation, and accident insurance.

Application Procedure: Applications can be sent to the above address from the beginning of April. Prospective volunteers from the UK can also apply through UNA Exchanges and Concordia UK. Contact through website.

Medasset (Mediterranean Association to Save the Sea Turtles)

Job(s) Available: Conservation volunteers.
Duration: Minimum period of work 3 weeks.
Cost: Volunteers pay for their own transport costs etc.
Job Description: Conservation volunteers needed to assist staff at central Athens office with campaigns and projects, filing, letter writing, database updating, fundraising, internet search and more.
Accommodation: Free accommodation is provided in central Athens.
Application Procedure: For further details contact the above addresses.

> **Head Office:** 1c Licavitou Str. 106 72 Athens
> ☎ +30 2 1036 13572
> ✆ medasset@medasset.org
> 🖳 www.medasset.org

Nine Muses Agency

Job(s) Available: Au pairs.
Duration: *Summer placements:* minimum period of work 1 to 3 months.
Working Hours: 30 hours per week.
Company Description: The owner Kalliope Raekou prides herself on her after-placement service, meeting regularly with au pairs at coffee afternoons.
Job Description: Au pairs to assist families with housework and look after children.
Requirements: Applicants should be young European or American women.
Additional Information: Hotel positions sometimes also available. Can also place candidates after arrival in Athens.
Application Procedure: For further details contact the above address.

> **Head Office:** Thrakis 39 and Vas. Sofias 2, 17121 Nea Smyrni, Athens
> ☎ +30 2 1093 16588
> ✆ ninemuses@ninemuses.gr
> 🖳 www.ninemuses.gr

ICELAND

The island of Iceland has a tiny population of about 300,000 inhabitants. The unemployment rate is at around 9%. Iceland is a member of the European Economic Area (EEA) and thus EEA citizens as well as European Union (EU) citizens have the right to live and work in Iceland without a work permit. Foreign nationals (not citizens of the EEA/EU) who wish to work and live in Iceland can only do so if they have arranged a contract of engagement with an Icelandic employer prior to entering Iceland; the employer will arrange for a limited work and residence permit. Summer is really the only time to get paid and unpaid temporary work as it gets much colder after that. Demand is greatest in the fish, farming, tourism and construction industries. The minimum period of work is usually three months.

There are eight regional employment offices in Iceland and EURES advisors can be consulted at Borgartuni, 7b, 105 Reykjavik, Iceland (+354 554 7600; eures@vmst.is). Efforts to recruit tend to be focused on the Scandinavian countries through the Nordjobb scheme (www.nordjobb.net), which arranges summer jobs for citizens of Scandinavia aged 18–25 able to work in Iceland for at least four weeks.

Red tape

ADDRESS: EMBASSY OF ICELAND
2A Hans Street, London SW1X 0JE
☎ 020 7259 3999
✆ icemb.london@utn.stjr.is
🖥 www.iceland.org/uk

Visa requirements: A visa is not required by citizens of the USA, Canada, Australia and most European countries, if they are entering Iceland as a visitor or as tourists. Visit www.utl.is/english for more information.

Iceland is a member of the Schengen countries and those with a Schengen visa may travel freely in the Schengen zone.

Residence permits: EEA citizens residing longer than three months, or six months if seeking work should register right of residence at the National Registry: Thjodskra, Borgartuni 24, 105 Reykjavik, Iceland (+354 569 2900; thjodskra@thjodskra.is).

Work permits: Work permits are not needed by nationals of the UK or any other EU country.

For up-to-date information about visa requirements check with the embassy before travel.

Voluntary work

Worldwide Friends

Job(s) Available: Volunteers for work camps.
Duration: 2–12 weeks.
Working Hours: 6 hours per day, 5 days a week.
Job Description: Projects fall into 4 broad categories: art projects, physical work such as building, planting and restoration. Social work, often with

Head Office: Einarsnes 56, 101 Reykjavik
☎ + 354 552 5214
✆ wf@wf.is
🖥 www.wf.is

children or people with handicaps. Work/study, where work and learning opportunities are integrated.
Requirements: Minimum age 18.
Accommodation: Places must be booked or else accommodation can be arranged in a sleeping bag at a cost.
Additional Information: Participation costs €90–€120 depending on the project and its duration.
Application Procedure: In order to join a work camp you need to contact the nearest partner organisation in your country www.iusgb.org.uk in the UK, www.vsiireland.org in Ireland or via the website.

Other employment in Iceland

Ninukot-work-study-Travel

Job(s) Available: This private work and travel agency originally found horticultural and agricultural jobs throughout Iceland but now also finds jobs babysitting, horse training, gardening and in tourism, plus other short-term jobs.

Duration: Minimum period of work 3 months.

Company Description: The website is in English and so offers the opportunity to pre-arrange a working holiday in Iceland.

Application Procedure: Only online applications to the above website.

> **Head Office:** Sidumuli 13,
> 108 Reykjavik, Iceland
> ☎ +354 561 2700
> ✆ ninukot@ninukot.is
> 🖳 www.ninukot.is

IRELAND

Unemployment is high in Ireland, at around 12%–13%.

Ireland offers a number of opportunities for seasonal work. The greatest demand for summer staff is in the tourist industry, which is concentrated around Dublin and in the west, south-west and around the coast. Unlike several other EU countries, Ireland has not imposed restrictions on the arrival of immigrants from the new (2004) member countries of eastern Europe. Consequently, seasonal jobs are rapidly filled by workers from these countries. Ireland is however a notoriously expensive country to live in and has high taxes but without the correspondingly high wages to compensate for such costs. Wages are, however, rising steadily.

There is a fair chance of finding paid work on farms and also scope for organising voluntary work. Two organisations can help those wishing to work voluntarily on Irish farms or who are interested in learning organic farming techniques; World Wide Opportunities On Organic Farms and the Irish Organic Farmers and Growers Association. About 80 Irish hosts can be found on the WWOOF independents list; this can be found at www.wwoof.org. For information on the Irish Organic Farmers and Growers Association, contact them at Main Street, Newtownforbes, Co Longford, Ireland (+353 043 334 2495; www.irishorganic.ie).

FAS is Ireland's training and employment agency. In addition to accessing details of Irish vacancies on their website www.fas.ie, jobseekers can also register their CV and state what type of job they would like to do. Jobseekers with a work permit in Ireland can call to the local FAS EURES office for details of vacancies. The main one for foreigners is the Dublin office (27–33 Upper Baggot Street, Dublin 4, Ireland; +353 1 6070500; info@fas.ie). Jobseekers from outside Ireland can also gain access to vacancies by using the European Commission's internet EURES placement system http://ec.europa.eu/eures/. There are also listings of private employment agencies in the *Irish Golden Pages* (www.goldenpages.ie).

Those seeking temporary work in Ireland's hospitality and leisure industry who don't want to be based in Dublin can try the main tourist regions including most of the south-west and County Kerry. Some vacancies can be found on EURES where prospective employees can leave their details. Potential employers can then access the website's database and contact you to invite you to apply for jobs they are offering.

Foreign students are under certain employment restrictions in Ireland with the exception of students from the USA, Canada, Australia and New Zealand, which have reciprocal agreements with Ireland. Students from other nations studying in Ireland may work up to 20 hours per week in term and full-time in vacations only if they are attending a full-time course of at least a year leading to a recognised qualification. As their primary cause for being in Ireland is study, work permits are not required but working beyond the above limits will be construed as a breach of the students' study visa. This change in the availability of casual work for students does not remove the financial support requirements for student visas.

In addition to the opportunities listed in this chapter voluntary work can be arranged by International Voluntary Service for British applicants and Service Civil International for Americans: see the *Worldwide* chapter for details.

Placing an advertisement in an Irish newspaper may lead to a job. Several newspaper websites carry information on job vacancies. You might also try the websites for job listings; these include the *Irish Examiner* (www.examiner.ie), the *Irish Independent* (www.independent.ie), the *Irish Times* (www.ireland.com), the *Sunday Business Post* (www.sbpost.ie) or the *Sunday Tribune* (www.tribune.ie).

Red tape

ADDRESS: EMBASSY OF IRELAND
17 Grosvenor Place, London SW1X 7HR
☎ 020 7235 2171
🖥 www.embassyofireland.co.uk

Visa requirements: If you are a citizen of an EU member state, you do not require a tourist visa to travel to Ireland. A number of other nationalities can enter Ireland without applying for a visa in advance including Australians, Canadians, New Zealanders and Americans. The full list of countries that do not require a visa in advance of entering Ireland is available on the Irish Naturalisation and Immigration Service website www.inis.gov.ie. Only nationals of EU/EEA countries can become workers in Ireland without a visa.

Residence permits: EU citizens do not require residence permits. However, nationals of the other EEA countries and Switzerland still need residence permits to stay in Ireland. On arrival in Ireland these citizens do not have to report their presence in the country immediately. However they must register within three months of their arrival and apply for a residence permit. If resident in Dublin, they should register with the Garda National Immigration Bureau. In other areas, they should register at the local Garda District Headquarters.

Work permits: A work permit is granted by the Department of Enterprise, Trade and Employment to an employer in order to employ a non-EU/EEA national in a specific position in their company or organisation for a specific period of time. For further information contact Employment Permits, Davitt house, 65a Adelaide Road, Dublin 2, Ireland, (+353 1 417 5333; employmentpermits@deti.ie).

'Work in Ireland' scheme for Americans and Canadians: 'Work in Ireland' is a reciprocal programme which allows US students to work in Ireland for up to four months, and Canadian students to work in Ireland for up to 12 months. For further information contact: BUNAC USA (+1 203 2640901; info@bunacusa.org; www.bunac.org/usa) or SWAP (www.swap.ca) for Canadians.

Working holiday permit for Australians and New Zealanders: Working holiday permits are available to Australians and New Zealanders for one year. This is also available for those travelling from Hong Kong and Canada. For further information and information about eligibility contact the relevant Irish embassy.

For up-to-date information about visa requirements check with the embassy before travel.

Hotel work and catering

Ardagh Hotel

Job(s) Available: Chambermaids, waiting/bar staff, chefs, kitchen porters, reception/bar staff.
Duration: Period of work 3 months. From Easter to November. Busy season mid-July to mid-September.
Working Hours: Flexible.
Pay: National minimum wage rates.

Head Office: Ballyconneely Road, Clifden, Connemara, Co Galway
☎ +353 9521 384
🖰 ardaghhotel@eircom.net
🖵 www.ardaghhotel.com

Requirements: Applicants must speak English. Must have 1 year's experience in the hotel trade, be flexible and have an interest in catering.
Accommodation: Provided.
Application Procedure: Send CV and telephone numbers for references by email.

Blue Haven Collection

Job(s) Available: Accommodation assistants (2–4), bar/restaurant staff (8), kitchen junior chefs (3–4), receptionist (3).
Duration: Minimum period of work is 3 months between 1 May and 31 October.
Working Hours: 39 hours per week, 5 days a week, subject to business.
Pay: Varies depending on role.

Head Office: 3 Pearse Street, Kinsale, Co Cork
☎ +353 2147 72209
🖰 info@bluehavenkinsale.com
🖵 www. bluehavencollection.com

Company Description: The Blue Haven Collection has 3 businesses under its name: Hamlets Café/Bar, a vibrant bar that also caters for outside BBQs, pizzaria and carvery; Old Bank House 4-star Guest House, a Georgian house with 18 rooms, with a recently opened café on the ground floor for the public and guests; and The Blue Haven Boutique Hotel which has 17 rooms with a 70-seated restaurant, a newly refurbished bar/bistro/conservatory and a popular Café Blue.
Job Description: *Accommodation assistants:* cleaning of all bedrooms and public areas. *Bar/restaurant staff:* responsible for service and hygiene. *Kitchen junior chefs:* preparation, presentation and service of food. Responsible for cleanliness in the kitchen. *Receptionist:* greeting, administration, hospitality.
Requirements: *Bar/restaurant staff:* relevant experience and fluent English essential. *Kitchen junior chefs:* experience preferred. *Receptionist:* computer skills necessary.
Accommodation: Not provided. Can be about €80 per week locally.
Application Procedure: By post to the above address with CVs and a recent photograph to info@bluehavenkinsale.com.

Castle Leslie

Job(s) Available: Food and beverage attendants.
Duration: Minimum period of work 3 months.
Working Hours: 5/7 days a week.
Pay: A competitive salary is provided.
Company Description: Irish country castle with

Head Office: Glaslough, Co Monaghan
☎ +353 478 8109
🖰 pa@castleleslie.com
🖵 www.castleleslie.com

specialist accommodation catering to local and international clientele.
Requirements: Restaurant and front-of-house staff should be fluent English speakers. Previous experience would be an advantage but further training will be given.

Accommodation: Board and lodging is available at a negotiable cost.
Application Procedure: Go to www.castleleslie.com/careers for up-to-date vacancies. Send a CV to Sinead Trainor at the above address or to pa@castleleslie.com.

Zetland Country House Hotel

Job(s) Available: Hotel staff (varying positions).
Working Hours: 10 hours per day, 5 days a week.
Pay: National minimum wage rates.
Company Description: A 4-star country house hotel on Ireland's west coast.
Requirements: Apart from the kitchen porter and

> **Head Office:** Cashel Bay, Connemara, Co Galway
> ☎ +353 953 1111
> 🖰 info@zetland.com
> 🖥 www.zetland.com

chambermaid positions, some previous hotel/catering experience is necessary. All staff should speak English. Staff must be able to work in the EU.
Application Procedure: Send CV by email.

Sports, couriers and camping

Errislannan Manor

Job(s) Available: Junior trek leader, pony child instructor, assistant gardener (2).
Duration: Minimum period of work 2 months. May to September.

> **Head Office:** Clifden, West Galway
> ☎ +353 952 1134
> 🖰 errislannanmanor@eircom.net
> 🖥 www.errislannan-manor.com

Working Hours: 5 days a week. Half-day Saturday.
Company Description: The manor is situated on Ireland's western seaboard, where the Gulf Stream allows palm trees and fuchsia to grow. It homes seabirds, sea shells and wildflowers.
Job Description: To work with 30 Connemara ponies on a trekking and riding centre mainly for children, the manor also breeds and schools ponies.
Accommodation: Provided. Some pocket money provided.
Application Procedure: Applications to Stephanie Brooks before March 2011.

Voluntary work

Barretstown

Job(s) Available: Activity leader, summer cara, volunteer cara. ('Cara' is the Irish word for friend.)
Duration: Length of contract for a summer cara is approximately from the end of May to the end of August. *Volunteer cara:* 9 or 12-day volunteer positions are available throughout the summer and 3 or

> **Head Office:** Barretstown Castle, Ballymore Eustace, Co Kildare
> ☎ +353 4586 4115
> 🖰 recruit@barretstown.org
> 🖥 www.barretstown.org

4-day weekends during our spring and autumn programmes.
Working Hours: Barretstown runs 7 10-day sessions each summer. There is no typical working day with contact hours varying, but staff can expect to work quite long days. Staff are given 3–4 days off between sessions with some time off every day during sessions including one 24-hour block.
Pay: Paid positions approximately €400 per week.
Cost: Travel costs are to be met by the applicant.

Company Description: Located in a castle in the foothills of the Wicklow mountains in Ireland, children with cancer and other serious illnesses come for some serious fun. The children and their families, from Ireland and 21 European countries, take part in a unique programme recognised by the medical world as playing an important part in their recovery from serious illness. Barretstown has developed a programme recognised as 'therapeutic recreation' by the medical world, it is internationally recognised as having a positive impact on the lives of children with serious illness and their families. Spring and autumn programmes focus mainly on the family, providing Family Camps, Bereavement weekends. The 10 and 7-day summer programmes cater for children and teens aged between 7 and 17. Barretstown's programmes help children to discover the courage they need to undertake the difficult journey of their illness and its treatment, and encourages them to take part more actively in their recovery process.

Job Description: *Summer cara and activity leader:* training period of 1 week before sessions start. *Activity leader:* responsible for designing, planning and directing one or more activities. Will have overall responsibility for the safety and age appropriateness of the activities. *Summer cara:* to be responsible for supporting and encouraging each child to participate fully in all aspects of camp to ensure they have the best experience possible and to look after their day and night time needs. *Volunteer cara:* required throughout the day to accompany the children in their activity group to scheduled activities and to look after their night time needs.

Requirements: Applicants must possess experience in people guidance and group work. Applicants must be over 18 and must be fluent in English. Some experience with children or young people, particularly in terms of social, creative or sporting activities would be an advantage. Background checks will be performed.

Accommodation: All posts are residential, full shared accommodation and all food is provided.

Additional Information: Volunteer interpreters and chaperones also required. On-site medical volunteers also needed.

Application Procedure: Application forms can be downloaded from the website or by request from Barretstown. Apply by the end of March.

Simon Communities of Ireland

Job(s) Available: Volunteers, part-time and full-time.

Duration: A minimum commitment of 6 months is required.

Working Hours: Volunteers work shifts. Regular holidays.

Head Office: St Andrew's House, 28-30 Exchequer Street, Dublin 2
☎ +353 1671 1606
volunteering@simoncommunity.com
www.simoncommunity.org.uk

Pay: Weekly pocket money allowance provided (full-time volunteers only).

Job Description: Volunteers required to work alongside the homeless in Ireland. The main duties of the volunteer include befriending residents and general housekeeping.

Requirements: Minimum age 18.

Accommodation: Full board and lodging for full-time volunteers only.

Application Procedure: Fill out an online application form. Interviews are necessary.

Voluntary Service International

Job(s) Available: Volunteers to work with VSI (the Irish branch of Service Civil International).

Duration: VSI organise 30 short-term voluntary work camps helping communities throughout Ireland each summer.

Company Description: The aim of the organisation is to promote peace and understanding through voluntary service in Ireland and throughout the world. VSI welcome the participation of volunteers from other countries.

Head Office: 30 Mountjoy Square, Dublin 1
☎ +353 855 1011
📧 info@vsi.ie
💻 www.vsi.ie

Application Procedure: Enquiries and applications must go through your local Service Civil International Branch www.sciint.org or work camp organisation.

Other employment in Ireland

Aillwee Cave Co Ltd

Job(s) Available: Catering staff (6), cave tour guides (5), sales staff (2). Throughout the year a variety of positions become available.

Duration: Minimum period of work 2 months. Work commences March. Majority of staff needed by the end of April. Please provide the exact dates which you are available to work.

Head Office: Aillwee Cave, Ballyvaughan, Co Clare
☎ +353 6570 77036
📧 fiona@aillweecave.ie
💻 www.aillweecave.ie

Working Hours: 39 hours per week, 5 days a week 10am–6pm. Half-hour lunch break and two 15-minute tea breaks to be taken in rotation with other staff.

Pay: *Catering staff:* from €1,100 gross per month. *Cave tour guides:* approximately €1,100 gross, per month plus tips. *Sales staff:* from €1,200 per month.

Company Description: Aillwee Cave is a show cave in Ireland and has a large amount of visitors each year. Its location is in the 'Burren' in Co Clare and is popular with visitors. Train and develop your sales and catering experience, customer service skills and gain experience as a member of a professional team.

Job Description: *Catering staff:* to work as counter hands for the salad bar, fast food outlet and potato bar. *Cave tour guides:* to lead a maximum of 35 persons on a 45-minute tour through the caves. *Sales staff:* to work in the gift shop or to work in a farm shop in which cheese is made daily on the premises.

Requirements: Proficiency in English essential and a genuine wish to work in tourism. Leaving certificate or equivalent desirable. A desire to be friendly, helpful and flexible is essential. *Catering staff:* experience necessary. *Cave tour guides:* training will be given. Knowledge of geology a help but not essential. *Sales staff:* previous sales experience an advantage.

Accommodation: Hostel-type accommodation is available. Rental charges are €50 per week.

Additional Information: Work is also now available from mid-November to the end of December for people with some drama/acting/singing experience to act as cave guide for the Santa Claus Project. Also opened a Bird of Prey Centre. See website for more details

Application Procedure: By post with full CV, colour photograph and contact numbers for references to Fiona Mellett at the above address or apply by telephone.

ITALY

The rate of unemployment in Italy has risen to 8%–9%. This can be misleading however as there is a sharp divide between northern and southern Italy in this respect. In the industrial power-house of the north, unemployment is lower, while in the far south it can be as high as 20% in some regions. The best chances of obtaining paid employment in Italy are probably with the tour operators in this and the *Worldwide* chapter. Other possibilities involve teaching English as a for-eign language, though most who get jobs have a TEFL qualification and are prepared to stay longer than a few months of the summer. If you want to try and find this sort of job once you are in Italy look up *Scuole di Lingue* in the *Yellow Pages*. Those with special skills are most likely to find work: for example an experienced secretary with a good knowledge of English, Italian and German would be useful in a hotel catering for large numbers of German, British and American tourists. Otherwise it is surprisingly difficult to find work in hotels and catering as there are many Italians competing for the jobs and now also people from eastern European countries that joined the EU in 2004 and 2007. People looking for hotel work while in Italy should do best if they try small hotels first: some large hotel chains in northern resorts take on staff from southern Italy, where unemployment is especially high, for the summer season and then move them on to their mountain ski resorts for the winter season.

Although Italy is the world's largest producer of wine, a similar problem exists with the grape harvest (*vendemmia*): vineyard owners traditionally employ migrant workers from North Africa and other Arab countries to help the local work force. Opportunities are best in the north-west of the country, for example in the vineyards lying south-east of Turin in Piemonte, and in the north-east in Alto Adige and to the east and west of Verona. The harvest generally takes place from September to October. For details of the locations of vineyards consult the *World Atlas of Wine* (Hugh Johnson and Jancis Robinson, Mitchell Beazley 2007). The same publishers also produce the useful *Touring in Wine Country: Tuscany* (Maureen Ashley, Mitchell Beazley 2000).

There are other possibilities for fruit picking earlier in the year, but again there will be stiff competition for work. Strawberries are picked in the region of Emilia Romagna in June, and apples are picked from late August in the region of Alto Adige and in the Valtellina, which lies between the north of Lake Como and Tirano. More information about finding casual farm work is given in *Work Your Way Around the World* by Susan Griffith (Vacation Work 2009; see *Useful publications*). When in Italy you should be able to get information on local harvest work from *Centri Informazione Giovani* (Youth Information Offices) which exist throughout the country for the benefit of local young people: consult telephone directories for their addresses.

EU nationals are allowed to use the Italian state employment service when looking for a job in Italy. To find the addresses of local employment offices in Italy either look up *Centro per L'Impiego* in the telephone directory of the area where you are staying, or go to www.centroimpiego.it. Note that these offices will only deal with personal callers. For further information consult the free booklet *Working in Italy* published by the UK Employment Service.

International Voluntary Service (IVS), UNA Exchange and Concordia can assist British applicants to find voluntary work in Italy, and Service Civil International can aid Americans; see the *Worldwide* chapter for details.

An advertisement in an Italian newspaper may produce an offer of employment. Smyth International (PO BOX 333, Hertford, SG13 9GU; www.smyth-international.com) deal with *La Stampa* (Turin daily), and other provincial papers. The Milan paper *Il Giornale* is published at Via Gaetano Negri 4, I-20123 Milan (www.ilgiornale.it). The Friday edition of *Corriere della Sera* (www.corriere.it) has a large section of employment adverts.

Red tape

ADDRESS: ITALIAN CONSULATE
38 Eaton Place, London SW1X 8AN
☎ 020 7312 2200
✆ ambasciata.londra@esteri.it
💻 www.conslondra.esteri.it

Visa requirements: Full citizens of the UK, the USA, Australia, New Zealand and most western European countries do not require a visa for visits of up to three months.

Italy is a member of the Schengen countries and those with a Schengen visa may travel freely in the Schengen zone.

Residence permits: Visitors staying in a hotel will be registered with the police automatically. Those intending to stay for more than three months should apply to the local police at the *Questura* (local police headquarters) for a *permesso di soggiorno* which is valid for 90 days. If you arrive with the intention of working, EU nationals must first apply to the police *(questura)* for a *Ricevuta di Segnalazione di Soggiorno* which allows them to stay for up to three months looking for work. Upon production of this document and a letter from an employer, you must go back to the police to obtain a residence permit – *Permesso di Soggiorno*. Then in some cases you will be asked to apply for a *Libretto di Lavoro* (work registration card) from the *Ispettorato del Lavoro* and/or *Ufficio di Collocamento* (although, in theory, this should not be necessary for EU nationals).

Special schemes for Australians and New Zealanders: Australians and New Zealanders aged 18–30 are eligible for a working holiday visa for up to 12 months in Italy. Further details can be obtained from the Italian embassy in Wellington (www.ambwellington.esteri.it).

Work permits: A work permit is issued by the local authorities to the prospective employer, who will then forward it to the worker concerned. Non-EU citizens must obtain the permit before entering Italy.

For up-to-date information about visa requirements check with the embassy before travel.

Hotel work and catering

Darwin SrL

Company Description: Darwin SRL is a recruitment organisation dealing with hotels, resorts and tourist villages all over the world.
Application Procedure: Email CV from February.

Head Office: Piazza Del Pesce 1, 50122 – Firenze
☎ +39 0 5529 2114
✆ darwinstaff@yahoo.it
💻 www.darwinstaff.com

Hotel Cavallino D'Oro

Job(s) Available: Assistant manager, chambermaids (2), dish washers (2), kitchen help (2) and waiters (2).
Duration: Minimum period of work 10 weeks. Staff needed all year, except November.
Working Hours: 7 hours per day, 6 days a week.
Pay: Dependent upon experience and qualifications.
Company Description: This renovated hotel in the old village square of Kastelruth, dates from 1326, giving it a history of hospitality spanning 680 years.
Requirements: Knowledge of German and/or Italian would be an advantage, and is essential for the managerial position.
Accommodation: Available upon request.
Application Procedure: Applications to the above address all year round by email.

> **Head Office:** I-39040 Castelrotto, Sudtirol, Dolomiti
> ☎ +39 0 4717 06337
> cavallino@cavallino.it
> 🖥 www.cavallino.it

Country Hotel Fattoria Di Vibio

Job(s) Available: Barman/waiter, chambermaid.
Duration: Minimum 2 month stay required between 15 June and 15 September.
Working Hours: 8 hours per day, 6 days a week.
Pay: Approximately £265 per month.
Company Description: A family-run country house.
Job Description: *Barman/waiter:* required to serve at tables in the restaurant/bar. *Chambermaid:* required to clean rooms and carry out other general cleaning jobs.
Requirements: Applicants should have relevant experience, be aged 20–35 and have a good knowledge of spoken Italian and English.
Accommodation: Board and accommodation provided.
Application Procedure: By post to Doglio, 05010, San Venanzo, Terni from February.

> **Head Office:** Doglio, I-06057 Montecastello di Vibio (PG)
> ☎ +39 0 7587 49607
> info@fattoriadivibio.com
> 🖥 www.fattoriadivibio.com

Hotel Des Geneys Splendid

Job(s) Available: Porters (2), 1 for day and 1 for night.
Duration: Minimum period of work July and August.
Working Hours: 6-day week of 48 hours.
Pay: €900 per month.
Company Description: A hotel with a youthful and family atmosphere. An ideal place to learn Italian, study and rest.
Accommodation: Free board and accommodation.
Application Procedure: Email CV to the above address.

> **Head Office:** Via Luigi Einaudi 21, 10052 Bardonecchia, Casella Postale 45
> ☎ +39 0 1229 9001
> info@hoteldesgeneys.it
> 🖥 www.hoteldesgeneys.it

IL Paretaio

Job(s) Available: Grooms, horse riding instructor, waiter/kitchen help.
Working Hours: 8 hours per day, 6 days a week (Monday to Saturday).
Pay: Salary negotiable.
Company Description: Country house accommodation and horse riding school half an hour from Florence and Siena.

> **Head Office:** Strada delle Ginestra 12, Barberino Velsa-Firenze
> ☎ +39 0 5580 59218
> ilparetaio@tin.it
> 🖥 www.ilparetaio.it

Job Description: *Grooms:* to look after horses. *Waiter/kitchen help:* to be in charge of breakfast and serving dinner for 20 people. No cooking, just serving and cleaning.

Requirements: *Grooms:* must be experienced with horses.

Accommodation: *Grooms:* lodging, food and horse riding. *Waiter/kitchen help:* board and lodging.

Application Procedure: Applications at any time to Giovanni de Marchi at the above address or email.

Hotel Tenuta Di Ricavo

Job(s) Available: Restaurant and reception assistant, waiter.

Duration: Minimum period of work is 2 months. Period of work from April to September/October. *Waiter:* from April/May to September/October.

Working Hours: 40 hours per week, 6 days a week.
Restaurant and reception assistant: for morning, afternoon and evening shifts.

Head Office: Loc Ricavo 4, 53011 Castellina in Chianti
☎ +39 0 5777 40221
📧 ricavo@ricavo.com
💻 www.ricavo.com

Pay: *Restaurant and reception assistant:* €1,100. *Waiter:* approximately €1,100.

Company Description: A 4-star hotel amidst typical Chianti landscape half an hour from both Siena and Florence.

Job Description: *Waiter:* to work at breakfast, lunch, dinner as service, room and pool service, filling up stock, stocking minibar, cleaning restaurant.

Requirements: *Restaurant and reception assistant:* besides English, knowledge of Italian requested.

Accommodation: Room in staff house at hotel. Lunch and evening dinner at staff mensa. Breakfast not included.

Application Procedure: To apply send CV with references and photo to the above address or email.

Sports, couriers and camping

Collett's Mountain Holidays

Job(s) Available: *Summer season in the Dolomites or Pyrenees:* artists, chalet hosts/cooks, resort managers, resort representatives (who can also speak Italian, German or Spanish) and walk and via ferrata 'organisers'. *Winter season:* chalet host/cooks, managers, ski guides and walk organisers.

Head Office: Harvest Mead, Great Hormead, Buntingford, Herts SG9 0PB, UK
☎ 01763 289660
📧 work@colletts.co.uk
💻 www.colletts.co.uk/work

Duration: From mid-May to late September. Applicants are preferred who are willing to work a full season.

Working Hours: Between 7 and 10 hours per day, 6 days a week.

Pay: *Walk and via ferrata 'organisers' and ski guides:* £85 per week. *Resort managers:* £95 per week. *Resort representatives:* £85 per week. *Chalet hosts/cooks:* £95 per week.

Company Description: Collett's Mountain Holidays offers specialist holidays to the Italian Dolomites and South Tyrol for walkers, climbers, wildflower enthusiasts and painters. Each year they recruit people for the summer to join their small resort teams to do a variety of jobs based in 3 Alpine villages in the Central Dolomites and one in the Spanish Pyrenees.

Job Description: *Artists:* keen walker with interest in the mountains and the outdoors. Optional participation in organised walks programme. Involvement with domestic tasks, cleaning, helping at dinner, kitchen assistance etc. Responsible for art programme as well as general care and well-being of guests. *Chalet hosts/cooks:* couples and individuals welcome to apply. Running an alpine chalet for between 10 and 20 guests and expected to fulfil cooking, hosting and hospitality. Must have a warm, engaging sociable and efficient manner. Provide breakfast and a 3-course evening meal 6 days a week, also responsible for domestic management of the chalet such as room cleaning, food ordering, chalet accounts, kitchen hygiene procedures etc. *Resort managers:* couples welcome as well as individuals. Required to perform various management tasks in one of three alpine resorts. Includes hospitality, staff support and general management. Overseeing the day-to-day running of the resort. Food and laundry ordering, accounts, cleaning rotas, airport transfers. Participate in the organised walk programme with guests. *Resort representatives:* required for office management, accounts, food and laundry ordering and management and supplier liaison. Participation in organised walks and/or via ferrata. Caring for well-being of guests, assistance, advice and suggestions. Booking restaurants and activities etc. Domestic tasks, cleaning and kitchen assistance. *Ski guides:* similar role to the summer walk organisers but spend time accompanying guests on ski day and snowshoes routes, with domestic chores every other day. *Walk and via ferrata 'organisers':* required to organise and accompany guests on high and low level walks or via ferratas in the area. Advising guests on suitable walking and/or via ferrata routes. Domestic commitment involving chalet cleaning, kitchen work and hosting assistance. Also involved with airport transfer driving.

Requirements: *Artists:* preferably qualifications up to degree level or experience of teaching art in some capacity. Untrained but talented individuals welcome to apply. *Chalet hosts/cooks:* applicants must have a good amount of cooking experience, but not necessarily professional. A passion for food and sharing it with other people is very important. Food hygiene certificate is a bonus. *Resort managers:* must have a good level of spoken Italian or German. Must have experience of managing people, excellent interpersonal skills and the ability to think on their feet, as well as the experience and interest needed for the walk organiser role. *Resort representatives:* applicants must have an excellent level of spoken Italian and a good manner with people. Must have a patient and helpful personality. Experience of accounting and/or Microsoft Excel a bonus. *Ski guides:* must be proficient skiers able to ski well on any grade of piste. *Via ferrata organisers:* must have good ropework skills and climbing experience. *Walk organisers:* must have excellent map reading and navigational skills. Outdoor and first aid qualifications are a bonus but not essential.

Accommodation: Board and lodging provided free of charge.

Application Procedure: Applications invited at any time of the year for summer and winter jobs. Go to the recruitment site www.colletts.co.uk/work and fill in an online application. For more information contact Phil Melia on 01763 289660 or email work@colletts.co.uk.

Interski

Job(s) Available: Classics coordinator, school and college coordinator, resort assistant, head resort assistant, resort rescue, snow coach assistants, resort support, ski hire coordinator/assistant, part-time ski instructors BASI Level 2 or national equivalent.

Duration: From December to April

Working Hours: Clients in resort 24/7 so working hours are dictated by the requirements of the position.

Pay: Dependent on position.

Head Office: 8 Acorn Park, Commercial Gate, Mansfield, Nottinghamshire
NG18 1EX, UK
☎ 01623 456333
✉ email@interski.co.uk
🖥 www.interski.co.uk

Company Description: With over 25 years of experience and over 150,000 clients, Interski is a unique tour operator offering all-inclusive snowsports holidays within the Aosta Valley, north-west Italy. One of the UK's leading schools and adult operators, based in the peaks surrounding Mont Blanc in the resorts of Courmayeur, Pila and La Thuile. Over 50 talented individuals are employed for the entire duration of the season plus over 1,000 part time snowsport instructors.

Requirements: Require talented and dynamic people. Ideally seeking individuals with experience in a customer related environment. Candidates must have an approachable nature, be able to demonstrate the ability to work under pressure, both independently and as part of a large team. But most importantly, must have enthusiasm and a genuine desire to make an impact on the clients' time in resort.

Accommodation: Good accommodation and full board provided for all positions.

Additional Information: Staff receive superb rewards and have the opportunity to spend time in an environment that will help develop your career in the sports/tourist industry. Travel to and from resort provided, along with lift pass and uniform without need for any retainer.

Application Procedure: Apply online for an application pack at www.interski.co.uk/resortteam.

Teaching and language schools

ACLE

Jobs Available: Summer camp English tutor.

Duration: From the beginning of June until mid-September. Usually 4–8 weeks.

Working Hours: Depending on the type of camp; 40+ hours per week, 5–7 days per week.

Pay: Weekly wage of €225–€275 net per week.

Head Office: Via Roma 54, 18083 Sanremo (IM)
☎ +39 0184 506070
✉ info@acle.it
🖥 www.acle.org

Company Description: Associazione Culturale Linguistica Educational (ACLE) is a non-profit educational organisation, officially recognised by the Italian Ministry of Education. ACLE promotes its own widely acclaimed innovative method of teaching English through drama, play and, most of all, fun!

Job Description: ACLE hosts 4–5 training Intro. to TEFL.TP (Teaching of English as a Foreign Language through Theatre and Play) orientation courses where you learn how to teach English through drama, games, sport and songs. Teaching at ACLE Camps throughout Italy is an intensive but rewarding summer experience where you can enjoy all that Italy has to offer and go home with some amazing memories. By working at ACLE Camps you will benefit from ACLE's 29 years of experience in this field; learn new teaching techniques based on emotional and physical involvement; obtain the TEFL.TP Certificate; improve your personal communication skills; visit different parts of Italy; discover Italian culture through direct contact with ACLE trainers and host families; make new friends from all over the world; gain a new perspective of your own culture; improve your self confidence and leadership skills and relax in magical, medieval Baiardo.

Requirements: ACLE recruits over 200 young (minimum age 19), responsible and enthusiastic native English speakers who love working with children. A university background combined with experience in volunteering, teaching and travelling are an advantage. Knowledge of Italian is not necessary. Prospective tutors must have successfully completed an online application, a demanding distance learning assignment and attended one of the Intro. to TEFL.TP Orientations organised by ACLE before being sent to camps.

Accommodation: During the orientation and camps ACLE provides meals, accommodation, insurance against work-related accidents and transportation between camps.

Application Procedure: Visit the website acle.org which has answers to your questions listed under FAQ, as well as application forms. Applications are due by 1 April 2011.

ACLE Theatrino

Job(s) Available: Native English-speaking TIE actors required.

Duration: Period of work January to June. Minimum period of work 6 months.

Working Hours: Flexible.

Pay: €230–€260 (plus a bonus) per week.

Head Office: Via Roma 54, 18038 Sanremo
☎ +39 0 1845 06070
✆ info@acle.org
🖥 www.acle.org

Company Description: Theatrino is part of ACLE, a non-profit organisation, which was the first to teach English to children and teenagers through Theatre in Education (TIE), and to organise drama courses recognised by the Italian Ministry of Education for Teachers. This small touring English-language theatre company recruit from the UK. Should be young, enthusiastic actors with plenty of energy to work in Italy on a 'Theatre in Education' tour.

Job Description: Actors tour Italian schools in groups of 3 and present graded interactive English-language shows. These are followed by workshops consisting of sketches adapted for a particular age group focusing on a particular theme and grammatical point. The overall emphasis is on promoting spoken English in a fun way.

Requirements: Applicants must be flexible, able to work in a team, be able to handle being 'on the road' and love working with children. Aged 20–30.

Accommodation: Provided. Food not included.

Application Procedure: Applicants must visit the website for details and an application form. Auditions are held in London in the autumn (date to be confirmed).

Keep Talking

Job(s) Available: English teachers for a language school in Italy.

Duration: 9-month contracts.

Working Hours: 25 hours per week, with an occasional maximum of 30.

Pay: Dependent on qualifications, experience and special skills.

Head Office: Via Roma 60, 33100 Udine
☎ +39 0 4325 01525 (Uldine)
✆ info@keeptalking.it
🖥 www.keeptalking.it

Company Description: Keep Talking was founded in Udine (north-east Italy) in 1989 and very quickly became a highly respected English-language training organisation in the area. Most of the students are adults (average age 20–40) learning English either for current or future jobs or personal interest/travel. Keep Talking also organises courses for children from 6 to 16. Large number of company clients. Keep Talking holds lessons at the school in the centre of Udine or out in companies.

Requirements: All applicants must have a university degree and CELTA or equivalent plus minimum 1 year of experience. Native English speakers. Applicants must have an EU passport or a current working visa and a clean driving licence.

Accommodation: Can be provided.

Application Procedure: For more information or to apply for a teaching post, please email a CV and covering letter to the above address.

Lingue Senza Frontiere

Job(s) Available: Camp tutors (60).

Duration: From early June for 2, 4 or 6 weeks.

Company Description: Italian non-profit association, officially recognised by the Ministry of Education.

Head Office: Corso Inglesi 172, 18038 Sanremo
☎ +390 184 533661
✆ christina@linguesenzafrontiere.org
🖥 www.linguesenzafrontiere.org

Job Description: Camp tutors for full-immersion summer camps. Camps are day camps and take place throughout Italy, north of Rome. In the morning children do worksheets and classroom games; in the afternoons arts, crafts and sports (all in English). At the end of the 2-week courses the children put on a show in English.

Requirements: All applicants must be fluent English speakers, over 21 and have experience teaching or working with children. Applicants should be able to lead sports, crafts or drama activities.

Accommodation: The association provides full board and accommodation, insurance, all materials, 3-day orientation and travel to and from the camps. Travel to Italy not included.

Application Procedure: Applications to Christina Niknejad at the above address/email.

Voluntary work

AGAPE

Job(s) Available: Volunteers for manual work alongside the permanent staff.

Duration: To work from 21 days to 5 weeks between the middle of June and September. Volunteers can work for weekends in spring and autumn seasons.

Working Hours: 6 hours per day, 6 days a week.

Company Description: AGAPE is an 'ecumenical centre', where believers of different faiths and

Head Office: Centro Ecumenico, I-10060 Prali (Torino)
☎ +39 0 12180 7514
✆ ufficio@agapecentroecumenico.org
or ufficio@campolaboragepe.
centroecumenico.org
🖳 www.agapecentroecumenico.org

denominational backgrounds can meet with non-believers in an open and relaxed atmosphere. AGAPE is situated in the village of Prali in the Germanasca valley, about 80 miles from Turin. The centre organises national and international 1-week seminars on theological, political, female, male and homosexuality issues. Its isolated position provides the opportunity to experience life away from modern stresses, although this means that the volunteers should be prepared to entertain themselves on occasions.

Job Description: Includes helping with cooking, cleaning, laundering and bar work etc.

Requirements: Minimum age 18. Knowledge of Italian or English an advantage.

Accommodation: Board and lodging provided.

Application Procedure: Applications should be sent to the above address.

Au pairs, nannies, family helps and exchanges

ARCE

Job(s) Available: Au pairs/mothers' helps for placements in Italy.

Duration: 6–12 months from September to June. 2–3 months in the summer.

Working Hours: 5–6 hours per day with 3 evenings babysitting.

Head Office: Via Molfino 64, 16032 Camogli, Genova, Italy
☎ +39 3386 161600
✆ info@arceaupair.it
🖳 www.arceaupair.it

Pay: €70 per week.

Job Description: To babysit and perform a little light housework.

Requirements: Aged 18–30. Single. Childcare experience essential. Knowledge of English and possibly Italian required. EU citizenship is also required.

Accommodation: Board and accommodation provided.

Application Procedure: Applications (male/female) from April to the above address.

LUXEMBOURG

The official language in Luxembourg is Luxembourgish but German and French are spoken and understood by almost everyone, and casual workers will normally need a reasonable knowledge of at least one of these. EU citizens can use the State Employment Service when they are looking for work and can get general information on the current work situation from them: Administration de l'Emploi (ADEM; +352 4785300; www.adem.public.lu). ADEM also operates an employment service for students and young people (Services Vacances; freephone in Luxembourg 80024646; info.jeu@adem.public.lu) offering jobs in warehouses, catering etc.

Employment agencies specialising in temporary work include Manpower-Aide Temporaire (42 rue Glesener, 1630 Luxembourg; +352 482323; luxembourghoreca@manpower.lu; www.manpower.lu). Employment agencies are listed in the yellow pages under *Agences de Travail*. In March or April of each year, a special forum for summer jobs is organised by the Youth Information Centre in Luxembourg City, where students can meet employees and firms offering summer jobs and be informed about their rights. The centre also runs a special service for summer jobs from April to August. The Youth Information Centre can be found at Centre Information Jeunes, 26 place de la Gare, L-1616 Luxembourg (+352 3200 2629 or +352 2629 3216; www.cij.lu).

The internet can be used for obtaining contact details of hotels in Luxembourg, for instance the directory www.hotels.lu or the website of the Luxembourg tourist office (www.luxembourg.co.uk).

People are sometimes needed to help with the grape harvest, which normally begins around 20 September and continues for four or five weeks.

To advertise in newspapers contact *Tageblatt* at 44 rue du Canal, L-4050 Esch-Alzette (+352 547131; www.tageblatt.lu) who also publish a French weekly called *Le Jeudi* aimed at foreigners living in Luxembourg.

Red tape

ADDRESS: EMBASSY OF LUXEMBOURG
27 Wilton Crescent, London SW1X 8SD
☎ 020 7235 6961
✆ londres.amb@mae.etat.lu
🖥 www.mae.lu _____

Visa requirements: No visa is necessary for entry into Luxembourg by members of an EU country or citizens of the USA, Canada, Australia or New Zealand. Nationals of Romania and Bulgaria still require an individual work permit.

Luxembourg is a member of the Schengen countries and those with a Schengen visa may travel freely in the Schengen zone.

Residence permits: If you wish to stay in Luxembourg for longer than three months, you must obtain permission in advance from the Administration Communale of the Municipality of Residence, unless you are an EU national. Non-EU nationals must produce a medical certificate and radiographic certificate issued by a doctor established in Luxembourg as well as the other documents required by all applicants: proof of identity and proof of sufficient means of support or a Déclaration Patronale.

Work permits: Necessary for any non-EU national wanting to work in Luxembourg. Permits (Déclaration Patronale) are issued by the Administration de l'Emploi to the prospective employer. Non-EU nationals must obtain a job and a work permit before entering Luxembourg. Foreigners are free to carry out voluntary work for recognised international bodies.

For up-to-date information about visa requirements check with the embassy before travel.

Hotel work and catering

Hotel Le Royal

Job(s) Available: Trainees (2).
Duration: 6-month placements.
Working Hours: 40 hours per week.
Pay: Staff will earn around £170 per month. As a trainee, staff will earn: 1–2 months, €150; 2–4 months, €200; 4–6 months, €300; 6–12 months, €450.

Head Office: 12 Boulevard Le Royal, L-2449
☎ +352 2416161
humanresources@hotelroyal.lu
www.hotelroyal.lu

Company Description: Located in the heart of Luxembourg City, this 5-star hotel has 210 rooms and suites, and prides itself on the attentive but discreet service of its staff.
Job Description: Trainees required to take up placements in this leading hotel. Successful candidates may be employed as restaurant and banquet waiting staff or assistant receipt controllers and auditors.
Requirements: Applicants should ideally speak French.
Accommodation: Board and lodging available.
Application Procedure: Applications are invited immediately and should be sent to the HR manager at the above address.

THE NETHERLANDS

The Netherlands has one of the lowest unemployment rates in the EU at only 5%. Most Dutch people speak excellent English, and so knowledge of Dutch is not essential for those looking for unskilled seasonal jobs. The tourist industry employs large numbers of extra workers over the summer: it is worth noting that the bulb fields attract tourists from spring onwards, and so the tourist season begins comparatively early for Europe. Early application is therefore important. Information on living and working in the Netherlands can be found on the Dutch Embassy's website (www.netherlands-embassy.org.uk)

There are also a number of opportunities for voluntary work. International Voluntary Service, Concordia and UNA Exchange recruit Britons and Service Civil International (see the IVS entry) in the USA recruits Americans for camps there; see the *Worldwide* chapter for details.

The Netherlands has many private employment agencies (*uitzendbureaus*) which are accustomed to finding short-term jobs for British and Irish workers. These jobs normally involve unskilled manual work, such as stocking shelves in supermarkets, working on factory production lines, or washing up in canteens. Most of the agencies will only help people who visit them in person. To discover nearby addresses look up *uitzendbureaus* in the *Gouden Gids (Yellow Pages;* www.goudengids.nl); Randstad, Unique and Manpower are among the best known names.

Some agencies handle vacancies for work in flower bulb factories, which need large numbers of casual workers from mid-April to October to pick asparagus, strawberries, gherkins, apples and pears: the peak period is between mid-June and the beginning of August. At the same time of year there are jobs in greenhouses and holiday parks. These jobs are popular with locals and usually can be filled with local jobseekers. From the end of September/beginning of October until January of the following year, jobs might be available in the bulb industry (bulb picking and in factories). Although bulbs are grown elsewhere in Holland, the industry is concentrated in the area between Haarlem and Lisse, especially around the town of Hillegom. There are also a limited number of jobs every year in the fruit and vegetable producing greenhouses of the 'Westland' in the province of Zuid-Holland.

EU nationals can make use of the service of the European Employment Services (EURES) represented in their own Public Employment Service and in the Netherlands. EURES provides jobseekers with information and advice about living and working in another country of the EU. The Euroadvisers also have an overview of temporary and permanent vacancies available in the Netherlands. Contact the nearby local employment office for more information. In the Netherlands addresses of local Dutch Euroadvisers can be obtained through the Landelijk Bureau Arbeidsvoorziening; look up *Arbeidsbureau* in a telephone directory. For further information consult the free booklet *Working in the Netherlands* published by the UK Employment Service (Jobcentre Plus).

Those wishing to place advertisements in Dutch newspapers may contact *De Telegraaf*, a major Dutch newspaper. There is a contact point on the website.

Red tape

ADDRESS: ROYAL NETHERLANDS EMBASSY
38 Hyde Park Gate, London SW7 5DP
☎ 020 7590 3200
✆ london@netherlands-embassy.org.uk
🖥 www.netherlands-embassy.org.uk

Visa requirements: Citizens of the UK, USA, EU countries, Canada, Australia, New Zealand, Switzerland and Japan do not need a visa. For more information see www.ind.nl. Members of countries needing a visa will have to apply for one at the Dutch embassy. The application will need to be accompanied by full details of means of support, accommodation and prospective employment. Entry may be refused to all travellers who are unable to show that they have the means to support themselves while in the Netherlands and to buy a return ticket.

The Netherlands are a member of the Schengen countries and those with a Schengen visa can travel freely in the zone.

Residence permits: Members of those countries not requiring a visa who intend to stay for more than three months must acquire a sticker in their passport from the local aliens police (*Vreemdelingenpolitie*) or town hall, normally over-the-counter, within eight days of arrival. Non-EU members may be required to undergo a medical check for tuberculosis, take out comprehensive medical insurance, submit evidence of suitable accommodation and means of support, and sign a statement that they do not have a criminal record. Short-term residence permits (MVVs) can be authorised for paid employment and au pair placements.

Work permits: Subjects of the EU do not need work or employment permits. North Americans, Antipodeans and others who require no visa to travel to the

Netherlands are allowed to work for less than three months, provided they report to the Aliens Police within three days of arrival and they and their employer has obtained a *tewerkstellingsvergunning* (employment permit). In practice, the *tewerkstellingsvergunning* is unlikely to be issued for casual work. Non-EU nationals wishing to work for longer than three months must obtain a work permit before arrival in the Netherlands from the local labour exchange in the Netherlands. Permission to take on voluntary work may be obtained on your behalf by the sponsoring agency in the Netherlands. Once a work permit has been issued a non-national can apply for a residence permit.

Working holiday scheme: The scheme is open to Australians, New Zealanders and Canadians who are aged between 18 and 30. They may obtain temporary work for up to a year to finance their holiday in the Netherlands. Applications must be made in person for a provisional residence permit (MVV) to the Dutch Embassy from which further details of personal requirements are available.

For up-to-date information about visa requirements check with the embassy before travel.

Hotel work and catering

Grand Hotel & Restaurant Opduin-Texel

Job(s) Available: Assistant waiters (2).
Duration: Applicants for these positions must be available for at least 3–4 months during the period March to November.
Company Description: A 4-star hotel with 100 rooms, 50 employees, restaurant, and swimming pool. It is just 200m from the beach on a beautiful island in 'the top of Holland'.

> **Head Office:** Ruyslaan 22, 1796 AD De Koog, Texel
> ☎ +31 2 2231 7445
> ✆ info@opduin.nl
> 🖳 www.opduin.nl

Job Description: Required for general work in the service department during breakfast, lunch and dinner.
Requirements: Knowledge of Dutch, English and German. Previous experience is essential. Good appearance is essential.
Accommodation: Available at a small charge.
Application Procedure: Applications with photograph from January to Luuk de Jong at the above address.

Other employment in the Netherlands

The Expat Company

Job(s) Available: Agency seeks staff for a number of temporary and permanent jobs around the Netherlands.
Company Description: Dutch recruitment and international employment agency specialising in international positions in the Netherlands.

> **Head Office:** Postbus 1459, 1300 BL Almere-Holland
> ☎ +31 3 6530 2000
> ✆ jobexpress@expatcompany.nl
> 🖳 www.expatcompany.nl

Requirements: EU citizen or valid work permit.
Application Procedure: Applications are invited all year round; contact the above address for more details.

Norway voted not to join the European Union, but it is a member of the European Economic Area (EEA) which means that EU nationals can enter and look for work for up to six months. They can seek work through local offices of the Norwegian employment service (now part of NAV; www.nav.no), and work without needing work permits. Citizens of other Scandinavian countries are also free to enter Norway. Visas are issued only for visitors to Norway; if one is required the person has to apply for that before entering Norway. Some nationals may apply for work and residence permits after arrival in Norway, however, the rules and regulations vary for each nationality and the purpose of stay. For full details check with the Norwegian Embassy (www.norway.org.uk).

There are a number of well-paid jobs available in Norwegian hotels over the summer. English is widely spoken but knowledge of Norwegian is advantageous. As elsewhere in Europe, the tourist industry appreciates people who can speak more than one language. People who are in Norway may also be able to find unpleasant but lucrative work in fish processing factories in such towns as Bergen, VardØ and BodØ, but over-fishing has reduced the possibilities of finding such work. When looking for work it is worth bearing in mind that Norwegian students are on vacation between 15 June and 15 August (approximately), and so there will be more opportunities before and after these dates. Those aged 18–30 can take advantage of a 'working guest' programme whereby visitors can stay with a Norwegian family in a working environment such as a farm, in tourism or as an au pair; details can be found under the Atlantis Youth Exchange Entry below, or at www.atlantis.no.

The Norwegian employment service is unable to help people looking for summer jobs. British citizens may be able to find voluntary work in Norway through Concordia or International Voluntary Service and Americans through Service Civil International (see the *Worldwide* chapter for details). A booklet entitled *Norway-A Guide to Living and Working in Norway* is published by NAV (www.nav.no).

Oslo has a Use It office (Ungdomsinformasjonen), who can find work and accommodation for young visitors while offering a range of services, which are all free of charge. The Oslo Youth Information Centre is located at MØllergata 3, 0179 Oslo (2414 9820; ida@ung.info; www.unginfo.oslo.no) and is open year round from 11am to 5pm with longer opening hours during the summer. Their website, in English, carries tips for living and working in Oslo.

Those wishing to advertise in Norwegian newspapers may contact Crane Media Partners Ltd (St Edmunds House, 13 Quarry Street, Guildford, Surrey, GU1 3UY; 0 1483 461770), who handle the national daily *Dagbladet* (www.dagbladet.no). *Aftenposten* (www.aftenposten.no/english) also has a job section.

Red tape

ADDRESS: ROYAL NORWEGIAN EMBASSY
25 Belgrave Square, London SW1X 8QD
☎ 020 7591 5500
✆ emb.london@mfa.no
🖥 www.norway.org.uk

Visa requirements: A visa is not required by citizens of most EU countries for a visit of less than three months, provided that employment is not intended. If you are from a country that is not an EU member you must obtain a work visa or permit to work in Norway.

Residence permits: This permit may be obtained before entering Norway through a Norwegian foreign service, or in Norway at the local police station for any stay of more than three months – your passport, two photographs and proof that you are financially self-supporting are required. Even if obtained before entering the country, you must report to the local police with a 'confirmation of employment' within three months of arrival. EU nationals, with the firm intention of taking up employment, may enter and stay in Norway for up to three months (extendable to six months, if you are financially self-supporting) while seeking work. Should you obtain long-term work during this period you must apply for a residence permit and report to the local police. If you are from the EU and you take up short-term employment for a period not exceeding three months, you do not need a residence permit, nor do you need to report to the police.

Work permits: British, Irish and nationals of other EU/EEA countries do not need work permits in Norway. Non-EU citizens must obtain a work and residence permit before entering Norway. Permits should be applied for at least three months before you intend to arrive in Norway. Having been offered a job and a place to live, you should obtain application forms for a work permit from the nearest Norwegian embassy or consulate general, which will send the completed applications to the directorate of immigration in Oslo for processing and must have proof of an 'offer of employment.' Applicants may not enter Norway during the period in which the application for a work-and-residence permit is under consideration.

Permits for skilled and seasonal workers: Skilled workers with higher-level training whose position cannot be filled by Norwegian nationals or EU members may be provided with a work permit for at least one year. Non-EU nationals looking for seasonally-determined work may be granted a work permit for a period of usually no greater than three months. Applications for such permits should be made to the Norwegian Embassy.

Working holiday visas: A working holiday visa scheme exists between Norway and Australia; applicants must be Australian nationals, intend primarily to holiday in Norway for up to a year, be aged between 18 and 30 years at time of application, possess reasonable funds and travel insurance. Applications can be made through the consular offices of the Royal Norwegian Embassies in Australia or London.

For up-to-date information about visa requirements check with the embassy before travel.

Agricultural work

Atlantis Youth Exchange

Job(s) Available: Working guest on a Norwegian farm, seasonal hospitality work.
Duration: *Farm guests:* Stays are for between 2 and 3 months all round the year. EU applicants can apply for up to 6 months or longer. *Hospitality:* work available May to October.
Working Hours: Maximum of 35 hours per week. Usually 6–7 hours per day, 5 days a week.

Head Office: Rådhusgata 4,
N-0151 Oslo
☎ +47 2 247 7170
✉ atlantis@atlantis.no
🖥 www.atlantis.no

Pay: Pocket money of approximately £97 per week.

Cost: £550–£850. If not placed after 2 months then applicants are fully refunded.

Company Description: Atlantis, the Norwegian Foundation for Youth Exchange, arranges stays on Norwegian farms and hospitality for people of any nationality to promote respect and understanding between cultures through youth exchange.

Job Description: *Farm guests:* participants share every aspect of a farmer's family life, both the work and the leisure. The work may include haymaking, weeding, milking, picking berries, fruit and vegetables, caring for animals etc. *Hospitality:* forms of hotel work eg porters, waiters, bar work.

Requirements: Applicants must be aged 18–30 and speak English. Applicants are accepted from all countries where there is an Atlantis Partner organisation.

Accommodation: Free board and lodging provided.

Application Procedure: Prospective applicants should contact WAVA, 67–71 Lewisham High Street, London SE13 5JX; 020 8297 3275; Ptalbot@workandvolunteer.com; www.workandvolunteer.com.

Hotel work and catering

Kvikne's Hotel

Job(s) Available: Bartender (5), chamber staff (10), chef (10), kitchen help (8), luggage porters (3), night porters (2), waiting staff (15).

Duration: Minimum period of work 1 June to 31 August.

Working Hours: 152 hours per month, 5–6 days a week.

Company Description: One of Norway's largest hotels with 190 rooms, 400 guests, conference facilities.

Requirements: Previous experience is an advantage as are languages (German, French, Scandinavian).

Accommodation: Accommodation is provided for NOK1,200 per month.

Application Procedure: Apply to the above address from 1 February.

> Head Office: Box 24, 6898 Balestrand
> ☎ +47 5 769 4200
> ✆ personnal@kviknes.no
> 🖳 www.kviknes.no

Lindstroem Hotel

Job(s) Available: Hotel staff (20).

Duration: Minimum period of work 6 weeks from 1 May to 30 September.

Working Hours: 8 hours per day, 5 days a week.

Pay: NOK116 per hour.

Job Description: To work in the kitchen, dining room and to clean rooms.

Requirements: No Norwegian necessary. Minimum age 18. Applicants should speak English.

Accommodation: Board and lodging available at a price.

Application Procedure: CV and cover letter to Knut Lindstrom at the above address from January.

> Head Office: Laerdal 6886
> ☎ + 47 5 766 6900
> ✆ post@lindstroemhotel.no
> 🖳 www.lindstroemhotel.no

Stalheim Hotel

Job(s) Available: Chefs, chambermaids, cooks, pantry boys/girls, sales girls, waiters/waitresses.
Duration: Minimum period of work 3 months, May to September.
Working Hours: 37.5 hours per week.
Pay: Competitive salary.

> Head Office: N-5715 Stalheim
> ☎ + 47 5 652 0122
> ⁀ info@stalheim.com
> ▨ www.stalheim.com

Company Description: This busy, high-class, family-run hotel is situated in the Fjord country of western Norway, 140km from Bergen. It has an international clientele.
Requirements: Fluent English necessary. Must be an EU citizen. Minimum age 19.
Accommodation: Board and accommodation provided at a cost.
Application Procedure: Email or send CV and reference to above address. Check website for vacancies.

PORTUGAL

Unemployment in Portugal is now at 10%–11%. The best chances of finding paid employment are in the tourist industry. Tour operators (see the *Worldwide* chapter), teaching English as a foreign language, or in hotels and bars etc in tourist areas such as the Costa do Sol and the Algarve are normally good starting points. A drawback is that the minimum wage in Portugal is one of the lowest in the EU and approximately half that of Britain or France and that living costs, once correspondingly low, are rising faster than wages. Private employment agencies such as Manpower (www.manpower.com) may be able to provide casual jobs for which knowledge of Portuguese is necessary.

Short-term voluntary work can be arranged for British travellers by UNA Exchange and Youth Action for Peace. American and British citizens can also arrange some voluntary work places through International Voluntary Service/Service Civil International, see their entry in *Worldwide* for details.

British and Irish citizens and other EU nationals are permitted to use the Portuguese national employment service: look under *Centro do Emprego* in a telephone directory. The website of Portugal's national employment institute (Instituto do Emprego e Formação Profissional), has an English version of their website (www.iefp.pt). There are also a number of private employment agencies, principally in Lisbon and Oporto: for agencies specialising in temporary work look under *Pessoal Temporàrio* in the yellow pages (*Pàginas Amarelas;* www.pai.pt). For further information consult the free booklet *Working in Portugal* published by the Employment Service.

An advertisement in the English-language *Anglo Portuguese News (APN)* may lead to an offer of a job (apn@mail.telepac.pt; www.the-news.net).

Red tape

ADDRESS: PORTUGUESE EMBASSY
11 Belgrave Square, London SW1X 8PP
☎ 020 7235 5331
⁀ london@portembassy.co.uk

Visa requirements: For holiday visits of up to three months a visa is not required by full citizens of EU countries. A visa is not required for either US, Canadian or

Australian citizens for holiday visits of up to three months but they do need a work permit for employment. Portugal is a member of the Schengen agreement.

Residence permits: If you want to stay for more than three months but not more than a year you must apply for a temporary residence permit to the Immigration and Border Control Department (Servico de Estrangeiros e Fronteiras), that will be issued for at least the duration of your employment. To obtain a residence permit, you must be able to provide a letter from your employer in Portugal confirming your employment. Non-EU nationals must provide a residence visa obtained from the Portuguese consulate in their home country.

Work permits: EU nationals do not require work permits to work in Portugal, only a residence permit as above. Non-EU nationals must provide an array of documents before they can be granted a work visa, including a residence visa obtained from the Portuguese consulate in their home country, a document showing that the Ministry of Labour (*Ministerio do Trabalho*) has approved the job and a medical certificate in Portuguese. The final stage is to take a letter of good conduct provided by the applicant's own embassy to the police for the work and residence permit. There are no restrictions applied to volunteer work.

For up-to-date information about visa requirements check with the embassy before travel.

Hotel work and catering

Mayer Apartments

Job(s) Available: Bar person.
Duration: From 1 May to 31 October.
Working Hours: 10am–7pm, 6 days a week.
Job Description: Outgoing, hardworking, independent individual to serve drinks and snacks at a busy poolside bar.
Requirements: No experience necessary as full training is given. Applicants must speak English.
Accommodation: Included.
Application Procedure: Send CV and photo to Mr Adrian Mayer at the above address from February onwards.

Head Office: Praia Da luz, 8600-157 Luz Lagos, Algarve
☎ +351 2827 89313
info@mayerapartments.com
www.mayerapartments.com

SPAIN

Unemployment has dogged the Spanish economy in recent years mainly due to regulations restricting fluidity in the job market. The unemployment figure currently stands at about 20%, one of the highest in the EU. There are reasonable opportunities for finding temporary work. For foreigners these are best sought in the tourist industry or teaching English, both of which count knowledge of another language as an asset.

Some of the best opportunities for work in Spain are in the tourist industry, so applications to hotels in tourist areas could result in the offer of a job. Since many of these hotels cater for tourists from northern Europe, a good knowledge of languages such as German, Dutch, French and English will be a great advantage to foreign workers. The website www.gapwork.com has information about working in Ibiza and provides the web addresses for clubs and other potential employers. It is estimated that about 6,000 Britons try to find work on Ibiza each year so it is important to offer a relevant skill.

It should be remembered that hotel workers in Spain work very long hours during the summer months and foreign workers will be required to do likewise. In many cases at the peak of the tourist season hotel and restaurant staff work a minimum of 10 hours per day and bar staff may work even longer hours. A 7-day week is regarded as perfectly normal during the summer. Despite these long hours, salaries are generally somewhat lower than elsewhere in western Europe.

English and Spanish may help an experienced secretary to get bilingual office work with companies in large cities. There are also a number of jobs for teachers of English: the definitive guide to this type of work is *Teaching English Abroad* by Susan Griffith (Vacation Work 2009; see *Useful publications*).

British and Irish citizens and other EU nationals who are in Spain and confident of their knowledge of Spanish may use the Spanish national employment service (www.oficinaempleo.com), for addresses consult the *Yellow Pages* (*Pàginas Amarillas*; www.paginas-amarillas.es), look under *Oficina de Empleo*. Private employment agencies are known as Empresas de Trabajo Temporal. For further information consult the jobs section of the EURES website (htpp://ec.europa.eu/eures), or click on Living & Working for details. Alternatively you can contact your nearest embassy: the Spanish embassy in London has information on its website.

It is always worth checking the English-language press for the 'sits vac' columns which sometimes carry adverts for cleaners, live-in babysitters, chefs, bar staff, etc. Look for *SUR* in English (www.surinenglish.com) which has a large employment section and is used by foreign and local residents throughout southern Spain. It is published free on Fridays and distributed through supermarkets, bars, travel agencies, etc. If you want to place your own ad, contact the publisher through the website. Advertisements can be placed in Spanish newspapers including *El Mundo*, a national daily, which is handled by Smyth International (020 8446 6400; mail@smyth-international.com; www.smyth-international.com). *El Pais* (www. elpais.com) is the leading national daily.

There are also opportunities for voluntary work in Spain arranged by Concordia, UNA Exchange, Youth Action for Peace and International Voluntary Service for British citizens, and Service Civil International for US nationals; see the *Worldwide* chapter for details.

Red tape

ADDRESS: SPANISH EMBASSY
20 Draycott Place, London SW3 2RZ
☎ 0207 589 8989
cog.londres@maec.es
www.conspalon.org

Visa requirements: A visa is not required by citizens of the EU and of citizens from countries included in Annex 1 of the Regulement CE no 539/2001 of the Council when visiting Spain with non-working purposes for a stay not exceeding 90 days within an annual period.

For those EU nationals that intend to stay in Spain for a longer period than 90 days, it is recommended that you register with the local Comisaría de Policía.

Non-EU nationals who are not included in the list of countries of the aforementioned Annex 1 must obtain a visa ('visado de estancia') from the Spanish Consulate of their home country, or where they have a legal residence permit. The 'visado de estancia' is for non-working purposes and for a stay not exceeding 90 days.

Non-EU nationals that want to reside in Spain for longer periods than 90 days a year or that are taking up a paid job must obtain a visa from the Spanish Consulate before travelling to Spain in the conditions established in the Spanish National Legislation.

Spain is a member of the Schengen countries and those with a Schengen visa may travel freely in the Schengen zone.

Residence permits: British and other EU citizens residing in Spain can register in the local Comisaría de Polícia or Oficina de Extranjeros. For further details visit Spain's Interior Ministry at www.mir.es.

NIE number: All foreign nationals need to apply for a foreigner's identification number (*numero de identificación de extranjeros*) from the police as soon as they start work. The NIE is a tax identification number that allows you to undertake any kind of employment or business activity in Spain.

Work permits: These must be obtained in Spain before applying for a visa under the conditions established by Spanish legislation. Information about work permits can be obtained from the Spanish Consulate (London, Manchester, Edinburgh) or by visiting www.conspalon.org. Spain has recently signed working holiday agreements for young people from New Zealand and Canada.

For up-to-date information about visa requirements check with the embassy before travel.

Hotel work and catering

Easy Way Association

Job(s) Available: Commis waiters, restaurant staff to work as fast-food staff, waiters.
Duration: Minimum period of work 4 weeks at any time of year.
Working Hours: Full and part-time positions available.
Pay: €250–€1,100 a month depending on hours worked and experience.

Head Office: Calle Gran Via 80, Planta 10 Oficina 1017 28013, Madrid
☎ +34 9 1542 8854
info@easywayspain.com
www.easywayspain.com or www.euroroom.net

Company Description: A non-profit association for international cultural exchanges, specialising in work placements (long and short stays) and all types of programmes with accommodation in youth centres, apartments, residences and family accommodation in Madrid, Barcelona and the rest of Spain.
Requirements: Applicants must be aged 18–32.
Accommodation: Available in shared flats or homestays. From €230–€630 per month.
Additional Information: For some programmes no Spanish is required. Spanish lessons are available through the Easy Way School of Spanish.
Application Procedure: Applications to the above address or apply online at www.easywayspain.com/ingles/registration.htm.

Emilio's Bar & Apartment Rentals

Job(s) Available: Live-in bar staff and chamber-maids required.
Duration: Seasonal job during summer.
Working Hours: 38 hours per week.
Pay: €100 per week pocket money plus tips.
Company Description: Located in El Puerto de Santa Maria Cadiz, Spain. A busy bar on the water-front, a few minutes walk from the beach. Offers

> Head Office: Paseo de la bahía N°77,
> Puerto Sherry, El Puerto de Santa Maria,
> 11500 Cadiz
> ☎ +34 956 540112
> or +34 692 643396
> 🖅 info@emiliosbar.com
> 🖥 www.emiliosbar.com

working holidays to students wishing to learn Spanish in Andalucía, Southern Spain.
Requirements: Applicants must speak Spanish and English. Bar experience is appreciated.
Accommodation: Shared accommodation provided within walking distance of the beach. Accommodation is free of charge in the Marina complex of Puerto Sherry.
Application Procedure: Email at info@emiliosbar.com for more information or send CV and a recent photo at the above address.

Sports, couriers and camping

Camping Globo Rojo

Job(s) Available: Qualified swimming pool guard, waiter/waitress and chef.
Duration: Work is available between 15 June to 30 August.
Working Hours: 8 hours a day, 6 days a week.
Pay: €900–€1,000 per month.
Company Description: Small and cosy campsite-

> Head Office: Barangé-Brun C.B.,
> Carretera Nacional II, km 660,9 08360
> Canet de Mar (Barcelona)
> ☎ +34 9 3794 1143
> 🖅 camping@globo-rojo.com
> 🖥 www.globo-rojo.com

bungalow park for families with small children as well as couples looking for a getaway. Located only 40 km north of Barcelona, on the Maresme coast, in Canet de Mar, a small vil-lage by the Mediterranean Sea famous for its beautiful beaches.
Job Description: *Qualified swimming pool guard:* to oversee safety of pool, and accident prevention. Other duties may include teaching swimming classes – may require knowledge of competitive swimming, water polo or water exercise. *Waiter/waitress:* to serve in the restaurant and bar. *Chef:* to prepare cold starters and desserts.
Requirements: Ideally applicants should speak English, German and Spanish.
Accommodation: Free board and lodging.
Application Procedure: Applications are invited from April onwards.

Pavilion Tours

Job(s) Available: Watersports instructors.
Duration: Minimum period of work between May and August.
Working Hours: Variable, 7 days a week.
Pay: Depending on qualification.

> Head Office: 1 Jubilee Street, Brighton,
> East Sussex BN1 1GE, UK
> ☎ 0870 241 0425/7
> 🖅 info@paviliontours.com

Company Description: An expanding, specialist activity tour operator for students, with bases in Spain. Watersports include: windsurfing, dinghy sailing and canoeing.
Job Description: Watersports instructors required to instruct sailing/windsurfing etc and to assist with evening entertainments.
Requirements: Highly motivated staff. Instructor qualifications are essential.

Accommodation: Board and lodging included as well as travel to and from resorts.
Application Procedure: Please send an up-to-date CV along with a copy of your qualifications through to Sue Lloyd at s.lloyd@stgmail.net

Teaching and language schools

The Farm Summercamp

Job(s) Available: Summer camp staff (20).
Duration: Required in July.
Company Description: The Farm organise summer English-language camps in the Basque country. They are not a language academy.
Job Description: Summer camp staff to organise activities for Spanish children aged 8–14.
Requirements: Minimum age 18. Applicants should be creative, good team workers, have an independent nature and be fluent in English.
Application Procedure: Applications, from EU citizens only, should be sent to the above address by mid-March.

> **Head Office:** Barrio Elizade 11, Erentxun, 01193, Alava
> ☎ +34 945063234
> ✆ mascha.thefarm@gmail.com
> 🖥 www.thefarmfun.com

English Educational Services

Job(s) Available: English teachers (80–110).
Duration: Standard length of contract 9 months. Summer contracts available.
Working Hours: 5 hours per day. Teaching mainly in the evenings from 5pm onwards.
Pay: Depends on the client school the teacher is employed by.
Company Description: Provide jobs in independent language schools in Spain.
Job Description: Positions available in various parts of the country including Madrid.
Requirements: English teachers with higher education and recognised EFL qualification such as CELTA or Trinity CertTESOL required by recruitment specialists for EFL in Spain. EU citizens are preferred.
Accommodation: Provision for accommodation depends on the client school the teacher is employed by. Most client schools will help their teachers find a place to live.
Additional Information: There is also an English-speaking theatre company operating from October to June, which has opportunities for candidates with a native speaker's standard of English.
Application Procedure: Applications with CV and 2 referees should be made to the above address. Interviews may be carried out in the UK and Ireland at peak times. Interviews also held in Madrid throughout the academic year.

> **Head Office:** c/ Alcalá 20-2, 28014 Madrid
> ☎ +34 9 1531 4783
> or +34 9 1532 9734
> ✆ richardinmadrid@gmail.com

Voluntary work

VaughanTown

Job(s) Available: Native English-speaking volunteers.
Company Description: VaughanTown is the brainchild of an established English-language school in Spain, Vaughan Systems. Founded by American Richard Vaughan in 1977, Vaughan Systems is a

> **Head Office:** Avda General Peron, 38, 2ª Planta, Madrid 28020
> ☎ +34 91 748595
> ✆ anglos@vaughantown.com
> 🖥 www.vaughantown.com

large in-company language training firm in Spain, with over 300 teachers providing more than 350,000 hours of language training per year to over 5,000 executives and technical personnel in more than 520 national and international companies.

Job Description: In VaughanTown, native English-speaking volunteers spend a week with 15 Spaniards, talking to them on an individual basis, in the morning, afternoon and evening. In return for this, volunteers will stay in a 4-star hotel in one of the many regions of Spain. A new 6-day program starts almost every Sunday of the year.

Application Procedure: If you have the gift of the gab and you are set for an adventure, check out the website where you will find all the necessary information and an application form.

Sunseed Desert Technology

Job(s) Available: Volunteers are required year round.

Duration: Short and long-term volunteer positions.

Cost: Volunteers make a weekly contribution of between €54–€84 (depending on length of stay and hours worked).

Head Office: Apdo. 9, E-04270 Sorbas, Almeria
☎ +34 9 5052 5770
✉ sunseedspain@arrakis.es
🖥 www.sunseed.org.uk

Company Description: Situated in a village in southern Spain, Sunseed Desert Technology aims to develop, demonstrate and communicate accessible, low-tech methods of living sustainably in a semi-arid environment. Working holiday makers, students and long-term volunteers can join the international community to learn about all aspects of low impact living. Sunseed is a registered Spanish association and a registered UK charity.

Job Description: Volunteers have the possibility to work in all 6 departments, taking part in specific projects or developing their own research in different Sunseed departments: organic gardening, dryland management, appropriate technology, sustainable living, eco-construction and education and publicity. Also they can take part in communal activities such as cooking including solar cooking, visits to other projects and leisure activities such as: going to the river, beach or doing yoga in the valley. Students frequently complete academic projects and dissertations at the project.

Application Procedure: Applicants should see website or contact the project directly for further details.

Other employment in Spain

Instituto Hemingway

Job(s) Available: Au pair, internships, hospitality management in Spain, France and Italy.

Duration: Minimum period of work 3 months.

Working Hours: *Au pair:* 25 hours per week. *Internships* and *hospitality management:* 30–35 hours per day.

Head Office: Bailen 5, 2 Dcha, 48003 Bilbao
☎ +34 9 4416 7901
✉ info@institutohemingway.com
🖥 www.institutohemingway.com

Pay: *Au pair:* €50 per week. *Internships* and *hospitality management:* €50 per week.

Company Description: Instituto Hemingway offers programmes that are designed for those who want to learn about other cultures while studying, travelling or working in Spain or other countries.

Requirements: Applicants should be aged 18–35 and should be from the EU, USA, Canada or Australia. Applicants should have a basic level of Spanish.

Additional Information: Spanish lessons can be provided. Also offers positions in France and Italy.

Application Procedure: Applications at www.institutohemingway.com/inscrip.htm.

SWEDEN

Sweden is a fully integrated EU member, and EU citizens are free to enter to look for and take up work. There are strict limits on the number of foreigners allowed to work in Sweden.

The Swedish Public Employment Service cannot help jobseekers from non-EU countries to find work in Sweden. General information and addresses of local employment offices may be obtained from Arbetsförmedlingen at SE-113 99 Stockholm, Sweden (+46 0771 416 416; www.arbetsformedlingen.se; in English at www.sweden.se). For further information consult the EURES website (http://ec.europa.eu/eures). It is up to the individual to get in touch with employers.

The Scandinavian Institute in Malmö (Box 3085; +46 40 939440; info@scandinavianinst.com; www.scandinavianinst.com) makes au pair placements in Swedish families and throughout Scandinavia.

There are also opportunities for voluntary work in Sweden arranged by International Voluntary Service for British people and Service Civil International for Americans: see the *Worldwide* chapter for details.

Advertisements in Swedish newspapers may be placed through Crane Media Partners Ltd St Edmunds House, 13 Quarry Street, Guildford, Surrey GU1 3UY; +44 (0)1483 461770; www.cranemedia.co.uk), who handle *Dagens Nyheter, Goteborgs Posten* and *Sydsvenska Dagbladet.*

Jobs are plentiful in hospitality roles in the holiday resorts in places such as Stockholm.

Red tape

ADDRESS: EMBASSY OF SWEDEN
11 Montagu Place, London W1H 2AL
☎ 020 7917 6400
✆ ambassaden.london@foreign.ministry.se
🖳 www.swedenabroad.com/london _____

Visa requirements: A visa is no longer required by many countries including all EU countries. Nationals of these countries are allowed to visit Sweden for up to three months. Visa information is available from the embassy website.

Sweden is a member of the Schengen countries and those with a Schengen visa may travel freely in the Schengen zone.

Residence permits: A permit is required if you are to live and work in Sweden for more than three months. EU citizens must register for the right of residence with the Migration Board (Migrationsverket; 60170 Norrköping; +46 771 235 235; migrationsverket@migrationsverket.se; www.migrationsverket.se).

Non-Europeans must submit to their local Swedish embassy a written offer of work on migration board form 232011, at least two months before their proposed arrival. The procedure involves an interview at the embassy. Immigration queries should be addressed to the Swedish Migration Board (see above for details). Full details are posted in English on their web pages or you can request printed leaflets.

Work permits: Citizens of EU countries do not need work permits in order to work in Sweden. For others a work permit requires an offer of employment; application forms for the necessary permit should then be obtained from your nearest Swedish embassy. The application will be processed by the Swedish Migration Board and the procedure can take one to two months. Applications for work permits are not accepted from foreign visitors who are already in Sweden.

Voluntary work

Hultsfred Festival

Job(s) Available: Volunteers, stewards etc (5,000).
Duration: 3 days in July. Minimum period of work 3 days.
Pay: Unpaid but volunteers receive free entry to festival.
Company Description: Hultsfred first started in 1986 and is one of the biggest and longest running youth-oriented music festivals within Scandinavia. It contains 7 stages and is located in a picturesque forest glade.
Job Description: Rockparty, a non-profit organisation, takes on 5,000 volunteers a year, with around 4,750 working only during the festival.
Accommodation: Volunteers receive a free ticket to the festival, as well as camping, uniform and free meals.
Application Procedure: Volunteers apply all year round but all volunteer places are taken by February, according to the organisers. Volunteers should send a CV and covering letter indicating their interest by January. Apply by email to info@rockparty.se.

Head Office: Hultsfred, Box 170 577 24, Hultsfred
☎ +46 4 956 9500
info@rockparty.se
www.rockparty.se

SWITZERLAND

Switzerland reached one of the lowest unemployment rates in the world at 4%, and to preserve that state it has traditionally imposes strict work permit requirements on all foreigners who want to work there. It is significant that unlike most of the other non-EU members of western Europe, Switzerland did not join the EEA a few years ago, although there are long-term plans for it to do so. However, a bilateral treaty on free movement of persons was concluded with the EU and the main obstacles to free movement of labour were removed in 2004. In the same year the seasonal worker category of permit was abolished. As a result, EU jobseekers are able to enter Switzerland to look for work for up to three months. Permits are extendable for a potential period of up to five years, depending on the contract. Information on this can be found online at www.bfm.admin.ch.

Switzerland has always needed extra seasonal workers at certain times of the year. The tourist industry in particular needs staff for both the summer and winter seasons (July to September and December to April). Jobs in the tourist industry are described both in this chapter and the *Worldwide* chapter. Students looking for hotel work should note the entries below for the Schweizer Hotelier-Suisse (Swiss Hotels' Association).

Farmers also need extra help at certain times of the year: see the entry below for the Landdienst-Zentralstelle, which can arrange working stays on Swiss farms. Opportunities in the short but lucrative grape harvest in October (particularly in the Lausanne area) are also worth seeking out although this takes place usually in October rather than summer. Some knowledge of German or French is normally needed, even for grape picking. Italian is also spoken, particularly in the canton of Ticino.

Switzerland is also covered by the EURES programme (http://ec.europa.eu/eures), and further information on jobseeking and living and working in Switzerland can be found on their website. There are opportunities for voluntary work in Switzerland with the organisations named at the end of this chapter and British applicants can also apply through Concordia and International Voluntary Service, and Americans through Service Civil International; see the *Worldwide* chapter for details.

Placing an advertisement in a Swiss paper may lead to the offer of a job. *Tribune de Geneve* is published at 11 rue des Rois, CH-1211 Geneva (www.tdg.ch).

Red tape

ADDRESS: EMBASSY OF SWITZERLAND
16/18 Montagu Place, London W1H 2BQ
☎ 020 7616 6000
✆ lon.vertretung@eda.admin.ch
🖥 www.swissembassy.org.uk

Visa requirements: Citizens of the UK, the USA, Canada, Australia, New Zealand and most other European countries do not normally require visas for tourism. Detailed information can be found online at http://ch.vfsglobal.co.uk.

Switzerland is a member of the Schengen countries and those with a Schengen visa may travel freely in the Schengen Zone.

Residence/Work permits: For non-EU citizens the situation is now a little bit more complicated as employers in Switzerland have to deal with sponsorship paperwork on their behalf and try harder to prove to the authorities that they need to employ a foreigner from outside Europe. An L permit has to be applied for by the employer in Switzerland and by the applicant at the Swiss embassy in his country of residence. Once approved an entry visa has to be issued to the employee by the Swiss embassy in the employee's own country.

The L permits cover both the right of abode and employment. These are required for all persons entering to take up employment and entitle the holder to live in a specific canton and work for a specified employer. They also entitle the worker to join the state insurance scheme and enjoy the services of the legal tribunal for foreign workers, should they require an arbitrator in a dispute with their employer. Accident insurance is compulsory and is largely paid by the employer. This does not obviate the need of the temporary foreign employee to take out their own health insurance policy. A work permit is required for volunteer work.

If successful, you will receive an entry visa and within the first eight days following your initial entry you will have to declare your arrival at the Foreigners Police or Town Registrar at your place of Residence. (German: Fremdenpolizei/Einwahnerkontrolle; French: Police des étrangers/Contrale des habitants; Italian: Ufficio degli stranien/Controllo degli abitanti). The permit to stay, study or work in Switzerland will be issued upon notification of your arrival.

For up-to-date information about visa requirements check with the embassy before travel.

Agricultural work

Agriviva _____

Job(s) Available: Farmers' assistants.
Duration: Minimum period of work 2 weeks between the spring and autumn; maximum period 2 months.
Working Hours: 8 hours per day, 6 days a week.
Pay/Cost: CHF16–CHF20 pocket money per day. Registration fee CHF40 or €25 to cover costs.

> **Head Office:** Postfach 1538, CH-8401, Winterthur
> ☎ +41 5 2264 0030
> ✆ info@agriviva.ch
> 🖥 www.agriviva.ch

Company Description: Agriviva is a non-profit-making, publicly subsidised organisation which each year places around 2,500 Swiss and foreign farmers' assistants.
Job Description: Farmers' assistants to work on family farms.
Requirements: Basic knowledge of German and/or French essential. Individual applicants should be aged 16–25. Individual applicants must be EU citizens.
Accommodation: Free board and lodging.
Application Procedure: Applications are invited at least 4 weeks prior to desired starting date. Apply online.

Hotel work and catering

Chalet-Hotel Adler _____

Job(s) Available: Barmaids, chambermaids, waitresses.
Duration: Minimum period of work 2.5 months from May/June to September/October.
Working Hours: 8 hours and 40 minutes per day, 5 days a week.
Pay: Net salary approximately £1,200 per month.

> **Head Office:** Fam. A & E Fetzer, CH-3718 Kandersteg
> ☎ +41 3 367 58010
> ✆ info@chalethotel.ch
> 🖥 www.chalethotel.ch

Company Description: This hotel is set in the mountains of Switzerland, with rail access allowing excursions across the country.
Requirements: Knowledge of German required.
Accommodation: Provided.
Application Procedure: By post or email with a photo, from April to the above address.

Grand Hotel Bellevue _____

Job(s) Available: Housekeeping, waiters, kitchen and office staff.
Duration: Winter season approximately from 15 December to 31 March. Summer season approximately from 11 July to 30 September.

> **Head Office:** 3789 Gstaad
> ☎ +41 3 3748 0000
> ✆ info@bellevue-gstaad.ch
> 🖥 www.bellevue-gstaad.ch

Working Hours: 42–45 hours per week. 5 days per week.
Pay: Approximately £900 per month.
Requirements: Applicants should speak German, English and French.
Accommodation: Free board and lodging subject to availability.
Application Procedure: By email to hr@bellevue-gstaad.ch.

Jobs in the Alps (Employment Agency)

Job(s) Available: Housekeepers, kitchen porters, porters and waiting staff. 150 in the winter, 50 in summer.
Duration: Periods of work from June to mid-September (minimum period of work 3 months including July and August), or December to April.
Working Hours: 5 days a week.
Pay: £500 per month.
Job Description: Staff for Swiss and French hotels, cafés and restaurants at mountain resorts.
Requirements: Good French and/or German required for most positions. Experience is not essential, but a good attitude to work and sense of fun are definite requirements.
Accommodation: Free board and accommodation provided.
Application Procedure: Applications should be sent by 30 April for summer and 30 September for winter to the above address.

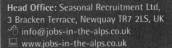

Head Office: Seasonal Recruitment Ltd, 3 Bracken Terrace, Newquay TR7 2LS, UK
info@jobs-in-the-alps.co.uk
www.jobs-in-the-alps.co.uk

Hotel Postillon

Job(s) Available: Waiting staff.
Working Hours: 42 hours, 5 days a week.
Pay: Dependent on responsibility.
Job Description: Waiting staff to work in a busy restaurant on a motorway.
Requirements: Knowledge of German and English is necessary.
Accommodation: Board and accommodation available for a small fee.
Application Procedure: Applications at the above address.

Head Office: CH-6374 Buochs
☎ +41 4 1620 5454
info@postillon.ch
www.postillon.ch

Residence and Bernerhof Hotels

Job(s) Available: Buffet assistants, general assistants, laundry maids, waiters/waitresses.
Duration: Period of work from December to April, and June to October.
Working Hours: 9 hours per day, 5 days a week.
Pay: Monthly salary.
Company Description: 2 hotel restaurants; à la carte, and pizzeria. Guests are usually English, German, American and Swiss. In the centre of Wengen.
Requirements: Knowledge of German required. Knowledge of French an advantage.
Accommodation: Available for 30 days. Lunch and dinner provided (no breakfast) for 22 days.
Application Procedure: By post to Miss Lidice Schweizer at the above address.

Head Office: CH-3823 Wengen
☎ +41 3 3855 2721
mail@behof.ch
www.behof.ch

Hotel Rigiblick Am See

Job(s) Available: Trainee assistant (waiter/waitress), trainee chef.
Duration: Period of work May/June to August/September.
Working Hours: 44 hours per week, 5 days a week.
Pay: €1,800–€2,000 per month.
Company Description: A 4-star hotel and restaurant on the lakeside.

Head Office: Seeplatz 3, CH-6374 Buochs
☎ +41 4 162 44850
info@rigiblickamsee.ch
www.rigiblickamsee.ch

Requirements: Applicants must hold an EU passport and have very good knowledge of German.
Accommodation: Board and accommodation provided for €600 per month.
Application Procedure: Applications throughout the year to the above address.

Romantik Hotel Säntis

Job(s) Available: Waiter/waitress.
Duration: Minimum period of work 4 months from June to October.
Working Hours: 9 hours per day, 5 days a week.
Pay: CHF3,300 approximately per month.

> Head Office: CH-9050 Appenzell
> ☎ +41 7 178 81111
> ✆ info@saentis-appenzell.ch
> 🖥 www.saentis-appenzell.ch

Company Description: A family-run 4-star hotel in Appenzell, which is in the German-speaking region. The staff are mostly young people of various nationalities.
Requirements: Applicants must have experience and speak German.
Accommodation: Board and accommodation available for €400 per month.
Application Procedure: Applications to Stefan A Heeb at the above address.

Hotelleri Suisse

Job(s) Available: General assistants.
Duration: Minimum period of work 3 months.
Pay: Varies according to position.
Company Description: The Swiss Hotel Association has around 2,500 hotels and restaurants as members. The association acts as a source for employment within hospitality.

> Head Office: Monbijoustrasse 130,
> Postfach, CH-3001 Bern
> ☎ +41 3 1370 4111
> ✆ info@hotelleriesuisse.ch
> 🖥 www.hotelleriesuisse.ch

Job Description: General assistants from EU countries to work in hotels in German-speaking Switzerland. Duties include helping with cooking, service and cleaning.
Requirements: EU citizens with good knowledge of German essential.
Accommodation: Board and accommodation available at a cost of approximately CHF900 per month.
Additional Information: Please note that jobs in the French and Italian speaking parts of Switzerland cannot be arranged.
Application Procedure: Applications to the above address.

Teaching and language schools

The Haut Lac International Centre

Job(s) Available: House staff, language teachers (English, French, German) and sports activity monitors.
Duration: Period of work mid-June until the end of August, with a minimum requirement of 4 weeks work.

> Head Office: CH-1669 Les Sciernes
> ☎ +41 2 692 84200
> ✆ jobs@haut-lac.com
> 🖥 www.myswisscamp.com

Working Hours: See website for specific working hours as each job varies.
Pay: All positions are from £120 per week according to qualifications and experience.
Company Description: The Haut Lac Centre is a family-run business organising language and activity courses for an international clientele. It is a holiday centre designed specifically for kids aged 8–18.

Job Description: *House staff:* for reception, cleaning, dishwashing or kitchen work. *Language teachers:* to organise and run classes for students and supervise them at all times. *Sports activity monitors:* to organise and run a wide variety of sports and excursions.

Requirements: Applicants should speak English, French or German. *House staff:* minimum age 18. A second language is preferable as is hotel experience. *Language teachers:* candidates should have a degree and a TEFL qualification or equivalent, or be studying for a language or teaching degree. *Sports activity monitors:* a second language is preferable as are coaching qualifications or camping experience.

Accommodation: Board and accommodation are provided.

Application Procedure: Apply to Mark Gallagher at the above email address.

Voluntary work

Gruppo Voluntari Dalla Svizzera Italiana

Job(s) Available: Volunteers (15 per camp).
Duration: Minimum period of work 1 week between June and September.
Working Hours: 4 hours work per day.

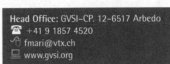

Head Office: GVSI-CP. 12-6517 Arbedo
☎ +41 9 1857 4520
🖰 fmari@vtx.ch
🖳 www.gvsi.org

Company Description: The Group of Volunteers of Italian Switzerland (GVSI) is an association of adults and youngsters, coming from Italian Switzerland. This organisation is open to all persons coming from other countries who believe it is useful to carry out a social activity, like the work of volunteers in emergency situations.

Job Description: Volunteers to take part in work camps in Maggia, Fusio and Borgogne helping mountain communities, cutting wood, helping the aged, in the orchards, etc.

Requirements: Applicants should speak Italian, German or French. Minimum age 18. Volunteers must be able to present valid documents and a residence permit.

Accommodation: Board and accommodation available.

Application Procedure: Applications to the above address.

CENTRAL & EASTERN EUROPE

CROATIA

The chances of finding paid summer work in Croatia are fairly low, although its tourist industry is burgeoning and teaching opportunities in private language schools can also be found. Voluntary projects also remain a popular option.

Red tape

ADDRESS: EMBASSY OF CROATIA
21 Conway Street, London W1T 6BN
☎ 020 7387 2022
✆ conlon@mvpei.hr
🖥 www.mvpei.hr

Visa requirements: British and EU citizens along with nationals from the USA, Canada, Australia, New Zealand and Japan do not require a visa for stays of up to 90 days. However, a work or business permit must be obtained before gaining employment. A useful website on these matters is www.mup.hr. Please contact the Embassy of Croatia for further details.

For up-to-date information about visa requirements check with the embassy before travel.

Boats

Setsail Holidays

Job(s) Available: Engineers, hostesses and skippers.
Duration: Starts April/May to end September/ October.
Pay: £120–£160 pocket money per week, depending on job and experience.

Head Office: 40 Burkitts Lane, Sudbury, Suffolk CO10 1HB, UK
☎ 01787 310445
✆ boats@setsail.co.uk
🖥 www.setsail.co.uk

Company Description: Setsail Holidays are a specialist tour operator providing flotilla sailing and bareboat charter holidays to Greece, Turkey and Croatia.
Job Description: Skippers, hostesses and engineers required to coordinate and run the flotilla sailing holidays, which can consist of up to 12 yachts.
Requirements: Must have sailing experience and/or qualifications plus the ability to work well with people.
Accommodation: Provided on the 'lead yacht'.
Application Procedure: Applications to John Hortop at the above address by fax or email. Applications must include a CV and recent picture.

Voluntary work

Research-Educational Centre for the Protection of Nature

Job(s) Available: Conservation volunteers.
Duration: Minimum period of work 1 week between 1 March and 31 October.
Cost: Volunteers have to pay for the cost of food, and also organise and pay expenses for travel to and from Croatia.

> Head Office: Beli 4, 51559 Beli, Island of Cres
> ☎ +385 5184 0525
> ✁ caput.insulae@ri.t-com.hr
> 🖵 www.supovi.hr

Job Description: Conservation volunteers help with a variety of projects including: 1. The protection of Eurasian griffons - cleaning and maintaining the sanctuary for sick and injured birds, watching over the Eurasian griffons when feeding on the cliffs in the ornithological reserve of the island of Cres and collecting data on their behaviour. 2. Restoration of dry stonewalls. 3. Rescuing freshwater ponds. 4. Managing the eco-traits and environment. 5. Work in the interpretation centre. 6. Helping local people. 7. Making souvenirs.
Requirements: Applicants should be healthy, able to swim and speak English. Minimum age 18.
Accommodation: Provided although there is a charge.
Application Procedure: Apply to the address above.

POLAND

TEFL teachers can find relatively abundant employment and reasonable working conditions in Poland. Teaching work in Poland can be found with the organisations listed below. Poland is also covered by the EURES programme http://ec.europa.eu/eures, and further information on jobseeking, living and working there can be found on their website. In addition, voluntary work in Poland can by arranged through Youth Action for Peace, UNA Exchange and International Voluntary Service for British people, and the CIEE and Service Civil International for Americans (see the *Worldwide* chapter for details).

Red tape

ADDRESS: POLISH EMBASSY
47 Portland Place, London W1B 1JH
☎ 0207 291 3520
✁ london@msz.gov.pl or london.visa@msz.gov.pl (visa information)
🖵 www.london.polemb.net or www.londynkg.polemb.net
(visa and consular information)

Visa requirements: Poland joined the EU on 1 May 2004. EU nationals do not require a visa, they need a valid passport or valid national identity card to enter Poland. For stays of longer than 90 days, EU citizens have to register at the local municipal office (*Urzad, Wojewódzki*) to obtain the certificate on registration of the residence. After five years of continuous residence an EU national can obtain the right of permanent residency in Poland. Nationals of the USA, Canada and New Zealand do not need a visa to enter Poland for stays up to 90 days. If they wish to stay in Poland longer than three months they need to apply for a residence permit. The website of the Polish Foreign Ministry is www.msz.gov.pl.

Teaching and language schools

Els-Bell School of English

Job(s) Available: Activity leaders (8), teachers (8).
Duration: Begins in July. Minimum period of work 2 weeks.
Working Hours: *Teachers:* lead 5 hours of class per day, 5 days a week.
Pay: *Activity leaders:* PLN700 net. *Teachers:* PLN1,400 net.

Head Office: Nowy Swiat 6/12, Warsaw
☎ +48 5 8551 3298
✆ recruitmentcamp@bellschools.pl
💻 www.bellschools.pl

Company Description: An international school of English based in Gdansk, Poland. Every summer residential camps are organised for mainly Polish students by the sea.
Job Description: *Activity leaders:* responsible for afternoon activities and other non-language sessions. *Teachers:* lead class and are also involved in drama, evening activities and excursions.
Requirements: *Activity leaders:* must have finished first year of university, and achieved Polish Kuratorium Camp Counsellors certificate C1 English. *Teachers:* Degree/CELTA certified or a native speaker of English.
Accommodation: Board and accommodation included.
Application Procedure: Contact Malgorzata Imbierowicz. Phone interviews from March 2011. Foreign applicants welcome, but only native speakers for teacher positions.

The English School of Communication Skills (ESCS)

Job(s) Available: Teachers of English (60).
Duration: Period of work from October to June.
Working Hours: Part-time positions.
Pay: Salary dependent on experience and qualifications.

Head Office: Attn. Personnel Department, St. Krakowska 47/5, 33-100 Tarnow
☎ +48 14 656 3737
✆ personnel@escs.pl
💻 www.escs.pl

Company Description: ESCS school in Tarnów.
Job Description: Job involves teaching English to Polish students of all ages.
Requirements: Applicants must hold an EFL methodology certificate and have a degree level of education. Minimum age 21.
Additional Information: ESCS holds EFL training courses in August and September.
Application Procedure: Applications to the above address or by email.

Program-Bell

Job(s) Available: Teachers of English/sports monitors.
Duration: 6 weeks from the end of June.
Working Hours: 20 hours of teaching per week, with a teaching hour of 50 minutes.
Pay: PLN1,900 net per month.

Head Office: UL. Fredry 1, 61-701 Poznan
☎ +48 6 1851 9250
✆ office@program-bell.edu.pl
💻 www.program-bell.edu.pl

Company Description: PROGRAM-Bell School of English is an ELT institution associated with the Bell Educational Trust. It operates a language school which is presently located in 2 centres in Poznan. PROGRAM-Bell offers tuition to approximately 1,000 students. PROGRAM-Bell employs about 30 full-time qualified teachers from Poland as well as Britain and the USA.

Requirements: Native English speakers with TEFL qualifications and a university degree.

Accommodation: Provided.

Application Procedure: Apply for a teaching post at PROGRAM-Bell by contacting the school by email. Selection is based on an interview.

ROMANIA

As of the 1 January 2007, Romania became a full member of the EU and is covered by the EURES programme. The National Agency for Employment works with the public employment services in the other 26 EU Member States to promote the mobility of the EU nationals within the European Union and increase the employment rate. There are mainly voluntary work opportunities in Romania, although paid positions can also be found, particularly in teaching.

Red tape

ADDRESS: EMBASSY OF ROMANIA
4 Palace Green, London W8 4QD
☎ 020 7937 9666
✆ roemb@roemb.co.uk
🖳 www.londra.mac.ro

Visa requirements: Romania joined the European Union on 1 January 2007 along with Bulgaria. Further to Romania's EU accession there are no restrictions for EEA nationals wishing to travel or work in Romania. However, EEA citizens wishing to reside in Romania for longer than three months must register with the relevant Romanian authorities. Non–EEA nationals may be subject to visa requirements. Contact your local embassy for up-to-date details.

Work permits: It is now not necessary for EEA nationals to apply for a work permit as they have free access on the Romanian labour market. The other categories of foreigners (Americans, Australians and Canadians) may be subject to the work permit obligation prior to their employment in Romania. For further information, visit the website of the Romanian Office for Immigration (http://ori.mai.gov.ro/home/index/en).

For up-to-date information about visa requirements check with the embassy before travel.

Teaching and language schools

Volunteers for Mental Health

Job(s) Available: Volunteers.
Duration: Minimum period of work 3 months. 6 month placements are preferred.
Cost: For volunteers on a 6-month placement, VfMH will cover the cost of flights to and from the UK to Romania, travel from the airport to the volunteer

Head Office: 7 Dewsbury Close, Pinner HA5 5JG, UK
☎ 020 8868 9612
✎ info@vfmh.org.uk
🖳 www.vfmh.org.uk

house, insurance, utility bills and rent of the volunteer accommodation as well as any calls made to VfMH. However, volunteers are expected to cover their daily expenses (food, travel and leisure). All volunteers are asked to fundraise £500 either before or during their placement. Volunteers must also pay £100 once they have accepted a placement.
Working Hours: 5 days a week (Monday to Friday).
Company Description: VfMH is a small, UK based charity which sends volunteers to Tarnaveni Hospital in Romania to work alongside the Romanian staff and to provide a programme of therapeutic activities for long-term male and female inpatients.
Job Description: Volunteers help with detained patients and drop in sessions in the club room and encourage them to engage in enjoyable activities like arts and crafts. Patients have a variety of problems, from learning difficulties and autism, to dementia and a variety of mental health problems such as depression and schizophrenia.
Requirements: Minimum age 18. Applicants must have at least 2 years' experience working with people with mental health problems and/or learning difficulties as well as good level of health and stamina. A professional qualification in this area is desirable. Applicants should also be based in the UK, have a UK or EU passport and the right to work in Europe.
Accommodation: Free accommodation is provided in a volunteer house.
Application Procedure: Download an application form from the website, or request an information pack by email or by sending a stamped, addressed envelope to the above address. Applicants must attend an information day and interview and then a training weekend. It is also necessary to complete an enhanced criminal records bureau check, as well as a medical and HIV test.

Dad International UK-Romania

Job(s) Available: Volunteer activity leaders/English teachers (50).
Working Hours: 4–6 hours per day.
Pay: Receive a benefits package while abroad, including full board, insurance, 24-hour support and assistance, transfers to place of work, training, inter-

Head Office: 1 Camil Petrescu, 705200 Pascani Iasi
☎ +40 7 8847 3523
✎ dad@dad.ro
🖳 www.dad.ro

net access, a phrasebook and excursions to Transylvania, Moldavia etc.
Company Description: DAD International UK-Romania is a non-profit charity organisation and is an official partner of the Romanian Ministry for Education and Research. Its mission is to provide the highest possible quality summer and winter activity programmes in Romania, in order to meet the needs of both the Romanian and UK communities.
Job Description: To teach Romanian students through informal classes, games and fun.
Requirements: Minimum age 17. No previous teaching experience or special qualifications are required.
Accommodation: Full board.
Application Procedure: Apply online at www.dad.ro/main.

While there are occasional opportunities for finding paid temporary work in Russia, it is still easier to find voluntary rather than paid work there. Even the English teachers in language schools are mostly home-grown non-native speakers, although there are still sufficient high-grade schools which are prepared to go to the expense of hiring foreign teachers with appropriate qualifications for TEFL. In addition to the opportunities listed below British people should contact Youth Action for Peace, International Voluntary Service, UNA Exchange and Concordia while Americans should contact the CIEE and Service Civil International; for details see the *Worldwide* chapter.

Red tape

ADDRESS: EMBASSY OF RUSSIA
5 Kensington Palace Gardens, London W8 4QS
☎ 0203 051 11 99
✆ info@rusemblon.org
🖥 www.rusemblon.org

Visa requirements: Any person wishing to travel to Russia must obtain a visa (visit www.rusemblon.org) in advance and register it within three working days of their arrival in the country (this does not apply to visits of three days or under). In order to obtain any sort of visa, you must first obtain a special invitation from an inviting party in Russia (company, organisation, tourist agency, private person). The tourist visa is valid for three months but does not entitle the holder to gain employment in Russia. Any person wishing to work in Russia (including voluntary work) must first receive an official invitation from the employer before they can apply for a working visa. As this takes time and effort, very few national companies are willing to go through the process. The Russian embassy has outsourced visa applications to a private company – visit http://ru.vsfglobal.co.uk to apply.

Work permits: In order to gain a work permit the foreign national must be able to produce a work contact from a company with an official invitation and the results of an HIV test. In certain cases a three-month stay can be lengthened to a year. It is advisable to contact your local embassy of Russia before travel for further information.

Teaching and language schools

Language Link

Job(s) Available: Camp teachers (6).
Duration: Staff required from the end of May to Mid August. Preference given to teachers who are available for this period.
Working Hours: 40 hours per week, 5 days a week. This includes 30 academic hours (22.5 hours) of teaching. The remaining time can be taken up with lesson preparation and camp activities. Overtime will be renumerated.
Pay: $400–$500, depending on qualifications and experience.

Head Office: Novoslobodskaya ultsa 5/2, 127055, Moscow
☎ +7 49 5250 6900
✆ jobs@languagelink.ru
🖥 www.jobs.languagelink.ru

Company Description: Language Link Russia, with its headquarters in London, has been teaching English as a foreign language since 1975. Each year it offers employment opportunities to more than 150 native speaking teachers. Language Link runs a number of English language summer camp programmes in Turkey, Bulgaria and the Moscow and St Petersburg regions.

Requirements: TEFL certificate is helpful but not necessary. All successful applicants will be put through a short training programme prior to undertaking their camp assignment. Minimum age 20. Experience working with children is an advantage but not essential.

Accommodation: Free room and board available.

Application Procedure: Applications are accepted year round. Apply online at the website above. References are mandatory and telephone interviews are conducted. Applicants are accepted from the UK, Ireland, USA, Canada, Australia and New Zealand.

Svezhy Veter

Job(s) Available: English teachers, au pair placement, work experience.

Duration: 2 weeks to 3 months (due to visa restrictions) from September to June.

Requirements: Native speakers of English, French, Spanish or German. Aged 18–55.

Accommodation: Provided.

Application Procedure: Application form available from website.

> Head Office: 426000 Izhevsk, Karla Marxa St. 288-a
> ☎ +73412 450037
> ✎ svezhyveter@gmail.com
> 🖥 www.svezhyveter.ru

SERBIA

Serbia recently regained its status as an independent state. Serbia and Montenegro, two former republics of former Yugoslavia, existed in a state union until Montenegro voted for separation from Serbia in June 2006. Short-term volunteer projects in Serbia can be arranged for British citizens by Youth Action for Peace and in Serbia by UNA Exchange. See their entries in the *Worldwide* chapter for more details.

Red tape

ADDRESS: EMBASSY OF SERBIA
28 Belgrave Square, London SW1X 8QB
☎ 020 7235 9049
✎ london@serbiaembassy.org.uk
🖥 www.serbianembassy.org.uk

Visa requirements: Citizens of all EU countries as well as the USA, Canada, Singapore, the Republic of Korea, Australia, Russia and New Zealand do not need a visa to travel to Serbia for stays of up to 90 days.

For up-to-date information about visa requirements check with the embassy before travel.

Teaching and language schools

Galindo Skola Stranih Jezika (Sava Centar & Vozdovac) ___

Job(s) Available: English teachers.
Working Hours: 6–7 hours per day, 5 days a week.
Pay: Minimum wage rates, approximately £280 per month.

Head Office: Milentija Popovica 9, 11070 Novi Beograd
☎ +381 1131 14568
✆ galindo@scnet.is
🖳 www.inlingua-beograd.com

Company Description: The first private language school in the country, located in Novi Beograd's congress and shopping centre. Excellent working atmosphere, with students from pre-school to executives. Also has 2 other locations.
Job Description: English teachers to work with children, adolescents and adults.
Requirements: Applicants should have a BA in English and TEFL, TESL or TESOL qualifications. Knowledge of some Serbo-Croatian would be an advantage.
Application Procedure: Applications online at www.interlingua.com.

Voluntary work

Exit Festival ___

Job(s) Available: Volunteers (600).
Duration: 1 week in July.
Pay: Unpaid but free entry to festival. Volunteers also receive free food and drink at the festival.

☎ +381 2147 54222
✆ volunteri@exitfest.org
🖳 www.exitfest.org

Company Description: This festival began life as an artistic anecdote to the Milosevic regime and has grown into one of Europe's largest musical celebrations. It takes place in the grounds of a citadel and attracts mainstream rock, indie and hip hop artists.
Job Description: During the festival, Exit organisers employ around 1,500 workers and volunteers to work as bartenders, promoters, security, stewards and so on. Most of the volunteers are Serbian students, but a growing number of volunteers from all over Europe attend each year in return for a ticket.
Requirements: Fluent English is not necessary.
Accommodation: Provided at Exit villager camping site for free.
Application Procedure: Those interested in volunteering should check the website from March each year when further details about volunteering are made available.

SLOVENIA

Slovenia is a great country to work in with a high standard of living. Most of the short-term possibilities for foreigners revolve around teaching English or voluntary work. The British Council in Ljubljana (www.britishcouncil.si) has a list of private language schools that may take teachers for summer schools. Slovenia is also covered by the EURES programme http://ec.europa.eu/eures, and further information on jobseeking, living and working there can be found on their website.

The following organisation organises voluntary work in Slovenia. British people can also find this type of work there through International Voluntary Service or UNA Exchange, while US citizens can apply to Service Civil International; see the *Worldwide* chapter for details.

Red tape

ADDRESS: EMBASSY OF SLOVENIA
10 Little College Street, London SW1P 3SH
☎ 020 7222 5700
✆ vlo@gov.si
🖳 www.london.embassy.si

Visa requirements: The citizens of a majority of countries may travel to Slovenia without obtaining a visa, including those from the USA, New Zealand, Canada, Japan and Australia. Slovenia joined the EU on 1 May 2004. EU citizens are able to work in Slovenia under the same conditions as Slovenians. EU citizens also have the right to live in Slovenia, but for stays of longer than three months a residence permit is obligatory. For EU citizens working in Slovenia, the employer has to register their employment with the Slovenian Employment Service. Nationals of other countries may stay up to 90 days in any half a year depending on their country of origin. For more information contact the embassy or go to the employment service of the Slovenia website, www.ess.gov.si.

For up-to-date information about visa requirements check with the embassy before travel.

Voluntary work

Zavod Voluntariat

Job(s) Available: International short-term work camp volunteers. Long-term voluntary work.
Duration: Most work camps are held during the summer and last 2 to 3 weeks. Long-term posts are announced in EVS information resource and last 6 to 10 months.

Head Office: Cigaletova, 9, 100 Ljubljana
☎ + 386 1239 1623 (624, 625)
✆ placement@gmail.com or
info@zavod-voluntariat.si
🖳 www.zavod-voluntariat.si

Pay: Applicants usually receive pocket money.
Company Description: Zavod Voluntariat is a non-profit and non-governmental organisation established in 1991 on the basis of the reorganisation of the Association MOST. Voluntariat organises voluntary work with the aim of providing programmes on social inclusion, environment protection and other activities that the state does not provide. They consider international voluntary work as a value for personal growth, promotion of social justice, intercultural learning and education for peace and solidarity.
Job Description: *Short-term work camps:* Voluntariat organises between 5 and 10 work camps in Slovenia each year. The work varies greatly from peace projects, nature conservation work, community projects with children, the elderly, refugees to community arts projects and restoration of historical monuments. *Long-term voluntary work:* volunteers help with promotional activities, with workshops and training for volunteers, with organising social activities including the projection of movies and photographic exhibitions.
Requirements: *Short-term work camps:* no special skills needed. *Long-term voluntary work:* there is a selection of required criteria for these positions, further details on request.
Accommodation: *Short-term work camps:* accommodation and food provided. *Long-term voluntary work:* accommodation not provided but applicants receive travel expenses and insurance.
Application Procedure: *Short-term work camps:* applications should be made through your local branch of International Civil Service at www.sciint.org. *Long-term voluntary work:* applications should be made directly to programi@zavod-voluntariat.si.

Opportunities for paid work in Turkey usually involve either teaching English or working for a tour operator. There are opportunities for volunteer work with the organisations listed below or through UNA Exchange, Youth Action for Peace, International Voluntary Service, and Concordia for British citizens, or the CIEE and Service Civil International for Americans; see the *Worldwide* chapter for details.

Red tape

ADDRESS: EMBASSY OF TURKEY
Rutland Lodge, Rutland Garden, Knightsbridge, London SW7 1BW
☎ 020 7591 6900
✆ turkcons.london@mfa.gov.tr
🖥 www.turkishconsulate.org.uk

Visa requirements: All British, Australian, American, Canadian and Irish nationals can obtain a three-months/multiple-entry visa at their point of entry to Turkey. Citizens of New Zealand, Denmark, Finland, France, Germany, Greece, Holland, Iceland, Israel, Japan, Sweden and Switzerland do not need visas for stays of up to three months as tourists. Any UK national entering Turkey is advised to have a minimum of six months validity on their passports from the date of their entry into Turkey. In the UK up-to-date details of visa and permit requirements can be obtained by telephoning 09068 347 348.

Work permits: Work permits are not granted for students seeking work for the summer months. They are only granted for permanent positions lasting more than a year. As there is currently not a temporary or student work visa available, the embassy advises students to make use of an exchange programme, or go as a tourist.

For up-to-date information check with the embassy before travel.

Voluntary work

Genctur

Job(s) Available: International voluntary work camps.
Duration: 2 weeks.
Company Description: Genctur is Turkey's leading youth and student travel organisation. Their main activities are international voluntary work camps in Turkey.

Head Office: Istiklal Cad. No 108,
Aznavur Pasaji, K: 5 34430, Istanbul
☎ +90 2 1224 46230
✆ workcamps.in@genctur.com
🖥 www.genctur.com

Job Description: Project volunteers are needed for mostly manual work, including repairing and painting schools, digging water trenches, constructing schools or health care centres, gardening and environmental development works or social schemes such as helping handicapped people or practising English with children. Projects take place mostly in small villages and towns where the traditional way of life can be seen through contact with the local people. The language spoken at the camps is English. Children's camps are for 10–14 years and teenage camps are for 15–17 years.

Requirements: Minimum age 18.

Accommodation: Full board and accommodation provided.

Application Procedure: Applications are only accepted through the following partner voluntary organisations: UNA Exchange, Concordia, IVS and Youth Action for Peace UK.

GSM Youth Services Centre

Job(s) Available: Work camp volunteers.

Duration: 2 weeks, from July until the end of September.

Working Hours: 5 hours per day.

Cost: Volunteers pay their own travel costs.

Head Office: Bayindir Sokak, No.45/9 Kizilay, 06450 Kizilay-Ankara
☎ +90 3 1241 71124
📧 gsm@gsm-youth.org
🖥 www.gsm-youth.org

Company Description: GSM-Youth Services Centre is a non-governmental, non-profit youth organisation that was founded by a group of young people in 1985, in Ankara, Turkey. Its main aim is to support common understanding, peace, friendship and intercultural learning among young people from different cultural backgrounds by organising international youth activities. They operate under the belief that these intercultural activities give space to young people to share their experiences and own cultural richness, which could help young people to break down barriers and prejudices. In order to achieve these aims available programmes include: international voluntary work camps, international youth projects under European programmes, NGO capacity building seminars, youth information. GSM is a member of the Alliance of European Voluntary Service Organisations and YEN-youth express network.

Job Description: GSM organises around 20 work camps throughout Turkey in cooperation with the local municipalities and universities. The projects, usually taking place in towns or on campus sites, can involve environmental protection, restoration, construction and/or festival organisations.

Requirements: Applicants aged 18–28.

Accommodation: Board and lodging provided in dormitories, small hotels/pensions, camp houses or with families.

Application Procedure: Applications through partner organisations including Concordia, Quaker International Social Projects and the United Nations Association (Wales).

Other employment in Turkey

ICEP (International Cultural Exchange Programs)

Job(s) Available: Au pairs, English teachers, interns with Turkish companies.

Duration: Minimum period of work 3 months.

Pay: *Au pair:* minimum $200 per month. *English teacher:* $50 per month. *Interns:* $150 per month.

Head Office: Karanfil Sk. 19/3, Kizilay, Ankara
☎ +90 3 1241 84460
📧 icep@icep.org.tr
🖥 www.icep.org.tr

Company Description: The International Cultural Exchange Programme (ICEP) Scholarship Foundation is a not-for-profit organisation which was established in Turkey in 1995 under the auspices of the Turkish Prime Ministry Department of Charitable Foundations. The purpose of the Foundation is to provide cultural exchange opportunities for young people and students around the world, with the added aim of introducing Turkey, its history, heritage and culture to young foreigners.

Job Description: *Au pair:* babysitting, some light housework, caring for children. This work can include but is not limited to: preparing meals for the children, feeding them, playing with them, taking them to the park, taking them and picking them up from school, keeping their room tidy, washing and ironing their clothes. Only provide vacancies for female applicants. You may be asked to teach English to the children of your host family.

Accommodation: Available free of charge.

Application Procedure: Apply by email to icep@icep.org.tr.

ICEPworld

Job(s) Available: Marketing assistant (2), student representative (2).

Duration: The end of May/beginning of June to September. Minimum period of work 2 months but can be longer.

Working Hours: 5 days a week, 7 hours per day.

Pay: $150.

Head Office: Cumhuriyet Cad. Pertev Apt. 3/1 Taksim, Istanbul
icep@icep.org.tr
www.icep.org.tr

Company Description: ICEPworld is an international network for youth and student, work and travel, au pair and language studies. ICEPworld partners are based all over the world including the UK, USA, Germany, Turkey, Ukraine and Romania.

Job Description: General office assistant position. Includes daily running of the office, completing projects assigned.

Requirements: 18–30 years old. Basic IT skills.

Accommodation: Provided. Lunch is provided during office hours, both free of charge.

Application Procedure: Applications to Mr Celemet Yener by email at info@icep.org.tr. Applicants can send their applications starting in April. There will be a phone interview. Foreign applicants welcome to apply.

PART 3: WORLDWIDE

ORGANISATIONS WITH VACANCIES WORLDWIDE

Agricultural work

IAEA/AgriVenture

Job(s) Available: Farming or horticultural working programmes.

Duration: Programmes depart all year round (applications required usually 2 months minimum before departure).

Costs: Start at approximately £2,100 which include return flights (and transfer to host family), full travel and work insurance, work permits, job placement, departure information meeting, seminar in host country and full emergency back-up through offices in hosting country.

Head Office: Speedwell Farm Bungalow, Nettle Bank, Wisbech, Cambridgeshire PE14 0SA, UK
☎ 01945 450999 or 0800 783 2186
📧 uk@agriventure.com
🖥 www.agriventure.net

Company Description: Agriventure arrange farming or horticultural working programmes to Australia, New Zealand, Canada, the USA and Japan.

Requirements: Applicants must be aged 18–30, have no dependents, be British citizens, have a full driving licence and have experience or an interest in agriculture or horticulture.

Application Procedure: For a free brochure or more information telephone or email with your name, address and postcode, or visit the website to find details of your local office.

WWOOF (World Wide Opportunities on Organic Farms)

Job(s) Available: Volunteering on organic properties in exchange for food and accommodation.

Company Description: WWOOF gives people the opportunity to gain first-hand experience of organic

📧 general.info@wwoof.org
🖥 www.wwoof.org

farming and gardening in return for spending a week or longer helping on a farm. Since WWOOF began in England in 1971, similar schemes have developed in other countries around the world. WWOOF organisations now cover more than 80 countries. Each WWOOF organisation has its own aims, system, fees and rules (eg WWOOF Australia, WWOOF Italy) but they all offer volunteers the chance to learn organic growing methods in a practical way from their hosts. WWOOF organisations supply a list of hosts; volunteers choose farms and contact them directly. Some volunteers have previous experience on an organic farm, but most volunteers are unskilled.

Some countries have a national WWOOF organisation (including Australia, Austria, Bulgaria, Canada, China, Costa Rica, the Czech Republic, Denmark, Estonia, France, Germany, Ghana, Hawaii, India, Israel, Italy, Japan, Korea, Mexico, Nepal, New Zealand, Spain, Sweden, Switzerland, Turkey, the USA and the UK).

Hosts in other countries are listed with WWOOF Independents (currently listing over 50 countries worldwide).

Requirements: Join the national WWOOF organisation of the country you want to visit (or WWOOF Independents where there is no national organisation) to obtain addresses of host farms. Membership fees are around €15–€25 per year.

Application Procedure: For further information, see www.wwoof.org, email general.info @wwoof.org, or write to WWOOF in the UK (PO Box 2154, Winslow, Buckingham MK18 3WS, UK).

Hotel work and catering

Club Med Recruitment

Job(s) Available: Receptionist, public relations, childcare activities counsellor, bartender, sport instructor, hostess, sales assistant and more.

Duration: Applicants must be available for a season (3–8 months).

UK office: Human Resources Gemini House, 10–18 Putney Hill, London SW15 6AA, UK

www.clubmedjobs.com

Company Description: By working at Club Med you choose to highlight your professional know-how and your personal competencies as you take part in the entertaining events in the resort and help to create the international atmosphere which makes Club Med holidays unique.

Job Description: Staff required for Club Med resorts in more than 40 countries.

Requirements: Applicants must have professional experience and/or diploma and excellent inter-personal skills. Good level of French and/or other foreign languages would be a plus. *Childcare activities counsellors:* should have NNEB qualifications and first aid knowledge. *Sport instructors:* should have relevant qualifications and experience. *Receptionist/PR:* should have relevant experience and be fluent in French (other foreign languages being a plus).

Application Procedure: Please apply online at the above website.

Crystal Ski

Job(s) Available: Resort representatives, chalet and hotel, chefs, chalet hosts, childcarers, hotel hosts and maintenance for the winter ski season.

Duration: November to April.

Crystal Ski Recruitment: King's Place, 12–42 Wood Street, Kingston-Upon-Thames, Surrey KT1 1JY, UK

☎ 020 8541 2223

sla.recruitment@tuiski.com

www.jobsinwinter.co.uk

Company Description: Crystal Ski is part of TUI UK, one of the top specialist tour operators in the UK. They offer a selection of catered chalet and hotel holidays on their winter ski programme featured in 140 resorts worldwide.

Requirements: Representatives need to be independent and have a thorough knowledge of customer requirements, be able to ski or showboard at solid intermediate level or above and be able to ski/ride confidently on Black and Red runs, as well as have group leadership skills. Chalet hosts need to be customer focused with excellent catering and housekeeping skills. Childcarers need to be qualified and have a passion for working with children.

Application Procedure: Apply online at www.jobsinwinter.co.uk/crystal.

Industrial and office work

Global Choices

Job(s) Available: Field-specific practical internships abroad, professional internships, teaching programmes, volunteering and working holidays.

Duration: From 2 weeks to 18 months.

Cost: Varies according to the individual programme.

Head Office: 420 Omega Works, 4 Roach Road, London E3 2LX, UK

☎ 020 85332777

info@globalchoices.co.uk

www.globalchoices.co.uk

Company Description: For over 14 years, Global Choices has arranged placements and cultural exchanges for students and young professionals from all over the world. Their mission is to find jobs where students can reach their maximum potential and chances for a bright future. To make this dream a reality, Global Choices aim to provide excellent service to their candidates by listening closely and immediately acting on their needs.

Job Description: *Field-specific practical internships abroad:* allows students or professionals to gain training and work experience in hospitality management or agriculture. *Professional internships:* work experience relevant to student's studies. Placements are offered in industrial, business, science, conservation, agriculture, travel, tourism, marketing, sales, finance and IT industries. *Teaching programmes:* native English speakers and professional teachers to teach where English is being acquired as a second language. *Working holidays:* opportunity for current students during summer, who are seeking to build work experience, travel abroad and earn money. Destinations include Argentina, Australia, Brazil, Canada, China, Greece, India, Ireland, Italy, Spain, the UK, the USA, Vietnam, Costa Rica, Guatemala, South Korea, Mauritius and Singapore.

Application Procedure: Varies according to different program structures. Visit the website for more details.

International Cooperative Education

Job(s) Available: Include retail sales, banking, computer technology, hotels and restaurants, offices etc.
Duration: 2–3 months.
Working Hours: 30–40 hours per week.
Pay: Depending on the particular employment students earn a modest salary or stipend.

Head Office: 15 Spiros Way, Menlo Park, California 94025, USA
☎ +1 650 3234944
✆ icemenlo@aol.com
🖥 www.icemenlo.com

Cost: Placement fee is $700 plus an application fee of $250.
Company Description: ICE provides American college and university students with the unique opportunity to become immersed in a culture other than their own, and gain practical cultural and work experience abroad.
Requirements: Aged 18–30. Full time students. Most jobs require knowledge of the relevant language.
Accommodation: Either live with a homestay or with an employer sponsored housing programme.
Application Procedure: Apply online at www.icemenlo.com/apply.

International Association for the Exchange of Students for Technical Experience (IAESTE)

Job(s) Available: Course-related traineeships.
Duration: Short-term contracts, usually between 6 weeks to 3 months.
Pay: Students are responsible for their own travel and insurance costs, but paid a salary by host employer to cover cost of living.

Head Office: IAESTE UK, 10 Spring Gardens, London SW1A 2BN, UK
☎ 020 7389 4114
✆ iaeste@britishcouncil.org
🖥 www.iaeste.org.uk

Company Description: IAESTE operate an exchange scheme whereby students in undergraduate degree level scientific and technical studies, are offered course-related traineeships in industrial, business, governmental and research organisations in over 80 countries.
Job Description: IAESTE selected trainees undertake specific scientific, or professional tasks.
Application Procedure: More information and applications available from the above address.

Sports, couriers and camping

Broadreach and Academic Treks

Job(s) Available: Language instructors in Spanish, French and Chinese (8–16), Scuba instructors (35), skippers (17), marine biologists (8) and wilderness leaders (8).

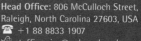

Head Office: 806 McCulloch Street, Raleigh, North Carolina 27603, USA
☎ +1 88 8833 1907
staffinquiry@gobroadreach.com
www.gobroadreach.com or www.academictreks.com

Duration: Required from June to August. Minimum period of work 3 weeks.

Working Hours: 24 hours per day, 7 days a week for the duration of the trip. Each trip has several days of preparation and debriefing.

Pay: Wages for all positions depend on instructor's level of experience in the skill area as well as experience level as a trip leader. Programme travel, housing and meals are included.

Company Description: Broadreach and Academic Treks provide summer adventure and educational programmes for teens. These inspirational programmes focus on teamwork, exploration and skill-building. Academic Treks, the academic and service adventure division of Broadreach, offers college-accredited summer programmes abroad for teenagers which combine experiential learning, traditional classroom learning and community service learning with wilderness adventure, international travel and cultural immersion to create enriching expeditions.

Job Description: All available positions are challenging. Instructors not only teach students about their area of expertise but also teach students all life skills required for life in a confined space in a group of people. This includes but is not limited to cooking, cleaning, interpersonal counselling and group dynamic facilitation

Requirements: Staff should be competent in their skill area. Should have experience travelling internationally, and working with teens on leading multi-day trips. Should enjoy working with teens, possess a positive, healthy attitude and be flexible. Fluent English is essential. *Language instructors in Spanish, French, Chinese:* must have Masters or PhD. *Skippers:* must be able to sail a 40ft–50ft sailboat. *Marine biologists:* must have Masters or PhD. *Wilderness leaders:* must have backcountry experience.

Accommodation: Board and lodging available. Meals, housing and some transportation are covered in addition to monetary wages.

Additional Information: Programmes are offered in more than one country but do not provide any sort of sponsorship nor reimbursement for visas.

Application Procedure: Apply by email or at www.broadreachstaff.com. Overseas applicants welcome to apply.

Contiki Holidays

Job(s) Available: Tour managers, drivers and site reps.

Head Office: Wells House, 15 Elmfield Road, Bromley BR1 1LS, UK
☎ 020 8290 6777
travel@contiki.co.uk
www.contiki.com

Duration: Seasonal basis from March to October.

Company Description: A company that specialises in coach tours holidays for 18–35 year olds throughout Europe and the UK.

Job Description: Tour managers and drivers are responsible for the day to day running of our tours pointing out the best sights and sounds of Europe and making sure everyone enjoys themselves along the way. Site reps are based in destinations in Europe and look after clients for duration of their stay.

Requirements: No experience necessary. All successful applicants receive thorough training in the form of a 10–week road trip in Europe. *Tour managers and site reps*: must hold an EU passport or a valid UK work visa. *Drivers*: must hold an EU passport.

Application Procedure: Apply online at www.contiki.com/jobs. Recruitment starts in September for the following year's summer season.

Monarch Holidays

Job(s) Available: Operations assistants, overseas representatives.

Duration: Summer season runs from April to October.

Pay: *Operations assistants:* from £650. O*verseas representatives:* from £415.

> **Head Office:** Wren Court, 17 London Road, Bromley, Kent BR1 1DE, UK
> ☎ 020 8464 3444
> 🖳 www.monarch.co.uk/jobs

Company Description: Cosmos/Monarch Holidays is an independent tour operator, providing holidays in the Mediterranean and further afield.

Job Description: *Operations assistants:* to provide administrative support to a busy resort and management team. *Overseas representatives:* customer service, sales, guiding excursions, airport duties.

Accommodation: Flights and accommodation provided.

Application Procedure: To apply send a CV and covering letter to overseasCV@cosmos.co.uk.

Dragoman

Job(s) Available: Crew to drive their expedition vehicles through developing countries.

Duration: Minimum of 15 months.

Pay: All crew on road (including trainees) receive daily living allowance. Once a qualified crew member you will start to earn a wage as well. When you

> **Head Office:** Camp Green, Kenton Road, Debenham, Suffolk IP14 6LA, UK
> ☎ 01728 862255
> ✎ recruitment@dragoman.co.uk
> 🖳 www.dragoman.co.uk

are leading trips and/or are a trip mechanic you will also be eligible for bonuses based upon your performance.

Company Description: Overland adventure tours worldwide. Dragoman Overland employ overland crew to drive their expedition vehicles through developing countries, showing travellers the wonders of the world.

Requirements: Minimum age 25. Valid driving licence essential.

Application Procedure: Download an application form at www.dragoman.com/documents/crew_application_form.pdf.

Explore!

Job(s) Available: Tour leaders.

Duration: 3–6 months. Work available throughout the year, minimum period of work 3 weeks. The peak periods of Christmas, summer holidays and Easter are most popular times.

Working Hours: On duty 24/7 but work is satisfying.

> **Head Office:** Nelson House, 55 Victoria Road, Farnborough, Hampshire GU14 7PA, UK
> ☎ 01252 391114
> ✎ hr@explore.co.uk
> 🖳 www.explore.co.uk

Cost: A £250 deposit.

Company Description: Explore! is a large adventure travel tour operator.

Job Description: Tour leaders for leading tour groups of 16–24 clients per group, to 100+ countries around the world.

Requirements: Applicants with language skills and previous travel experience essential. Full training given. Must be available to leave the UK for certain set periods of time.

Application Procedure: Applications to the above address are accepted all year round and must be on an application form, which can be downloaded from the website.

Kumuka Worldwide

Job(s) Available: Tour leaders, tour drivers.
Duration: Minimum period of work 6 months.
Working Hours: 24/7 with tour groups. Time off between tours.
Pay: Minimum £100 per week plus daily allowance, accommodation, transport and some meals. Increases with experience.

> **Head Office:** 40 Earls Court Road, London W8 6EJ, UK
> ☎ 020 7937 8855
> ✍ humanresources@kumuka.com
> 🖥 www.kumuka.com

Company Description: Leading specialists in worldwide adventure travel, Kumuka have been successfully operating exciting tours for the enthusiastic traveller for more than 25 years. Covering Africa, Latin America, North America, Asia, Europe, the Middle East, Australia, New Zealand and Antarctica, Kumuka recruits outgoing people with a strong interest in travel.

Requirements: *Tour leaders:* minimum age 23. Chosen according to experience and personality. *Tour Drivers:* minimum age 25, with HGV license (or equivalent) and mechanical experience.

Application Procedure: Applications via the above email address.

Mark Warner

Job(s) Available: Accountants, aerobics instructors, bar staff, chefs, handymen, kitchen porters, nannies, nightwatch, receptionists, restaurant staff, tennis instructors, watersports instructors.
Duration: *Corsica, Sardinia, Greece, Portugal, Turkey and France:* during the summer from April to November. *Egypt:* all year round.
Pay: Varies according to role plus staff benefits.

> **Head Office:** 20 Kensington Church Street, London W8 4EP, UK
> ☎ 020 7795 8375 (for childcare recruitment)
> ✍ recruitment@markwarner.co.uk
> 🖥 www.markwarner-recruitment.co.uk

Company Description: Mark Warner is an independent tour operator with hotels in Europe and beach resorts in the Mediterranean. They have 35 years of experience and offer many new opportunities and activities.

Job Description: Work in hotels in Corsica, Sardinia, Greece, Portugal, France, Turkey and Egypt, Sri Lanka and Mauritius.

Requirements: Requirements for languages, experience, qualifications etc vary according to the job applied for.

Accommodation: Full board, medical insurance, travel expenses, free use of watersports and activity facilities and more.

Application Procedure: Please apply online.

Powder Byrne

Job(s) Available: Children's club managers/assistants, crèche managers/assistants, resort drivers and resort managers.

Head Office: 250 Upper Richmond Road, London SW15 6TG, UK
☎ 020 8246 5342
📧 oliver@powderbyrne.co.uk
🖥 www.powderbyrne.com

Duration: Duration of contracts vary from 2 weeks to 6 months between April and October plus the winter season.

Working Hours: Long hours. You will be expected to be up early and full of enthusiasm.

Pay: Dependent on job and experience.

Company Description: Powder Byrne is an exclusive tour operator offering tailor-made holidays, working alongside 4 and 5-star luxury hotels, to provide a top of the range holiday package. They are looking for highly motivated customer-focused team players to work in their summer resorts programme in overseas holiday destinations, in Europe mainly around the Mediterranean. Winter season destinations are Switzerland, Austria, France and Italy.

Job Description: *Children's club managers/assistants:* to organise and run the kids' clubs for 4–9 and, 9–14-year-olds. *Crèche managers/assistants:* required for managing resort crèches for children aged 6 months to 3 years. *Resort drivers:* required for transporting guests in exclusive company minibuses and assist the resort manager in providing a high level of customer service to Powder Byrne clients. *Resort managers:* required for managing a team of staff in resort, to provide a high calibre of services to Powder Byrne clients and to liaise with head office.

Requirements: Knowledge of French, German, Italian and Spanish are desirable but not essential. No formal qualifications required. *Crèche managers/assistants:* NNEB or equivalent is required. Training is provided.

Accommodation: Accommodation, flights, transport, resort insurance and uniform provided. Certain meals included while working.

Application Procedure: Applications are made online at www.powderbyrne.com/resort_staff.php.

Sunsail Ltd

Job(s) Available: Activities assistants, BWSF waterski instructors, mountain bike leaders, qualified nannies (NNEB/BTEC/CACHE), RYA windsurf/dinghy/yacht instructors, watersports managers, lifeguards, Flotilla crews including RYA qualified skippers, engineers and hosties.

Head Office: The Port House, Port Solent, Portsmouth, Hampshire PO6 4TH, UK
☎ 02392 334600
📧 recruitment@sunsail.com
🖥 www.sunsail.co.uk

Duration: From April to November, certain vacancies also available for summer holiday periods.

Working Hours: 6 days a week.

Company Description: Sunsail provide worldwide sailing holidays with 29 bases worldwide employing around 1,000 staff. Most positions are seasonal, but as Sunsail is part of the TUI Travel Plc, there are opportunities for year round employment.

Job Description: All positions are in Greece, Turkey and Croatia. In addition to the specific responsibilities of the role, staff also commit a great deal of time to socialising with guests and providing exceptional customer care. *Watersports managers, RYA windsurf/dinghy/yacht instructors and BWSF waterski instructors:* required to instruct RYA courses and provide rigging assistance and rescue cover for beach operations.

Requirements: Minimum age 18. Relevant qualifications essential.

Accommodation: Benefits include shared accommodation, all meals in the club, paid holiday, return flights on successful completion of the contracted period, full uniform, discounted holidays, bar discount in the club and free use of all the equipment.

Application Procedure: To apply or for more information visit www.sunsail.co.uk/hr and fill in an online application form.

Tucan Travel and Budget Expeditions Recruitment for South America

Job(s) Available: Tour leaders, drivers.

Duration: All year round.

Company Description: Tucan Travel is a leading adventure travel specialist for Latin America, operating tours all year round throughout South and Central America, including Cuba. In recent years,

Head Office: 316 Uxbridge Road, Acton, London W3 9QP, UK
☎ 020 8896 6704
✆ sara@tucantravel.com
🖥 www.tucantravel.com

extended tours include Europe, Asia, Africa, Northern Africa, Russia, the Middle East, Southeast Asia and many more to come. This is an exciting opportunity to relocate to a fascinating and very interesting part of the world, to gain some fantastic travel experience and have a great adventure.

Job Description: *Tour leaders:* required to guide international groups on published itineraries. *Drivers:* to drive passengers safely and responsibly. Roles vary depending on the destination.

Requirements: Applicants must have some leadership experience, be a keen traveller, be self motivated and enthusiastic, speak at least a moderate level of Spanish, have travelled to one or more of our destinations previously and have an understanding or participated in group travel. Minimum age 25 (in Latin America). Responsible for the welfare and general enjoyment of our clients, this entails being very friendly, helpful, outgoing and organised. Must display excellent communication skills and will be on call 24 hours a day.

Application Procedure: Please send CV and job application (this can be found on the Employment section of website) to Sara at sara@tucantravel.com.

TUI-UK Ltd (Thomson and First Choice Holidays)

Job(s) Available: Holiday advisor (rep), children's representative, resort admin staff, football coaches, swimming instructors and entertainment staff.

Duration: They recruit for the summer season with the potential for winter working opportunities.

Company Description: TUI Travel PLC is a FTSE 100 company that makes special holidays happen for

Head Office: TUI Travel UK & Ireland Recruitment Team, Jetset House, Lanfield Heath, Cranley, West Sussex RH11 0PQ, UK
☎ 0800 169 5692 or 01293 816899
✆ tuitravel.recruitment@tuitravel.com
🖥 www.tuitraveljobs.co.uk

more than 30 million customers. The business was founded in 2007 following the merger of First Choice Holidays and Thomson holidays. It operates in 180 countries worldwide with 20 leading brands offering a wide range of leisure travel experiences.

Requirements: If you're flexible, responsible and have a passion for delivering excellent customer service, visit the website to find out more about the positions available and the specific requirements for each role.

Application Procedure: Please apply online at the above website.

VentureCo

Job(s) Available: Expedition leaders (8).
Duration: Up to 4 months. Work available year round.
Working Hours: 24/7.
Pay: £800–£1,300 per month, plus expenses.
Company Description: VentureCo is a Gap Year and Career Gap provider operating in South America, the Galapagos and Africa.

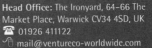

Head Office: The Ironyard, 64–66 The Market Place, Warwick CV34 4SD, UK
☎ 01926 411122
mail@ventureco-worldwide.com
www.ventureco-worldwide.com

Job Description: About 275 gap year students per year and those on a career break participate in projects which combine language schools, local aid projects and expeditions.
Requirements: Minimum age 25. Must be group-oriented and enjoy working with 18–25-year-olds.
Accommodation: Board and accommodation provided.
Additional Information: Each venture includes a travel safety course held in the UK, and expedition skills training in country.
Application Procedure: Apply to the above address or email.

Weissman Teen Tours

Job(s) Available: Tour leaders (11).
Pay: All expenses paid while on tour plus pay of $125 per week.
Company Description: Family-oriented teen tour company personally supervised by owners. The company offers programmes in the USA, Canada, England, France, Holland, Belgium, Switzerland Italy and Hawaii.

Head Office: 517 Almena Avenue, Ardsley, New York 10502, USA
☎ +1 91 4693 7575
wtt@cloud9.net
www.weissmantours.com

Job Description: Trips include snorkelling, surfing or scuba diving in Hawaii, cruising to Mexico or horseback riding in Bryce Canyon. Plus TV tapings, Hearst Castle, and West End Theatre tours in London.
Requirements: Minimum age 21. Relevant work visas and fluent English necessary. Must truly enjoy working with teens. No smoking or drinking alcohol permitted.
Accommodation: Accommodation and board provided.
Application Procedure: Apply by fax at +191 4693 4807. Own transportation to interview required. Must attend interview in person.

World Challenge Expeditions

Job(s) Available: Expedition leaders and expedition assistants.
Duration: Period of work 8 days to 4 weeks between June and late August.
Pay: Fee negotiable and all expenses paid.
Company Description: World Challenge run expe-

Head Office: 17–21 Queens Road, High Wycombe HP13 6AQ, UK
☎ 01494 444996
rbrounhill@world-challenge.co.uk
www.world-challenge.co.uk

ditions and adventure activities overseas. All expeditions and activities are designed to enable education through exploration and to raise motivation in young people through developing skills in leadership, team building, decision-making and problem solving.
Job Description: World Challenge Expeditions requires male and female leaders for expeditions to Central and South America, Africa and Asia.
Requirements: Should be trained in an NGB award eg WGL or ML. Leaders with good facilitation and youth development skills are also welcome and considered for expedition assistant positions.
Application Procedure: Apply online at www.world-challenge.co.uk.

Boats

Global Crew Network

Job(s) Available: Professional and amateur yacht crew wanted for permanent or temporary postions worldwide. Working holidays and working passages available for beginners. Ideal for gap year students or people seeking some experience or low cost/free travel.

Head Office: 23 Old Mill Gardens, Berkhamsted, Hertfordshire HP4 2NZ, UK
☎ 07773 361959
✆ info@globalcrewnetwork.com
🖳 www.globalcrewnetwork.com

Job Description: Luxury yacht jobs worldwide.

Application Procedure: For more info visit www.globalcrewnetwork, email CV or call John on the above number for more information.

P&O Cruises Carnival UK

Job(s) Available: Port presenters, shore excursion staff.

Head Office: Carnival House, 100 Harbour Parade, Southampton SO15 1ST
🖳 www.oceanopportunities.com

Job Description: Staff required on board cruise ships to promote and manage operations of shore excursions in the Mediterranean, Caribbean and Americas.

Application Procedure: Applications should be made by sending a CV and covering letter to human resources-hotel services at the above websites.

Voluntary work

Africa and Asia Venture

Job(s) Available: Work experience in teaching, community, sports coaching and environment conservation in Latin America, Africa, the Indian Himalayas, Nepal, China, Thailand and Mexico.

Head Office: 10 Market Place, Devizes, Wilts SN10 1HT, UK
☎ 01380 729009
✆ av@aventure.co.uk
🖳 www.aventure.co.uk

Duration: 3 weeks to 5 months. You can also take part in shorter expeditions in Kenya, Uganda, Thailand and Mexico.

Company Description: AV has 16 years of experience offering 18–24-year-old volunteers rewarding projects that combine community work with travel and adventure and opportunities for those keen to improve their Spanish in Mexico.

Job Description: Volunteers with AV will start with an in-country orientation course covering customs, then the experience of a rewarding project, followed by 3 weeks independent travel, and a 6–8 day safari, including travelling in game reserves, deserts, or white water rafting. All this supported by excellent back-up enabling you to experience first hand countries away from the tourist trail.

Application Procedure: Apply at the above number or online.

Càlédõñiâ (Latin America)

Job(s) Available: Volunteer work in Latin America, plus work experience in Europe and Latin America.
Duration: 3 weeks to 9 months.
Cost: Dependent on programme and location.

Head Office: The Clockhouse, 72 Newhaven Road, Edinburgh EH6 5QG, UK
☎ +44 (0)131 621 7721
info@caledonialanguages.co.uk
www.caledonialanguages.com

Company Description: Caledonia has 12 years' experience of organising trips in 50 locations world-wide including Europe, Latin America and the Caribbean. Caledonia maintains a close working relationship with all their overseas partners and can recommend the places to go according to your particular interests.

Job Description: Work experience placements with local partners eg Admin/secretarial work or social volunteer placements helping with local communities such as helping young children in orphanages and teaching English. There are also placements in national parks, nature reserves and in the rainforest.

Requirements: Minimum age 18. Experience of the language of the country that volunteers wish to travel to is required.

Accommodation: Accommodation is provided depending on project.

Additional Information: Applicants can choose the type of work they would like to do but Caledonia will make the final decision of where you are placed. Your experience and language level, however, will be taken into consideration.

Application Procedure: Request an application form via Caledonia and further information can be found on the website.

Cultural Embrace

Job(s) Available: *Paid work placements:* hospitality/tourism, non-technical, agricultural, clerical throughout Australia and New Zealand. *Paid Au Pair placements:* France, Germany, Italy, Netherlands, Spain. *Paid teaching placements:* Chile, China, Thailand and Latin America *Unpaid professional internships:* Argentina, Australia, Brazil, Chile, Costa Rica, Ecuador, France, Spain, South Africa. *Humanitarian Service Work:* South Africa, Kenya, Ghana, Australia, New Zealand, China, India, Latin America, Southeast Asia.

Head Office: 7201 Bill Hughes Road, Austin, Texas 78745, USA
☎ +1 51 2469 9089
info@culturalembrace.com
www.culturalembrace.com

Duration: Placements are varied, ranging from 1 to 52 weeks. Most employers require minimum period of work 3 months for paid position, but many placements depend on visa requirements.

Working Hours: Positions vary with each employer or school. *Childcare/au pair:* 40–50 hours per week. *Hospitality/tourism work:* approximately 35–50 hours per week. *Teaching English:* approximately 20–30 hours per week. *Farm/administrative:* approximately 20–40 hours/week.

Company Description: Cultural Embrace pre-arranges and guarantees placements for individuals and groups to work, intern, volunteer, teach, take cultural classes, travel and live abroad. Offers programmes to Asia, Africa, Australia/New Zealand, Europe or Latin America, including major medical traveller's insurance, housing and visa assistance, pre-departure and local support. Specialise in programmes that integrate the authenticity of the local community, highlighting educational, cultural and/or humanitarian projects. Customise an itinerary to fit your schedule, budget, interests, needs and academic curriculum.

Requirements: Requirements vary with programme and employer. *Hospitality/tourism work and internship work placements:* in Europe require intermediate/advanced language level (language lessons usually included or available upon request). *Work and internship placements:* in Asia and Latin America prefer language knowledge, but not required (language lessons usually included or available upon request). *Teaching English:* requires fluent English, and classroom experience preferred but not required (TEFL online preparatory course included). Visa requirements for New Zealand/Australia are 18–30 years old or full-time students.

Accommodation: Most placements include accommodation. If not, Cultural Embrace will assist with pre-arranging a clean, safe, comfortable and affordable housing.

Application Procedure: Recommend application by email at least 3 months in advance. Expedited fees apply for prior 12 weeks of departure date. Phone interview required.

Global Vision International

Job(s) Available: Volunteers and interns.

Duration: Length of projects varies from 1 week to 2 years.

Pay: Internship positions available for a working insight into ground operations within Global Vision International.

Job Description: Volunteers for projects including conservation, community and construction work in over 40 countries and 5 continents.

Requirements: No special qualifications required. Minimum age 18.

Application Procedure: Applications are taken online via the projects page. Applicants should be contacted 2 to 3 days after their application is submitted.

Head Office: 3 High Street, St Albans, Herts AL3 4ED, UK
☎ 01727 250 250
info@gviworld.com
www.gvi.co.uk

Head Office: GVI North America, 66 Long Wharf, Suite 562 S, Boston, MA 02110, USA
☎ + 1 88 8653 6028

Head Office: GVI Australasia, Suite 206, 530 Little Collins Street, Melbourne, VIC, 3000, Australia
☎ +61 1300 795 013

Inter-Cultural Youth Exchange UK (ICYE-UK)

Job(s) Available: Voluntary placements available, (50+ per year) in developing countries, mainly in Latin America, Africa and Asia.

Duration: *Long-term:* (6–12 months) volunteers begin their placement in either January or August each year. *Short-term:* (3–16 weeks) volunteers can begin their placement at any time throughout the year.

Head Office: ICYE-UK, Latin America House, Kingsgate Place, London NW6 4TA, UK
☎ 020 7681 0983
info@icye.org.uk
www.icye.org.uk

Working Hours: Monday to Friday, 4–8 hours per day but some flexibility may be required.

Pay: All placements are on a voluntary (non-paid) basis and are self-funded. *Long-term:* volunteers receive monthly 'pocket' money.

Cost: *Long-term:* £4,495 for 12 months and £3,795 (subject to change) for 6 months. Fee is inclusive of return flights, full medical travel insurance, accommodation (with host family or local lodgings), 3 daily meals, pre-departure training in the UK and in-country training and support throughout the placement, visa support and 30 hours' worth of language lessons. *Short-term:* 3–16 weeks, from £1,200 to £2,550, depending on host country and length of placement, inclusive of return flights, board and lodgings, travel insurance, visa support, in-country support and induction.

Company Description: ICYE-UK is a member of the international ICYE Federation which has over 50 years of experience in sending and hosting volunteers worldwide. ICYE-UK works exclusively through its network of local ICYE partners meaning that voluntary placements are sourced and run by local experts ensuring a worthwhile voluntary experience and the development of sustainable community-based projects.

Job Description: ICYE can offer volunteers a huge range of different projects across Europe, Latin America, Asia and Africa. Examples include working with children in schools and orphanages, conservation work, human rights projects, HIV/AIDS awareness and lots more.

Requirements: No previous experience required but volunteers must have enthusiasm, flexibility, dedication and desire to experience a new culture.

Accommodation: Volunteers experience total cultural emersion by living with a host family, with local staff at the project or in local lodgings.

Additional Information: To find out more come along to an information day, check the website or call to find out the date of the next day.

Application Procedure: In the first instance, contact by phone or email to discuss opportunities in more detail. Volunteers will be required to complete an application form, attend an informal interview, provide 2 confidential references and a Police check (CRB).

Mercy Ships

Job(s) Available: Volunteer positions range from photographers, cooks, stewards, accountants, engineers, deck officers, nurses, surgeons, supply assistants and more.

Duration: Placements available from 2 weeks to 2 years. (Longer terms preferred).

Cost: Crew fees range from $650 to $900 per month.

Head Office: Mercy Ships UK, The Lighthouse, 12 Meadway Court, Stevenage SG1 2EF, UK
☎ 01438 727800
info@mercyships.org.uk
www.mercyships.org.uk

Company Description: Mercy Ships, a global charity, has operated a fleet of hospital ships in developing nations since 1978. It brings hope and healing to the poor, mobilising people and resources across West Africa to countries such as Liberia, Benin, Togo, and Sierra Leone.

Job Description: All positions are skills-based. Training in working with the poor and maritime safety training is provided.

Requirements: A working knowledge of French is beneficial. Applicants must be at least 18 and be in good physical condition.

Accommodation: Accommodation provided on board the ship.

Application Procedure: Download an application form from the website www.mercyships.org/pages/volunteer and post to above address.

Mondo Challenge

Job(s) Available: Volunteers.

Duration: A normal stay lasts 1–4 months and start dates are flexible.

Cost: Varied.

Head Office: Town Hall, Market Place, Newbury RG14 5AA, UK
☎ 01635 45556
info@mondochallenge.co.uk
www.mondochallenge.co.uk

Company Description: Mondo Challenge promotes sustainable development in local communities. Volunteers are sent to projects all over the world. Projects have included teaching, HIV awareness, business advice, community development and much more.

Job Description: Programmes are community based, providing volunteers with an insight into local cultures and a chance to experience a different way of life. Destinations include: Nepal, India, Sri Lanka, Tanzania, The Gambia, Senegal, Chile, Ecuador and Romania. All nationalities and ages accepted (average age 34). About half of all volunteers are non-UK based with a large number of volunteers from North America, Europe and Australia.

Requirements: For teaching projects, the minimum qualification is A-level or equivalent in the subject to be taught. For business development, a minimum of 4 years of business experience is required. Must be able to cope with remote posting and to relate to people of other cultures. Enthusiasm, flexibility and good communication skills are essential.

Accommodation: Board and lodging with a local family.
Application Procedure: Further information from the above address.

Projects Abroad

Job(s) Available: Projects Abroad send over 5,000 people abroad annually. Volunteers are needed in Argentina, Bolivia, Brazil, Cambodia, China, Costa Rica, Ethopia, Fiji, Ghana, India, Jamaica, Mexico, Moldova, Mongolia, Morocco, Nepal, Peru, Romania, Senegal, South Africa, Sri Lanka, Tanzania, Thailand and Togo.

> **Head Office:** Aldsworth Parade, Goring, Sussex BN12 4TX, UK
> ☎ 01903 708300
> 📧 info@projects-abroad.co.uk
> 🖥 www.projects-abroad.co.uk

Duration: 2 weeks to 1 year.

Cost: Projects start at £895.

Company Description: Projects Abroad was established to help those who wanted to learn conversational English in the lesson developed world. Later, other projects were added as many organisations requested volunteers with a special interest in the work they were doing. Volunteers can currently be found working on biodiversity studies in the Amazon rainforest in Peru; they are also saving sea turtles on the Pacific Coast of Mexico.

Job Description: Projects available include teaching, conservation, environment, culture and community, healthcare, veterinary medicine and animal care, sports, journalism, archaeology, business, law and human rights, language, enterprise and group trips.

Requirements: Minimum age 16. No TEFL, teaching qualifications or local languages are required, just good spoken English and university entrance qualifications.

Accommodation: Included in the price.

Additional Information: Volunteers can choose their dates. Price also includes food, insurance, placement and in-country support.

Application Procedure: Via the above email.

Quest Overseas

Job(s) Available: Gap Year and summer team projects and expeditions in South America and Africa.

> **Head Office:** 15A Cambridge Grove, Hove, East Sussex BN3 3ED, UK
> ☎ 01273 777206
> 📧 info@questoverseas.com
> 🖥 www.questoverseas.com

Duration: Gap adventures are 3 months long and are a combination of project and expedition. Summer trips are 4–6 weeks and are just project or expedition.

Cost: Prices range between £1,600 and £4,950 depending on the duration and destination – prices include all accommodation, food, in-country transport and activities as well as a donation to support the project long-term. Flights and insurance are not included.

Company Description: Be inspired – Quest overseas specialises in team projects and expeditions in South America and Africa. They focus in long-term partnership with project partners and have extensive knowledge of remote expedition routes.

Job Description: 3-month expeditions are a combination of language learning (where relevant), volunteer work and an adventurous expedition. Project work is always with a long-term partner, where the work to be carried out by each team is a specific objective within the context of a longer-term plan. Projects vary from work with children and construction of school buildings, to care for wild animals and conservation of threatened forests, depending on which team volunteers join. Expeditions are packed with all kinds of activities - ice climbing, white water rafting, trekking, mountain biking, surfing, safaris, scuba diving, the lot!

Additional Information: Quest regularly recruit project and expedition leaders to lead teams in Africa and South America. Contact the office for more information.

Application Procedure: All applicants must complete an application form online, followed by an interview. The interview is to make sure they fully understand what they are committing to.

Raleigh

Job(s) Available: If you are aged 17–24 you will have the opportunity to work on sustainable community and environmental projects, plus an adventure challenge. Those aged over 25 will have the opportunity to become volunteer managers to help lead and facilitate the expedition. Roles include project managers, medics, logistics, finance officers, administrators, communications officers, interpreters, photographers and drivers.

Head Office: Third floor, 207 Waterloo Road, London SE1 8XD, UK
☎ 020 7183 1270
✆ info@raleigh.org.uk
🖥 www.raleighinternational.org

Duration: Adventure and challenge expeditions for 4, 5, 7 and 10 weeks. For those over 25 the commitment is either for 8 or 13 weeks.

Company Description: Raleigh is a well-established charity with over 25 years' experience of providing adventure and challenge expeditions to destinations including Borneo, Costa Rica, Nicaragua and India.

Job Description: Join a community of over 30,000 people from all backgrounds and nationalities, including those from the host country. Volunteers are taken out of their comfort zone into remote areas where they'll learn about different cultures, make a valuable contribution and develop key life skills which will enhance your professional and educational prospects.

Requirements: Full training provided in-country.

Application Procedure: Apply online or go to an open event to find out more. More information is available on the website: www.raleighinternational.org.

Scripture Union

Job(s) Available: Volunteers for holidays and missions in the UK and Europe.

Head Office: 207-209 Queensway, Bletchley MK2 2EB, UK
☎ 01908 856120
✆ countmein@scriptureunion.org.uk
🖥 www.scriptureunion.org.uk

Duration: Throughout the summer for 1-3 weeks.

Cost: Prices range from free to £250. International missions do not include flights.

Job Description: Volunteers guide groups of children or young people and help in activity whilst engaging with Bible teachings. Volunteers also needed for kitchen work, technical support, special needs and admin.

Requirements: Applicants must identify with the aims of Scripture Union, be committed Christians and over 18. Qualifications or interest in outdoor activites, sports, first aid, life saving and working with the disabled an advantage. All volunteers working with young people must complete Enhanced CRB checks.

Application Procedure: Contact via email for appropriate application form.

Travellers Worldwide

Job(s) Available: Structured voluntary placements.

Duration: Placements last from 2 weeks to a year, with flexible start dates all year round.

Head Office: 2A Caravelle House, 17/19 Goring Road, Worthing, West Sussex BN12 4AP, UK
☎ 01903 502595
✆ info@travellersworldwide.com
🖥 www.travellersworldwide.com

Cost: Costing from £595. Sample charges for 4 weeks in Kenya is £895 and £1,195 in China.

Company Description: Founded in 1994, with 16 years organising volunteer placements abroad and a founder member of the Year Out Group. They operate over 200 projects across 20 countries so have something for everyone.

Job Description: Structured voluntary placements involving teaching conversational English (also music, sports, drama and other subjects), conservation (with orangutans, elephants, lions, dolphins etc), language courses, structured work experience (journalism, law, medicine etc) and cultural courses (photography, tango etc) in Argentina, Australia, Brazil, Brunei, Cambodia, China, Ecuador, Ghana, Guatemala, India, Kenya, Malaysia, Mauritius, New Zealand, Peru, South Africa, Sri Lanka, Thailand, Zambia and Zimbabwe. Hundreds of projects are available worldwide and are described in detail on their website. If you have something not currently provided in mind, Travellers Worldwide will attempt to arrange it for you, so don't hesitate to ask.

Requirements: No formal qualifications required.

Accommodation: Prices include food and accommodation, meeting at the nearest airport, plus support and back-up from local staff in destination countries, but exclude flights, visa costs and insurance. Travellers can arrange the latter but many volunteers prefer the flexibility of organising their own.

Application Procedure: Applications should be made to the above address or online.

Conservation and the environment

African Conservation Experience (ACE)

Job(s) Available: Volunteers.

Duration: Voluntary conservation work placements last 2–12 weeks throughout the year.

Costs: Vary, depending on reserve and time of year; support and advice are given on fund-raising.

Company Description: Have you ever dreamed of tracking wild leopard and cheetah through the bush, or assisting a marine biologist in whale and dolphin research? ACE support vital conservation projects in South Africa and with over 10 years of experience are able to offer every volunteer the benefits of their personal knowledge.

> Head Office: Unit 1, Manor Farm, Churchend Lane, Charfield, Wotton-under-edge, Gloucester GL12 8LJ, UK
> ☎ 01454 269182
> info@conservationafrica.net
> www.conservationafrica.net

Job Description: Placements for people on game reserves in southern Africa, including South Africa and Botswana. Tasks may include darting rhino for relocation or elephants for fitting tracking collars. Game capture, tagging, assisting with wildlife veterinary work, game counts and monitoring, animal care and rehabilitation may be part of the work programme. Marine projects involve dolphin and whale research, seal and sea bird monitoring. Elephant and leopard monitoring is often involved.

Requirements: Applicants must have reasonable physical fitness and be able to cope with mental challenges. Enthusiasm for conservation is essential. No previous experience or qualifications necessary.

Additional Information: The programme may be of special interest to students of environmental, zoological and biological sciences, veterinary science and animal care.

Application Procedure: Applicants are invited to attend open days at various venues across the UK. Applications to the above address or via the online form.

Coral Cay Conservation Ltd

Job(s) Available: *Expedition site:* education officer, expedition leaders, community officer, medical officer, project scientist, science officer and scuba instructors. *London office:* events intern, graphics and web intern, PR and marketing intern, science intern.

Head Office: Elizabeth House, 39 York Road, Waterloo, London SE1 7NQ, UK
☎ 020 7620 1411
info@coralcay.org
www.coralcay.org

Duration: 4–6 months.

Pay: Unpaid voluntary work.

Cost: Expenses.

Company Description: Coral Cay Conservation (CCC) is a recognised leader in the field of conservation. Volunteers are at the forefront of our work, gathering key information about the condition of tropical forests and coral reefs, all for the benefit of communities that depend on these ecosystems for their livelihood.

Job Description: *Expedition leaders:* to oversee running of marine or forest expeditions. *Medical officers:* to oversee all aspects of expedition medical health. *Science officers:* to oversee coral reef and/or tropical forest scientific training and survey programmes. *Scuba instructors:* to provide scuba training for expedition personnel and host country counterparts. *Project Scientist:* to assist expedition leader, liaise with in-country partners, ensure goals are achieved. *Community Officer:* deals with all community related work on expedition.

Requirements: *Expedition leaders:* management experience is desirable. For marine expeditions scuba diving qualifications are required and for forest expeditions a Mountain Leader qualification is preferable. *Medical officers:* minimum qualification paramedic, registered nurse or doctor with A&E experience. *Science officers:* minimum qualification degree and proven field research experience. *Scuba instructors:* PADI OWSI and EFRI as minimum. *Volunteers:* provided with full training; no previous experience required. *Project scientist:* relevant postgraduate qualification in marine or terrestrial biology, Scuba diving certification or minimum of Advanced Open Water (AOW).

Accommodation: CCC covers accommodation, food and other subsistence costs out on expedition.

Application Procedure: Either email a CV and cover letter to operations@coralcay.org or post applications to the above address.

Earthwatch Institute (Europe)

Job(s) Available: Volunteers.

Duration: Over a period of 5 to 18 days.

Cost: Project fees range from £500–£1,800.

Job Description: Volunteers to work with scientists as part of a team conducting research into a variety of environmental conservation and heritage projects in the UK, and all over the world.

Head Office: Mayfield House, 256 Banbury Road OX2 7DE, UK
☎ 01865 318831
info@earthwatch.org.uk
www.earthwatch.org/europe

Requirements: No formal qualifications or experience required.

Application Procedure: For further details contact the above email address.

Ecovolunteer Programme

Job(s) Available: Volunteers (500–600).

Duration: Projects lasting from 1 week to 6 months.

Company Description: The Ecovolunteer Programme organises wildlife conservation projects and wildlife research projects operated by local conservation organisations worldwide.

info@ecovolunteer.org
www.ecovolunteer.org or
www.ecovolunteer.org.uk (British)

Job Description: Work varies from practical fieldwork to production and support jobs in wildlife rescue centres, to visitor education, maintenance work and household duties, dependent on each individual project.

Requirements: Minimum age 18. Participants must be in good physical health and speak English.

Accommodation: Provided.

Additional Information: A list of the national agencies can be found at www.ecovolunteer.org/contact or obtained from the above address as there are offices in Austria, Belgium, Brazil, Canada, France, Hungary, Italy, the Netherlands, Spain, Switzerland and the UK.

Application Procedure: Applications should be made to the national Ecovolunteer agency of the country in which the applicant is resident. If there is no agency in your home country, then apply through www.ecovolunteer.org.

Explorations in Travel

Job(s) Available: Volunteers.

Duration: Periods of work by arrangement; most placements are available throughout the year.

Company Description: Explorations in Travel arrange volunteer placements around the world, throughout the year, with placements arranged individually.

Head Office: 2458 River Road, Guilford, Vermont 05301, USA
☎ +1 80 2257 0152
explore@volunteertravel.com
www.volunteertravel.com

Job Description: Volunteers to work with wildlife and domestic animal rescue organisations, rainforest reserves, organic farms, environmental and conservation projects, sustainable tourism and schools. Placements are in Belize, Costa Rica, Ecuador, Guatemala and Puerto Rico.

Requirements: Minimum age 18.

Accommodation: Volunteers most often pay a local family for room and board.

Application Procedure: For further details contact the programme director, at the above address.

Frontier

Job(s) Available: Work in coral reefs, African savannahs, forests and mangrove areas as part of conservation programmes in far-off destinations. Over 250 placements per year.

Head Office: 50–52 Rivington Street, London EC2A 3QP, UK
☎ 020 7613 2422
info@frontier.ac.uk
www.frontier.ac.uk

Duration: Placements are for 2 weeks or longer and take place throughout the year.

Cost: Depending on location and duration, costs are between £1,100 and £3,950. This covers all individual costs, including a UK training weekend, scientific and dive training, all internal travel and airport pick-ups, visas, food and accommodation, but excludes international flights and insurance.

Company Description: Frontier is a non-profit international conservation and development NGO operating since 1989.

Job Description: Programmes are established in response to problems; surveys of damaged areas are carried out so that possible solutions can be identified. For example, dynamite fishing in Tanzania was destroying the delicate web of marine life so Frontier volunteers carried out more than 6,000 dives in order to establish a marine park where marine life will be protected. As Frontier is a professional agency, volunteers get the chance to work on real wildlife and habitat conservation programmes. Volunteers also work on capacity-building initiatives aimed at developing sustainable livelihoods for the world's most impoverished and marginalised communities.

Requirements: Minimum age 18. No specific qualifications are needed as training is given.

Accommodation: Provided.

Application Procedure: Contact the above website for more details, a free information pack and application form.

BTCV International Conservation Holidays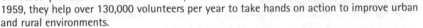

Job(s) Available: Volunteers.

Duration: Projects take place throughout the year and last from 1 to 8 weeks.

Cost: Volunteers must pay their own travel expenses.

Company Description: BTCV is an experienced UK-based practical conservation charity. Founded in 1959, they help over 130,000 volunteers per year to take hands on action to improve urban and rural environments.

> **Head Office:** Sedum House, Mallard Way, Potteric Carr, Doncaster DN4 8DB, UK
> ☎ 01302 388883
> ✆ information@btcv.org.uk
> 🖳 www.btcv.org

Job Description: Volunteers to take part in international conservation projects in Albania, Bulgaria, France, Estonia, Germany, Iceland, Italy, Japan, Portugal, Romania and the USA.

Requirements: Minimum age 18. Knowledge of languages not essential.

Accommodation: Board, accommodation and insurance provided, from around £350 per week.

Application Procedure: For full details of BTCV's Conservation Holiday programme, contact BTCV for an up-to-date brochure. Full project details are also available on the BTCV website.

Gapforce

Job(s) Available: Volunteers for remote conservation projects, teaching placements and challenging expeditions in the rainforest. Trek through remote locations, around the world.

Duration: Minimum period of work 1 week. Some expeditions can last 1 year.

> **Head Office:** 21 Heathmars Road, London SW6 4TJ, UK
> ☎ 020 7384 3028
> ✆ info@gapforce.org
> 🖳 www.gapforce.org

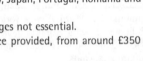

Company Description: Gapforce has 20 years of experience in offering extreme, worthwhile and challenging rainforest expeditions, projects and placements. Projects and placements actively protect sustainable and vulnerable environments and assist rural communities throughout the world.

Job Description: Concentrating on conservation and community development, the project could be anything from building ranger stations to discourage illegal logging, to building tourist huts and clearing trails to increase visitors to the area, or painting and restoring school classrooms. Teachers needed to teach traditional subjects including English and maths as well as an opportunity to run a drama group or art club.

Requirements: All training is provided. Minimum age 17.

Accommodation: For many of the expeditions applicants will be camping on site while trekking. Host families provide accommodation for teachers, who are placed in pairs for the duration of the placement.

Additional Information: Paid work available through work abroad programme in Australia.

Application Procedure: Call above telephone number for a one-to-one briefing. Events are held which offer information about projects. Gapforce also provide a scheme whereby they will put applicants in contact with past volunteers for a first-hand account of their experiences.

Gap year organisations

Lattitude Global Volunteering

Job(s) Available: International voluntary work opportunities.

Duration: Placements range from 3 to 12 months (typically 4–6). Departures throughout the year.

Pay: Work is voluntary, but a small living allowance is paid on some placements.

> **Head Office:** 42 Queen's Road, Reading, Berkshire RG1 4BB, UK
> ☎ 01189 594914
> ✆ volunteer@lattitude.org.uk
> 🖥 www.lattitude.org.uk

Company Description: Lattitude Global Volunteering is a registered charity which places young volunteers (17–25) on projects around the world. Lattitude volunteers have been making a difference overseas since 1972, with around 1,500 young people taking up placements each year. Lattitude also offers bursary schemes providing financial assistance for those who might struggle to afford to volunteer overseas.

Job Description: Currently opportunities exist in Argentina, Australia, Brazil, Canada, China, Ecuador, Fiji, Ghana, India, Japan, Malawi, Mexico, New Zealand, South Africa, Tanzania, Vietnam and Vanuatu. A wide variety of projects are available, including teaching, assisting with English lessons, working in care homes and orphanages, helping in Red Cross hospitals, participating in outdoor camps and conservation work. Specialist placements are suitable for graduate applicants.

Requirements: Lattitude welcomes applications from all young people who are keen to volunteer and make a difference in communities around the world.

Accommodation: Food and accommodation provided in almost all placements.

Application Procedure: Applications accepted year round with numerous departures throughout the year. All applicants are interviewed either by phone or in person to ensure they are matched with a suitable project. Apply online or by email to the above address.

Outreach International

Job(s) Available: Volunteers.

Duration: Programmes range from 1–6 months. Departures are throughout the year but the most popular times are January, April, June and September.

Cost: The cost of £2,965 (for 3 months) includes full health, baggage and public liability insurance, a

> **Head Office:** Bartletts Farm, Hayes Road, Compton Dundon, Somerset TA11 6PF, UK
> ☎ 01458 274957
> ✆ info@outreachinternational.co.uk
> 🖥 www.outreachinternational.co.uk

generous food allowance and comfortable accommodation, a comprehensive language course on arrival and a CD language course in the UK, full in-country support, all project-related travel, a weekend trip, and training in the UK including a fundraising awareness day. This cost does not include the cost of international flights. For full details see the cost section of the website.

Company Description: A small, specialist gap organisation with carefully selected projects in specific parts of Cambodia, Sri Lanka, Costa Rica, Ecuador, Galapagos Islands, Nepal and on the Pacific Coast of Mexico. The projects have enough variety to ensure that the interests and skills of individual volunteers can be put to good use.

Job Description: Placements include helping at orphanages, supporting a busy centre for street children, horse riding with disabled children, teaching English in coastal schools, helping at a medical centre and offering support at a busy children's hospital, humanitarian work, physiotherapy, carrying out conservation work in the Amazon rainforest, working at a centre for rescued wild animals and arts and crafts projects. These are humble, grass-root initiatives where you can make a significant difference to the lives of local people. The projects are well organised and have a clear and genuine need for volunteer support. Each one is regularly visited and assessed by the Outreach International director. In addition to providing a challenging experience a number of volunteers have used this as a stepping-stone towards a career in overseas work.

Requirements: No specific skills or qualifications are normally required and most placements are ideal for people taking a gap year. However trained physiotherapists and people with office skills are needed for some projects.

Accommodation: Accommodation is shared with fellow volunteers or with a local host family.

Application Procedure: Applications would be welcome from confident, energetic people with a desire to travel, learn a language and offer their help to a worthwhile cause. All potential volunteers are interviewed informally to help them make an informed decision about whether the placement is right for them. Further details available from www.outreach international.co.uk or from the UK head office on 01458 274957.

Project Trust

Job(s) Available: There are a wide variety of projects on offer: childcare, development work, healthcare, teaching and outward bound activities.
Duration: Placements are from 8 to 12 months.
Working Hours: Varies by project.
Cost: The cost for 8 months is £4,350 and for 12 months is £4,950 which includes insurance and travel, full support overseas, food and accommodation. Fundraising workshops are held throughout the country to help volunteers raise the necessary finance.

> **Head Office:** The Hebridean Centre, Isle of Coll, Argyll PA78 6TE, UK
> ☎ 01879 230444
> ✉ info@projecttrust.org.uk
> 🖥 www.projecttrust.org.uk

Company Description: Project Trust arranges for volunteers to spend a whole year in an exciting country, becoming part of a community and learning another language.

Project Trust is an educational charity, which sends 200 school leavers overseas every year to over 20 countries around the world. At present these are: Bolivia, Botswana, Cambodia, Chile, China, the Dominican Republic, Guyana, Honduras, Hong Kong, Jamaica, Japan, Mauritius, Malaysia, Namibia, Peru, South Africa, Sri Lanka, Swaziland, Thailand and Uganda.

Requirements: Minimum age 17–19 at time of project. Scottish Highers students can apply at 16.

Accommodation: Food and accommodation provided.

Additional Information: All volunteers attend a selection course on the Isle of Coll in the autumn before they go overseas. Week-long training courses take place on the Isle of Coll after final exams in the summer, and following a year overseas the volunteers assemble again on the Isle of Coll to debrief on their experiences.

Application Procedure: Apply online at www.projecttrust.org.uk. Apply as early as possible to avoid disappointment.

Social and community schemes

Concordia Worldwide

Job(s) Available: The International Volunteer Programme offers volunteers aged over 18 the opportunity to join international teams of volunteers working on community-based projects in over 60 countries worldwide. There are a selection of teenage programme projects available for 16–17 year olds.

Head Office: 19 North Street, Portslade, Brighton BN41 1DH, UK
☎ 01273 422218
✉ info@concordiavolunteers.org.uk
🖥 www.concordiavolunteers.org.uk

Duration: Projects last for 2–4 weeks with the main season from June to September and a smaller winter/spring programme.

Cost: Volunteers pay a registration fee of £180 and fund their own travel and insurance. For projects in Africa, Asia and Latin America only there is an additional preparation weekend fee of £40 and an extra fee payable to the in-country host of approximately £80–£150.

Company Description: Concordia is a small not-for-profit charity committed to international youth exchange.

Job Description: Projects are diverse ranging from nature conservation, restoration, archaeology, construction, art and culture to projects that are socially based including work with adults or children with special needs, children's play-schemes and teaching.

Requirements: Generally the work doesn't require specific skills or experience, though real motivation and commitment to the project are a must. Applicants must be aged over 19 to participate on a project in Latin America, Africa and Asia. Concordia can only place volunteers who are resident in the UK.

Accommodation: Food and basic accommodation free of charge for all projects in Europe, North America, Russia, Japan and South Korea. For projects in Africa, Asia and Latin America only, food and accommodation are provided by the host and covered by the in-country extra fee mentioned in the cost section above.

Additional Information: Concordia also recruits volunteers (20+) to act as group coordinators on UK based projects, for which training is provided and all expenses are paid. This training takes place in spring each year. Early application is advised. See website for details.

Application Procedure: For further information on volunteering or coordinating please check the website or contact the international volunteer coordinator at the above address. Volunteers applying from abroad should contact a volunteer organisation in their own country or country in which they are based.

Cross-Cultural Solutions

Job(s) Available: Volunteers.

Duration: Volunteer programmes operate year round in Africa, Asia, Latin America and Russia and range from 1 to 12 weeks.

Head Office: Tower Point, 44 North Road, Brighton BN1 1YR, UK
☎ 0845 458 2781 or 0845 458 2782
✉ infouk@crossculturalsolutions.org
🖥 www.crossculturalsolutions.org

Cost: Prices start at £1,514 for a 2-week programme.

Company Description: Established in 1995, Cross-Cultural Solutions is a registered charity and a recognised leader in the field of international volunteering, sending thousands of volunteers overseas every year.

Job Description: Volunteers work side-by-side with local people on locally designed and driven projects, enabling them to participate in meaningful community development and see a country from a whole new perspective. The CCS experience also includes cultural and learning activities so that volunteers learn about the local culture. These include an in-depth orientation, language training, guest speakers and more. There is also plenty of free time to relax, reflect, or explore the community.

Accommodation: CCS provides a home base for all volunteers. Here, all daily needs are taken care of, including lodging, meals and transportation. Through each of these elements volunteers are able to immerse themselves in the culture of the country and fully realise their experience. Programme fees cover the costs of accommodation in the CCS home base, meals and ground transportation, plus individual attention and guidance from an experienced and knowledgeable programme manager, coordination of the volunteer placement, cultural and learning activities, a 24-hour emergency hotline in the USA, and medical insurance.

Application Procedure: For more information about Cross-Cultural Solutions, please visit the website above.

Global Citizens Network

Job(s) Available: Volunteers.
Duration: Volunteer trips last 1–3 weeks and are ongoing throughout the year.
Cost: Volunteers pay a programme fee of $1,100–$2,450 (£700–£1,500). The airfare is extra.
Company Description: Connect with indigenous peoples and contribute to peace throughout the world with Global Citizens Network, an organisation offering short-term volunteer trips that last a lifetime.

Head Office: 129 North Second Street, Suite 102, Minneapolis, Minnesota 55401, USA
☎ +1 800644 9292
🖂 info@globalcitizens.org
🖳 www.globalcitizens.org

Job Description: Volunteers for projects in Kenya, Tanzania, Guatemala, Nepal, Thailand, Ecuador, Peru, Brazil, Canada, the USA and Mexico. Build, plant, grow and learn. Programmes involving volunteers include building a health centre, teaching in a school, harvesting shade grown coffee and working with a women's co-op.
Requirements: No special qualifications required. Minimum age 18. Volunteers under 18 years must be accompanied by parent or guardian.
Accommodation: Cost includes most in-country costs (food, lodging, transportation etc).
Application Procedure: For more information contact the programme director at the above address.

Habitat for Humanity Great Britain

Job(s) Available: Teams of 10–15 volunteers.
Duration: 1–2 weeks.
Cost: Applicants pay their direct costs and also raise a donation for the charity.
Company Description: The charity Habitat for Humanity seeks to eradicate poverty housing and

Head Office: 46 West Bar Street, Banbury, Oxon OX16 9RZ, UK
☎ 01295 264240
🖂 globalvillage@habitatforhumanity.org.uk
🖳 www.habitatforhumanity.org.uk

homelessness, working with community groups worldwide to build or renovate homes.
Job Description: Work alongside local people to help build or renovate homes. A British team leader is provided. A local construction manager will show you what to do. Learn about issues of poverty housing first hand, from people who face them every day, and play a part in helping to solve them.
Requirements: Minimum age 18. No experience or building skill is necessary.
Accommodation: Provided in a 3-star hotel or guest house.
Application Procedure: By phone or visit the website.

VOLUNTARY WORK

WORLDWIDE

Learning Enterprises

Job(s) Available: Volunteer English teacher (130).
Duration: From mid-June to mid-August. Minimum period of work 4–6 weeks.
Working Hours: Approximately 3–6 hours. Depends on the village.

Head Office: PO Box 58217, Washington DC 20037, USA
info@learningenterprises.org
www.learningenterprises.org

Company Description: Learning Enterprises sends university-aged students overseas to teach English in underdeveloped areas. Its mission is to expand the horizons of disadvantaged youth through global volunteerism.

Job Description: Most volunteers are University students, who are placed with host families. Each volunteer will teach in a rural or underdeveloped area to students, whose ages range from 6 through to adults. Volunteers are required to develop their own lesson plans. Positions are available in Camodia, China, Croatia, Hungary, Mauritius, Mexico, Panama, Poland, Romania, Slovakia, Thailand and Turkey.

Requirements: No teaching experience necessary. Minimum age 18. Latin American countries require basic Spanish.

Accommodation: Room and board provided free of charge. Volunteers are responsible for their airfare and in-country costs.

Application Procedure: Apply online. Applications open 1 January to 1 February. Strong applicants will be chosen for the general interview then passed on to the programme director for the final interview before the final decision is made. Applicants will be contacted by early March with the result of their application.

ProWorld Service Corps

Job(s) Available: Interns.
Duration: Minimum period of work 2 weeks.
Working Hours: 4–6 hours per day.
Cost: Fee of $1,795–$1,895 required for first 2 weeks, $490–$585 for each week thereafter. Cost includes full room and board with a local family, domestic

Head Office: 324 East Oak St, Fort Collins, CO 80524, USA
+187 7429 6753
info@myproworld.org
www.myproworld.org

transportation, Spanish classes in Peru and Mexico, Portuguese classes in Brazil, cultural and adventure activities, project funding and support and travel insurance.

Company Description: Promotes social and economic development, empowers communities and cultivates educated, compassionate global citizens. Participants will work abroad with the community and one of the affiliated non-governmental organisations (NGOs), government social programmes, or a ProWorld-initited project. Projects are determined by community need and participants' skills and interests. Programmes are offered in Belize, Brazil, Ghana, India, Mexico and Peru.

Job Description: Interns are needed for public healthcare, public health education and assistance, health research, environmental conservation, environmental tourism, cultural and museum work, archaeology, construction, education and teaching, women's rights, human rights and social assistance.

Accommodation: Included in cost.

Application Procedure: Apply to Adam Saks, placement adviser, 1–3 months before participation. Phone interview necessary once accepted.

Tearfund Transform International Programme _____

Job(s) Available: Volunteers.
Duration: Volunteers to work for 4–6 weeks from early July to the end of August.
Cost: A contribution is required of between $1,000–$1,200 which includes food, accommodation and orientation. Volunteers are responsible for paying their own airfare and visas.

Head Office: 100 Church Road, Teddington, Middlesex TW11 8QE, UK
☎ 020 8943 7777
✆ transform@tearfund.org
🖥 www.tearfund.org/transform

Company Description: Tearfund is an evangelical Christian development charity working with partners overseas to bring help and hope to communities in need.
Job Description: Volunteers to join teams of 8–12 people. Assignments are in a number of countries and include practical work, renovation and work with children.
Requirements: Applicants should be over 18 and committed Christians.
Accommodation: Provided as part of cost.
Application Procedure: Details are available on the website from the enquiry unit at the above address. Applications should be received by 1 March.

Work camps

International Voluntary Service (British Branch of Service Civil International) _____

Job(s) Available: Volunteers.
Duration: Volunteers work for 2–4 weeks. Most work camps are between April and September and last 1–4 weeks. There are some short-term projects.
Cost: Volunteers must pay for membership of IVS,

Head Office: Thorn House, 5 Rose Street, Edinburgh EH2 2PR, UK
☎ 0131 243 2745
✆ scotland@ivs-gb.org.uk
🖥 www.ivsgb.org.uk

a registration fee of £195 for projects abroad and £105 for projects in Britain. This includes annual membership to IVS. Volunteers pay for their own travel costs.
Company Description: IVS-GB aims to promote peace and intercultural understanding through volunteering and international voluntary projects. IVS-GB organises international short-term projects in Britain and across a choice of 45 countries around the world.
Job Description: Volunteers work for 2–4 weeks in an international team of 6–20 people, sharing domestic and social life as well as the work. The projects include work with children, with socially disadvantaged, north-south solidarity, arts and culture, and the environment and conservation. For example helping an intercultural centre in Guatemala, helping at a centre for disabled children in Latvia or building a solar water heater on a Scottish island.
Requirements: English is the language of most projects, (languages are required for the North/South programme). For their North/South programme (Africa, Asia and Latin America for over 21s) previous experience of voluntary work is required or preferred.
Accommodation: Projects provide food and accommodation.
Additional Information: If you want to receive more information, please contact an IVS-GB office. To find an IVS/SCI branch in your country please see www.sciint.org or contact IVS-GB at the above addresses.
Application Procedure: IVS can only accept applications from people with an address in Britain. Applications should be posted to IVS at the relevant address. Application forms are available online or from an office. Project listings for each summer are compiled by April of each year and available from March on the website, which has all the up-to-date project information. IVS is working towards equal opportunities.

VOLUNTARY WORK

WORLDWIDE

UNA Exchange

Job(s) Available: Volunteer projects.

Duration: Most projects last 2–4 weeks between April and September but there are also projects at other times of year. There are longer-term (3–12 month) projects available, mainly in Europe, through the European Voluntary Service (EVS) and Medium Term Volunteer (MTV) programmes.

> **Head Office:** Temple of Peace, Cathays Park, Cardiff CF10 3AP, UK
> ☎ 02920 223088
> ✒ info@unaexchange.org
> 🖳 www.unaexchange.org

Cost: There is a volunteer contribution of £150–£175 to UNA Exchange for projects abroad and £200 for longer term projects. Volunteers pay for their travel. All food and accommodation is covered by the host organisation during the project.

Company Description: Organises projects in Wales for international volunteers and sends volunteers to projects abroad.

Job Description: Projects include a huge variety of social, environmental and renovation work from helping to set up a festival in France to working with children in the Ukraine. UNA Exchange also operates a North-South programme of projects in Africa, Latin America and South East Asia.

Requirements: To participate in the North-South programme, volunteers need to attend a training weekend in Cardiff.

Accommodation: Provided in cost.

Application Procedure: Further details available on the website www.unaexchnage.org.

Volunteers for Peace, International Voluntary Service (VFP)

Job(s) Available: International voluntary service projects.

Duration: *Short term voluntary service projects:* (2–3 weeks) and a smaller number of medium-term projects (1–3 months) and long-term projects (3–6 months).

> **Head Office:** 1034, Tiffany Road, Belmont, Vermont 05730, USA
> ☎ +1 80 2259 2759
> ✒ vfp@vfp.org
> 🖳 www.vfp.org

Company Description: Coordinates international voluntary service projects in over 100 countries worldwide.

Job Description: There are many types of work available because projects arise from grassroots local community needs (construction, environmental, agricultural and social work).

Accommodation: Varies widely but usually volunteers share the same living space, doing all their own cleaning and food preparation on a rotating basis.

Application Procedure: A full listing of VFP's programmes can be found in VFP's international projects online directory ($30 annual membership fee) or online at www.vfp.org). For further details phone, write or email for a free newsletter.

VAP (Volunteer Action for Peace)

Job(s) Available: Volunteers needed to take part in voluntary work projects.

Duration: Projects from 2 weeks to 12 months, all year found.

Working Hours: Participants will usually work 30–35 hours per week.

> **Head Office:** VAP, 16 Overhill Road, East Dulwich, London SE22 OPH, UK
> ☎ 0844 2090 927
> ✒ action@vap.org.uk
> 🖳 www.vap.org.uk

Cost: Projects in Europe, North America, Japan, South Korea and Taiwan cost £150. Projects in Africa, Asia and Latin America cost £180. There is a hosting fee (approx. £200) payable on arrival in Africa, Asia and Latin America. Volunteers to organise their own travel.

Company Description: Voluntary work projects organised in 80 countries worldwide.

Job Description: Work with local people on grassroot community projects. The work undertaken varies from entertaining children in need to environmental, artistic or restoration work.

Requirements: No particular qualifications are necessary, but normally minimum age is 18.

Accommodation: Food, accommodation and leisure activities are provided.

Application Procedure: For further details check the above address.

Au pairs, nannies, family helps and exchanges

A-One Au-Pairs and Nannies

Job(s) Available: Au pairs and au pairs plus.
Working Hours: 5 days a week.
Pay: Varies according to hours worked.
Job Description: Au pairs/au pairs plus required for light housework and childcare. Places available throughout Europe and America.
Requirements: Applicants should be 18–27 years old.
Accommodation: Board and lodging vary according to hours worked.
Application Procedure: Contact Hillary Perry, proprietor, for details.

> **Head Office:** 35 The Grove, Edgeware, Middlesex HAB 9QA, UK
> ☎ 0800 298 8807 or 020 8905 3355
> info@aupairsetc.co.uk
> www.aupairsetc.co.uk

Childcare International

Job(s) Available: Au pair and nanny in the USA.
Duration: Visa-supported 1-year stay.
Pay: Families provide full round-trip air fare, medical insurance and part-time college course plus 2 weeks paid holiday. Salary is up to $250 per week for qualified nannies and a minimum salary of $195.75 per week for au pairs.
Company Description: Childcare International offers placements to applicants aged 18–26 with good childcare experience. Full local counsellor support is provided to introduce friends and give guidance with every aspect of the stay.
Job Description: Choose from a wide range of approved families from across the USA. 4 days' orientation is provided in the USA.
Requirements: Applicants must be able to drive.
Application Procedure: Apply online at www.aupairinamerica.com.

> **Head Office:** Childcare International Ltd, Trafalgar House, Grenville Place, London NW7 3SA, UK
> ☎ 020 8906 3116
> sandra@childint.co.uk
> www.childint.co.uk

Inter-Sejours

Job(s) Available: Au pairs placed in Australia, Austria, Canada, Denmark, France, Germany, Ireland, Italy, the Netherlands, New Zealand, Spain, Sweden, and the UK.
Duration: We accept stays for 2–3 months during the summer holidays and from 3–12 months during the rest of the year. An immediate start is possible.

> **Head Office:** 179 Rue de Courcelles, F-75017 Paris, France
> ☎ +33 1 47 63 06 81
> aideinfo.intersejours@wanadoo.fr
> www.inter-sejours.fr

Working Hours: 15–30 hours per week.

Pay: Pocket money minimum €300 per month.

Company Description: Inter-Sejours is a non-profit making organisation with 42 years of experience.

Requirements: Applicants should be aged 18–30. Previous childcare experience an advantage.

Accommodation: Full board and lodging provided.

Additional Information: Also offer work placements in hotels and restaurants in England and Spain for 2 months to 1 year. Pay varies according to age and hours worked. Accommodation provided by the employer. See website for further details.

Application Procedure: Application forms available at www.inter-sejours.fr.

Neilson

Job(s) Available: Children's club staff.

Duration: Summer and winter (ski) work is available.

Working Hours: 6 days a week.

Pay: Competitive seasonal package.

Company Description: Neilson is a holiday company committed to providing excellent quality activ-

Head Office: Locksview, Brighton Marina, Brighton, East Sussex BN2 5HA, UK
☎ 0870 241 2901
✆ recruitment@neilson.com
🖥 www.neilson.com/recruitment

ity holidays. They pride themselves on having a high staff/client ratio and the exceptional calibre of their overseas staff.

Job Description: To care for 0–17 year olds in the resorts.

Requirements: NNEB, BTEC or equivalent preferred. Applicants should be at least 18 years old with experience of working with children, a sense of fun, and be creative team players.

Accommodation: Flights paid to and from resort, accommodation, insurance and uniform provided.

Application Procedure: Please complete on online application form at www.neilson.co.uk.

Roma Au Pair Associazione Culturale

Job(s) Available: Au pair, au pair plus, mother's help in Italy.

Duration: Throughout the year. Minimum stay 6 weeks (summer), long-term (9–12 months).

Working Hours: 6–8 hours per day.

Pay: €70–€100 per week depending on position. Monthly bus card provided.

Head Office: Via Pietro Mascagni, 138 00199 Roma, Italy
☎ +39 0 6863 21519
✆ info@romaaupair.com
🖥 www.romaaupair.com

Company Description: Roma au pair has been working with the youth cultural programme since 1998. Arrange good placements for both the au pairs and families.

Job Description: The au pair programme is a cultural exchange for young people willing to live abroad and who wish to learn a new culture and life style of their host country. A perfect way to visit abroad without the expensive costs and learning new languages. Language classes provided for free.

Requirements: Minimum age 18. Childcare experience is an advantage. Fluent English and driving licence would be an advantage.

Accommodation: Full board and lodging paid for by host family.

Application Procedure: Apply to Giuseppina Pamphili at info@romaaupair.com between March and May. Phone interview required.

Solihull Au Pair & Nanny Agency

Job(s) Available: Au pairs in Europe.

Pay: *Au pairs in Europe:* pocket money £180–£240 per month. Pocket money is paid in euros.

Company Description: Now based in Birmingham and established for more than 45 years, Lorraine uses her vast experience to place au pairs abroad.

> **Head Office:** 5 Parklands, Blossomfield Road, Solihull B91 1NG, UK
> ☎ 07973 886979
> ✉ aupairs1@btconnect.com or lorraine@nannies4u.co.uk

Job Description: *Au pairs in Europe:* placed in major European countries. France, Italy and Spain are the most popular. Work with overseas contacts to locate bona fide host families.

Requirements: Applicants should have some childcare experience. Not necessary to speak language of the country as many families wish to have au pairs who can speak English to their children. References required and police check if available. Driving licence can be an advantage.

Accommodation: Private room and full board, with carefully screened host family, plus medical insurance provided.

Application Procedure: Contact www.nannies4u.co.uk and fill in the online pre-application form.

Travel Active

Job(s) Available: Au pair high school programmes, and work exchange worldwide.

Company Description: Travel Active is Holland's largest youth exchange organisation. Travel Active is a member of the World Youth Student & Educational (WYSE) Travel Confederation, Wyse Work Abroad Association, Association of Language Travel

> **Head Office:** PO Box 107, 5800 AC Venray, The Netherlands
> ☎ +31 4 7855 1900
> ✉ info@travelactive.nl
> ▢ www.travelactive.nl

Organisations (ALTO) and a founding member of the International Au Pair Association (IAPA).

Job Description: Travel Active receives students from all over the world on its incoming high school, au pair and work exchange programmes. For these programmes Travel Active also offers its own tailor-made insurance. Applicants may choose from a variety of work programmes worldwide, with or without job placement. Internships are also available. Several programmes combine a language course with a job placement.

Application Procedure: For further details contact the above address.

Other employment worldwide

Alliance Abroad Group

Job(s) Available: Customised internship, work, teach and volunteer programmes.

Duration: 2 weeks to 12 months.

Company Description: Founded in 1992, Alliance Abroad Group, offers programmes for students and graduates in and outside of the USA. Opportunities

> **Head Office:** 1221 South Mopac Expressway, Suite 100, Austin, TX 78746, USA
> ☎ +1 512 457 8062 or +186 66 ABROAD
> ▢ www.allianceabroad.com

include working in Australia and New Zealand, teaching in China, Argentina and Spain, working and interning in the USA and volunteering in South America and South Africa. Placements include North, Central and South America, Europe, Asia and Oceania.

Accommodation: For most programmes airport pickup, salary/stipend, meals and accommodation are provided.

Anywork Anywhere

Anywork Anywhere provides an online Job Search, Volunteer Guides and Resources for Work & Travel throughout Europe and Worldwide, via the web site www.anyworkanywhere.com .

It is free to search and apply for jobs, as well as to access the resources sections, with no need to register first. Many jobs provide accommodation and sometimes meals as well. You may need to turn up for a face to face interview, but many employers are willing to interview over the phone, accompanied by a solid CV and checkable references.

Whilst the majority of positions are full-time temporary, with contracts running from a couple of weeks to 12 months, there are also a handful of advertised permanent positions, and it's not unlikely - where the employee/employer relationship has been good - for some 3/5 month summer/winter positions to turn into long term working relationships.

You could find work in Summer Resorts, Ski Resorts, Fruit Picking & Packing, Pubs & Bars, Catering, TEFL, Education, Hotels, Entertainment, Activity Centres, Voluntary & Conservation, Holiday & Theme Parks, Care Work, Childcare and other varied and exciting opportunities we come across which we feel are interesting and of value to the site...

If you fancy something with a little moral depth, there are an abundance of Voluntary opportunities, with a wide range of fees to suit all budgets. Either going via a mainstream "Western World" based organisation, many of which you would have heard already, or for the more adventurous, going direct to a local NGO or even smaller project on the ground, we try to maintain a balance of the two, knowing that everyone has their own ideal environment for this kind of expeditionary experience.

The site is vast. As well as listing Jobs or Voluntary opportunities, our comprehensive Guides section has lots of helpful info on Visas, Working Holiday Visas and other varied Work & Travel resources. From our embassy directory, listed by host country, easy to navigate map links, Country specific links sections, Voluntary Guides, and Training & Courses from Snowboarding to Cookery – find all this and much, much, more.

www.anyworkanywhere.com

Additional Information: All programmes include guaranteed placement, visa assistance, orientation materials, health and travel insurance, 24/7 emergency support, and personal in-country coordinators.

Application Procedure: Apply using the online form. Applications should be made 3 months in advance.

Anywork Anywhere

Job(s) Available: All levels of hotel and pub staff, chalet chefs and hosts, construction and horticultural staff, nannies, barge and yacht crew, teachers,

> 🖵 www.anyworkanywhere.com

nurses, tour guides, ski/board instructors and guides, care workers, farm workers, helpdesk, sales and customer service operatives, cabin crew, holiday and theme park, campsite and summer resort staff, are among the many jobs listed as well as a variety of new opportunities being added daily.

Company Description: This organisation provides a free international job search and a good starting point for people looking to work and travel throughout the UK and worldwide via an easy-to-navigate site. The site provides a broad range of other resources for work and travel, including visa info, worldwide work guides, an embassy directory and a huge bank of hand-picked useful and relevant links.

Accommodation: Jobs advertised mostly offer accommodation and sometimes meals. Check first what is included and what deduction from your wage/fee is levied for this.

Application Procedure: Interested candidates can simply contact their chosen advertiser from the worldwide job search and apply direct. You do not need to pay or register to browse and apply for jobs. For further information visit: www.anyworkanywhere.com.

BUNAC

Job(s) Available: There are a great variety of programmes on offer including summer camp counselling in the USA and work and volunteer programmes to the USA, Canada, Australia, New Zealand, India, South Africa, Ghana, Costa Rica, Peru, Cambodia and China.

> Head Office: 16 Bowling Green Lane, London EC1R 0QH, UK
> ☎ 020 7251 3472
> 🔎 enquiries@bunac.org.uk
> 🖵 www.bunac.org.uk

Company Description: Established in 1962, BUNAC is the UK's leading non-profit travel club, offering great value work, travel and volunteering opportunities around the world.

Accommodation: BUNAC provides help and advice on jobs, accommodation and travel as well as providing back-up services while working and travelling.

Application Procedure: For further information contact the above address or visit www.bunac.org.uk.

InterExchange

Job(s) Available: Cultural exchange programmes including work and travel, camp USA, work abroad, career training and language school programmes within the USA and around the world.

> Head Office: 161 Sixth Avenue, New York, NY 10013, USA
> ☎ +1 212 9240446
> 🔎 info@interexchange.org
> 🖵 www.interexchange.org

Company Description: InterExchange is a non-profit organisation dedicated to promoting cultural awareness.

Job Description: In the USA they offer J-1 Visa programmes for au pair, seasonal work, internship, camp counsellor and staff positions. InterExchange also offer working abroad placements for US residents to travel to Australia, Costa Rica, France, Germany, Chile, China, India, Namibia, Peru, Netherlands, South Africa, Spain, New Zealand and Thailand. InterExchange also offer H-2B Visa programmes for seasonal work. Most InterExchange programmes include placements.

Application Procedure: For further details contact InterExchange at the above address.

i-to-i

Job(s) Available: Paid work overseas, teaching English as a foreign language (TEFL) and TEFL training plus supported volunteer projects. More than 5,000 volunteers are placed each year.

Head Office: 261 Low Lane,
Leeds LS18 5NY, UK
☎ 0800 011 1156
✆ info@i-to-i.com
🖥 www.i-to-i.com

Duration: *Paid jobs and internships (TEFL):* 3–12 month contracts depending on the country of choice. *Volunteer projects:* 1–24 weeks in duration. Projects are available all year round from 1 week to a complete year out. TEFL training included where applicable.

Pay: *Paid jobs (TEFL):* up to £1,100 per month depending on the country of choice. *Volunteer projects:* self-funded volunteer projects. No pay is received as applicants are assisting at a local project in a developing country.

Cost: *TEFL training:* courses start from £179 and can be studied online or over a weekend. *Paid jobs (TEFL):* free when you complete 100-hour training course (£395). *Volunteer projects:* from £549 including meals, accommodation, arrival transfer and support from in-country team throughout your stay. TEFL training included where applicable.

Company Description: i-to-i is an award-winning organisation providing worthwhile work and travel opportunities throughout the world. i-to-i offers over 200 volunteer projects across 32 countries worldwide along with paid work, teaching English as a foreign language (TEFL). i-to-i also provides on-site and online TEFL training for those who want to combine teaching as part of their travel experience or find work overseas. All projects are thoroughly researched and volunteers are met and supported while away by in-country coordinators.

Job Description: *Paid jobs (TEFL):* assistance in arranging paid TEFL work in a variety of schools in 14 countries worldwide. Job involves teaching English to children and/or adults. *TEFL training:* in the UK, the USA, Ireland and Australia. An online TEFL course is also available at www.onlineTEFL.com allowing study from any location worldwide. Further courses add practical training with teaching practice sessions overseas. All courses are designed for travellers and include a module on finding work abroad. i-to-i also offers a database of more than 8,000 job contracts for TEFL tutees. *Volunteer projects:* project types include voluntary teaching, conservation, community development, building, sports and media as well as humanitarian tours. Current projects include a panda conservation project in China, surfing programmes in South Africa, reporting for an English newspaper in Sri Lanka, and teaching English to orphans in India.

Requirements: *Paid jobs (TEFL):* opportunities for both graduates (any discipline) and undergraduates. No previous teaching experience is necessary. *TEFL training:* open to anyone who wants to learn the fundamentals of TEFL either online (with tutor support) or over a weekend in a small group environment. *Volunteer projects:* i-to-i projects are suitable for all ages. As long as you have a desire to help out and give something back to a developing country and a locally run project you are more than welcome.

Accommodation: *Paid jobs (TEFL):* accommodation is either included (free of charge) or assisted subject to chosen destination/school. *Volunteer projects:* food and accommodation are included. Accommodation varies from home stays with local families to guesthouses, and apartments. Food is local cuisine and can include up to 3 meals per day.

Application Procedure: For further details contact the above address or phone for more details.

Overseas Development Institute

Job(s) Available: 40 fellowships are awarded annually.

Duration: 2 years.

Company Description: ODI runs the Overseas Development Institute Fellowship Scheme which enables recent young economics graduates to gain practical experience in the public sectors of developing countries in Africa, the Caribbean and the Pacific.

Requirements: Candidates may be of any nationality but must have a postgraduate qualification with a very strong background in economics.

Application Procedure: Online applications are accepted from November each year via the website at www.odi.org.uk/fellows.

> **Head Office:** 111, Westminster Bridge Road, London SE1 7JD, UK
> ☎ 020 7922 0300
> ✉ fellows@odi.org.uk
> 🖥 www.odi.org.uk

The SeasonWorkers Network

Job(s) Available: Gap year opportunities, rep, ski, outdoor, education, TEFL, cruise ship and childcare jobs.

Company Description: SeasonWorkers is a website that lists hundreds of jobs and has won various awards including best recruitment website at the Travel and Tourism Web Awards in London.

Job Description: You can use SeasonWorkers to thoroughly research every avenue and apply online for hundreds of different summer jobs both in the UK and overseas.

Requirements: Whatever your age, experience or aspirations there will be a summer job on the SeasonWorkers Network for you.

Additional Information: The site also includes a vibrant message board for help and chat about summer jobs and thousands of pages of help on finding summer work.

Application Procedure: Go to www.seasonworkers.com.

> **Head Office:** Houdini Media Ltd, PO BOX 29132, Dunfermline KY11 4YU, UK
> ☎ 0845 6439338
> ✉ info@seasonworkers.com
> 🖥 www.seasonworkers.com

AFRICA AND THE MIDDLE EAST

GHANA

Voluntary work for Britons in Ghana can be organised by UNA Exchange or Concordia. A summary of their work is listed along with their addresses in the *Worldwide* chapter. The Student and Youth Travel Organisation in Accra works with many partner organisations to bring volunteers to Ghana, but individuals can also apply directly via the website, though this must be done 10 weeks in advance. Projects Abroad offers opportunities for Gap Year, summer placements, work experience and career breaks. Visit www.projects-abroad.org or call 1 888 839 3535 for more details. The organisations listed below also offer opportunities to work in Ghana.

Red tape

ADDRESS: OFFICE OF THE HIGH COMMISSIONER FOR GHANA
The Chancery 13 Belgrave Square, London SW1X 8PN
☎ 020 7201 5900
✆ information@ghanahighcommissionuk.com
🖥 www.ghanahighcommissionuk.com

Visa requirements: The citizens of most countries are required to apply for a visa/work permit before travelling to Ghana and taking up employment. A visa can be applied for in person at the nearest consulate of Ghana. In the UK a visa can be applied for in person or through the post.

For up-to-date information about visa requirements check with the embassy before travel.

Voluntary work

Rural Upgrade Support Organisation (RUSO)

Job(s) Available: Volunteers for community projects in Ghana.

Duration: 4–8 weeks, throughout the entire year.

Cost: There is an initial registration fee of $200, which includes administration costs and return

Head Office: PO Box CE 11066, Tema, Gt Acca
☎ +233 2447 60826
✆ ruralupgrade@yahoo.com
🖥 www.ruso.interconnection.org

transfers from the airport. Additional charges for extended periods of stay: 1–3 months $25 per week, 3–6 months $15 per week. No financial support is given by RUSO. Volunteers are to provide their own insurance.

Company Description: RUSO is a non-political, non-sectarian and non-governmental organisation that aims to assist community upgrading using sustainable and environmentally friendly means. RUSO is a recently established NGO formed by members within the community offering a fresh perspective on solving rural problems. RUSO offers general information and training on communication development. RUSO have qualified personnel and project supervisors available to assist volunteers.

Job Description: Projects include providing healthcare, education, cultural exchange and social development. Volunteers can work alone and also with others.

Requirements: Minimum age 18. Volunteers must be in good health, willing to work hard and live within the rural community.

Accommodation: Accommodation with a host family is £300 per month including dinner. RUSO will organise all aspects of transport to the village upon arrival for free. Tour programmes available on request.

Application Procedure: Apply direct, or via email, but not through the website, throughout the year. An interview may be necessary.

Voluntary Work Camps Association of Ghana (VOLU)

Job(s) Available: Around 1,500 volunteers needed for work camps.

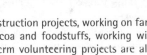

Head Office: PO Box GP 1540, Accra
☎ +233 2166 3486
✉ voluntaryworkcamp@yahoo.com
🖳 www.voluntaryworkcamps.org

Duration: Easter, Christmas and from June to October. Volunteers can stay throughout each period.

Cost: Volunteers pay their own travelling costs. Inscription fee of approximately €250 per camping project and €150 for any additional project.

Company Description: VOLU organises work camps in the rural areas of Ghana for international volunteers.

Job Description: Tasks involve mainly manual work; construction projects, working on farm and agro-forestry projects, tree planting, harvesting cocoa and foodstuffs, working with mentally disabled people, teaching, etc. Medium/long term volunteering projects are also available. Areas of placement include hospitals, health centres, local schools, psychiatric hospitals. Placements in orphanages are available across Ghana.

Requirements: No special skills or experience are required but volunteers should be over 16 years old and fit to undertake manual labour.

Accommodation: Accommodation and food provided at the camps.

Application Procedure: Join through a partner organisation located in your country of residence. Information on the website. VOLU supplies official invitations to enable volunteers to acquire visas before leaving for Ghana. In emergencies call 0233 244 544526.

Volunteer in Africa

Job(s) Available: Volunteers.

Head Office: P.O. Box 602, OSO Accra
✉ ghana@volunteeringinafrica.org
🖳 www.volunteeringinafrica.org

Duration: Programmes last between 1 and 21 weeks. Students can do internships during the summer.

Working Hours: 5 days a week, 5-8 hours per day, depending on the number of hours volunteers want to work daily.

Cost: Participation fees £397 (1-4 weeks), £597 (6 weeks), £797 (8 weeks).

Job Description: Volunteer programmes social welfare, teaching, healthcare education (HIV/AIDS education), conservation, media, journalism and law.

Requirements: Volunteers aged 18-65, of any religion, race or nationality.

Accommodation: Host families provide accommodation.

Application Procedure: Contact above email or address for application forms.

BUNAC: Volunteer Ghana

Job(s) Available: Volunteer placements.
Duration: Departures are all year round. Spend between 2–3 months working and travelling in West Africa.
Cost: Programme costs start at £799 for 2 months including food and accommodation.

Head Office: BUNAC, 16 Bowling Green Lane, London EC1R 0QH, UK
☎ 020 7251 3472
🖰 enquires@bunac.org.uk
🖳 www.bunac.org.uk

Job Description: Placements range from teaching positions or development projects to childcare or HIV/AIDS awareness.
Requirements: Residents of the UK and Ireland only. Minimum age 18.
Application Procedure: For further details about this programme contact BUNAC at the above address or visit www.bunac.org.uk and download our application pack. Orientation interviews will take place.

Wava (Work & Volunteer Abroad)

Job(s) Available: Volunteer construction projects in Ghana.
Duration: From 3 weeks to 1 year.
Working Hours: From 5 to 8 hours per day, 5 days per week.
Cost: Varies depending on programme.

Head Office: 67-71 Lewisham High Street, London SE13 5JX, UK
☎ 020 8297 3278
🖰 ptalbot@workandvolunteer.com
🖳 www.workandvolunteer.com

Company Description: WAVA is an independent company which specialises in providing participants with memorable travel experiences around the world.
Job Description: There are normally several construction projects on the go at once ranging from building brand new learning centres from scratch, to helping update existing sites. Tasks such as running in power supplies (both solar and electric) and general renovation work are all possible during the project.
Requirements: Minimum age 18. Must be physically fit, hard working and have a good sense of humour. International volunteers must have a tourist visa.
Accommodation: All volunteers will stay in accommodation close to the building project. It is basic but clean and will have electricity and running water, though power cuts are normal. Most volunteer accommodation has a lady who will clean and prepare the meals and generally be available for help and advice. The meals are a mixture of Ghanaian and western cuisine and vegetarians can be catered for.
Additional information: Pre-departure briefing events are arranged every month in order to inform and adequately prepare the applicants for their upcoming journeys.
Application Procedure: Visit the above website, choose a programme you like, and then apply online. A member of WAVA will then provide applicants with further details.

ISRAEL

The number of foreigners wishing to work in Israel has dwindled considerably due to the explosive conflict between the Israelis and Palestinians that goes on interminably and seems irresolvable, at least to foreigners' eyes. Even more recently, the conflict between Israel and Lebanon has made travelling to this region an extremely dangerous prospect. The Foreign and Commonwealth Office advises against all travel to Gaza and to Sheba's Farms and Ghajar along the border with Lebanon (www.fco.gov.uk). Despite this tourists flock to Israel each year, and almost all visits are trouble-free. If you do decide to visit Israel, maintaining a high level of vigilance and taking security precautions for your personal safety is essential.

A special visa exists for volunteers to Israel to work on kibbutzim and moshavim, and there are organisations sending volunteers to Palestine though it is becoming increasingly difficult for such organisations to operate there because of the instability of the Palestinian territories.

There are some opportunities for paid employment in the tourist industry, especially around the resort of Eilat on the Red Sea and the Old City in Jerusalem. However, most people who wish to work in Israel for a few months choose to work on kibbutzim or moshavim. These are almost wholly self-sufficient settlements which take on volunteers for a normal minimum of eight weeks. The main difference between the two is that the property is shared on a kibbutz, while most houses and farms are privately owned on a moshav. So on one, volunteers work and share the farm tasks with permanent staff, while on the latter they are paid and there is less communal spirit. However, the whole kibbutz system has undergone so many dramatic changes since its beginnings in socialist, state-owned, pioneering communities, to private ownership.

On a kibbutz the work may consist of picking olives, grapes or cotton in the fields, domestic duties, or factory work; on a moshav the work is usually agricultural. In return for a six-day week volunteers receive free accommodation, meals, laundry and cigarettes. Volunteers are normally given pocket money on kibbutzim, while on a moshav a small wage is paid but the working hours are liable to be longer. Other programmes available on kibbutzim include Kibbutz Ulpan (which is intensive Hebrew study) and Project Oren Kibbutz Programmes (which is intensive Hebrew study, as well as travel and study of Israel).

Anyone interested in working on a kibbutz is advised to contact the Kibbutz Programmes Centre in Israel (kpc@volunteer.co.il). Americans can contact Kibbutz Program Center at 114 West 26th Street Suite 1004, New York, NY 10001 (212 462 2764; mail@KibbutzProgram Center.org); volunteers need to bear in mind that with this organisation they must be prepared to make a commitment of at least six weeks. There are many other placement offices around the world: Israel's diplomatic missions should be able to advise on the nearest one to you.

The following organisation may be able to place people who are actually in Israel. In recent years the authorities have been discouraging volunteers from travelling to Israel on one-way tickets without having a written assurance of a place on a kibbutz, and with insufficient money for their fare home: the official line is that volunteers must have a return ticket and a reasonable sum of money (around £150/$225) in their possession when they enter the country. Contact the Kibbutz Program Centre: Department of the Kibbutz Volunteer Movement; 6 Frishman Street, Tel Aviv 61030 (972 5246 15416; kpc@volunteer.co.il; www.kibbutz.org.il); it is open 9am–2pm, Sunday to Thursday. The centre advises people who do not pre-arrange a place before entering Israel that there might be a wait of days or even weeks before one is found, especially in the summer. However in the current political circumstances, there is a general shortage of foreign volunteers. All volunteers must be available for a minimum of two months, be between the ages of 18 and 35, speak a reasonable level of English and be in good mental and physical health.

The other major form of voluntary work in Israel consists of helping with archaeological excavations, often of Old Testament sites. The minimum stay for volunteers is normally two weeks. In the majority of cases volunteers must pay at least £15/$25 a day for their expenses on a dig. British citizens wishing to find voluntary work in Israel can obtain placements through Concordia.

Placing an advertisement in the English-language paper The Jerusalem Post may also lead to an offer of a job. They can be contacted at the Jerusalem Post Building (PO Box 81, Romena, Jerusalem 91000 (www.jpost.com).

Red tape

ADDRESS: EMBASSY OF ISRAEL IN LONDON, 2 PALACE GREEN LONDON W8 4QB
☎ 020 7957 9500
✆ consulate@london.mfa.gov.il
🖥 http://london.mfa.gov.il/mfa

Visa requirements: Citizens of EU countries, including the UK, and citizens of the USA, Australia and Ireland can visit Israel for up to three months without a visa. However, in order to travel to Israel from any country including those which do not need a visa, a passport valid for at least six months, a return ticket from Israel and medical insurance are required. If a tourist visa is required, the fee is £13. To work in Israel, however, you must have a foreign worker's visa or work permit. This is the only visa that allows a visitor to work (other than for voluntary work eg kibbutz) in Israel. For volunteer work a work visa is not normally required prior to arrival by citizens of the UK, USA and some western European countries.

Work permits: If you wish to work in Israel you must first find secure employment in Israel and ask your prospective employer to obtain the necessary permit from the Ministry of the Interior in Israel. You should have the permit with you when you enter the country or apply when in Israel with a tourist visa. Your work visa will be limited to the period set out in your employment permit.

Residence permits: On entering the country, a visitor is likely to be given permission to stay for up to three months. Permission for a longer stay should then be obtained from the Ministry of the Interior.

Voluntary work: A B4 Volunteer Visa is required of participants doing voluntary work (which includes kibbutzim and moshavim). The organisation that the applicant will attend should apply for a B4 visa in the Ministry of Interior in Israel. The Ministry of Interior will send a confirmation to the relevant Israeli Consulate that will be able to issue that visa abroad. Once the Consulate has that confirmation, the applicant should come to the Consulate with one passport photo, fill in the forms and wait for the visa to be issued.

For up-to-date information about visa requirements check with the embassy before travel.

Kibbutzim and moshavim

Kibbutz Programme Centre

Job(s) Available: Kibbutz volunteers.
Duration: Required all year round. Period of work 2 months (minimum) to 6 months.
Working Hours: 7–8 hours per day, 6 days a week.
Pay/Cost: Volunteers need to pay a registration fee of NIS360, NIS110 for the visa and NIS340 for health insurance.

Head Office: 6 Frishman Street (corner of Hayarkon Street), Tel Aviv 61030
☎ +972 3524 6156/4
✆ kpc@volunteer.co.il
🖥 www.kibbutz.org.il

Company Description: The Kibbutz Programme Centre is the only office officially representing all the kibbutzim. The centre is responsible for their volunteers and provides for them from arrival until they leave the kibbutz.

Requirements: Volunteers must be able to converse in English. Applicants must be aged between 18 and 35.

Accommodation: Volunteers receive full board and accommodation and free laundry.

Application Procedure: To apply contact the centre with details of your name and date of birth, date of arrival, passport number, a covering letter describing yourself and a medical form. Applications are accepted all year round, but apply at least 4 weeks in advance of your arrival in Israel.

Teaching and language schools

Unipal

Job(s) Available: English teachers.
Duration: The programmes take place each summer from mid-July and usually last 4–5 weeks.
Cost: Summer volunteers are expected to pay around £500 to cover air fare and insurance. Extra spending money should be budgeted for.

> **Head Office:** BCM Unipal, London WC1N 3XX, UK
> ⁀ info@unipal.org.uk
> 🖳 www.unipal.org.uk

Company Description: Unipal (Universities' Trust for Educational Exchange with Palestinians) seeks to facilitate a two-way process of education, providing English-language teaching in Palestinian refugee camps in the West Bank, Gaza and Lebanon and introducing British students to a knowledge and understanding of the situation and daily lives of refugees.

Job Description: English teachers to teach school children aged 12–15. Sometimes additional teaching with older students or with women's groups can be arranged.

Requirements: Previous experience with children is essential and previous teaching experience would be a real advantage. TEFL/TESL qualifications are also an advantage but are not necessary. Personal qualities needed include sensitivity, tolerance, adaptability, readiness to learn, political awareness, reliance and tenacity. It is also vital that each volunteer is able to work successfully as part of a team. Minimum age 20.

Accommodation: Food and accommodation provided.

Application Procedure: Via the website www.unipal.org.uk. Closing date for applications at the end of February.

Other employment in Israel

Weizmann Institute of Science

Job(s) Available: Undergraduate students to join a research project.
Duration: Projects last between 8 to 10 weeks in the summer.
Pay: A small stipend is provided.

> **Head Office:** Academic Affairs Office PO Box 26, Rehovot 76100
> ☎ +972 8934 4578
> ⁀ undergraduate.summer@ weizmann.ac.il
> 🖳 www.weizmann.ac.il

Company Description: The Weizmann Institute of Science's annual Kupcinet-Getz International Science school was established in 1971.

Job Description: A research project involving the life sciences, chemistry, physics and mathematics.

Requirements: Applicants must have finished at least 1 year of study at university. Students in their final year must apply for the summer immediately after graduation. Overseas students must have a grade point average of at least 3.6 out of 4.0 or equivalent.

Application Procedure: Application forms should be downloaded and completed online. Forms will be available at the end of September 2010. The deadline for applications is 31 December 2010.

KENYA

Chances of finding a paid summer job in Kenya are minimal, but there are opportunities to participate in voluntary work with the following organisations. In addition, Concordia and UNA Exchange can place British, and Service Civil International, American nationals in voluntary work in Kenya: see the *Worldwide* chapter for details. For short-term teaching assignments in rural areas of Kenya, Americans can apply to Global Citizens Network.

Red tape

ADDRESS: EMBASSY OF KENYA
45 Portland Place, London W1B 1AS
☎ 0207 636 2371
✒ immigration@kenyahighcommission.net
💻 www.kenyahighcommission.net

Visa requirements: According to the Kenyan High Commission in London, all non-Kenyan citizens require a visa to go to Kenya and must complete Form V1, which can be downloaded from the website. In order to take up paid or unpaid work in Kenya, you must apply for a work/entry permit which can be done by downloading Form 3 from the website.

For up-to-date information about visa requirements check with the embassy before travel.

Voluntary work

Action for Cheetahs in Kenya

Job(s) Available: Volunteers.
Duration: Minimum 2 weeks.
Cost: $1,500 for 2 weeks, includes internal transportation, room and board. Volunteers will be expected to pay their own airfare to and from Nairobi.

Head Office: Cheetah Conservation Fund, c/o ACK, PO Box 1611, 00606, Nairobi
☎ +254 733 997910
✒ cheetah@africaonline.co.ke
💻 www.cheetah.org

Company Description: ACK was established under the umbrella of Cheetah Conservation Fund Namibia to evaluate the pressures of habitat change and rapid human population growth and to understand issues facing cheetahs as they come into greater contact with mankind. Specifically, ACK conducts field research to understand predator conflict issues. The project implements educational programmes to increase community awareness of cheetah issues. The ACK, in conjunction with the Kenya Wildlife Service, also evaluates the overall status of cheetahs within Kenya.
Job Description: Administrative work such as filing, writing articles, cooking, cleaning, database entry, weekly food shopping as well as field work such as game counts and habitat analysis, education programmes and tourist outreach programmes.
Requirements: Minimum age 18. Must be flexible, adaptable and patient. Students and volunteers of all backgrounds are welcome.
Accommodation: Accommodation, bedding and bathroom linen are supplied at no charge.
Application Procedure: Download a 'Kenya Questionnaire' from the website, complete and email it to the address above.

Kenya Voluntary Development Association (KVDA)

Job(s) Available: Volunteers.

Duration: Short-term voluntary service programme takes 21 days. The schedule runs from January to December every year. Medium and long-term projects take between 3 months and 1 year.

Working Hours: *Short-term:* 6 hours per day, 6 days a week.

> **Head Office:** PO Box 48902 - 00100, GPO Nairobi
> ☎ +254 2025 00120 or
>   +254 7216 50357 (mobile)
> ✆ kvdakenya@yahoo.com
> 💻 www.kvda.or.ke

Pay: There is a registration fee to be paid on arrival. *Short-term:* approximately €300. *Medium and long-term:* volunteers pay €200 every month.

Company Description: KVDA is a non-political, membership organisation which is non-sectarian and non-profit-making which started in 1962 as a work camp organisation. In 1993, KVDA was registered as a non-governmental organisation by the establishment of the NGO Coordination act.

Job Description: *Short-term:* volunteers will work on projects in remote villages aimed at improving amenities in Kenya's rural and needy areas, working alongside members of the local community. The work may involve digging foundations, building, making building blocks, roofing, awareness campaigns, or environmental programmes and every project is based on specific themes relevant to the socio-economic challenges of the local communities. This brings together 20–25 volunteers per project. The projects are thematic in nature, focusing on socio-economic situations of the local people. They are motivated to provide impetus for empowerment of the marginalised segments of the local population. *Medium and long-term:* entailing placement of both professional and non-professional volunteers drawn from various countries in the world. The projects are based on themes such as awareness on HIV/AIDS, drug abuse, agriculture, income-generating activities, renovation of learning institutions and infrastructure in general, conservation of the environment, volunteering in hospitals and more.

Requirements: Minimum age 18.

Accommodation: Normally provided in school classrooms or similar buildings by the local community; foreign participants must be able to adapt to local foodstuffs and cultures. Participation fee is inclusive of meals, accommodation and general administration.

Additional Information: Volunteers participating in KVDA projects are invited to participate in the KVDA educational tour designed to take them to places of interest that include historical and archaeological sites, wildlife and game parks. The participation fee is €100 per day and there are different packages for 3–10 days. Details about this programme are available on request by contacting kvdakenya@yahoo.com.

Application Procedure: For further information visit the website. For more information about the work of KVDA volunteers in the UK can apply through KVDA partner organisations like Concordia-UK, Youth Action for Peace (YAP-UK), and UNA-Exchange. You can also get links to KVDA partner organisations through the global voluntary service network, the coordinating committee for International Voluntary Service (CCIVS) based in Paris, France: secretariat@ccivs.org. Please visit the KVDA website above for an overview of the voluntary service program.

MADAGASCAR

Opportunities for paid temporary work in Madagascar are rare. The following organisations can arrange voluntary placements there: Blue Ventures Expeditions and Reefdoctor.

Red tape

ADDRESS: EMBASSY OF THE REPUBLIC OF MADAGASCAR
33 Stadium Street, London SW10 0PU
☎ 075 538 75128
✆ contact@embassy-madagascar-uk.com
🖳 www.embassy-madagascar-uk.com

Visa requirements: Visas are required for anyone wishing to enter Madagascar. Those wishing to volunteer can apply for a tourist visa from their nearest Madagascan embassy in their home country a buy the visa upon arrival in Madagascar. Volunteers do not currently need to provide an official letter of invitation from the NGO they are joining. Tourist visas are issued for up to a maximum 90 days and are valid for six months from date of issue. Forms and further information can be found on the website.

For up-to-date information about visa requirements check with the embassy before travel.

Voluntary work

Blue Ventures Expeditions

Job(s) Available: SCUBA and PADI diving research volunteers.

Duration: Minimum period of 3 weeks.

Cost: *Madagascar*: from £1,500 for 3 weeks. *Belize*: from £1,600 for 3 weeks. *Malaysia:* from £2,100 for 3 weeks.

Head Office: 309 Aberdeen Centre, 22-24 Highbury Grove, London N5 2EA, UK
☎ 0203 176 0548
✆ madagascar@blueventures.org
🖳 www.blueventures.org

Company Description: A non-profit organisation dedicated to coral reef and sustainable development in Madagascar, Fiji and Malaysia. Volunteers work with the field research team and in partnership with local communities.

Requirements: Minimum age 18.

Accommodation: Included in cost and locally owned.

Application Procedure: Complete web form at above website. Applications ongoing, telephone interview required and foreign applicants welcome.

ReefDoctor

Job(s) Available: Volunteers (4–12).

Duration: Minimum of 4 weeks and a maximum of 3 months, (4, 6, 8, 12 weeks).

Cost: £950 for 4 weeks, £1,400 for 6 weeks, £1,800 for 8 weeks, £2,200 for 3 months, excluding travel to Madagascar, driving and medical insurance and in-

Head Office: 14 Charlwood Terrace, Putney, London SW15 1NZ, UK
☎ 07866 250740
✆ volunteer@reefdoctor.org
🖳 www.reefdoctor.org

country personal expenses. As of 2010 going into 2011 up to 20% discounts on expeditions for students and experienced scuba divers are available; discounts decided upon application.

Company Description: ReefDoctor is a small not-for-profit organisation conducting coral reef research, implementing marine management principles, community education and social development work in conjunction with Madagascar's only marine research institute, the IHSM. It is based on the lagonall reef system of the Bay of Ranobe part of the 'Toliara coral reef system of SW Madagascar', the third largest coral reef system in the world. Volunteers receive 1–2 weeks training in marine species identification, underwater survey techniques, marine biology principles, marine management, conservation principles and local community history, dynamics and more.

Requirements: ReefDoctor has opportunities for gap, graduate and postgraduates as well as general enthusiastic people to support the projects. Volunteers need to be qualified up to PADI Advanced Open Water to conduct the research and dive courses from PADI Open Water to Rescue Diver are given to volunteers for free. Volunteers can also hire dive equipment from ReefDoctor for a small extra fee. Ages 18–60.

Accommodation: In reed huts on the beach 100m from the fishing village of Ifaty. Volunteers are made aware that heat, humidity and insects are the norm.

Application Procedure: Applications to the above address.

MOROCCO

Work permits are necessary for employment in Morocco; but there are no restrictions on foreign workers.

There are, however, possibilities of seasonal work in the expanding tourist industry, especially around the resorts of Saidia, Agadir, Marrakesh and Tangier. Several European holiday companies operate in Morocco and employ summer staff. Knowledge of French will normally be expected: this is also the language most likely to be used in voluntary work camps, although English should be understood.

In addition to the voluntary opportunities listed below, Concordia, International Voluntary Service, Volunteer Action for Peace and UNA Exchange can help UK nationals, and the CIEE and Service Civil International Americans, find voluntary work in Morocco: see the *Worldwide* chapter for details.

Red tape

ADDRESS: THE CONSULATE GENERAL OF THE KINGDOM OF MOROCCO
Diamond House, 97-99 Praed Street, Paddington, London W2 1NT
☎ 020 7724 0624
✆ ambalondres@maec.gov.ma
🖥 www.moroccanembassylondon.org.uk

Visa requirements: A visa is not required by citizens of most EU countries and some other countries, including Australia, Canada, New Zealand, the USA, the Russian Federation, Turkey and Switzerland if they are entering Morocco as tourists for up to three months.

Residence permits: Those planning a stay of over three months must register with the local Police station and apply for a visa extension within 15 days of arrival, and be able to provide evidence of how they are supporting themselves.

Work permit: Any foreigner taking up paid employment in Morocco must have a valid work permit: this will be obtained by the prospective employer from the

Ministry of Labour (or by applying directly to the Ministry of Labour if self-employed). Work permits (*Permis de travail*) can be obtained while in Morocco if a job is found. Check with the embassy for relevant visa/work permit requirements before travel.

Passports must be valid for at least six months after your arrival and it is advised to get your passport stamped.

For up-to-date information about visa requirements check with the embassy before travel.

Teaching and language schools

American Language Centre

Job(s) Available: Teachers (45).
Duration: Typically 1 year contracts starting in September of each year. Occasionally offer summer hires for highly qualified teachers.
Working Hours: 18–24 contract hours per week during the main terms. Teaching takes place on weekday evenings and Saturdays.

Head Office: 4 Zankat Tanja, Rabat 10000
☎ +212 3776 7103
dir@alcrabat.org
www.alcrabat.org

Pay: Full-time salaries offered by ALC Rabat usually allow teachers to live comfortably in Rabat. Salaries are in Moroccan dirhams.
Company Description: Member of a non-profit association of language schools. A large association with 10 schools in Morocco.
Requirements: Bachelor's or Master's degree plus classroom experience, preferably in an overseas environment. A certificate in TEFL or TESL and participation in our teacher orientation programme before teaching begins.
Application Procedure: Application forms available from www.alcrabat.org/jobs.

SOUTH AFRICA

The government is, understandably, not keen to hand out work permits to Europeans and other nationalities when so many of their own nationals are unemployed; the current rate stands at 22.5%. Work permits are granted only in instances where South African citizens or permanent residents are not available for appointment or cannot be trained for the position. The weakness of the land has lead to a 'brain drain' out of the country and positions existing for professionals.

Red tape

ADDRESS: SOUTH AFRICAN HIGH COMMISSION
South Africa House, Trafalgar Square, London WC2N 5DP
☎ 020 7925 8900
london.general@foreign.gov.za
www.southafricahouse.com

Most European and North American citizens do not require a visa to visit South Africa. Nationals of these countries may take up casual work for up to three months. A 90-day extension can be obtained from the Department of Home Affairs for a fee. Once you have done this a few times though the authorities will become suspicious.

One solution to the problem is to consider BUNAC's work and travel programme in South Africa. Full-time students or those within 12 months of graduation aged 18 or over may be eligible for a 12-month working holiday permit (see entry) which allows them to look for work on the spot. Unfortunately for summer jobseekers, the time when jobs are likely to be found is the high season of October to March.

Voluntary work is organised for British citizens in South Africa by UNA Exchange. See their entries in the *Worldwide* chapter for details. Work can be found in South Africa through the organisations below. A Letter from the organisation stating the duration of the visit must be presented to the immigration officer upon entry into South Africa. For further information either write to: South African High Commission, 15 Whitehall, London SW1A 2DD, enclosing an s.a.e. or visit the above website.

For up-to-date information about visa requirements check with the embassy before travel.

Voluntary work

BUNAC: Volunteer South Africa

Job(s) Available: Local Community Volunteer projects including the environment, community development, education and social welfare as well as sports projects in and around Cape Town.

Duration: Placements last from 5 to 33 weeks. Participants may then stay on in South Africa to travel. Departures are available on a year-round basis.

Head Office: BUNAC, 16 Bowling Green Lane, London EC1R 0QH, UK
☎ 020 7251 3472
✉ enquires@bunac.org.uk
🖥 www.bunac.org.uk

Cost: Programme costs range from £969 to £2,299 depending on length of placement.

Requirements: British or Irish passport holder. Minimum age 18.

Accommodation: Accommodation is with a host family and meals are included in the programme fee.

Application Procedure: For further details contact BUNAC at the above address or visit their website to download an application form.

Cape Town Garden Volunteers

Job(s) Available: Garden volunteers.

Duration: Minimum period of work 2 weeks from mid-August. Dates can be extended to accommodate independent travel around South Africa.

Head Office: 8 Bisham Gardens, London N6 6DD,UK
☎ 020 7209 1659
✉ patricia@capetowngardenvolunteers.co.uk
🖥 www.capetowngardenvolunteers.co.uk

Cost: From £1,850. Includes airfare, accommodation, transport, insurance and excursion fees.

Company Description: Set up to offer volunteer opportunities at Kirstenbosch, Cape Town's world-renowned botanical gardens. Projects range from working in the gardens themselves – designing and planting borders – to greening and farming projects in the townships that fall under the umbrella of Kirstenbosch and its staff. Fun sessions to learn about the botany of the unique Cape flora are also included.

Job Description: Greening the community, help farmers in townships turn wasteland into market gardens, assist with projects within Kirstenbosch botanical gardens, replant arterial borders of the gardens, collect, sort and preserve seed for posterity, nursery work, cycad fertilising.

Requirements: The trip is aimed at students and practising professionals in garden design, landscape architecture and horticulture and related areas.

Accommodation: 4-star luxury bed and breakfast included in price.

Additional Information: Volunteers also have the opportunity to travel to famous, beautiful sites in Cape Town including Cape Point, Table Mountain and the winelands. Volunteers of all ages from 19–70+ welcome.

Application Procedure: Apply by email to Patricia Walby at the above address.

SANCCOB – The Southern African National Foundation for the Conservation of Coastal Birds

Job(s) Available: Volunteers.

Duration: The period between May and October is the busiest but help is needed year-round. Minimum period of work 6 weeks.

Cost: Volunteers must meet their own living costs (approximately $30–$40).

Head Office: PO Box 11116, Bloubergrant 7443, Cape Town
☎ +27 2 1557 6155
carole@sanccob.co.za
www.sanccob.co.za

Company Description: The coastal waters of South Africa are a major shipping route and oil pollution is a recurrent problem, the main bird types dealt with are African penguins, gulls, gannets, terns and cormorants.

Job Description: Volunteers are required to help with the cleaning and rehabilitation of injured, oiled, ill and abandoned coastal birds, in particular, the African penguin. The main tasks involve keeping the rehabilitation centre clean (scrubbing pools and pens), feeding and caring for the birds.

Requirements: Volunteers must be willing to work in hard conditions with wild and difficult birds. Minimum age 18.

Accommodation: Help is given with finding bed and breakfast accommodation.

Application Procedure: To apply contact SANCCOB at the above address.

TANZANIA

Some paid work may be found in Tanzania in the form of teaching, however most work placements are within the voluntary sector. In addition to the following entries, Concordia and UNA Exchange can offer short-term volunteer projects to Britons wishing to work in Tanzania for a few months, while Americans may be able to apply through Service Civil International (their entries in the *Worldwide* chapter give more details). There are other organisations which operate in a similar way to Volunteer Africa (below), ie you pay the organisation for your voluntary work placement of four weeks or longer: try also the UK-based Frontier (www.frontier.ac.uk) and Madventurer (www.madventurer.com).

Visa requirements: All visitors wishing to enter The United Republic of Tanzania need to obtain a visa, which must be obtained before entering Tanzania. A tourist or visitor visa is valid for up to three months (90 days).

Work permits: There are several types of visa available. If you are volunteering a permit is required which must be applied for by your host organisation in Tanzania. Alternatively you can apply for an entry visa in your home country and then request a permit upon arrival in Tanzania. Enquire at the consular section of the high commission for details.

For up-to-date information about visa requirements check with the embassy before travel.

Voluntary work

Art in Tanzania

Job(s) Available: Over 300 volunteer placements and internships in areas such as education, vocational training, medicine, sports, music, journalism, arts, construction and environmental projects.

Duration: Any time throughout the year.

Cost: Volunteering in mainland Tanzania costs $230 (£160) per week; internships cost $240 (£167) per week. Volunteering/internships in Zanzibar cost $250–$260 (£174–£180) per week. Volunteering/internships in Masai Land cost $300–$310 (£208–£215) per week. Fees include airport transfers, accommodation, breakfast and dinner, orientation, project guidance, 24 hour security and a dedicated team leader.

Head Office: Silver Sands Road, Bahari Beach, Kunduchi, Dar Es Salaam
☎ +255 755 36 33 98
✎ info@artintanzania.org
💻 www.artintanzania.org

Company Description: Art in Tanzania is a Tanzanian/Finnish NGO which began with a few grassroots projects in 2001. It has grown into an organisation which attracts around 1,500 volunteers and interns annually. Its vision is to be at the heart of community development.

Job Description: Tasks vary based on the project chosen. Volunteers can also structure their own programme. See website for further details.

Requirements: No formal requirements.

Accommodation: Included in cost.

Additional Information: Safari community work packages are also available where safari fees form part of the volunteer donation.

Application Procedure: Apply by sending an email to the above address.

VolunteerAfrica

Job(s) Available: Volunteers.

Duration: Volunteers can participate for 2–10 weeks.

Cost: The cost of participating during 2010 is £600 for 2 weeks and £1,895 for 10 weeks. Of these fees, approximately 60% goes to the host organisations to support development work in Tanzania. Participants also need to budget around £600 for flights and medical insurance.

Company Description: Providing volunteers and fundraising to community-based organisations working in Tanzania, VolunteerAfrica is run largely by volunteers to keep down running costs.

Job Description: Singida rural development. Fundraising advice is given and the first week is spent in language and cultural training.

Requirements: Minimum age 18.

Application Procedure: Applications can only be made through the organisation's website.

> **Head Office:** Silver Sands Road, Bahari Beach, Kunduchi, Dar Es Salaam
> ☎ +255 755 36 33 98
> ✑ info@artintanzania.org
> 🖳 www.artintanzania.org

UGANDA

Most jobs on offer for people seeking to work in Uganda are unpaid. The following organisations can arrange voluntary placements in Uganda: Skillshare International Uganda, United Children's Fund Inc and Uganda Volunteers for Peace. The FCO (www.fco.gov.uk) currently advise against all travel to the Karamoja region in north eastern Uganda.

Red tape

ADDRESS: THE UGANDAN HIGH COMMISSION
58–59 Trafalgar Square, London WC2N 5DX
☎ 020 7839 5783
✑ info@ugandahighcommission.co.uk
🖳 www.ugandahighcommission.co.uk

Visa requirements: The citizens of most countries (except notably nationals from the Republic of Ireland) are required to apply for a visa before entering Uganda. Visas can be applied for from your local consulate or consular section at high commission or embassy of Uganda. It is advisable to seek information on visa types from your local embassy before travelling.

Voluntary work

United Children's Fund Inc

Job(s) Available: Volunteers.
Duration: Placements last 1 month at any time of year.
Cost: $2,150 for 1 month. This covers all food, transportation and local fees when in Uganda.
Company Description: United Children's Fund provides volunteer opportunities in East Africa for those wanting to use their talents and skills to make a difference in someone's life.

> **Head Office:** PO Box 20341, Boulder, Colorado, 80308-3341, USA or 300-1055 West Hastings, Vancouver BC V6E 2E9
> ☎ +180 0615 5229 (toll-free in the US and Canada)
> ✆ united@unchildren.org
> 🖥 www.unchildren.org

Job Description: United Children's Fund places volunteers on projects in Uganda including healthcare, working in village clinics, teaching in local village schools, assisting teachers, school construction, working with women's groups on income-generating projects and more. Volunteers are needed to work on projects where they think they can make the biggest difference.
Requirements: Special skills are not prerequisite. Minimum age 18.
Accommodation: Provided at no extra cost.
Application Procedure: For further details check the website above.

THE AMERICAS

CANADA

The employment of foreigners in either short or long-term work in Canada is strictly regulated. Even with Canada's relatively strong economy (unemployment is currently at 8%), it is illegal to work in Canada without a work permit; with some exceptions, a job must be obtained from outside the country, and even then the employer will face difficulty in obtaining permission to employ you unless they can show that they are not depriving a Canadian citizen or permanent resident of the job.

Anyone seeking employment in Canada should write directly to Canadian employers before arrival to enquire about employment prospects. Information on how to find a job in Canada, obtain a Labour Market Opinion and apply for a work permit is available from the website www.cic.gc.ca and the HRSDC website www.hrsdc.gc.ca. Further information on jobs can also be obtained from Canadian newspapers or trade journals, which are available at larger newsagents. Addresses of potential employers can also be found in the *Canadian Trade Index* or the *Canadian Almanac and Directory*, both of which can be found at large libraries.

Teachers from British Commonwealth nations may be able to arrange exchange placements by contacting The League for the Exchange of Commonwealth Teachers (60 Queens Road, Reading RG1 4BS, www.lect.org.uk).

To work legally in Canada, you must obtain a work permit from a Canadian high commission or embassy before you leave your home country. Most work permits must be applied for at a local Canadian embassy before entering Canada. Work permits are not issued for the purpose of seeking employment in Canada. The applicant must include a confirmed job offer with the application. A foreign national must not work in Canada without permission. It is also advised not to make any definite travel plans before obtaining the work permit. Applicants from the UK or Ireland may be eligible to apply for an open work permit through one of the Youth Mobility Programme (YMP) (formerly The Student General Working Holiday Program (SGWHP); consult the website www.london.gc.ca for up-to-date information on these programmes. Applications must be sent to BUNAC (UK) or USIT (Ireland) and applied for before travelling to Canada. BUNAC's Work Canada programme offers about 3,000 students and non-students the chance to go to Canada for up to a year and take whatever jobs they can find. Participants on this programme can depart at any time between February and January. The great majority of participants go to Canada without a pre-arranged job and spend their first week or two job-hunting. The Canadian High Commission in London administers the scheme for British and Irish passport holders. There are similar schemes for Australians and New Zealanders. Note: if you applying to work in Québec, there are separate and additional immigration procedures.

Concordia arrange voluntary placements in Canada, and UNA Exchange can organise voluntary work in French-speaking Québec; the CIEE can arrange voluntary work in Canada for Americans. For details of these, see the *Worldwide* chapter.

Red tape

ADDRESS: CANADIAN HIGH COMMISSION
Immigration Division, 38 Grosvenor Street, London W1K 4AA
☎ 020 7258 6600
✆ ldn.consular@international.gc.ca
🖥 www.unitedkingdom.gc.ca

Visa requirements: Citizens of the UK and most other countries in western Europe, of UK dependent territories, Australia, New Zealand, the USA and Mexico do not normally require a visa for a visit to Canada. Citizens of other countries may need to obtain one. No matter what the length or purpose of the proposed stay, permission to enter and remain in Canada must be obtained from the immigration officer at the port of entry. If the purpose is any other than purely for a tourist visit to Canada, you should consult the Canadian high commission or embassy abroad before departure. The length of stay in Canada is decided at the port of entry. Normally entry is granted for six months and extensions must be applied for from inside Canada at least 30 days before the status expires. Please visit the immigration websites www.cic.gc.ca or www.canada.org.uk for a full list of visa exemptions before travelling.

Work permit: In almost all cases it is necessary to have a valid work permit which authorises an individual to work 'at a specific job for a specific period of time for a specific employer'. It must be applied for before arrival. Non-students aged 18–35 may be eligible for a 12-month general working holiday permit.

Student General working holiday programmes: Open to full-time students aged 18–30 from the UK and 18–35 from Ireland, Sweden and Finland. Citizens of the latter three countries can apply directly to the immigration section of their local embassy, providing a letter of university acceptance and a letter confirming return to studies or proof that they have completed their studies within the previous 12 months and sufficient funds must be proven for voluntary work. There is also the Student Work Abroad Programme (SWAP) available for Australian and New Zealand citizens. This programme is coordinated through STA (travel) offices in Australia and New Zealand. Prospective SWAP applicants must contact the STA office for information on the programme for that year.

Voluntary work: A special category of work permit covers voluntary work which takes about two to four months to process if you have found a placement through a recognised charitable or religious organisation.

For up-to-date information about visa requirements check with the embassy before travel.

Agricultural work

Agricultural Labour Pool

Job Description: Seasonal and permanent agricultural jobs in Canada.
Application Procedure: See website for details.

☎ +1 60 4823 6222
✆ info@agri-labourpool.com
🖥 www.agri-labourpool.com

World Wide Opportunities on Organic Farms (WWOOF Canada)

Job(s) Available: Volunteers to work on organic farms.
Duration: Opportunities may be available all year round.
Company Description: Hundreds of young people, from 30 different countries, every year

Head Office: 4429 Carlson Road, Nelson, British Columbia, VIL 6X3
☎ +1 25 0354 4417
✆ wwoofcan@shaw.ca
🖥 www.wwoof.ca

go 'WWOOFing' in Canada. 750 hosts available from the east to the west coast of Canada.

Job Description: Volunteers to work on 750 organic farms in Canada ranging from small homesteads to large farms. Duties include general farm work and may include going to market, working with horses, garden work, milking goats, etc.

Requirements: Minimum age 16. Only EU nationals with valid tourist visas need apply.

Accommodation: Board and lodging provided free of charge.

Application Procedure: See 'How to Apply' on website: www.wwoof.ca.

Sports, couriers and camping

Camp Artaban

Job(s) Available: Head guard (1), kitchen helpers (3), lifeguards (2), maintenance workers (2).

Duration: Mid-June to beginning of September.

Company Description: Camp Artaban has been providing Christian camping on its Gambier Island site since 1923, making it one of the oldest camps in British Columbia. The site was chosen by a group of ministers and businessmen under the leadership of Bishop Heathcote and the first camp was held in 1923.

Head Office: Camp Artaban Society, 1058 Ridgewood Drive, North Vancouver, BC V7R 1H8
☎ +1 60 4980 0391
✉ hiring@campartaban.com
🖥 www.campartaban.com

Job Description: Camp Artaban encourages living in a Christian community, and that the very act of living is a religious experience. Camp Artaban offers a programme that provides a greater understanding of the Christian faith, not only through relationships, but also through appropriately structured periods of instruction. Camp helpers would have to instruct and abide by this programme.

Requirements: Fluent English is necessary. *Head guard:* NLS and Pleasure Craft Operator card required. OFA Boat level III an asset. Boating experience an advantage. *Kitchen helpers:* must have food safe level 1. *Lifeguards:* pleasure craft operator card required. Boating experience an asset. *Maintenance workers:* previous construction or other related experiences an asset. Must have a valid driver's licence.

Accommodation: Board and accommodation available.

Additional Information: Also accepts volunteers.

Application Procedure: Email at the above address. Application deadline is mid-March. See website for further details.

Voluntary work

Frontiers Foundation/Operation Beaver

Job(s) Available: Volunteers.

Duration: Minimum period of work 12 weeks. The greatest need for volunteers is in June, July and August. Long-term placements of up to 18 months are possible provided that the volunteer's work is deemed satisfactory after the initial 12 week period.

Head Office: 419 Coxwell Avenue, Toronto, Ontario M4L 3B9
☎ +1 41 6690 3930
✉ frontiersfoundation@on.aibn.com
🖥 www.frontiersfoundation.ca

Pay: Living allowance of C$50 per week.

Company Description: Frontiers Foundation is an aboriginal non-profit voluntary service organisation supporting the advancement of economically and socially disadvantaged communities in Canada and overseas. The organisation works in partnership with requesting communities in low-income rural areas. Projects help to provide and improve housing, to provide training and economic incentives and to offer recreational/educational activities in developing regions.

Job Description: Volunteers are recruited from across the world to serve in native and non-native communities across Canada for a variety of community construction and educational projects.

Requirements: Minimum age 18. Skills in carpentry, electrical work and plumbing are preferred for construction projects. Previous social service and experience with children are sought for recreational/educational projects.

Accommodation: All accommodation, food and travel within Canada is provided. Travel to and from Canada is the responsibility of the volunteer. Accommodation is normally provided by the community; volunteers must be prepared to live without electricity, running water or roads in some communities. Medical insurance is provided.

Application Procedure: Application forms available at www.frontiersfoundation.ca/node/19. Once an applicant has sent in an application form there can be a delay of 3–12 weeks as references come in and possible placements are considered. Acceptance cannot be guaranteed.

Other employment in Canada

BUNAC: Work Canada

Job(s) Available: BUNAC offers a work and travel scheme to Canada.

Duration: The Work Authorisation is valid for 3 months to 1 year.

Cost: Programme costs are approximately £200. Must also have support funds of £500 on arrival in Canada.

Head Office: BUNAC, 16 Bowling Green Lane, London EC1R 0QH, UK
☎ 020 7251 3472
enquines@bunac.org.uk
www.bunac.org.uk

Job Description: Enables participants to work and travel anywhere in Canada. Approximately 90% of participants go to Canada without a pre-arranged job and take an average of 6 days to find one.

Additional Information: BUNAC also offers advice on job-hunting, various travel deals and on-going support services while in Canada.

Application Procedure: For further details contact the above address or visit the website www.bunac.org.uk to apply online or download an application form.

COSTA RICA

Under Costa Rican law, it is illegal for foreigners to be offered paid work and therefore the only work opportunities available are within voluntary work. US nationals may be able to obtain voluntary work through the CIEE allowing for yearly changes in their project planning. Britons may find opportunities arranged by UNA Exchange. See their entries in the *Worldwide* chapter for details.

Red tape

ADDRESS: COSTA RICAN CONSULATE
Flat 1, 14 Lancaster Gate, London W2 3LH
☎ 020 7706 8844
consul@costaricanembassy.co.uk

Work permits: For paid employment foreigners may apply for temporary residency. The application should be made to the General Directorate of Migration (GDM) and presented through the Costa Rican consulate of the country of residence or nationality of the applicant. The application documentation requires that the applicant provide information about the employer in Costa Rica (name, corporate id number, and other details). Other requirements include legalised birth certificates and police checks.

Voluntary work: EU nationals may volunteer for up to three months without a visa.

For up-to-date information about visa requirements check with embassy before travel.

Voluntary work

BUNAC: Volunteer Costa Rica

Job(s) Available: Volunteer placements.
Duration: Allows participants to spend 2–3 months working as a volunteer in Costa Rica.
Cost: Programme costs start at £1,149 for 2 months including food and accommodation.
Job Description: Placements can be in areas such as conservation, childcare, tourism or teaching.
Requirements: Applicants should have an interest in Spanish and must be either a UK or Irish resident. Minimum age 18.
Accommodation: Accommodation is provided with a host family as part of the programme fee.
Application Procedure: Visit www.bunac.org.uk and download an application form.

> **Head Office:** BUNAC, 16 Bowling Green Lane, London EC1R 0QH, UK
> ☎ 020 7251 3472
> ✆ enquiries@bunac.org.uk
> 🖳 www.bunac.org.uk

The Ara Project

Job(s) Available: Volunteers at The Ara Project main release site in Tiskita.
Duration: Minimum period of work 2 months.
Cost: $8 a day which contributes to project maintenance. Volunteers are responsible for paying their own airfare and travel to and from Tiskita.
Company Description: The Ara Project began in 1982. They have an 83% breeding success rate in the wild and have released nearly 100 hand-reared birds with a 94% survival rate. The main release site is situated in a private reserve on the South West coast near to the Panamanian border. It is owned by the Aspinall family who are working closely with The Ara Project. The first scarlet macaws were released in 2002 and are now an established flock of birds.
Job Description: Monitor birds and feeding stations, nest observations, clean feeding stations, spot counts, boundary walks and roost site observations.
Requirements: A biology-related qualification will help but is not essential, and previous experience with birds is preferred. Candidates must be responsible, dedicated, fit for hiking and camping and patient as long hours will be spent monitoring the birds. Spanish is not essential, but it would help to have a small understanding of the language.

> **Head Office:** Apdo 1904 – 4050, Alajuela
> ☎ +506 8339 4329
> ✆ thearaproject@gmail.com or hatchedtoflyfree@gmail.com
> 🖳 www.thearaproject.org

Accommodation: Provided free of charge.

Application Procedure: Apply to Marti at the above email address with a CV and 2 references. Please state the reasons for applying, avicultural experience, availability and for how long.

Tropical Adventures

Job(s) Available: Volunteers
Duration: Throughout the year.
Cost: Between $995–$2,495.

Company Description: The Tropical Adventures Foundation is a non-profit organisation that helps individuals and communities inside and outside of Costa Rica. They provide volunteers for helping with local projects that include community development, working and teaching children plus conservation and wildlife work.

> Head Office: 1775 E Palm Canyon Drive, Ste 110-341, Palm Springs, CA 92264-1613, USA
> ☎ +1 425 329 3345
> ✆ volunteer@tropicaladventures.com
> 🖥 www.tropicaladventures.com

Job Description: Depending on the project, volunteers will prepare lesson plans, teach English, patrol beaches to protect and aid sea turtles, maintain trails, provide care for children in a daycare and nutrition centre, provide support for the local community, help in the retirement home and work with animals in their wildlife refuge centre.

Requirements: Minimum age 16.

Accommodation: Accommodation and meals normally provided by the host family. Some projects do allow a choice of lodging.

Additional Information: Costs include airport pick-up, in-country support, placement, training and much more.

Application Procedure: Apply online via the website.

CUBA

The chances of finding paid work in Cuba are minimal for people travelling from abroad. However, there are opportunities available for those seeking voluntary and teaching jobs.

Red tape

ADDRESS: EMBASSY OF CUBA
167 High Holborn, London WC1V 6PA
☎ 020 7240 2488
✆ embacuba@cubaldn.com
🖥 www.cubaldn.com

Visa requirements: Any person wishing to enter Cuba must be in possession of the relevant visa, which must be obtained before travel. For information on how to obtain these visas please contact the embassy of the Republic of Cuba. A Tourist Visa Card is necessary for almost all visitors, which is sometimes issued by the airline or agency from whom you buy your tickets.

For up-to-date information about visa requirements check with embassy before travel.

Voluntary work

The Cuba Solidarity Campaign

Job(s) Available: Volunteers.
Duration: 2–3 weeks work. There are 2 working holidays organised each year, one in the summer and one in the winter.
Working Hours: Approximately 6 mornings in total.
Cost: *Summer brigade:* £945 (approx). *Winter brigade:* £999 (approx). Costs include flights, accommodation, full board, full programme of guided visits, special visa and 3 days of rest and relaxation in another part of the island.

Head Office: c/o Unite T&G, Woodberry, 218 Green Lanes, London N4 2HB, UK
☎ 020 8800 0155
✆ finance@cuba-solidarity.org.uk
🖥 www.cuba-solidarity.org.uk

Company Description: The Cuba Solidarity Campaign (CSC) works in the UK to raise awareness of the illegal US blockade of Cuba, and to defend the Cuban people's right to self-determination. It publishes a quarterly magazine, *Cuba Si*, in addition to organising meetings, cultural events, and specialist tours to Cuba.
Job Description: Volunteers are needed to take part in a scheme in Cuba on a self-contained camp near Havana. The work involves light agricultural work, a programme of guided visits to schools, hospitals and community projects, with excursions arranged and transport to Havana provided during time off. There are many opportunities to meet Cubans, and enjoy vibrant Cuban culture first hand.
Accommodation: Included in cost.
Additional Information: The campaign organises the necessary visa.
Application Procedure: Contact the above address for application deadlines and further information.

ECUADOR

As well as the following entries, Concordia, UNA Exchange and Volunteer Action for Peace offer short-term international volunteer projects to Britons in Ecuador, while the CIEE can do the same for US citizens. See their entries in the *Worldwide* chapter for details.

Red tape

ADDRESS: CONSULATE OF ECUADOR
58–59 Trafalgar Square, Ist Floor, Uganda House, London WC2N 5DX
☎ 020 7451 0040
✆ gov.ecceulondres@mmrree.gov.ec
🖥 www.consuladoecuador.org.uk

Visa requirements: For voluntary work a category 12-VII visa must be obtained. These must be applied for in person at the consulate. This visa is granted for a maximum of one year.

Work permits: At the moment, the Consulate in the UK does not issue working visas. If you would like to work in Ecuador you will need to process this visa directly in Ecuador in person or by the employer.

For up-to-date information about visa requirements check with the embassy before travel.

Voluntary work

Bolívar Education Foundation

Job(s) Available: Volunteers.
Duration: Varies based on programme.
Cost: $25 registration fee and $250 participation fee which includes a personal adviser, 1 free pick-up at the airport, social events, dancing and cooking lessons, free internet access and an orientation meeting.

Head Office: Centro de Capacitación Simón Bolívar, Mariscal Foch E9-20 y Leonidas Plaza, Quito
☎ +593 2 223 4708
✉ jorge@ecuadorvolunteers.org
🖥 www.ecuadorvolunteers.org

Company Description: The Bolívar Education Foundation is a private, non-profit organization that is not associated with any political or religious activities. The foundation was created in January 2008 with the objective of channeling more efficiently our volunteers' work through several organizations. By doing so, the foundation creates a bridge between our volunteers and the organizations; volunteers benefit from the experience acquired through the projects and the organizations benefit from the time, love, and energy volunteers offer. Besides, the Simón Bolívar Volunteer Program has many programs within varied fields including children and youth, health, environment and agriculture, teaching, gender, elderly, development and animal welfare. Most of the work takes place in the capital of Ecuador but also in Cuenca, coast, jungle and the Galapagos.
Job Description: Volunteers may work with children and youths, the elderly, and teach or work in health, development or animal welfare.
Requirements: Minimum age 18. No previous experience or educational qualifications needed.
Accommodation: Volunteers are required to pay for their own accommodation but the foundation will help them find host families, apartments or hostels.
Application Procedure: Apply online at the above email address.

Planet Drum

Job(s) Available: Volunteers in greenhouse.
Duration: Minimum period of work 1 month, preferably 2–3 months.
Working Hours: 20 hours per week, 5 days per week, 8am–12 pm.
Cost: Volunteers are responsible for paying their own travel expenses. $15 per month for house expenses and $10 per week for communal dinners.

Head Office: Planet Drum Foundation, PO Box 31251, San Francisco, California 94131, USA
☎ +1 415 285 6556
✉ planetdrumecuador@yahoo.com
🖥 www.planetdrum.org

Company Description: Planet Drum seeks to be a voice for bioregional sustainability, education and culture. Eco Ecuador is an ongoing project in collaboration with an urban community located in Ecuador to create a sustainable local ecology.
Job Description: Greenhouse duties including planting seeds, mixing soil, watering and maintaining on-site composite facility as well as re-vegetation tasks such as clearing trails with a machete, digging holes for trees, planting trees and watering.
Requirements: Desire to help restore damaged biosphere. The following qualities are preferred but not necessary: previous travel experience, some degree of Spanish language ability and a background in environmental education.
Accommodation: Accommodation provided in a communal house for up to 6 volunteers at a time. $15 (£10) per month for wear and tear of apartment.
Application Procedure: Apply to Clay Plager-Unger, field projects manager, at the above email address. Include CV and letter explaining relevant experience, skills, travels, summary of intent, available dates, explanation of why you are drawn to this type of work and if you are comfortable living communally.

Rainforest Concern

Job(s) Available: Volunteers (4).
Duration: Minimum period of work 7 days. Required at any time.
Cost: For costs and availability please see the website for individual project details.

Head Office: 8 Clanricarde Gardens, London W2 4NA, UK
☎ 020 7229 2093
✉ info@rainforestconcern.org
🖥 www.rainforestconcern.org

Company Description: Rainforest Concern is a non-political charity dedicated to the conservation of vulnerable rainforest and the biodiversity they contain.

Job Description: Volunteers for reforestation/trail maintenance and the establishment of organic agriculture. The work involves an element of monitoring and of physical labour, such as reforestation or compiling species lists, or trail maintenance, depending on the projects being undertaken at the time. Current volunteer opportunities are in the cloud forests of western Ecuador and in Amazonian Ecuador. Volunteers are encouraged to help out with research and reserve maintenance and are invited to sponsor acres of forest for protection.

Requirements: No special skills are required, although Spanish would be helpful. Applicants must have a sincere interest in conservation, and be generally fit. Minimum age 18.

Additional Information: Further volunteer opportunities in endangered sea turtle conservation are available at our projects in Costa Rica and Panama; see www.rainforestconcern.org/how_can_i_help/volunteering for further volunteering information.

Application Procedure: To apply visit the above website at any time of year.

EL SALVADOR

The smallest Central American country, El Salvador is still most known for the Civil War, despite the fact that is has been over since 1992. There is a US$10 entrance fee, which is paid when applying for the tourist card. On leaving the country by air, a tax of US$30 is payable.

Red tape

ADDRESS: EL SALVADOR EMBASSY
8 Dorset Square, London NW1 6PU
☎ 020 7224 9800
✉ elsalvador.embassy@gmail.com

Visa requirements: Visitors entering El Salvador must have a passport which is valid for at least six months after departure, in addition to either a visa or a tourist card. Visas are issued by the consulate of El Salvador and the tourist card is generally issued for 90 days although this period will be evaluated according to the applicant's nationality and type of passport.

Visas are not required by nationals from Britain and other EU countries, Australia, Canada and the USA for stays of up to 30 days. However, for stays of over 30 days, all nationals need to apply for a multiple-entry visa in advance. 30 day extensions are available from the Salvadoran immigration department.

Teaching and language schools

Centro De Intercambio Y Solidaridad

Job(s) Available: Volunteer English teachers (7).
Duration: Minimum period of work 9 weeks, with 1 week vacation. See website for details of dates.
Working Hours: 16–20 hours per week, classes 3 days a week (Monday, Tuesday and Thursday, 5.15pm–7pm). Plus staff meetings and preparation time.

Head Office: Colonia Libertad, Avenida, Bolivar #103, San Salvador
☎ +503 2226 5362
✉ volunteer@cis-elsalvador.org
🖥 www.cis-elsalvador.org

Company Description: A multi-faceted non-profit organisation that supports education and social justice and promotes solidarity and cultural exchange across borders between the Salvadoran people and others in the search for development and diginity.

Job Description: Classes are small with 6–9 students per class. Additional teaching and volunteer opportunities are available. TEFL and popular educational methodology training provided. Volunteers receive a 50% discount on Spanish classes if there is one other person in their class, and 2 free weeks in the political-cultural programme to learn more about El Salvador and its history.

Requirements: Minimum age 18. Spanish and ESL training not necessary but useful. Fluent English necessary.

Accommodation: Room and board available for $80 per week with host family. Includes breakfast and dinner. Lunch costs $1.50–$3 per day.

Application Procedure: Apply to the English school coordinator at the above email address at least a month prior to start date. Interview not required but application and reference letter are. Applicants must qualify for a tourist visa in El Salvador.

GUATEMALA

Volunteers will find little work in Guatemala city but there are other openings in the surrounding areas. Some travellers find work in bars, restaurants and places to stay in Antigua, Panajachel or Quetzaltenango but on minimal wages. Volunteers can occasionally pick up yacht work around the Rio Dulce area. Check the notice boards at Bruno's Marina in Fronteras for such opportunities. Approximately 29% of the population lives below the poverty line and there is a 3.2% unemployment rate. Guatemala is particularly recommended for those who speak Spanish well and are seasoned travellers.

Red tape

ADDRESS: THE EMBASSY OF GUATEMALA
13 Fawcett Street London SW10 9HN
☎ 020 7351 3042
🖳 http://guatemala.embassy-uk.co.uk

Visa Requirements: Visas are not required by British, Canadian, Australian or US citizens to enter Guatemala and they can visit freely for up to 90 days. If your stay in Guatemala is longer than 90 days you should go to the General Directorate of Migration in Guatemala to apply for an extension to the 90-day rule. British tourists can also travel within any of the CA-4 countries (Honduras, Nicaragua, El Salvador and Guatemala) for a period of up to 90 days without completing entry and exit formalities at border Immigration checkpoints. Passports must have at least six months validity before travel. There is also a security tax payable at the airport of US$3.

For up-to-date information about visa requirements check with the embassy before travel.

ARCAS

Job(s) Available: Volunteers.
Duration: Flexible and ongoing. Minimum period of work 1 week. In Hawaii, sea turtle nesting season is July–December, though there is other work to be done year round.
Working Hours: *Peten:* roughly 4 hours per day 7 days per week. *Hawaii:* nightly patrols, daily data entry, environmental education. Schedules at both projects are flexible.

> **Head Office:** Asociación de Rescate y Conservación de Vida Silvestre, 4 Ave. 2-47, Sector B5, Zona 8 Mixco, San Cristobal
> ☎ +502 247 840 96
> 🖂 arcas@intelnet.net.gt
> 🖳 www.arcasguatemala.com

Cost: $250 additional charge for reservation, airport pick-up and transportation to project site. *Peten:* $125 per week for food and lodging. *Hawaii:* $70 per week for lodging.
Company Description: Asociación de Rescate y Conservación de Vida Silvestre (Wildlife Rescue and Conservation Association) is a Guatemalan non-governmental, non-profit organisation, legally registered with the Guatemalan government and the IUCN, committed to preserving wildlife and its habitat.
Job Description: *Peten:* at the Rescue Centre, volunteers will help feed and care for animals that have been confiscated from illegal wildlife traffickers. Animals include spider and howler monkeys, parrots, macaws, jaguars, kinkajous and coatimundis among others. Volunteers have an opportunity to see the difficulties of conserving endangered species in a developing country. The centre encourages volunteers to come up with ideas for the better care of the animals. Volunteers will also spend time working with Guatemalans. *Hawaii:* at ARCAS's sea turtle conservation project in the village of Hawaii on the Pacific coast, volunteers help in conducting nightly patrols in search of nesting olive ridley and leatherback sea turtles and collecting research
Accommodation: Provided.
Application Procedure: See details on website.
Additional Information: Email arcas@intelnet.net.gt for up-to-date information. Information available on the website as well.

Maya Pedal

Job(s) Available: Volunteers in cycle mechanics, producing PDF instructions, sales and marketing, translation and workshop engineers.

Duration: Volunteers can decide length of stay.

Working Hours: 8am–4pm, Monday to Friday.

Cost: A small weekly fee. Volunteers are responsible for their own airfare and food.

Head Office: Asociación Maya Pedal, Cantón San Antonio, San Andrés Itzapa, Chimaltenango
☎ +502 7489 4671
✉ mayapedal@hotmail.com
🖥 www.mayapedal.org

Company Description: Maya Pedal is a NGO that works to recycle used bicycles and build pedal-powered machines called bicimaquinas which support the work of local, small-scale, self-sustainable projects.

Job Description: Tasks may include making pedal-powered machines, mixing concrete, painting, finishing, fixing up bikes brought in by the public, taking donated bikes and making them ready for sale, selling bikes at local markets and events, making links with Guatemalan NGOs and local cooperatives, writing and photographing instructions for each bicimaquina, and translating all instructions from English to Spanish and other languages.

Requirements: Must have previous relevant experience and have reasonable Spanish comprehension.

Accommodation: Provided.

Application Procedure: Download an application form from the website and email to the above address. Applications should be written in English.

MEXICO

Paid employment is difficult to find in Mexico and must be approved by the Mexican government before a visa will be issued to enter Mexico. Permits are generally issued to people who are sponsored by companies in Mexico. Visitors entering Mexico as tourists are not permitted to engage in any paid activities under any circumstances though this does not stop private language schools employing English teachers who have tourist visas. This is illegal.

There are a growing number of opportunities for voluntary work in Mexico. British applicants can find voluntary work in Mexico through Outreach International (www.outreachinternational.co.uk), Concordia, UNA Exchange or Volunteer Action for Peace, US nationals through the CIEE.

Red tape

ADDRESS: MEXICAN EMBASSY
16 St George Street, London W1S 1FD
☎ 020 7499 8586
✉ consulmexuk@sre.gob.mx
🖥 www.sre.gob.mx/reinounido

Work permits: A Mexican firm or company must apply on the employee's behalf. Further details can be found at the Mexican Consulate website www.sre.gob.mx/reinounido or contact the embassy for more information.

Voluntary work: A Non-Immigrant Visitor carnet (FM3) is necessary for anyone entering Mexico wishing to perform activities of social assistance or voluntary work in private or public institutions. The FM3 is not available to all nationalities, check with your local Mexican consulate for details.

For up-to-date information about visa requirements check with the embassy before travel.

Industrial and office work

Proworld Service Corps _____

Job(s) Available: Interns.
Duration: Minimum period of work 2 weeks.
Working Hours: 4–6 hours per day.
Cost: Fee of $1,795–$1,895 required for first 2 weeks; $490–$585 for each week thereafter. Cost includes full room and board with a local family,

Head Office: 324 East Oak St, Fort Collins, Colorado 80524, USA
☎ +187 7429 6753
🖷 info@myproworld.org
🖥 www.myproworld.org

domestic transportation, Spanish classes in Peru and Mexico, cultural and adventure activities, project funding and support, and health and travel insurance.
Company Description: Promotes social and economic development, empowers communities, conserves the environment and cultivates educated, compassionate global citizens. Participants will work abroad with the community and one of the affiliated non-governmental organisations (NGOs), government social programmes, or a Proworld initiated project. Projects are determined by community need and participants' skills and interests. Programmes are offered in Belize, Brazil, Ghana, India, Mexico, Peru and Thailand.
Job Description: Interns are needed for public healthcare, public health education and assistance, health research, environmental conservation, environmental tourism, cultural and museum work, archaeology, construction, education and teaching, women's rights, human rights and social assistance.
Accommodation: Included in cost.
Application Procedure: Apply to Adam Saks, placement adviser 1–3 months before participation. Phone interview necessary once accepted.

Teaching and language schools

Ahpla Institute _____

Job(s) Available: English teachers (35).
Duration: Minimum period of work 6 months.
Working Hours: 7am–9am and 5pm–7pm.
Requirements: Applicants must be educated, flexible, willing to work with a team and travel. People skills and personality are a must.

Head Office: Juan Escutia No 97, Colonia Condesa, C P 06140 D.F
☎ +555 286 9016, (extension 113)
🖷 kallen@ahpla.com
🖥 www.ahpla.com

Accommodation: Ahpla Institute offers no help with accommodation or flights, however help is given with working papers when teacher has shown a commitment to Ahpla.
Application Procedure: Applications to Karen Julie Allen, operations manager.

Culturlingua Language Center _____

Job(s) Available: English teachers.
Duration: Minimum 5 months.
Working Hours: 6 hours per day, 5 days a week, Monday to Friday.
Company Description: Culturlingua is a small, privately owned institution dedicated to teaching both English and Spanish.

Head Office: Morelos 636 Sur, C P 59680 Zamora, Michoacàn
☎ +52 351 516 0659
🖷 cebe1962@prodigy.net.mx
🖥 www.culturlingua.com

Requirements: Native English speaker with TESOL, ESL or any teacher's certificate. Must be adaptable to teach children, adolescents or adults. Must be positive and friendly.
Accommodation: Can be provided.
Application Procedure: Applications to the above address/email at any time.

Dunham Institute

Job(s) Available: English teachers (4).
Duration: To work minimum 5 months.
Working Hours: 3–4 hours in the afternoon teaching. Study Spanish in the mornings.
Pay: Unpaid.
Requirements: English teachers required with ESL certificate. Must be a native English speaker.
Accommodation: Available with a local family and with 2 hours of Spanish tuition a day.
Application Procedure: Applications to Joanna Robinson, academic coordinator at above address.

Head Office: Avenida Coronel Urbina 30, Chiapa de Corzo, Chiapas
☎ +52 9 6161 61498
✆ academic-coordinator@dunhaminstitute.com

Teachers Latin America

Job(s) Available: Various positions.
Duration: Minimum period of work 4 weeks.
Pay: $600–$1,000 per month.
Company Description: A TEFL organisation specialising in job placements around Latin America.
Job Description: Each position differs; applicants will be given job or internship details based on where they would like to work. The website details several of the positions.
Requirements: Minimum high school qualification and teaching credential (TEFL or CELTA). Other experience considered. High degree of fluency in English required.
Accommodation: Accommodation and board available at cost of $150–$300 per month.
Application Procedure: To apply contact Guy Courchesne, employment adviser. Telephone or email interviews only.

Head Office: Avenida Cuauhtemoc 793, Colonia Narvarte
☎ +52 5 5256 4108
✆ teachers@innovative-english.com
🖥 www.innovative-english.com

PERU

Chances of finding paid summer work in Peru are minimal. However, there are some opportunities to be found within the voluntary and teaching sectors.

Red tape

ADDRESS: EMBASSY OF PERU
52 Sloane Street, London SW1X 9SP
☎ 020 7838 9223
✆ peruconsulate-uk@btconnect.com
🖥 www.peruembassy-uk.com

Visa requirements: British, Irish and EU nationals do not need a visa when travelling to Peru. The same is true for nationals of the US, Australia or New Zealand. You are allowed to stay in Peru for up to 183 days. For stays beyond 183 days you must renew your visa. Volunteers who do not receive a wage can travel on a tourist visa. However, anyone hoping to take up paid employment in Peru requires a working permit.

Voluntary work

Hampy

Job(s) Available: Volunteers: chocco project, colibrí street kids project, coordinator, ecological school project, shelter for domestic violence project and website developer.

Duration: After 1 week training, a minimum of 1 month is required except for the volunteer coordinator which requires a minimum of 3 months and the website developer which requires a minimum of 2 months.

> **Head Office:** Urb. Santa Mónica, Jr. José Carlos Mariategui B-22, Wanchaq, Cusco
> ☎ +51 84 984 761072
> ✆ info@hampy.org
> 🖳 www.hampy.org

Cost: $300 for 1 week training programme. Spanish lessons not included in the price but Hampy does offer study options.

Company Description: Hampy is a self-sustaining organisation providing volunteer and academic experiences to local people and foreigners with a principal goal: to improve the lifestyle and well-being of the rural and economically depressed populations under the concept of self-sustaining development.

Job Description: *Chocco project:* assist with community projects, water and sanitation, education, hikes and many other jobs. *Colibri street kids project:* assist in setting up a market where kids can offer their services like shoe shining in appropriated hours and with all the regular permissions from the local government and police. *Coordinator:* assist with all the logistics involved in coordinating volunteers. *Ecological school project:* assist with the greenhouse, basic hygiene education and practising the three 'Rs' (reducing, recycling, reusing), at the Huacarpay ecological school, help them improve a rocket stove for the kitchen and teach primary school kids how to purify water. *Shelter for domestic violence project:* provide support for victims; assist in art therapy, legal counselling and emotional support. *Website developer:* help with all aspects of technology and promotion.

Requirements: Minimum age 18. Must complete at least 1 week training programme before volunteering.

Accommodation: Hampy helps volunteers to find accommodation with a host family, in a hostel, or in an apartment. The cost to stay with a family is $15 per day, including 3 meals and full board. Hostel prices vary but maximum price is $25 per day, including breakfast.

Application Procedure: Apply to the email address above.

Kiya Survivors

Job(s) Available: Volunteers.

Duration: Placements of 1–6 months, starting all year round.

> **Head Office:** Suite 41, 41–43 Portland Road, Hove BN3 5DQ, UK
> ☎ 01273 721092
> ✆ andrew@kiyasurvivors.org
> 🖳 www.kiyasurvivors.org

Cost: Cost ranges between £800 and £2,999. A full 1-month programme costs £1,950 and includes; 4 day Inca trail, return flights from Cusco to Lima, 1 night in a Lima hotel, UK training, Lima city tour, Spanish lessons while in Peru, 2 nights in a Cusco hotel, Cusco city tours and a trip to the Sacred Valley.

Company Description: Kiya runs a volunteer placement programme at the Rainbow Centre (1 hour's drive from Cusco) which supports children who have been abused, neglected or have special needs. Recent placements include a counselling internship, occupational therapy, physiotherapy and speech therapy. However, new projects start all the time and all types of help are required to maintain the running of the centre.

Requirements: Minimum age 18.

Accommodation: Included in cost. The volunteer house has cooking facilities and local markets provide cheap fresh food.

Application Procedure: Contact Andrew at the above address or email.

BUNAC: Volunteer Peru

Job(s) Available: Volunteer placements.

Duration: Allows participants to spend 8–12 weeks working as a volunteer in Peru.

Cost: Programme costs start at £1,299 for 8 weeks and includes accommodation and most food.

> Head Office: BUNAC, 16 Bowling Green Lane, London EC1R 0QH, UK
> ☎ 020 7251 3472
> ✆ enquiries@bunac.org.uk
> 🖥 www.bunac.org.uk

Job Description: There is a great need for volunteers with specific practical skills, for example IT. Placements can also be education or based on manual/unskilled labour.

Requirements: Applicants are expected to have basic conversational Spanish language skills. The programme is open to UK residents. Minimum age 18.

Accommodation: Provided with a host family as part of the programme fee as are all support services in the UK and in Peru for the duration of your trip.

Application Procedure: For further details contact BUNAC at the above address or visit www.bunac.org.uk to download an application pack. Orientation interviews will be held.

USA

Despite a slowing economy relative to most other countries, the USA has low unemployment and there is still a strong demand for workers to fill a wide variety of specialised summer jobs. Opportunities for summer work in the USA are so numerous that in addition to those listed below, there are thousands listed on websites including www.j1jobs.com, www.coolworks.com, www.apexusa.org, www.greatcampjobs.com and www.seasonalemployment.com/summer to name but a few. National and state parks in the USA list their recruitment needs on their websites; a list of parks and their contact details can be found at www.nps.gov.

Placing an advertisement in an American paper may lead to the offer of a job. *The New York Times* (www.nytimes.com) is published by A O Sulzberger, and has a UK office at 66 Buckingham Gate, London SW1E 6AU, UK (020 7799 2981).

Au pairing in the USA differs from au pairing in Europe since the hours are much longer. The basic requirements are that you be between 18 and 26, speak English, show at least 200 hours of recent childcare experience and provide a criminal record check.

Voluntary work in the USA can be arranged through the Winant-Clayton Volunteer Association, Volunteer Action for Peace, UNA Exchange, Concordia, International Voluntary Service, the CIEE, and Service Civil International.

Red tape

ADDRESS: EMBASSY OF THE UNITED STATES
24 Grosvenor Square, London W1A 1AE
☎ 020 7499 9000
🖳 www.usembassy.org.uk

Visa requirements: Since the introduction of the Visa Waiver Program, the tourist visa requirement is waived in the case of over 20 nationalities, including British and Australian passport holders (see the website www.usembassy.org.uk for full listings and conditions). Nationals of these countries may enter the USA for up to 90 days for tourism or business, provided they meet all of the regulations for visa free travel. It is particularly important to note that certain travellers are not eligible to travel visa free, for instance those who have been arrested and/or convicted of an offence, those with passports indicating that the bearer is a British subject, British Dependent Territories Citizen, British Overseas Citizen or a British national (Overseas) Citizen. As of 26 October 2006, all passports issued on or after this date must be biometric (electronic) in order to qualify for visa free travel.

Since 1 October 2004 visitors from 27 countries including Britain have been digitally photographed and electronically fingerprinted by US immigration before being given permission to enter the USA. Anyone entering the USA to work requires the appropriate work visa. Under no circumstances can a person who has entered the USA as a tourist take up any form of employment paid or unpaid.

Work permits: Anyone taking up temporary employment, whether paid or unpaid, requires the appropriate work visa. There are a number of possible visas for temporary workers, au pairs, exchange visitors and cultural exchange visitors on EVPs (recognised Exchange Visitor Programmes such as BUNAC and Camp America). Most of the opportunities listed in this chapter are covered by the Exchange Visitor visa (J), which is arranged by the organisations with entries or the Temporary Worker visa (H). Employment-based H-2B visas are available through major employers of seasonal workers (such as in ski resorts) only after the employer receives Labor certification from the Department of Labor (which takes three to six months).

Au pair: Visa (J1) is available through officially approved exchange visitor programmes overseen by the Public Affairs Division of the Department of State.

Voluntary work: Individuals participating in a voluntary service programme benefiting US local communities, who establish that they are members of and have a commitment to a particular recognised religious or non-profit charitable organisation may, in certain cases, enter the USA with business (B-1) visas, or visa free, if eligible, provided that the work performed is traditionally done by volunteer charity workers. No salary or remuneration will be paid from a US source other than an allowance or other reimbursement for expenses incidental to the stay in the USA, and they will not engage in the selling of articles and/or solicitation and acceptance of donations. Volunteers should carry with them a letter from their US sponsor, which contains their name and date and place of birth, their foreign permanent residence address, the name and address of their initial destination in the USA, and the anticipated duration of the voluntary assignment. The US embassy defines a voluntary service plan as 'an organised project conducted by a recognised religious or nonprofit charitable organisation to provide assistance to the poor or the needy or to further a religious or charitable cause'.

For up-to-date information about visa requirements check with the embassy before travel.

Agricultural work

Surfing Goat Dairy

Job(s) Available: Internship.
Duration: Minimum period of work 3 months.
Working Hours: 7:30am–5:30pm, Monday to Friday.
Pay: $5 per hour.

Head Office: 3651 Omaopio Rd, Kula, Hawaii 96790
☎ +1 808 878 2870
📠 info@surfinggoatdairy.com
🖥 www.surfinggoatdairy.com

Company Description: A small goat dairy farm located on the island of Maui in Hawaii with over 10 years in the business.
Job Description: Assist with all aspects of running a dairy farm and making cheese.
Requirements: Must not be afraid of hard work. Candidates need to have experience with at least one of the following: cheese making, goat care or animal husbandry, agri-tourism or hospitality experience, or a culinary background.
Accommodation: Room and board provided.
Application Procedure: Contact Angela at the above email address for application and complete program information. Write a bit of information about yourself in your introduction email.

WWOOF Hawaii (Willing Workers on Organic Farms)

Job(s) Available: Volunteers on organic farms in Hawaii. Over 125 choices.
Duration: Opportunities may be available all year round.
Pay: Pocket money is not provided.
Cost: Hawaii membership is $20. Cash or cheques

Head Office: 4429 Carlson Road, Nelson, British Columbia V1L 6X3, Canada
☎ +125 0354 4417
📠 wwoofcan@shaw.ca
🖥 www.wwoofhawaii.org

are accepted, or through Paypal. WWOOF will then send you the WWOOF Hawaii booklet.
Company Description: US youths and hundreds of people from all over the world go 'WWOOFing' every summer. Farm hosts are available in most states and on 5 of the Hawaiian islands.
Job Description: Volunteer experiences range from small homesteads to large farms. Duties include general garden work, etc.
Requirements: Minimum age of 16. If not a US citizen, only EU nationals with valid tourist visas need apply.
Accommodation: Free board and lodging provided.
Application Procedure: Applications can be made online, or send full name, mailing address and registration fee.

Sports, couriers and camping

Camp America

Job(s) Available: Camp America is looking for enthusiastic, outgoing individuals who are willing to get stuck in and have a laugh as camp counsellors. There are numerous roles and positions available across the USA, from lifeguarding, arts and crafts, football coach, rock climbing and jet skiing.

Head Office: Camp America, 37A Queen's Gate, London SW7 5HR, UK
☎ 020 7581 7373
🖥 www.campamerica.co.uk

Duration: Applicants must be available to leave the UK between 1 May and 27 June for a minimum of 9 weeks.

Cost: Approximately $474.

Pays: Dependent on age, rate and experience, ranges from approximately $575–$1,650.

Company Description: Camp America is one of the world's leading summer camp programmes, offering its counsellors over 40 years of experience placing people from Europe, Asia, Africa, Australia and New Zealand at American summer camps.

Job Description: *Camp counsellors:* required to undertake childcare and/or teaching sports activities, music, arts, drama and dance.

Requirements: No experience required. Any coaching or childcare experience would be an advantage. Must like kids, be open minded and willing to work hard and play even harder. Minimum age 18. Fluent English speaker.

Accommodation: Counsellors are offered return flights from London and other selected airports worldwide to New York and transfers to particular camp, free accommodation and meals, up to 10 weeks' travel time after camp, plus 24-hour support and medical insurance.

Application Procedure: Visit www.campamerica.co.uk and complete an online application form. You will then choose an interview location and date. Early application is advised.

CCUSA (Camp Counsellors USA)

Job(s) Available: Camp counsellor, support staff.

Duration: From May/June to August/September. Minimum period of work 9 weeks.

Working Hours: Work weekly shift patterns which vary from camp to camp. *Camp counsellor:* a typical day runs from 7am–10.30pm.

Support staff: a typical day runs from 6.15am–11pm.

Head Office: 2330 Marinship Way, Suite 250, Sausalito, CA 94965
Office: Unit 6.04, 6 Morie Street, Wandsworth Town, London SW18 1SL, UK
☎ 020 8874 6325
✆ info@ccusa.co.uk
🖳 www.ccusa.com

Pay: Wages are dependent on age and range from $800–$1,296.

Company Description: CCUSA has been sending young people to work on international work/travel placements since 1986. CCUSA is a visa sponsoring company and find the best job on an individual basis.

Job Description: Working at an American summer camp is a fun and rewarding experience. If you want to do something completely different with your summer and are keen for a new challenge then contact CCUSA.

Requirements: Minimum age 18. Both students and non-students welcome. Fluent English is necessary. *Camp counsellor:* enthusiastic with a love of children. *Support staff:* hardworking and enthusiastic.

Accommodation: Included.

Additional Information: CCUSA also offers programmes in South America, South Africa, Canada and Russia. *Camp Counsellors Russia*: work in Russia at a children's summer camp for 4 or 8 weeks between June and August. Flights and insurance included in package – applicants do not have to speak Russian. *Volunteer Experience South Africa*: work in 1 of 18 projects in South Africa or Namibia, with something to suit all tastes from community building to riding for the disabled or caring for orphans. *Camp Counsellors Canada*: work in Canada in a children's summer camp for at least 9 weeks starting from June or July. Camp placements tailored to suit your experiences and preferences. *Work and Play Canada*: spend time in the ski-fields of Canada. Work is available with ski resorts, hotels and inns, restaurants and shops.

Application Procedure: Apply online at www.ccusa.com. Interviews will be held. Foreign applicants are welcome to apply but it is down to the discretion of the US embassy whether a visa is granted.

USA

THE AMERICAS

321

Camp Kirby

Job(s) Available: Kitchen aid/dish washers, counselor-in-training director (1).

Duration: From June to August.

Company Description: Since 1923 Camp Kirby has been providing children the opportunity to grow, make friends, have fun, and come home with memories to last a lifetime. Camp Kirby has 47 acres, including beautiful, pristine forest and 1.5 miles of beach, is located on Samish Island in Skagit County. Owned and operated by Camp Fire USA, Camp Kirby is constantly growing to meet the needs and excite the imagination of Kirby campers.

Requirements: All staff must have current CPR and first aid cards.

Accommodation: Accommodation and meals included.

Application Procedure: Download an application form from www.campkirby.org.

> **Head Office:** Camp Fire USA Samish Council 2217 Wabum st Bellingham, WA 98229
> ☎ +1 360 733 5710
> ✆ info@campfiresamishcouncil.org
> 🖥 www.campkirby.org

Campower (Resort America programme)

Job(s) Available: Support staff at American summer camps.

Duration: Applicants must be available to leave the UK between 1 May and 27 June for a minimum of 9 weeks.

Cost: £474.

Pay: $900–$1,200 (dependent on age and experience).

Company Description: Campower, a programme of Camp America, is open to full-time students who want to work behind the scenes of American Summer camps.

Job Description: Typical job roles involve assisting in kitchen/laundry duties, administration and general camp maintenance. This supportive role represents an ideal camp alternative for those not wishing to work directly with children.

Requirements: No experience required. Experience in administrative roles, maintenance, health care and catering would be helpful but not mandatory. Must be full-time student.

Accommodation: Participants are offered free return flights from London and other selected airports worldwide to New York and transfer to their camp, free accommodation and meals, up to 10 weeks of travel time after camp, 24 hour support and medical insurance.

Application Procedure: Visit www.campamerica.co.uk and complete online application form.

> **Head Office:** Camp America, 37a Queen's Gate, London SW7 5HR, UK
> ☎ 020 758 7373
> 🖥 www.campamerica.co.uk

BUNAC: KAMP

Job(s) Available: KAMP (Kitchen and Maintenance Programme) is a low cost programme for people looking to work behind the scenes in a support role at a US summer camp.

Duration: 8–9 weeks.

Cost: The programme fee is approximately £287 and includes return flights to the US.

Pay: Highly competitive salary. Receive approximately $1,350 for 9 weeks' work.

Job Description: BUNAC places applicants, arranges the special work/travel visa, flight and travel to camp. In addition, participants are given free board and lodging at camp, a salary and up to 6 weeks of independent travel afterwards.

> **Head Office:** BUNAC, 16 Bowling Green Lane, London EC1R 0QH, UK
> ☎ 020 7251 3472
> ✆ enquiries@bunac.org.uk
> 🖥 www.bunac.org.uk

Requirements: The programme is open to those who are currently enrolled at a British university, studying full-time at degree (or advanced tertiary or postgraduate) level. Gap year students are not eligible. Minimum age 18.

Accommodation: Provided.

Application Procedure: Apply for a BUNAC account at www.bunac.org.uk and complete an application form.

BUNAC: Summer Camp USA

Job(s) Available: Counsellor positions in US summer camps.

Duration: Up to a 9 week work period.

Cost: The programme fee is approximately £287.

Job Description: A low-cost, non-profit camp counsellor programme run by BUNAC. Provides job, work papers, flights, salary, board and lodging, and a flexible length of independent holiday time after the work period.

> Head Office: 16 Bowling Green Lane, London EC1R 0QH, UK
> ☎ 020 7251 3472
> ✆ camps@bunac.org.uk
> 🖳 www.bunac.org.uk

Requirements: Applicants must have experience of working with children and be living in the UK at the time of making their application. Must have a full, valid passport and be able to speak English fluently. Minimum age 19.

Accommodation: Provided.

Application Procedure: Apply online at www.bunac.org.uk.

Geneva Point Centre

Job(s) Available: Food service staff, housekeeping, maintenance, guest services.

Company Description: Geneva Point Centre believe that all persons are called to wholeness of spirit, mind and body, so that they may become effective stewards and leaders in a complex world.

> Head Office: 108 Geneva Point Road Moultonboro, NH 03254
> ☎ +1 603 2534366
> ✆ pclaypoole@genevapoint.org
> 🖳 www.genevapoint.org

Geneva Point is a conference centre and camp serving Christian and non-profit groups for conferences, retreats, personal and family events and camps.

Application Procedure: Contact Peter Claypoole at pclaypoole@genevapoint.org.

UK Elite Soccer

Job(s) Available: Seasonal soccer coach (40), summer soccer coach (70).

Duration: *Seasonal coach:* March to November 2009, July to November 2009. *Summer coach:* 2 months, July and August 2009.

> Head Office: 210 Malapardis Road, Suite 201, Cedar Knolls, NJ 07927
> ☎ +1 97 363 19802 ext.206
> ✆ AndyB@UKElite.com
> 🖳 www.UKElite.com

Working Hours: *Seasonal coach:* full-time, 20+ hours per week. *Summer coach:* full-time, 20+ hours per week.

Pay: *Seasonal coach:* $9,000 salary, $11,000 expenses. *Summer coach:* $1,700 salary, $4,000 expenses.

Company Description: Provide high-quality soccer programmes in the USA with highly trained and diverse staff. All general information can be found on www.UKElite.com or on the employment homepage.

Requirements: Fluent English is necessary. *Seasonal coach:* coaching qualifications, teaching qualifications. *Summer coach:* experience working with children, full clean driving license preferred.

Accommodation: Board and accommodation provided.

Application Procedure: Apply to Jobs@UKElite.com or contact David Boyd +197 3631 9802 extension 209 or Andy Broadbent extension 206. Interviews will take place in November. Foreign applicants welcome to apply.

Voluntary work

Buddhist Work-Study Programs at Nyingma Centers

Job(s) Available: Volunteers.
Duration: Minimum 3 months. Longer programmes also available.
Working Hours: Monday–Saturday.
Pay: Housing, vegetarian meals, and free evening classes in various aspects of Buddhist study and practice.

Location: Northern California
☎ +1 512 981 1987
✆ contact@nyingmavolunteer.org
🖳 www.nyingmavolunteer.org

Cost: Travel expenses to and from Nyingma Centers.
Company Description: The Nyingma Volunteer Programs offer individuals the opportunity to live, work, practise and study in a Buddhist community. Two locations: city centre in Berkeley, CA or at a country retreat centre in the Redwood Coastal region of Sonoma county, CA (100 miles north of San Francisco).
Job Description: These residential volunteer programs are a rigorous and challenging experience combining work, spiritual practice and study with community living. Volunteers work with various projects, ranging from landscaping to publishing, and fundraising to book binding.
Requirements: Volunteers do not need to be Buddhist or have specific skills to apply. An appreciation for work and a sincere interest in the Buddhist teachings is required. Minimum age 21.
Accommodation: Shared accommodation provided, usually two to a room.
Application Procedure: Email the above address for an application form.

Gibbon Conservation Center

Job(s) Available: Voluntary primate keepers (up to 3 at any time).
Working Hours: 6.30am–5pm, 7 days a week. Opportunities for time off depend on the number of volunteers.

Head Office: PO Box 800249, Santa Clarita, CA 91380
☎ +1 661 296 2737
✆ volunteer@gibboncenter.org
🖳 www.gibboncenter.org

Company Description: This non-profit organisation houses the largest group of gibbons in the Americas. It is devoted to the study, preservation, and propagation of this small ape.
Job Description: Voluntary primate keepers to work with gibbons at the centre. Duties include preparing food and feeding, changing water, cleaning enclosures, observing behaviour (if time permits), entering data into computer (Apple Mac), maintaining grounds etc.
Requirements: Minimum age 20. Applicants must be well motivated, love animals, be capable of retaining unfamiliar information, get along with a variety of people, be in good physical condition and able to work outside in extreme weather conditions. They will need to have the following medical tests: stool cultures, ova and parasite stool test, standard blood chemistry and haematology, tuberculosis (or written proof from a doctor certifying that they have been vaccinated against tuberculosis) and Hepatitis B. Also required are vaccinations against tetanus (within the last 5 years), rubella, measles and Hepatitis B (if not already immune).
Accommodation: Provided. Volunteers must make their own travel arrangements and buy their own food locally.
Application Procedure: Applications to Volunteer Coordinator at the above address/email.

Kalani Oceanside Retreat

Job(s) Available: Opportunities for volunteering exist in food service, agriculture/landscaping maintence, and housekeeping.
Duration: Minimum of 1, 2 or 3 months.
Working Hours: *1, 2 or 3-month terms:* 30 hours of volunteer time per week, or 4 shifts a week.
Cost: *3-month term:* $1,800 lodging or $1,500 camping. *2-month term:* $1,500 lodging or $1,200 camping. *1-month term:* $1,000 camping.
Company Description: Kalani Oceanside Retreat is a non-profit, yoga, agricultural and inter-cultural conference retreat centre located on the big island of Hawai with 120 acres along the pacific coast, surrounded by tropical forest and walkways to explore.
Job Description: The retreat centre operates with the assistance of approximately 80 resident volunteers who help to provide services to the guests of the retreat.
Requirements: Volunteers must be in good health and have some form of health insurance. Experience in the area for which the applicant volunteers is preferred. Minimum age 18.
Accommodation: In exchange for volunteering, participants receive 3 buffet meals, activities and classes and shared lodging. *3-month term:* receive a week long vacation *2-month term:* gets 2 days vacation.
Application Procedure: Application form is available from the above address and the website www.kalani.com/volunteer/apply.

> **Head Office:** RR 2 Box 4500, Pahoa, Hawaii 96778
> ☎ +1 80 8965 0468 (extension 117)
> ✆ volunteer@kalani.com
> 🖥 www.kalani.com

Childcare America/Au Pair in America

Job(s) Available: Au pair and nanny stays in the USA.
Duration: Visa-supported 1-year stay.
Pay: Families provide full round-trip air fare, medical insurance and part-time college course plus 2 weeks paid holiday. Salary up to $250 per week for qualified nannies and a minimum of $195.75 per week for au pairs.
Company Description: Childcare America offer positions to applicants aged 18–26 with good childcare experience. Full local counsellor support is provided to introduce friends and give guidance with every aspect of the stay.
Job Description: Choose from a wide range of approved families from across the USA. 4 days' orientation is provided in the USA.
Requirements: Applicants must be able to drive.
Application Procedure: Apply online through www.aupairinamerica.com.

> **Head Office:** Childcare International Ltd, Trafalgar House, Grenville Place, London NW7 3SA, UK
> ☎ 020 8906 3116
> ✆ office@childint.co.uk
> 🖥 www.childint.co.uk

Other employment in the USA

BUNAC: Work America

Job(s) Available: The programme enables students to take virtually any summer job in the USA.
Duration: A special work and travel visa allows students to work and travel between May and October.
Cost: Approximately £259 plus support funds upon arrival in US.

> **Head Office:** BUNAC, 16 Bowling Green Lane, London EC1R 0QH, UK
> ☎ 020 7251 3472
> ✆ enquiries@bunac.org.uk
> 🖥 www.bunac.org

Job Description: Work America is a general work and travel programme open to students through BUNAC. Provides the opportunity to earn living and travelling costs. BUNAC provides a job directory, which is packed with jobs from which to choose and arrange work before going.

Requirements: The programme is open to those who are currently enrolled at a British university or college studying at degree (or advanced tertiary or postgraduate) level; unfortunately gap year students are not eligible. Minimum age 18.

Application Procedure: Visit www.bunac.org for more details and to download an application form. First time application will be required to attend an interview with the US Embassy. Early application is strongly advised.

CIEE (Council on International Educational Exchange)

Jobs Available: Opportunities for international work experience.

Duration: A student's work experience can last for up to 4 months and they can travel around the USA for a further month. For US students going abroad it varies according to visa restrictions.

Cost: Varies depending on the type and length of programme.

> **Head Office:** 300 Fore Street, Portland, ME 04101
> ☎ +1 20 755 34000 or +1 800 40 STUDY (toll-free)
> 🖰 info@ciee.org
> 🖥 www.ciee.org

Company Description: The Council on International Educational Exchange is the leading US non-governmental international education organisation. CIEE creates and administers programs that allow high school and university students and educators to study and teach abroad. It also sponsors numerous international exchange opportunities for young people to live, study, train, work and travel in the USA.

Application Procedure: For more information please contact CIEE at the above address. To find a CIEE representative in your country, check out the directory at www.ciee.org/representatives.

Dolphins Plus

Job(s) Available: Internships.

Duration: Minimum period of work 4 weeks throughout the year.

Pay: Unpaid.

Company Description: Dolphins Plus is committed to the conservation and protection of marine mam-

> **Head Office:** 31 Corrine Place, Key Largo, Florida 33037
> ☎ +1 305 451 1993
> 🖰 education@dolphinsplus.com
> 🖥 www.dolphinsplus.com

mals worldwide through education, research, experiential learning and environmental awareness.

Job Description: Work with educated researchers and animal care staff members, assist with ongoing research projects, aspects of animal care and husbandry, guest relations and day-to-day operations. Includes diet preparation, overseeing swim sessions, basic cleaning and maintenance.

Requirements: Minimum age 18, must have completed at least 1 semester of university and have an interest in the marine mammalogy field.

Accommodation: Accommodation not provided but the internship coordinator can assist interns in finding affordable housing in close proximity.

Application Procedure: Apply by sending a completed application form (available on the website) university transcript, CV, photograph, 2 letters of reference and a $25 application fee by post to Crystal at the above address.

Internship USA Programme

Job(s) Available: Course-related work experience/training placements. IST Plus can give applicants access to an employer database. Work and Travel programme now open.

Head Office: IST Plus Rosedale House, Rosedale Road, Surrey TW9 2SZ, UK
☎ 020 8939 9057
✆ info@istplus.com
🖳 www.istplus.com

Duration: *Work experience/placements:* period of work up to 12 months in the USA, with an optional travel period of up to 30 days following placement. *Work and Travel:* from May to October.

Cost: Participants pay a programme fee of £540 with £40 increments for each additional month of stay. This includes insurance and US government SEVIS fee. *Work and Travel:* £460 including medical insurance and SEVIS.

Job Description: *Work experience/placements:* this scheme enables students and recent graduates to complete a period of course-related work experience/training in the USA. *Work and Travel:* take up almost any job and work for up to 4 months, then travel another 30 days.

Requirements: Minimum age 18. Applicants must be enrolled in full-time further or higher education (HND level or above). Students may participate after graduation. Participants must find their own training placements, related to their course of study, and either through payment from their employer or through other means, finance their own visit to the USA.

Additional Information: IST Plus' US partner, CIEE provides the legal sponsorship required to obtain the J-1 visa. All participants must attend an interview at a US embassy or consulate. There are also comprehensive orientation materials for such issues such as social security, taxes, housing and transportation. CIEE maintains a 24/7 emergency assistance service for all participants in the USA. See www.istplus.com for more details.

Application Procedure: Applications can be made at any time of year, but should be made 6–10 weeks before desired date of departure. Applications can be downloaded from IST Plus website or candidates can email to ask for an application form.

Jacob's Pillow Dance

Job(s) Available: Summer festival internships (30).
Duration: From 24 May to 1 September.

Head Office: The Intern Programme at Jacob's Pillow, 358 George Carter Road, Becket MA, 01223
☎ +1 413 243 9919
✆ info@jacobspillow.org
🖳 www.jacobspillow.org

Pay: $500 (£347) stipend and a $150 (£104) travel/sundry expense allowance. Interns also receive 3 free meals a day, free accommodation, free performances and dance classes, staff-led seminars and training and mentoring.

Company Description: Jacob's Pillow Dance is a national history landmark and home to America's longest running international dance festival. Each year thousands of people from around the world visit to experience the festival with more than 50 international dance companies and 200 free performances, talks and events; observe classes at Jacob's Pillow Dance School, a professional dance training centre; explore the Pillow's rare and extensive dance archives, and take part in community programmes designed to educate and engage dance audiences of all ages.

Job Description: Interns may take on roles in areas such as archives/presentation, artist services, business, development, education, graphic and web design, house management/ticket sales, marketing, photojournalism, press/editorial, production, special events, ticket services and video documentation. Please see the website for specific duties within each intern area.

Requirements: Please see the website for specific requirements for each intern area.
Accommodation: On-campus accommodation provided.

Application Procedure: To apply download an application form from the website above. Post this along with a CV, 2 work-related references, 2 letters of recommendation and a cover letter explaining why you wish to apply, what position(s) you are applying for and in what priority order, your qualifications and interests and your goals and expectations for the internship to the address above. Applicants must include 2 copies of every role applied for in 1 envelope.

Portals of Wonder

Job(s) Available: Various positions, which range from archivists, librarians, project managers, executive personal assistants and fund raisers to theatrical producers and performers, as well as opportunities for internships.

Head Office: New York City
www.portalsofwonder.org

Duration: Varies according to individual project, from 6 weeks to several years.

Working Hours: 10am–7pm, 5 days a week. Part and full-time positions are available.

Pay: Depends on position. Stipend available for some internships.

Company Description: Portals Of Wonder is a dynamic volunteer driven non-profit community organisation that brings magic, mime, music and myth to critically ill and homeless children since 1999. Portals of Wonder is working to put smiles on 10,000 more faces of disadvantaged children. Situated within 35 minutes of Wall Street, Manhattan. Applicants can share in Portals of Wonder's mission by lending their valuable skills and expertise together with many others. Portals of Wonder's primary revenue-making programme is Adventures of a Wizard. It is an epic romantic adventure on the backdrop of the Ragtime Era and the Golden Age of Vaudeville extravaganza in Broadway musicals.

Job Description: Portals of Wonder offers a variety of positions and unique benefits for a dedicated candidate who is willing to work hard and responsibly. There are opportunities to continue working in long-term paid positions.

Requirements: Candidates must be of a professional calibre and have adaptable skills and abilities for a number of challenging situations in order to gain the most of their experience with Portals of Wonder.

Accommodation: Can be provided.

Application Procedure: First contact is by email only, via website. Please include a direct telephone number as there will be a telephone interview. A CV with covering letter and writing samples should also be included.

ASIA

BANGLADESH

Work available in Bangladesh is mainly voluntary projects and environmental or educational programmes.

Red tape

ADDRESS: HIGH COMMISSION FOR THE PEOPLE'S REPUBLIC OF BANGLADESH
28 Queen's Gate, London SW7 5JA
☎ 020 7584 0081
✆ info@bhclondon.org.uk
🖥 http://www.bhclondon.org.uk _____

Visa requirements: Visas are required for UK visitors to Bangladesh. A tourist visa can last for two months. Other types of visa are available; please enquire at the Bangladesh High Commission for up-to-date information.
Work permits: A letter from any business organisation in the UK endorsing the eligibility of the applicant and a letter of invitation from a Bangladeshi organisation mentioning the applicant's name and passport number are required in conjunction with a working visa application.

For up-to-date information about visa requirements check with the embassy before travel.

Voluntary work

Bangladesh Work Camps Association (BWCA) _____

Job(s) Available: Volunteers.
Duration: BWCA conducts short-term work camps with a duration of 10–15 days each year from October to March, and from 1–6 months from October to February. A Round The Year Programme (RTYP) is also available to medium-term volunteers staying for a minimum period of 1 month.

Head Office: 289/2 Work camp Road, North Shajahanpur, Dhaka-1217
☎ +88 0 2 935 6814
✆ bwca@bangla.net
🖥 www.mybwca.org

Working Hours: 30 hours per week.
Pay: $250 per camp per person. Volunteers must pay all other expenses including insurance and travel. RTYP registration is $300 for 3 months plus $2.50 per day per person for food.
Company Description: Bangladesh Work Camps Association (BWCA) promotes international solidarity and peace through organising community development, which takes the form of national/international work camps for volunteers in rural and urban areas of Bangladesh.
Job Description: The projects include environmental and health education, literacy, sanitation, reforestation, community work, development and construction, etc. At least 120 volunteers a year are recruited onto one of the 9 international work camps and 20 volunteers through RTYP.
Requirements: Volunteers aged 18–35, must be able to speak English, be adaptable to any situation and be team-spirited.
Accommodation: Accommodation and simple local food is provided for $2.50 a day. Volunteers must provide own sleeping bag/mat.

Application Procedure: Applications to BWCA 1 month in advance of scheduled camp/ programme date. Applications must come through a BWCA partner organisation in the applicant's country; if this is not possible individual, direct applications may be accepted and should be accompanied by a payment of $25. Apply in the first instance for the address of the nearest partner organisation. Application form available at www.mybwca.org/BWCA_APP_FORM.rtf.

CHINA

British nationals can find voluntary work in China through the UNA Exchange. Americans can check programmes such as Volunteers in Asia (VIA, Stanford University; www.viaprograms.org) which sends volunteer teachers to China and Vietnam and Princeton in Asia (www.princeton.edu/~pia) though these programmes are likely to be for longer than a summer. However, VIA in particular is looking for ways to expand volunteering in China. The following organisations offer the opportunity to work in China. Opportunities are found in main cities and usually come in the form of teaching English as well as volunteering. The following websites offer job information: http://english.zhaopin.com and www.chinajob.com.

Red tape

ADDRESS: EMBASSY OF THE PEOPLE'S REPUBLIC OF CHINA
49–51 Portland Place, London W1B 1JL
☎ 020 7299 4049
✆ ukcentre@visaforchina.org
🖳 www.chinese-embassy.org.uk

Visa requirements: Visas are required for any visit to China especially if travellers wish to work there. Applicants must submit an application form and supporting documents to the Chinese Visa Application Service Centre (CVASC) in London or Manchester. Alternatively you can apply online at www.visaforchina.org.uk. An interview may be required by the visa officer.

For up-to-date information about visa requirements check with the embassy before travel.

Voluntary work

International China Concern (ICC)

Job(s) Available: Volunteers to fulfil a variety of roles. Roles vary depending on duration of volunteering: administration assistant, accounts assistant, communications, education, management, medicine, physical or occupation therapy coordinator, special education teachers, social workers, special needs nursing carer.

Head Office: PO Box 20, Morpeth NE61 3YP, UK
☎ 01670 505622
✆ uk@chinaconcern.org
🖳 www.chinaconcern.org

Duration: From 3 weeks to 5 years or more.
Cost: Volunteers must be self-supporting.
Company Description: International China Concern (ICC) is a Christian development organisation which offers a service to improve the lives for more than 200 disabled and

abandoned children and young adults. Their services include housing, medical, therapy, special education plus vocational training. ICC offer training programmes for social welfare workers across China.

Job Description: Volunteers to help care for people who are disabled and abandoned.

Requirements: Knowledge of Mandarin Chinese is helpful but not essential. Volunteers are needed with a wide range of skills in OT, PT, nursing, music and art therapy, special education, counselling, social work and those who genuinely want to serve China's disabled and abandoned.

Application Procedure: To apply contact personnel@chinaconcern.org.

Teaching and language schools

Teach in China

Job(s) Available: TEFL teachers.

Duration: 5 or 10 months teaching English in a university, college or school in China. IST Plus sends participants on this programme in late August and early February in accordance with the Chinese semester system.

> **Head Office:** IST Plus Rosedale House, Rosedale Road, Surrey TW9 2SZ, UK
> ☎ 020 8939 9057
> ⌂ info@istplus.com
> ▱ www.istplus.com

Pay: Host institutions in China provide a monthly salary, which is generous by Chinese standards.

Cost: Participants are responsible for paying their outward air fare and programme fee to IST Plus to cover the costs of arranging the placement, processing all paperwork required for visas and work permits, visa fees, the training centre and 24-hour emergency support while in China. Return fare is paid by the host institution on completion of a 10-month contract.

Company Description: Sending more graduates to China than any other organisation, IST Plus is an organisation helping people develop skills and acquire knowledge for working in a multicultural, interdependent world.

Job Description: Successful applicants attend a 1-week training course on arrival in Shanghai focusing on learning Chinese, understanding Chinese culture and acquiring the basic skills to teach English. Participants are awarded a TEFL certificate upon completion of their teaching contracts.

Requirements: There is no age limit, a degree is required and a TEFL certificate is preferred.

Accommodation: Host institutions in China provide private accommodation (usually a teacher's apartment on or near the campus).

Application Procedure: Applicants are encouraged to return forms and application materials at least 3 months beforehand in order to ensure that a suitable placement is found. US applicants should apply to the CIEE in the USA.

INDIA

Despite its vast size India offers few opportunities for paid temporary work, particularly for those without any particular skill or trade to offer an employer: there are untold thousands of Indians who would be delighted to do any unskilled job available for a wage that would seem a pittance to a westerner. Anyone determined to find paid employment there should explore the possibility of working for tour operators who specialise in organising holidays to India, and they would normally only consider applicants who are familiar with the country.

There are, however, a number of opportunities for taking part in short-term voluntary schemes in India. The worldwide fame of *Mother Teresa's Missionaries of Charity* in Calcutta means it has no shortage of volunteers to take on part-time work to care for and feed orphaned children, the sick and dying, mentally or physically disabled adults and children or the elderly at its children's home in Calcutta (Shishu Bhavan, 78 AJC Bose Road), in the Home for Dying Destitutes at Kalighat and other houses run by the Missionaries of Charity in Calcutta and other Indian cities, but no accommodation can be offered. To register, visit the Mother House at 54A AJC Bose Road, Calcutta 700 016. Further information is also available from their London office at 177 Bravington Road, London W9 3AR (020 8960 2644).

Council International Volunteer Projects and Service Civil International can place Americans on voluntary schemes in India, and Concordia and UNA Exchange can offer similar placements for Britons. Please note that as is normal with short-term voluntary opportunities, those taking part must pay for their own travel expenses, and will often be required to put something towards the cost of board and lodging, though generally in India this is a modest amount. The organisation Aid India (www.aidindia.org) carries volunteer requests on its website.

Red tape

ADDRESS: OFFICE OF THE HIGH COMMISSIONER FOR INDIA
India House, Aldwych, London WC2B 4NA
☎ 020 7836 8484
✆ info.inuk@vfshelpline.com
🖥 www.hcilondon.in
(follow the link to in.vfsglobal.co.uk for visa information)

Visa requirements: A tourist visa is required by all non-Indian nationals entering India for a visit as tourists.

Residence permits: Those planning a stay of over three months must register with the Foreigners Regional Registration Office within 14 days of arrival and be able to provide evidence of how they are supporting themselves. It is not possible to change a tourist visa to a long stay visa within India.

Employment visas: Any foreigner taking up paid employment in India must have a valid work permit before they enter the country. They should apply (ideally in person) to the nearest Indian consulate, enclosing a copy of their contract, as proof of employment.

Voluntary work: Details of the voluntary work to be undertaken should be sent to the Indian consulate when applying for a visa at least two months in advance as they have to be forwarded to India. If you do want to attach yourself to a voluntary organisation for more than three months, you should aim to enter India on a student or employment visa (see Indian embassy website). There are Visa Centres in Edinburgh, Birmingham and London. Addresses can be found on the website.

For up-to-date information about visa requirements check with the embassy before travel.

Voluntary work

Dakshinayan

Job(s) Available: Volunteers.
Duration: Between 4 weeks and 6 months. Help is needed throughout the year.
Working Hours: Volunteers normally work 4–6 hours per day, 6 days a week.
Pay/Cost: Dakshinayan charges a fee of $300 per month. Volunteers are expected to cover travel expenses.

Head Office: Midadali Chadderjee, 2/1A Mahenbra Road, Kolkata 700 025, India
☎ +9199345 72399
dakshinayan@gmail.com
www.dakshinayan.org

Job Description: Volunteers to work with a registered trust engaged in providing education assistance to tribes in the Rajamhal Hills and the surrounding plains. Education is of primary level and volunteers are expected to assist in teaching English or arts and crafts, sports, poetry or singing. Participants must arrive in Kolkata in the first week of the month where they travel together to the project.
Requirements: No formal teacher training is needed. Minimum age 18. All applicants must be socially sensitive and willing to work in remote locations. Knowledge of Hindi is an advantage although not mandatory.
Accommodation: Cost includes food and accommodation while at the project, and no additional fee is charged. Living conditions on most rural development projects are very basic.
Application Procedure: Applications at least 30 days in advance of desired departure date, to Siddharth Sanyal, executive trustee, at the above email address.

Nomad Travel

Job(s) Available: Volunteer nurse/doctors.
Duration: Minimum period of work 6 weeks. Work is available all year round.
Cost: Funds are raised in the UK to pay for nurse, board and lodging and pharmaceuticals.
Company Description: Help is needed on the West Bengal/Sikkim borders, in the foothills of the

Head Office: Nomad Travel Store, 3–4 Wellington Terrace, Turnpike Lane, London N8 0PX, UK
☎ 0845 310 4470
cathy@nomadtravel.co.uk
www.nomadtravel.co.uk

Himalayas, approximately 3 hours from Darjeeling. This is a small clinic set up in Karmi Farm to help the indigenous population with day-to-day healthcare and childcare.
Job Description: Volunteer nurse/doctors to help in rural communities. The clinic currently caters for 210 families from the surrounding area. There is also outreach work. Situated in the foothills of the Himalayas, transport is all on foot. The main illnesses are skin disorders, chest problems, dehydration and childhood illnesses. Midwifery plays a big part. People turn up at the clinic any time night or day. However, there are long spells when it is quiet.
Accommodation: Comfortable accommodation and organic food provided.
Application Procedure: Applications should be made to Cathy Goodyear on the above details at any time.

INDIA

ASIA

Rural Organisation for Social Elevation (ROSE)

Job(s) Available: Volunteers (1–10).

Working Hours: 5 hours per day, 5 days a week.

Cost: Volunteers must pay their own travel costs and about £6 (500 rupees) a day towards board and lodging costs. Volunteer administration, guide, internet, phone, electricity, rent and other expenses covered by a one off registration fee of 6,000 rupees.

Head Office: Vill.–Sonargaon, PO Kanda, Bageshwar, Uttarakhand
☎ +915 9632 41081 (international) or +955 9632 41097 (mobile).
✉ jlverma_rosekanda@hotmail.com or jlverma.rosekandaegmail.com (infrequent internet access)
🖥 www.rosekanda.org

Company Description: ROSE is a small charity based at the foot of the Himalayas. It provides volunteers with the opportunity of experiencing true rural Indian life while providing education and improving local sanitation and healthcare facilities. ROSE offers many opportunities for students to conduct research in various subjects such as geography, anthropology, development, conservation and environmental studies as well as in the education development programme. Facilities include a library and learning participation. ROSE received the First Choice Responsible Tourism Award for Best Volunteering Programme in 2005.

Job Description: Volunteers to carry out work in rural areas including teaching children English, construction, poultry farming, environmental protection, organic farming, agricultural work, recycling paper to make handmade greetings cards, office work, compiling project proposals, reports and healthcare. Groups of volunteers can be organised into work camps lasting 10–30 days, but individuals are also welcome to apply for 6 months. An individual will need a tourist visa.

Accommodation: Provided in a family house in addition to 3 meals a day, the family will provide everything you need unless they don't have it themselves. *Individual 6 months stay:* accommodation avaliable in Jeevan Paying Guest Unit as a paying guest.

Additional Information: International phones and internet facilities are available in JPGU/Kanda/Bageshwar (1.5 hours by bus). Please note that the phone line may be hard to reach for international phone calls. Keep persevering.

Application Procedure: Application form available at www.rosekanda.info/Application Form.pdf.

JAPAN

The range of short-term casual jobs open to westerners in Japan is extremely limited, even with unemployment in Japan having rapidly fallen in recent years. However, longer-term opportunities do exist, particularly in the area of teaching English. A native English-speaker therefore possesses a marketable skill if he or she has a degree; experience or qualifications in teaching English as a foreign language are added advantages. One way of getting a teaching job is to advertise in the English-language *Japan Times* (www.japantimes.co.jp).

For further information on teaching work in Japan see *Teaching English Abroad* (see *Useful publications*). Anyone who is serious about wanting to spend some time in Japan should read *Live and Work in Japan* (Erica Simms, Crimson Publishing 2008), a thorough guide for anyone hoping to live and work there.

There is a support organisation for those wishing to visit Japan on a working holiday visa – the Japanese Association for Working-Holiday Makers with offices in Tokyo, Osaka and Kyushu (Tokyo office: Ichigaya KT building 5F, 4-7-16 Kudanminami, Chiyoda-ku, Tokyo, 102-0074; +81 3 3265 3321; www.jawhm.or.jp).

CIEE and Service Civil International can help US residents, Concordia, UNA Exchange and International Voluntary Service can help UK residents find short term voluntary work in Japan.

Red tape

ADDRESS: EMBASSY OF JAPAN
101–104 Piccadilly, London W1J 7JT
☎ 020 7465 6500
✆ info@ld.mofa.go.jp
🖥 www.uk.emb-japan.go.jp

Visa requirements: Nationals of the UK, the USA, Ireland, Germany, Switzerland and Austria can visit Japan as tourists without a visa for up to 90 days and extend this for a further 90 days. Most other nationalities can visit for up to 90 days, as long as they have a return or onward ticket and sufficient funds.

Work permits: A position must be secured and working visa obtained before you enter the country. Applicants for working visas must submit their application to the Consulate in person. If the person obtains a Certificate of Eligibility from the Japanese immigration authorities a visa can be issued in three days.

Working holiday visas: Holders of British, Australian, Canadian and New Zealand passports can apply for working holiday visas: these must be applied for at the Japanese embassy of their home country. The rules are generally the same, but full details can be obtained from the nearest Japanese embassy or consulate. They issue up to 1,000 to UK nationals a year. There is a small, non-refundable processing fee for a working holiday visa. Working holiday visas are available to British citizens between April and the following March, applications are accepted from April. Application forms and explanatory material can be obtained from the Japanese consulate-general in London or Edinburgh (www.uk.emb japan.go.jp).

Japanese working holiday visas are single entry, so if you have to leave Japan for any reason you must obtain a re-entry permit from the relevant immigration authorities before leaving. Travellers who stay in Japan longer than 90 days have to register with the local municipal office, and keep them informed of any subsequent change of address. They can also register with their embassy or consulate on arrival or later during their stay but this is not obligatory, merely advisable. For clarification of these points and news of any changes in the regulations please contact the nearest Japanese embassy or consular mission.

Voluntary work: A volunteer visa scheme allows British nationals to undertake voluntary work in Japan, working for charitable organisations for up to a year. Work should be unpaid but pocket money and free board and lodging are permitted. Details and application forms are available from the consulate general of Japan in London and Edinburgh.

For up-to-date information about visa requirements check with the embassy before travel.

JAPAN

ASIA

335

Teaching and language schools

The Japan Exchange and Teaching (JET) Programme ____

Job(s) Available: Positions in Japan promoting international understanding at a grass-roots level and to improve foreign language teaching in schools.
Duration: Minimum 12 month contract. Departure the following July/August after applying between September/November.
Pay: Participants are provided return air travel and an annual salary of ¥3,600,000 (about £25,000).

Head Office: JET Desk, Embassy of Japan, 101-104 Piccadilly, London W1J 7JT, UK
☎ 020 7465 6668
✑ info@jet-uk.org
🖳 www.jet-uk.org

Company Description: Established in 1987 and run by the Japanese Government, the Japan Exchange and Teaching (JET) Programme has placed over 50,000 participants from more than 50 different countries into Japan.
Requirements: UK nationals from any degree discipline can apply through the website between September and November.
Application Procedure: Applications can be made online through the above website from late September until the end of November. Please note that only UK passport holders can apply through the UK JET office. Non-UK passport holders should visit www.mofa.go.jp/j_info/visit/jet/apply.html for a list of countries offering the Programme or contact the Embassy of Japan in their home country. Contact the above address or email for more information.

REPUBLIC OF KOREA

Work opportunities in The Republic of Korea are found in teaching English in public primary/secondary schools.

Red tape

ADDRESS: EMBASSY OF THE REPUBLIC OF KOREA
60 Buckingham Gate, London SW1E 6AJ
☎ 020 7227 5500
✑ visas@koreanembassy.org.uk
🖳 http://gbr.mofat.go.kr ____

Visa regulations: Most countries, including European nations and the USA, may travel to South Korea without a visa. British passport holders do not require a visa for the entry purpose of a short-term visit up to 90 days. After this time a long-term visa will be required. Young Australians and New Zealanders are eligible for a working holiday visa for Korea. The Ministry of Education in Korea administers the English Programme in Korea (EPIK) through its embassies in the UK, the USA, Ireland, New Zealand, South Africa, Canada and Australia. Details of the scheme are given below. Visas must be obtained in the home country of the traveller.

Work permits: If possible, you should obtain a work visa, Teaching Foreign Languages, (E2) which is available only to graduates with a four-year BA or BSc. The E2 is valid only for employment with the sponsoring employer. You can obtain the permit in advance or you can enter on a tourist visa, find a job and then leave the country while the permit is being processed. The process time is five working days. Enquire at the embassy for more details.

For up-to-date information about visa requirements contact the embassy before travel.

Teaching and language schools

English Program in Korea (EPIK)

Job(s) Available: English teachers in Korea to teach during regular school hours.
Duration: Contracts are for a year (52 weeks).
Working Hours: 8 hours per day, 5 days a week. Excluding Saturdays, Sundays and Korean national holidays. Total instructional hours will not exceed 22 hours per week.
Pay: KRW2,700,000–KRW1,800,000 per month depending on experience and qualifications.

Head Office: The Education Centre, Embassy of the Republic of Korea, 60 Buckingham Gate, London SW1E 6AJ, UK
☎ 020 7227 5547
✆ edu@korean.embassy.org.uk
or epik2@mest.go.kr
🖥 www.educationinuk.org.kr
or www.epik.go.kr

Requirements: English speakers with an undergraduate degree. 9 day orientation must be completed (unpaid). By E2 visa law, EPIK teachers should have a citizenship from one of the following countries: Australia, Canada, Ireland, New Zealand, United Kingdom, United States or South Africa.
Accommodation: Furnished apartment provided free of charge.
Additional Information: Benefits include entrance and exit allowance, medical insurance, one-off settlement allowance, severance pay, paid vacation.
Application Procedure: Send application to the nearest embassy in designated countries or EPIK office in Korea.

TALK (Teach and Learn in Korea)

Job(s) Available: English teachers in Korea to teach in the after-school programme.
Duration: 6 months or 1 year contracts.
Working Hours: 15 hours per week, Monday to Friday.
Pay: 1.5 million KRW/month (approx. £740).
Requirements: Must be a citizen of a country where the national language is English and have completed two or more years of education at an accredited university.

Head Office: The Education Centre, Embassy of the Republic of Korea, 60 Buckingham Gate, London SW1E 6AJ, UK
☎ 020 7227 5500
✆ edu@koreanembassy.org.uk
or talkkorea@gmail.com
🖥 http://talk.go.kr

Accommodation: Furnished studio-type room, or a home-stay provided free of charge. Benefits include round-trip airfare, one-off settlement allowance, opportunities to participate in cultural programs, paid sick leave, Korean University Volunteer-aid system.
Application Procedure: Apply online at http://talk.go.kr.

MALDIVES

The Maldives are composed of just over 1,000 islands, 200 of which are inhabited and another 80 which are tourist resorts. Tourism is the main industry of the islands, and finding a placement or seasonal job is a possibility. This year the Government has launched a volunteering programme, in response to the need for teachers and health care workers on the islands, details of which can be found in the Maldives International Volunteer Programme entry.

It should be noted that the island's only religion is Sunni Muslim. While private worship of other religions is permissible, bringing in items such as Bibles, crosses, Buddhist statues or similar items is strictly illegal. The consumption of alcohol is strictly prohibited, except in the tourist resorts.

Red tape

ADDRESS: HIGH COMMISSION OF MALDIVES
22 Nottingham Place, London W1U 5NJ
☎ 0207 224 2135
✆ ivp@maldiveshighcommission.org
🖳 www.maldiveshighcommission.org

Visa Requirements: A 30-day tourist visa is provided to most nationalities provided that the following conditions are met:

1. Possession of a passport valid for the duration of the stay.
2. Possession of a valid return or onward journey ticket.
3. Having confirmation of a reservation in a tourist resort, or sufficient funds to cover the stay (US$100 plus US$50/day).

Work Permits: It is not permitted to enter the Maldives on a tourist visa and switch to a work visa. A work permit must be obtained from the Ministry of Employment and Labour before departing for the Maldives. Successful applicants for the International Volunteer Programme will have their visa arranged for them by the organisation.

For up-to-date information about visa requirements check with the embassy before travel.

Voluntary work

Maldives International Volunteer Programme

Job(s) Available: Education volunteers, health volunteers.
Duration: From January to November for teachers. Minimum period of work 9 months. Health volunteers 6 months to one year at any given date.
Pay: US $500 (approx. £309) per month to cover living costs. Volunteers will need to raise the cost of their airfare to the Maldives - advice will be given on how to do this.

Head Office: High Commission of Maldives, 22 Nottingham Place, London W1U 5NJ, UK
☎ 0207 224 2135
✆ ivp@maldiveshighcommission.org
🖳 www.maldiveshighcommission.org

Company Description: The International Volunteer Programme is an initiative founded by the Government of Maldives and Friends of Maldives, intended to provide volunteers to assist the Maldives and is part of the Maldives Volunteers Corps (MVC). The Maldives is one of the world's newest democracies and needs help in all sectors - particularly health and education.
Job Description: *Education volunteers:* volunteer as teachers in schools, and will also train teachers to improve the education level in the islands. *Health volunteers:* would be determined by the scope of your qualification (doctor, nurse, counsellor etc).
Requirements: The basic requirement to apply is a university degree, and preferably PGCE or TEFL qualifications. Applicants will be selected for their proficiency in English. Health volunteers will need to be qualified as appropriate in their field.
Accommodation: Provided, most likely with a local family.
Additional Information: Currently only applications from UK citizens are accepted.
Application Procedure: Email above address for more information.

NEPAL

Nepal is one of the most promising destinations for young people who want to spend a few months as a volunteer in a developing country, however they may face a visa problem. The first tourist visa will be issued for 30 days, and costs £35 for multiple entries. 90 days costs £75 and 15 days costs £20. Processing takes a few days. A tourist visa can be extended from the Department of Immigration and Pokhara Immigration Office for a total of 120 days. An additional 30 days visa may be granted on reasonable grounds from the department. Over the course of a visa year, a tourist cannot stay in Nepal more than cumulative 150 days.

People who overstay their visas have in the past been fined heavily or even put in prison. More information is available at www.nepembassy.org.uk. This applies to all except Indian nationals who do not require a visa to visit Nepal. An impressive range of non-governmental organisations makes it possible for people to teach in a voluntary capacity. Although volunteers must bear the cost of travel and living expenses, the cost of living is very low by western standards.

Concordia, UNA Exchange and Volunteer Action for Peace can arrange short-term voluntary work placements in Nepal. The following organisations are also looking for volunteers to work in Nepal.

ADDRESS: NEPALESE EMBASSY
12A Kensington Palace Gardens, London W8 4QU
☎ 020 7229 1594
✆ eon@nepembassy.org.uk
🖳 www.nepembassy.org.uk

A tourist visa is initially granted for 15, 30 or 90 days, which may be further extended on reasonable grounds from the Department of Information in Nepal not exceeding more than 150 days in total in a visa year (Jan 01 – Dec 31). Please see the embassy website for further information.

For up-to-date information about visa requirements check with the embassy before travel.

Voluntary work

Kathmandu Environmental Education Project (KEEP)

Job(s) Available: Volunteers in Nepal.
Duration: Minimum of 2 months. Registration fee is US$120 which cover general administration and annual KEEP membership.
Cost: Volunteers are required to be totally self-funding.

Head Office: PO Box 9178, Jyatha Thamel, Kathmandu
☎ +977 1421 6775/776
✆ volunteer@info.com.np
🖳 www.keepnepal.org

Job Description: Volunteers are sought to go to various trekking villages in Nepal to teach English to lodge owners, trekking guides and porters and also as teachers in government schools. KEEP also sends volunteers to NGOs operating in the field of conservation or health and community development according to the interest and experience of the volunteers.
Accommodation: Provided with community-based village families.
Application Procedure: Applications to the above email address.

Insight Nepal

Job(s) Available: Volunteer teachers (25).

Duration: Volunteer placements for 7 weeks and 3 months will be arranged. Work available all year round except in October.

Working Hours: 5-6 hours per day, 5-6 days a week.

Cost: There is a programme fee.

Head Office: PO Box 489, Zero KM, Pokhara, Kaski
☎ +977 61 530266
✆ insight@fewanet.com.np or insightnepal@gmail.com.np
🖳 www.insightnepal.org.np

Company Description: Insight Nepal was established with a view to providing an opportunity to those who are interested in gaining a unique cultural experience by contributing their time and skills for the benefit of worthwhile community service groups.

Job Description: Volunteer teachers to teach various subjects in primary, secondary and vocational schools or community development projects in Nepal.

Requirements: Applicants should be aged 18-60 and be educated to at least A-level standard. Experience of teaching is advisable but not essential. Applicants with games, sporting and artistic skills preferred.

Accommodation: Insight Nepal organises homestays for the volunteers, and the host family provide accommodation and all meals, also includes a 1-week trekking and 3-day jungle safari.

Application Procedure: Please submit applications online.

Volunteer Nepal

Job(s) Available: Volunteers.

Duration: 1-16 weeks, available year round. Also longer projects depending on volunteers' interest.

Working Hours: 3-6 hours per day.

Company Description: Volunteer Nepal, National Group is a community-based, non-governmental, non-profit organisation that coordinates local and international work camps with community groups or institutions in need of voluntary assistance.

Head Office: c/o Anish Neupane, PBN 10210 KTM, Bagmati Zone
Head Office: 84 De Beauvoir Road, Reading, Berkshire RG1 5NP, UK
☎ +977 1661 3724
✆ info@volnepal.np.org or volunteer@volnepal.np.org or shekharbhattarai@volnepal.np.org
🖳 www.volnepal.np.org

Job Description: Volunteers needed for teaching, working in orphanages, health centres, youth/women's organisations and environmental care.

Requirements: Volunteers should be aged 18-60 and educated to at least A-level standard.

Additional Information: Travel and tours in Nepal also arranged.

Application Procedure: For further details and costs, contact the above address.

Work & Volunteer Abroad

Job(s) Available: Volunteer projects in Nepal.

Duration: From 3 weeks to 1 year.

Working Hours: From 5 to 8 hours per day, 5 days per week.

Cost: Varies depending on programme.

Company Description: WAVA is an independent

Head Office: 67-71 Lewisham High Street, London SE13 5JX, UK
☎ 020 8297 3278
✆ rtjones@workandvolunteer.com
🖳 www.workandvolunteer.com

company which specialises in providing participants with memorable travel experiences around the world.

Job Description: Volunteers will work with local people on sustainable development projects. There is a choice of four different volunteer projects in Nepal ranging from ecotourism, school and community to environmental conservation.

Requirements: Minimum age 18. Must be physically fit, hard working and have a good sense of humour. International volunteers must have a tourist visa.

Accommodation: Accommodation is in Kathmandu during the training and orientation is in a hotel. Accommodation during the volunteer placements ranges from staying with a host family, a hostel or a volunteer house. Volunteers must bring their own sleeping bag. All accommodation is located near to the volunteer placements and is usually based on twin share. Three meals are provided a day.

Additional Information: Pre-departure briefing evenings are arranged every month in order to inform and adequately prepare applicants for their upcoming journeys.

Application Procedure: Visit the above website, choose a programme you like, and then apply online. A member of WAVA will then provide applicants with further details.

SRI LANKA

Work opportunities are available in Sri Lanka as volunteers who can teach English. Agencies who advertise for jobs are www.lankaweb.com, and www.sri-lankan.net.

Red tape

ADDRESS: HIGH COMMISSION FOR THE DEMOCRATIC SOCIALIST REPUBLIC OF SRI LANKA

13 Hyde Park Gardens, London W2 2LU

☎ 020 7262 1841

✒ mail@slhc-london.co.uk

🖥 www.slhclondon.org

Visa requirements: British and Irish citizens can get a landing endorsement valid for 30 days free of charge on arrival at the port of entry in Sri Lanka, so need not get a visa prior to departure. A visa is required for a stay exceeding 30 days, which will be granted for 90 days at www.immigration.gov.uk. If the passports and documents are to be returned by post, you should provide a self-addressed prepaid special delivery envelope to the weight of 500g along with your application form. The special delivery cover should not be stamped with a postage printout issued by the post office for same day use. Applications sent without prepaid special delivery cover/or postage will be retained until the applicant collects it personally. Irish passport holders should include an additional amount of £6 if they require their passports to be sent back to Ireland by registered airmail. If a visitor wishes to extend his stay in Sri Lanka, they should apply to the Department of Immigration & Emigration, 41, Ananda Rajakaruna Mawatha, Colombo 10 before the expiry of visa.

Volunteers: As volunteers are used informally to help with social, economic and technical development activities in villages, this works reasonably well for both parties. Volunteers usually pay something towards their keep while volunteering. This also applies to the nationals of most EU countries, the USA, Canada, New Zealand and China. The NGO operating in Sri Lanka should make an application on behalf of the applicant with the applicant's CV and passport details to the controller/immigration and emigration.

Working holiday scheme: As a citizen of a commonwealth country you may be eligible to apply for a UK working holiday visa.

For up-to-date information about visa requirements check with the embassy before travel.

Voluntary work

VESL (Volunteers for Educational Support and Learning) __

Job(s) Available: Volunteers (60).

Duration: Projects run from 4/6 weeks during July/August or 3/6 months at various times throughout the year.

Working Hours: 2–4 hours teaching per day, 5 days a week.

Head Office: 17 Silk Hill, Buxworth, High Peak SK23 7TA, UK
☎ 0845 094 3727
✆ info@vesl.org
🖳 www.vesl.org

Cost: Varies depending on project length, starting from £850. Volunteers are encouraged to fundraise towards costs and are given fundraising support and advice. Project cost covers set-up, food, accommodation, comprehensive medical and travel insurance, training, 24-hour back-up and support costs.

Company Description: VESL is a charity (no. 1117908) that sends volunteers to teach English in rural Indian, Thai and Sri Lankan communities, and trains UK teachers to run workshops for local teachers.

Job Description: Volunteers usually work in pairs to plan and run activities and games focusing on spoken English. Volunteers are also able to run after-school games and activities.

Accommodation: Volunteers are usually placed with a family for a homestay experience.

Application Procedure: Applications details can be obtained from the website.

THAILAND

In addition to the conservation project listed below Concordia, UNA Exchange and Volunteer Action for Peace offer British volunteers the chance to work in Thailand. English teaching jobs can be found on the website of the *Bangkok Post*, an English-language newspaper, at www.bangkokpost.net.

Red tape

ADDRESS: ROYAL THAI EMBASSY
29–30 Queen's Gate, London SW7 5JB
☎ 020 7589 2944
✆ csinfo@thaiembassyuk.org.uk
🖳 www.thaiembassyuk.org.uk

Visa requirements: Nationals of the following countries may enter Thailand without a visa for a maximum stay of 30 days for purpose of tourism only: Australia, Austria, Bahrain, Belgium, Brazil, Brunei, Canada, Denmark, Finland, France, Germany, Greece, Hong Kong, Indonesia, Iceland, Ireland, Israel, Italy, Japan, the Republic of Korea, Kuwait, Luxembourg, Malaysia, the Netherlands, New Zealand, Norway, Oman, Peru, Philippines, Portugal, Qatar, Russia, Singapore, South Africa, Spain, Sweden, Switzerland, Turkey, United Arab Emirates, the UK, the USA and Vietnam. This applies only if they are entering the country through the International Airport; if they are entering on foot from a neighbouring country it is 15 days. Nationals from countries not mentioned above will need a visa to visit Thailand. These travellers must have a valid return ticket. A tourist visa will allow a 60–day stay and can apply for another 30 days at a price. These nationals are not allowed to stay over 90 days within six months of first entry within one year.

A foreigner holding a Thai tourist visa is not permitted to work in Thailand, even on a voluntary basis. Applicants from English-speaking countries wanting paid employment in Thailand must apply for a Type B non-immigrant visa from the Royal Thai Embassy. With this visa it is possible to stay for up to 90 days; on arrival a work permit must be applied for at the Ministry of Labour. A Type B visa is necessary for a traveller on business even if they are visiting for two days. For voluntary work, a Type O visa as well as a volunteer work permit is required; the applicant will be permitted to stay for a maximum of 90 days. Any person wishing to exceed that time must apply to the Office of Immigration Bureau. Most foreign nationals must apply for their visa before entering the country; however there are a few countries whose citizens may apply for a 15-day visa once inside Thailand (visa on arrival).

For up-to-date information about visa requirements check with the embassy before travel.

Teaching and language schools

Teach in Thailand

Job(s) Available: TEFL teachers.
Duration: Opportunity for graduates to spend 5 or 10 months teaching English in primary and second-ary schools in Thailand. IST Plus sends participants on this programme in late October and early May in accordance with the Thai semester system.

> **Head Office:** IST Plus Rosedale House, Rosedale Road, Surrey TW9 2SZ, UK
> ☎ 020 8030 0067
> info@istplus.com
> www.istplus.com

Pay: A monthly salary which is generous by local standards.
Cost: Participants are responsible for paying their outward air fare and a programme fee to IST Plus to cover the costs of arranging the placement, processing all paperwork required for visas and work permits, visa fees, the training centre and 24-hour emergency support while in Thailand. Return fare is paid by the host institution on completion of a 10-month con-tract if the participant starts in May.
Company Description: Sending more graduates to Thailand than any other organisation, IST Plus is an organisation helping people develop skills and acquire knowledge for working in a multicultural, interdependent world.
Job Description: Successful applicants attend a 1-week training course on arrival in Bangkok focusing on the language and culture and acquiring the basic skills to teach English. Participants are awarded a TEFL certificate upon completion of their teaching contracts.
Requirements: There is no age limit, a degree is required and a TFL certificate is preferred.
Accommodation: Host institutions provide private accommodation (usually a teacher's apartment on or near the campus).
Application Procedure: Applicants are encouraged to return forms and application mate-rials at least 3 months beforehand in order to ensure that a suitable placement is found. US applicants should apply to CIEE in the USA.

Voluntary work

The Mirror Foundation _____

Job(s) Available: Indoor work, teaching English volunteer placements and outdoor work volunteer placements.

Duration: 2 weeks to 6 months. Minimum period of work of 1 month recommended.

Working Hours: Tuesday to Saturday, 8:30am–5pm.

Head Office: Mirror Art Group, 106 Moo 1 Ban Huay Khom, T. Mae Yao, A. Muang, Ching Rai 57100
☎ +66 53 737 412
✆ moo@bannok.com
🖥 www.mirrorartgroup.com

Cost: Starts at £320 for 2 weeks. Price includes meals from Tuesday to Saturday (lunch), accommodation, pickup, transportation for volunteer program, elephant ride, home stay program and volunteering support.

Company Description: The Mirror Foundation is an NGO working in the northern Thai province of Chiang Rai. The Foundation operates a number of projects and programs to help the hilltribe peoples of Mae Yao sub-district to combat their everyday struggles with unemployment, poverty, drug addiction and lack of Thai citizenship. The Foundation also tries to give the hilltribes of Mae Yao the skills, education and support required to adapt to a co-existence with lowland Thais without sacrificing their cultural identity.

Job Description: *Indoor work; teaching English:* teaching in childcare centres, primary schools, a special school for special kids, a hospital, a temple, as well as giving lessons for local Hilltribe tour guides, staff and local children. *Outdoor work; community development program:* building water tanks; extending waterpipe systems; building check dams, school classrooms, new houses, staff offices and toilets; painting; developing agricultural projects; helping in the vegetable garden; working on plantations; road repairs.

Requirements: Minimum age 17 but if candidate is under age they are welcome to join with a family member or teacher as a group. Must love to teach, love children, be open minded, flexible, polite and able to follow rules. Candidates should also be fit and healthy, have a positive attitude and be willing to live in another culture.

Accommodation: Provided at no extra cost at the foundation.

Application Procedure: Apply by sending an email to the above address.

The Wild Animal Rescue Foundation of Thailand _____

Job(s) Available: Volunteers.

Duration: Minimum period of work 3 weeks.

Head Office: 65.1 Third Floor, Sukhumvit 55, Klongton, Wattana, Bangkok 10110
☎ +662 712 9515
✆ volunteer@warthai.org
or war@warthai.org
🖥 www.warthai.org

Company Description: The foundation is dedicated to the protection and provision of welfare to all wild animals in need. The foundation operates 2 sanctuaries in the south of Thailand. The first sanctuary is a gibbon rehabilitation project, which was set up in 1992 and deals exclusively with gibbons that may have been rescued from situations of abuse and cruelty. The aim of the project is to release selected gibbons from the sanctuary into the wild plus provide ongoing care to those who through their association with humans are now unfit for release. The second sanctuary in the province of Ranong provides a home to all wild animals common to Thailand which have suffered at the hands of humans. These projects are ongoing projects which house gibbons, a large colony of macaques and many other species.

Job Description: At both projects, volunteers are involved in the day-to-day operation of the unit including food preparation, cage cleaning and maintenance, assisting with health inspections, behavioural observation and informing people who call at the visitors centre of the work of the foundation.

Requirements: Volunteers should be in good physical condition and be able to live and function in field station conditions. It is essential that volunteers are enthusiastic and able to live and work with people of different cultures. Volunteers are required to have had all relevant vaccinations for Hepatitis A & B, Tuberculosis (TB), Diptheria, Rabies, Pertissus, Tetanus and Japanese Encephalitis before arriving and Malaria for WAREN.

Application Procedure: For current placement rates and opportunities, please contact by email.

AUSTRALASIA

AUSTRALIA

The short length of this chapter does not bear any relation to the vast range and number of temporary opportunities available in Australia: there are many, as unemployed Australians don't want to do the jobs that working holiday visa visitors are willing to do. However, there are a few factors to bear in mind when considering Australia as a destination for a summer job. The first factor is the reversal of seasons: the Australian summer takes place in what is winter to much of the rest of the world and so jobs on their fruit harvests and at the peak of their tourist industry occur at the wrong time of year for anyone hoping to find work between July and September. There is also the financial factor: the cost of a return ticket to Australia makes going there for a paid job for just a few weeks very uneconomical – even though in real terms the cost of getting to Australia is at its cheapest ever, the cost is still such that it makes better financial sense to stay for months rather than weeks.

Luckily for the foreigner, Australia has a reciprocal working holiday scheme with certain countries that can ease the formalities for those going there to pick up casual work. Some guidelines for those hoping to do so are given below, but working holidays in Australia are covered in greater depth in *Work Your Way Around the World* by Susan Griffith, (see *Useful publications* section), in the information available from Australian high commissions and embassies or through the Australia government immigration website at www.immi.gov.au. A third point to consider is that Australia is one of the most popular destinations for working travellers, and you need to begin the application process well in advance of your intended travel: 144,000 people apply for visas every year and the processing usually takes six days. The fee at present is £135. It is important to remember that your first working holiday maker visa can only be obtained in your country of origin, you cannot apply for a WHM visa once you are in Australia, although you can renew it.

Although Australia now has a declining unemployment rate, jobseekers must be prepared to devote time and energy to the job-hunt. One tip is to look for work away from the big cities, where other new arrivals from overseas may be competing for the same jobs. A valuable source of rural jobs is www.jobsearch.gov.au which includes harvest work jobs at jobsearch.gov.au/harvesttrail, to which the Department of Immigration and Citizenship (DIAC) normally directs general job inquiries. Enquiring in one office will allow you to uncover harvest work near one of the more than 200 other offices across the country. Employment National encourage working holiday-makers to contact their specialist fruit and crop-picking department or to check their website, which has details of the EN offices all over the country and the types of work that these may offer.

The fruit harvests of northern Victoria employ a massive 10,000–12,000 people in the Australian summer (January to March). The city of Shepparton is in the Goulburn Valley, about two hours north of Melbourne with easy accessibility via rail or bus services. Information can be obtained from the Northern Victoria Fruitgrowers' Association Ltd (NVFA), PO Box 612, Mooroopna, Vic 3629 (+61 3 58253700; administrator@nvfa.com.au; www.nvfa.com.au) and The Victorian Peach and Apricot Grower's Association (VPAGA) 30 A Bank Street, Cobram, Vic (+61 3 58721729). There is also a National Harvest Hotline number: 1800 062 332. This number gives the option of states and areas within Australia where current seasonal work is available. By following the prompts, callers are able to obtain accurate updated information to a particular area or are able to speak directly with a person in a particular area.

Searching the web for employment leads is especially productive in Australia. There are dozens of routes to finding out about job vacancies. A wide search can be done by looking at

Employment under Google's regional directory at http://directory.google.com/Top/Regional/Oceania/Australia. Before leaving home, you might like to register (free) with www.gapwork.com which is updated regularly and lists employers who hire working holidaymakers. See www.jobsearch.gov.au for a government source of information with details of the National Harvest Trail. One of the best sites is a free service by the Wayward Bus Company (www.waywardbus.com.au). If in Queensland check the adverts in *Queensland Country Life* magazine (http://qcl.farmonline.com.au). The magazine also has an online jobs guide (www.jobsguide.com.au). Some properties also function as holiday ranches and they often take on domestic staff and guides.

Hard-working travellers can earn A$100 a day doing harvest work, although A$9 an hour would be more typical. The cost of living in Australia is a lot lower than in Britain so those wages go further than it sounds if you convert them into sterling at the current rate (£1 is worth A$1.64 at the time of writing).

Some city-based employment agencies deal with jobs in outback areas, primarily farming, station, hotel/motel and roadhouse work. In Western Australia, Pollitt's (+61 8 93252544) say that experienced farmworkers and tractor drivers are paid A$12–A$14 an hour for 10–12 hours per day, seven days a week at seeding time (April to June) and harvest time (October to December). Housekeeping, nannying and cooking positions are available for two to three months at a time throughout the year. The standard wage is A$300 a week after board, most of which can be saved. For work in outback roadhouses and hotels, previous experience in kitchen, food and beverage service is essential to earn A$400 a week after lodging. The three-month commitments enable travellers to experience the regional country towns while saving most of their earnings.

In urban areas the usual range of jobs exist (bar, restaurant, office and factory work), available through the many private employment agencies such as Bligh, Adecco and Drake Personnel. It is also worth investigating tourist areas such as the coastal and island resorts of Queensland for jobs in hotels, restaurants, etc especially during the Australian winter from June to October.

One of the best sources of job information for working holidaymakers in Australia is the extensive network of backpackers' hostels, some of which employ young foreigners themselves and all of which should be able to advise on local possibilities. One such is Brook Lodge Dackpackers (3 Bridge Street, Donnybrook, WA 6239; +61 8 97311520; info@brooklodge.com.au; www.brooklodge.com.au) in Western Australia, which provides accommodation and can arrange hourly or weekly contract seasonal work including seasonal work in the apple harvest between November and May. Details of lodges like this can be found on the internet at http://backpackingaround.com, a website set up by backpackers which carries job and visa information as well as links and info on accommodation around Western Australia. Another useful source is the work exchange called Workstay Australia, which is based in Western Australia and can be found at www.workstay.com.au. There is a membership fee and members are guided to a network of hostels when work is available. The group HNH Travellers Australia (18 Withington St, East Brisbane, Queensland 4169; +61 7 34115955; www.hnh.net.au) can arrange fruit picking in some areas. They offer a Travellers Discount Card for A$5 which will enable travellers a 10% discount at restaurants along with corporate car hire rates etc.

Either before you leave or once you are in one of the major cities, get hold of the free 200-page booklet *Australia and New Zealand Independent Traveller's Guide* published by the London-based travel magazine *TNT* (www.tntmagazine.com) It includes a section on work and some relevant advertisements as well as travel advice.

Most newspapers advertise jobs on one or two days each week – varying from paper to paper and state to state. *The Sydney Morning Herald* can be contacted at www.smh.com.au, *The Australian* at www.theaustralian.com.au, and *The West Australian* at www.thewest.com.au.

Information and application forms for visitor and working holiday visas may be obtained in the UK from the high commission's designated agent, Consyl Publishing. For an application form and

AUSTRALIA

AUSTRALASIA

a free copy of *Travel Australia*, a newspaper aimed at those planning a working holiday in Australia, the DIAC prefers people be referred to its own website at www.immi.gov.au to ensure clients access the most up-to-date forms and information.

Red tape

ADDRESS: AUSTRALIAN HIGH COMMISSION
Migration Branch, Strand, London WC2B 4LA
☎ 09065 508 900 (£1 pm)
🖳 www.uk.embassy.gov.au

Visa Requirements

The Department of Immigration and Citizenship specifies that non-Australian citizens travelling to Australia should enter Australia on an appropriate visa for their intended purpose of stay and length of stay.

Tourist Visas

eVisitor

About this visa: An eVisitor is designed for people who want to visit Australia for tourism or business purposes. Tourism includes holidays, recreation and seeing family and/or friends.

How it works: The eVisitor is valid for multiple entries into Australia for a 12-month period from the date of grant or until your travel document expires (if it expires before the eVisitor expiration date). Each time you enter Australia within the 12 months you can stay for a period of up to 3 months from the date of entry. Please note that if your visa is due to expire after you arrive in Australia you can still remain for the 3 months.

An eVisitor does not require a physical visa label or any paperwork for travel. The eVisitor is electronically linked to your travel document number.

Eligibility: UK citizens are eligible for eVisitor. Visit www.immi.gov.au for a list of eVisitor eligible countries.

How to apply: There is no application or service charge for an eVisitor application.

ETA: Visitor – subclass 976

About this visa: A Visitor ETA subclass 976 is designed for people who are outside Australia and want to visit Australia for holidays, tourism, recreation and informal studies or training.

How it works: Visitor ETAs and Business (Short Validity) ETAs are valid for multiple entries to Australia for a 12-month period from the date of grant or until your travel document expires (if it expires before the ETA expiration date). Each time you enter Australia within the 12 months you can stay for a period of up to 3 months from the date of entry.

An ETA does not require a physical visa label or any paperwork for travel. The ETA is electronically linked to your travel document number.

Eligibility: US and Canadian citizens are eligible for ETAs. Visit www.immi.gov.au for the full list of ETA-eligible countries.

How to apply: When the ETA is applied for online through www.immi.gov.au there is a service charge of A$20. Third parties such as travel agents and airlines may charge a different amount.

Working Holiday Visas

Working Holiday Visa – Subclass 417

About this visa: This visa is for people who intend to travel to Australia for the purpose of a holiday. The visa allows you to do incidental work but you will be prohibited from working for one employer for more than six months.

How it works: You have 12 months to enter Australia from the date the visa is granted. This visa permits you to stay in Australia for 12 months from the date that you first enter Australia. The Working Holiday Visa allows multiple entries into Australia. This means that you can leave Australia and re-enter as many times as you wish during your 12-month stay. However if you depart Australia during your 12-month stay you are not able to recover the period of time you spend outside Australia.

Eligibility: The age requirement for a Working Holiday Visa is 18–30. You must hold a passport for a country participating in the program. UK, Canadian and most European citizens are eligible. Visit www.immi.gov.au for a complete list of eligible countries.

US citizens are eligible for a similar visa, the Work and Holiday Visa – Subclass 462. Visit www.immi.gov.au for more information.

You may not be accompanied by dependent children at any time during your stay in Australia if granted a Working Holiday Visa.

You must have enough funds to be able to support yourself while you are looking for work and in between work, while travelling in the country. These funds should be easily accessible at any time. An amount of A\$5,000 plus a return airfare is generally considered to be sufficient in this regard.

You may be eligible for a Second Working Holiday Visa if you complete a minimum of 3 months of approved seasonal work in a regional area (ie fruit picking, harvesting, farming etc). Visit www.immi.gov.au for further information.

How to apply: The visa application charge is A\$230.

For up-to-date information about visa requirements check with the embassy before travel.

Agricultural work

Go Workabout

Job(s) Available: Farm work/fruit picking (200), hospitality (bar, chefs, waiting staff etc) (50).

Duration: All year round. Minimum period of work 1–3 months.

Working Hours: *Farm work/fruit picking:* 40–50 hours per week. *Hospitality:* 40–50 hours per week.

Pay: *Farm work/fruit picking:* A\$15–A\$20 per hour. *Hospitality:* A\$18–A\$25 per hour.

Cost: Total price for package is A\$699.

Head Office: Lot 87 Market Street, Fremantle, West Australia, 6160 or PO Box 1865, Fremantle, West Australia, 6959
☎ +61 864 205 000
📧 info@goworkabout.com
🖥 www.goworkabout.com

Company Description: Go Workabout arranges jobs in Australia for working holidaymakers before they leave their home countries. They provide assistance with all the administration issues involved (eg visa, tax file number, accommodation). The jobs come packaged with the 'Complete Working Holiday Maker Starter Pack'. This pack includes the arrangement of your working holiday visa, tax file number, bank account, mailing service, accommodation and starter pack booklet (and job of course).

Requirements: *Farm work/fruit picking:* minimum age 18. Must be prepared to work outdoors. No experience necessary. *Hospitality:* relevant hospitality experience necessary.

Accommodation: Available at cost of A$50 to A$125 per week.

Additional Information: Also fully assist fully qualified carpenters and farm workers.

Application Procedure: See website for more details on how to sign up.

RJ Cornish and Co

Job(s) Available: Fruit pickers.

Duration: Work period is from late January to mid-March/early April.

Working Hours: 5–6 days a week, 7am–4pm (weather and crop permitting).

Pay: Australian Worker's Union rates are paid per bin of fruit harvested.

> Head Office: 174 Cottons Road, Cobram, Victoria 3644
> ☎ +61 3 5872 2055
> ⌨ picking@rjcornish.com
> 💻 www.rjcornish.com

Company Description: RJ Cornish and Co is a family-owned and operated business located at Cobram on the Murray River on the border of Victoria and New South Wales. As one of Australia's largest producers of apples, pears and canned peaches the company employs a large number of overseas backpackers each year.

Requirements: The work is heavy physical labour and may be unsuitable for some people. New pickers will participate in an induction programme which covers picking skills as well as health and safety prior to starting work.

Accommodation: Accommodation (2 or 3 persons per room) including meals for approximately A$138.70 per week.

Application Procedure: Apply online at www.rjcornish.com.

Outback International/Industrial

Job(s) Available: Farmers, farm managers, farm mechanics and tractor drivers. Also trade qualified personnel; welders, fabricators, boiler makers, mechanics, diesel fitters and experienced engineers.

Duration: *Farm/trade personnel:* required all year. Minimum period of work 2 weeks.

Working Hours: 8–12 hours per day, 5–7 days a week.

Pay: *Farm staff:* around £8–£12 per hour. *Trade personnel:* £10 + per hour.

> Head Office: PO Box 1142, Toowong, QLD 4066
> ☎ +61 737 208 504
>   or +61 737 208 645
> ⌨ admin@outbackinternational.com
> 💻 www.outbackinternational.com
>   or www.outbackindustrial.com

Company Description: Outback International is an Australia-wide rural employment agency. The experience of working within the primary industries overseas aims to broaden your knowledge of technology and work practices. Outback Industrial is a recruitment and labour hire services provider specialising in trade qualified personnel.

Job Description: *Farm staff:* numerous vacancies for personnel to operate farm machinery, drive tractors/harvesters, or work on irrigation schemes, in addition to farm management roles. *Trade qualified:* temporary or permanent vacancies in the industrial industry for trade qualified personnel.

Requirements: It is essential that applicants speak English. *Farm staff:* applicants must have an agricultural background. *Trade personnel:* must be trade qualified.

Accommodation: *Farm workers:* board and lodging is usually included but depends on the location. *Trade personnel:* board and lodging is generally not included.

Application Procedure: Applications are invited at any time to the above address or via website.

Torrens Valley Orchards

Job(s) Available: Cherry picking and packing from November until mid-January. Tree planting, pruning, irrigation installation and maintenance, and general orchard work.

Head Office: PO Box 1659, Gumeracha, South Australia 5233
✆ tvo@hotkey.net.au
🖳 www.tvo.com.au

Company Description: Farm business that has used a lot of student and backpacker workers over the last 16 years particularly during the cherry harvest. The company has had German, English, Japanese, Korean and French employees.

Requirements: Anyone who stays at TVO should be quick, polite and clean and look after the facilities provided.

Accommodation: Provides hostel-type accommodation for travellers.

Additional Information: Owner organises trips to barbecues, football, beach etc. The farm is 30 minutes from Adelaide on the local bus.

Application Procedure: Apply to Tony Hannaford, owner, at the above mail or email address.

VISITOZ

Job(s) Available: Opportunities for working holidays in Australia.

Head Office: Springbrook Farm,
8291 Burnett Highway, Goomeri,
Queensland, 4601
☎ +61 7 4168 6185
✆ info@visitoz.org or will@visitoz.org
or jules@visitoz.org
🖳 www.visitoz.org

Duration: Staff are needed around the year but working holiday regulations limit the time with any one employer to 6 months. For those completing 3 months' outback work, a second visa is on offer which can be taken straight away or at any time before the participant's 31st birthday.

Pay: Varies according to the work, the skills and the state of employment, but the minimum of about A$350 goes into the bank at the end of the week, plus food, accommodation and tax paid.

Cost: Participants in the scheme must pay for their own air fare, visa costs and the VISITOZ training fee of A$1,990. This includes a 500km Greyhound Pass and covers being met at the airport on arrival, 3 days jet lag recovery at a beach resort, 5 days on the training farm and help with the red tape paperwork once in Australia.

Company Description: VISITOZ offers an introduction to Australia for those who would like to have a working holiday in Australia. This is coupled with a 9-day introduction, which includes a short course in either agricultural or hospitality skills. Well-paid jobs are guaranteed for the whole of the 365 days of the visa, plus a friendly helping hand from the Burnet family on Springbrook Farm. The Burnets moved from Argyll to Queensland in 1991 after Dan had a full career as a British army officer.

Job Description: Work can be provided as distance education teachers, horse riders, hospitality workers, mothers' helps, stockworkers, tractor drivers and positions on cattle and sheep stations. Money made can be saved as there is nothing to spend it on! After 3 months or so this money can be used by the participant, who can take a holiday and enjoy all that Australia has to offer. Participants are encouraged to phone the Burnets again and are given another job and can thus work around Australia.

Requirements: Applicants must be aged 18–31 and all are assessed and/or trained for the job required.

Application Procedure: For further details contact Dan and Joanna Burnet. Their son, William and his wife Jules, based in the UK, can also be contacted. Call 07966 528664 or email above address. Jobs are guaranteed - the company states that in over 18 years no one has left VISITOZ without a job.

AUSTRALIA

AUSTRALASIA

Sports, couriers and camping

Thredbo Resort

Job(s) Available: Cashiering and sales staff (5), chefs/commis/demis, childcare, lift attendants, room attendants, ski hire staff (5).

Head Office: Kosciusko Thredbo Pty Ltd, PO Box 92, Thredbo, New South Wales 2625
☎ +61 2 6459 4100
📧 jobs@thredbo.com.au
🖥 www.thredbo.com.au

Duration: The period of work from around 1 July to 21 September (depending on snow), with a minimum period of work of 12 weeks.

Working Hours: Hours of work vary between 28 and 38 per week according to position.

Pay: *Cashiering and sales staff:* £853 per month. *Chefs/commis/demis chefs:* approximately £1,400 per month. *Childcare:* dependent on qualifications, from approximately £1,500 per month. *Lift attendants:* approximately £1,290 per month. *Room attendants:* approximately £1,080 per month. *Ski hire staff:* £1,250 per month.

Company Description: Thredbo is Australia's premier ski resort, with a season from mid-June to the end of September. They employ over 700 staff in winter, and have a ski village population of over 4,400.

Job Description: *Cashiering and sales staff:* to sell ski lift passes, ski school products and assist in retail. *Chefs/commis/demis chefs:* to work for the Thredbo Alpino Hotel, including bistro, à la carte, fine dining and conferences. *Childcare:* trained and untrained staff who are prepared to assist in all aspects of caring for children 6 months to 5 years. *Room attendants:* to do all aspects of cleaning hotel rooms and apartments. *Ski hire staff:* to fit customers with skis and snowboards and hire out clothing and equipment.

Requirements: *Cashiering and sales staff:* applicants should have sales and cash handling skills, accurate balancing and computer experience. *Lift attendants:* must be willing to work outdoors in all weather conditions. Some heavy work required. Good customer service skills. *Room attendants:* friendly and courteous disposition required. *Ski hire staff:* should have some cash handling experience and be willing to work split-shifts.

Accommodation: Board and lodging available for a cost of £67 per week.

Application Procedure: Applications to the above address are invited from January and close in early April, with interviews in Sydney, Brisbane and Thredbo in early April.

Voluntary work

Conservation Volunteers Australia (CVA)

Job(s) Available: Volunteers.

Head Office: CV International Booking Office, PO Box 423, Ballarat, Victoria 3353
☎ +61 3 5330 2600
📧 info@conservationvolunteers.com.au
🖥 www.conservationvolunteers.com.au

Duration: CVA offers overseas volunteers the Conservation Experience package. Packages run in blocks of 4 weeks and 6 weeks. Extra weeks can be added if required.

Cost: Volunteering with CVA costs approximately A$33 a night.

Company Description: Conservation Volunteers Australia is Australia's largest practical conservation organisation. CVA welcomes everyone who is enthusiastic about the outdoors and hands-on conservation.

Job Description: Volunteers are part of a team of 6–10 people under the guidance of a CVA team leader. Projects undertaken by CVA include: tree planting, native seed collection, endangered flora and fauna surveys, constructing and maintaining walking tracks in national parks, weed control. Projects are run in every state and territory of Australia throughout the year.

Accommodation: Costs include, all meals, project related travel and accommodation and recreational activity on alternate Sundays.

Application Procedure: For more information visit the website or email or write to CVA.

Other employment in Australia

BUNAC: Work Australia

Job(s) Available: BUNAC offers a gap year support package for people looking to work and travel around Australia on the Working Holiday Visa.

Duration: For up to a year. Group departures from the UK are monthly.

Cost: Programme costs are £349.

Head Office: 16 Bowling Green Lane, London EC1R 0QH, UK
☎ 020 7251 3472
enquiries@bunac.org.uk
www.bunac.org.uk

Job Description: The package includes an airport transfer, accommodation on arrival in Sydney, and orientation with guidance on jobs, housing, health, taxes, etc plus back-up services. Participants have the option to travel on a BUNAC group flight with an organised stopover in Hong Kong or to arrange independent travel.

Requirements: Travellers must be aged 18–30 inclusive, citizens of the UK and Ireland, and will need to be able to show that they have reserve funds of at least £2,000.

Application Procedure: For further details and to book visit www.bunac.org.uk.

Work and Travel Australia Programme

Job(s) Available: Opportunities in casual work, internships and teaching positions across the world.

Duration: Visa valid for 12 months from entry to Australia. Wide variety of work available, for up to 6 months per position.

Cost: Programme fee is £310 and includes 2 guaranteed jobs.

Head Office: IST Plus, Rosedale House, Rosedale Road, Surrey TW9 2SZ, UK
☎ 020 8939 9057
info@istplus.com
www.istplus.com

Company Description: IST Plus is an organisation offering people opportunities in work. This programme allows participants to travel in Australia, taking up work along the way to support themselves. IST Plus offer assistance at every stage, from obtaining the visa, to helping find work and accommodation in Australia. Ongoing services include mail receiving and holding, 24-hour emergency support, and access to office facilities and free internet at their partner's resource centre in Sydney.

Requirements: This programme is open to British, Canadian, Dutch and Irish passport holders resident in the UK as well as certain other nationalities, aged 18–30, who have not been on a working holiday to Australia before.

Application Procedure: Apply online at www.istplus.com.

NEW ZEALAND

New Zealand offers many job opportunities and has the lowest unemployment rate in Australasia. If you intend to work in New Zealand you will require a work visa, but some visas such as working holiday visas are very easy, quick and cheap to obtain. You don't need a visa if you want to go to New Zealand on holiday for up to six months and hold a UK passport.

The Working Holiday Scheme allows Britons aged 18–30 to work in any role for up to 23 months, although most Britons choose a one year visa, as this does not require a medical certificate nor police check. The scheme has proved so successful in allaying seasonal shortages of labour that the yearly ceiling of working holiday visas has been removed completely and applications are welcomed throughout the year. If you are already abroad you can apply online and pay by credit card (about £58) at the time of application. This entirely online application procedure was introduced in 2005 and keeps in touch with working holidaymakers by email, sending them information about jobs and requesting feedback to keep the service up to scratch. You do not need a job offer when applying as the scheme allows you to pick up any sort of work when you get to New Zealand. You can work in your profession or in casual work, changing jobs as many times as you like. Go to the immigration website for information and to apply www.immigration.govt.nz/whs.

There are working holiday schemes for a wide range of other nations including German, French, Irish, Canadian, Japanese and Malaysian nationals. Details of each scheme are also on www.immigration.govt.nz/whs.

There are a lot of jobs in New Zealand, and it is particularly easy to find casual work in horticulture and hospitality. Links to jobs are on the website www.immigration.govt.nz/whs. While wages are lower on average than in Australia, the cost of living is cheaper.

Either before you leave or once you are in one of the major cities, get hold of the free 200-page booklet *Australia and New Zealand Independent Traveller's Guide* published by the London-based travel magazine *TNT* (www.tntmagazine.com).

Red tape

ADDRESS: IMMIGRATION NEW ZEALAND
Mezzanine Floor, New Zealand House, 80 Haymarket, London SW1Y 4TQ
☎ 09069 100 100 (£1 pm)
✆ aboutnz@newzealandhc.org.uk
🖳 www.newzealandnow.govt.nz

Tourist visa requirements: New Zealand has visa waiver agreements with 30 countries so citizens of the UK, Ireland, USA and most European countries do not need a visa for bona fide tourist or business visits of up to three months (six months for UK citizens). On arrival, visitors must have valid passports, return tickets and evidence of sufficient funds (about £300 per month of stay). Renewals of permits will be considered to allow stays of up to a maximum of 12 months: approval is not automatic.

Working holiday visa: Available for people aged 18–30 years; you must be under 31 at the time of application. To be eligible you must not have had a working holiday visa to New Zealand before. Visas are obtained online from www.immigration.govt.nz/whs and usually granted within days. You then have 12 months to enter New Zealand, and your visa period begins only when you enter NZ. You can study for up to three months. There are no restrictions on the work you can do, nor the number of jobs that you undertake. You may be asked to demonstrate that you have access to funds to support yourself in NZ, a minimum of NZ$350 per month of intended stay. You must have an outward ticket to leave NZ, or evidence of funds to purchase an onwards ticket.

Work visas and permits: It is now possible for people on working holiday visas (or any type of visa) to apply to extend their stay or even apply for residence without having to leave the country.

Work visas are required for au pairs and any form of voluntary work.

Permanent migration: New Zealand welcomes people with skills to help with its expanding economy. The skilled migrant category is a points based system, with young, qualified professionals scoring well, particularly if they have previously worked in New Zealand.

It should be noted that, like all countries, visa rules are liable to change and that there is a fee for all visas, including visitor visas. For further information, contact Immigration New Zealand.

For up-to-date information about visa requirements contact the embassy before travel.

Agricultural work

Farm Helpers in New Zealand (FHINZ)

Job(s) Available: Farm stays.
Duration: Varies from 3 days to several months, depending on the needs of the farm.
Working Hours: Free farm stays to visitors in exchange for 4–6 hours help per day.
Company Description: FHINZ is a voluntary group of over 240 farms throughout New Zealand.

> **Head Office:** 31 Moerangi Street, Palmerston North, 4410
> ☎ +64 6 354 1104
> ✑ info@fhinz.co.nz
> 🖥 www.fhinz.co.nz

Job Description: Dependent on season and type of farm. Volunteer work, no paid work available.
Requirements: No experience is necessary and all equipment is provided. Visitors need to each have a membership booklet (revised every month), with full details of all the farms, the family and what kinds of work visitors will be helping with. These are $25 each, valid for 1 year and available either by mail order or through some agents.
Accommodation: Board and lodging provided in the family home in return for daily farm work. Most farms will collect visitors from the nearest town at no cost, and return them.
Application Procedure: For more information contact the address above.

Voluntary work

Conservation Volunteers New Zealand (CVNZ)

Job(s) Available: Volunteers
Duration: CVNZ offers overseas volunteers the Conservation Experience package. This package runs in blocks of 4 weeks and 6 weeks, but extra weeks can be added if required.
Costs: Volunteering with CVNZ costs approximately A$33 a night. International volunteers book via the

> **Head Office:** CV International Booking Office, PO BOX 423, Ballarat, Victoria 3353
> ☎ +61 3 5330 2600
> ✑ info@conservationvolunteers.com.au
> 🖥 www.conservationvolunteers.com.au

Conservation Volunteers International Booking office in Australia and pay in $A.

Company Description: Conservation Volunteers New Zealand was founded in 2006 by Conservation Volunteers Australia. CVNZ welcomes everyone who is enthusiastic about the outdoors and hands on conservation.

Job Description: Volunteers are part of a team of 6–10 people under the guidance of a CVNZ team leader. Projects undertaken by CVNZ include: tree planting, native seed collection and endangered flora and fauna surveys. Projects are run on both the North and South Islands throughout the year.

Accommodation: Cost includes all meals, project related travel and accommodation.

Application Procedure: For more information visit the website or email the above address.

Other employment in New Zealand

Bunac: Work New Zealand

Job(s) Available: BUNAC offers a gap year support package for people looking to work and travel around New Zealand.

Duration: Up to 23 months.

Cost: The Essentials support package costs £349.

Job Description: The package includes an airport

Head Office: 16 Bowling Green Lane, London EC1R 0QH, UK
☎ 020 7251 3472
✆ enquiries@bunac.org.uk
🖥 www.bunac.org.uk

transfer, accommodation on arrival in Auckland and orientation with guidance on jobs, housing, health, taxes, etc plus back-up services. Members have the option to travel on a BUNAC group flight with an organised stopover in Hong Kong or to arrange independent travel.

Requirements: Travellers must be aged 18–35 inclusive and citizens of the UK and Ireland. Those who have already used their once-in-a-lifetime, 2-year working holiday visa can apply for BUNAC's exclusive, 1-year IEP visa.

Application Procedure: For further details and to book, visit www.bunac.org.uk.

Useful publications

Work Your Way Around the World
Susan Griffith
Vacation Work 2009

Teaching English Abroad
Susan Griffith
Vacation Work 2010

Hands-on Holidays
Guy Hobbs
Vacation Work 2007

The Au Pair & Nanny's Guide to Working Abroad
Susan Griffith
Vacation Work 2006

The Directory of Jobs & Careers Abroad
Guy Hobbs
Vacation Work 2006

Working in Tourism
Verité Reily Collins
Vacation Work 2004

Prospects Work Experience
www.prospects.ac.uk

The Archaeological Fieldwork Opportunities Bulletin (AFOB)
Archaeological Institute of America 2007

The Archaeology Abroad Bulletin
www.britarch.ac.uk/archabroad

Back Door Guide to Short-Term Job Adventures
Michael Landes
Ten Speed Press 2005

100 Paid Summer Adventures for Teachers
Jill Frankfort
Benefit Press 2007

Guide to Summer Camps and Summer Schools, 30th edition
Porter Sargent Publishers 2010/2011

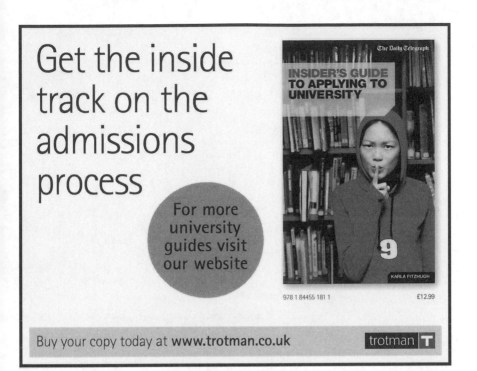
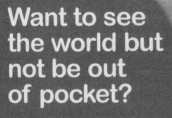

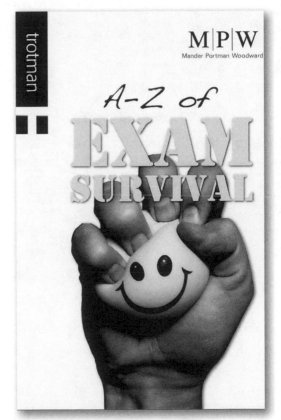